Greatly to be Praised

Greatly to be Praised
The Old Testament and Worship

Michael E. W. Thompson

◆PICKWICK *Publications* • Eugene, Oregon

GREATLY TO BE PRAISED
The Old Testament and Worship

Copyright © 2016 Michael E. W. Thompson. All rights reserved. Except for brief quotations in critical publications or reviews, no part of this book may be reproduced in any manner without prior written permission from the publisher. Write: Permissions, Wipf and Stock Publishers, 199 W. 8th Ave., Suite 3, Eugene, OR 97401.

Pickwick Publications
An Imprint of Wipf and Stock Publishers
199 W. 8th Ave., Suite 3
Eugene, OR 97401

www.wipfandstock.com

PAPERBACK ISBN: 978-1-4982-3412-2
HARDCOVER ISBN: 978-1-4982-3414-6
EBOOK ISBN: 978-1-4982-3413-9

Cataloguing-in-Publication data:

Names: Thompson, Michael E. W.

Title: Greatly to be praised : the Old Testament and worship / Michael E. W. Thompson.

Description: Eugene, OR: Pickwick Publications, 2016 | Includes bibliographical references and index.

Identifiers: ISBN 978-1-4982-3412-2 (paperback) | ISBN 978-1-4982-3414-6 (hardcover) | ISBN 978-1-4982-3413-9 (ebook)

Subjects: LSCH: 1. Bible. Old Testament—Criticism, interpretation, etc. | 2. Worship in the Bible. | 3. Public worship in the Bible. | 4. Bible. Old Testament—Prayers.

Classification: BS1199.P93 T466 2016 (paperback) | BS1199.P93 (hardcover) | BS1199.P93 (ebook)

Manufactured in the U.S.A.   06/20/16

For Hazel

"Let us go to the house of the Lord!"
Psalm 122:1b

For great is the Lord, and greatly to be praised.

(PSALM 96:4)

Seraphs were in attendance above him;
each had six wings:
with two they covered their faces,
and with two they covered their feet,
and with two they flew.
And one called to another and said:
"Holy, holy, holy is the Lord of hosts;
the whole earth is full of his glory."

(ISAIAH 6:2–3)

This shall be an everlasting statute for you,
to make atonement for the people of Israel
once in the year for all their sins. And Moses
did as the Lord commanded him.

(LEVITICUS 16:34)

Contents

Preface | ix
Abbreviations | xi

Introduction | 1

Part I: The Place of Worship | 17
1. Holy Places | 19
2. Temples | 26
3. Other Places of Worship | 49

Part II: The People at Worship | 57
4. The Worshipping People | 59
5. Priests and Levites | 71
6. The King and Worship | 89

Part III: The Liturgy of Worship | 103
7. Prayers | 105
8. Psalms | 119
9. Sacrifices | 162
10. Feasts, Festivals and Calendars | 179
11. Evidences of Liturgies | 191

Part IV: Visions and Warnings | 209
12. Visions of Worship | 211
13. The Prophets and Worship | 240

Part V: Worship in the Hebrew Bible | 277
14. Concluding Reflections | 279

Bibliography | 297
Index of Subjects | 317
Index of Authors | 321
Index of Biblical References | 327

Preface

This work is offered as a survey of the worship spoken about and set forth in the Old Testament. It eschews detailed historical considerations of the subject for reasons stated in the Introduction, and is organized on a thematic basis, as the Contents page makes clear. This arrangement of materials does inevitably bring about certain repetitions, but I trust that the book in this form will be useful both for those whose need is to refer to certain parts, to consider particular aspects of worship, and at the same time for those who wish to read the whole work.

I seek to write for two main groups of people: those in the Academy and those in the Church. I would like to think that among the former group this work could make a small contribution to a renewed study of this aspect of the Hebrew Bible, and in particular lead to new researches in the subject. Among the latter group my earnest hope is that my writing may make some small contribution to a fresh appreciation of the centrality of worship in the Old Testament, and that study of it may lead to the ongoing renewal of the Church's worship.

In general my biblical quotations are from the New Revised Standard Version, chapter and verse enumerations being those of the English versions. No knowledge of Hebrew is presupposed for the reading of this work, and those who wish to do so can read on without attention to the details about Hebrew texts. At the same time certain Hebrew words find a place in what follows for those who find them helpful. Where a Hebrew word is indicated, the form of transliteration is that of the *SBL Handbook of Style*, with minor exceptions.

Once again I am deeply grateful to those who have encouraged me in the writing of this work, and in the study over a number of years that lies behind it. I can only hope that they are not too disappointed with what is now offered. Once again, I am most grateful for the provisions of, and the helpful staffs at various libraries, in particular at the University of Sheffield, at the Nazarene College in Manchester, and at St John's College in Nottingham. For a second time I am most grateful to Wipf & Stock for accepting a work for publication under their Pickwick Publications imprint, and in particular to Noah Crabtree, Robin Parry, Calvin Jaffarian and their colleagues for much expertise and help. My thanks go to my friend Adrian Curtis for his scholarly reading of an earlier version of the work, and for all his helpful comments and observations. Above all, I thank my wife Hazel once again for her encouragement and support, her love and intellectual companionship, and yet again for her readiness to come to my aid on those not-infrequent occasions when my computer skills were found to be inadequate for the task.

Michael E. W. Thompson

On the Festival of Gregory the Great,
Servant of the servants of God
September 3, 2015

Abbreviations

ABD	*Anchor Bible Dictionary.* 6 vols. Edited by David Noel Freedman. New York: Doubleday, 1992
ANET	*Ancient Near Eastern Texts Relating to the Old Testament.* Edited by James B. Pritchard. 3rd edition. Princeton: Princeton University Press, 1969
BDB	Brown, Francis, S. R. Driver and Charles A. Briggs, *Hebrew and English Lexicon of the Old Testament,* Oxford: Clarendon, 1907
BJRL	*Bulletin of the John Rylands Library*
CBQ	*Catholic Biblical Quarterly*
DCH	*Dictionary of Classical Hebrew.* Edited by David J. A. Clines. Sheffield, UK: Sheffield Academic / Sheffield Phoenix, 1993–2011
EDB	*Eerdmans Dictionary of the Bible.* Edited by David Noel Freedman. Grand Rapids: Eerdmans, 2000
EQ	*Evangelical Quarterly*
EVV	English versions
ExpT	*Expository Times*
FAT 2	Forschungen zum Alten Testament 2
IDB	*Interpreter's Dictionary of the Bible.* 4 vols. Edited by George Arthur Buttrick. Nashville: Abingdon, 1962
IDBSup	*The Interpreter's Dictionary of the Bible. Supplementary Volume.* Edited by Keith Crim. Nashville: Abingdon, 1976
IEJ	*Israel Exploration Journal,* Jerusalem
Int	*Interpretation: A Journal of Bible and Theology*
JBL	*Journal of Biblical Literature*
JJS	*Journal of Jewish Studies*

JSNTSup	Journal for the Study of the New Testament: Supplement Series
JSOT	*Journal for the Study of the Old Testament*
JSOTSup	Journal for the Study of the Old Testament: Supplement Series
JSS	*Journal of Semitic Studies*
JTS	*Journal of Theological Studies*
KB	*Lexicon in Veteris Testamenti Libros.* Edited by Ludwig Koehler and Walter Baumgartner. Leiden: Brill, 1953
KTU	Dietrich, Manfried, Oswald Loretz, and Joaquín Sanmartín. *The Cuneiform Alphabetic Texts from Ugarit, Ras Ibn Hani, and Other Places.* 2nd enlarged edition. Münster: Ugarit-Verlag, 1995.
LHBOTS	Library of Hebrew Bible/Old Testament Studies (Formerly Journal for the Study of the Old Testament: Supplement Series)
LXX	Septuagint (Greek translation of the Old Testament)
MT	Masoretic Text (Hebrew Text)
NRSV	New Revised Standard Version of the Bible, 1989
OTS	Oudtestamentische Studiën
PEQ	*Palestine Exploration Quarterly*
PIBA	*Proceedings of the Irish Biblical Association*
REB	Revised English Bible, 1989
RHPR	*Revue d'Histoire et de Philosophie religieuse*
SBL	Society of Biblical Literature
SJT	*Scottish Journal of Theology*
TDOT	*Theological Dictionary of the Old Testament.* 15 vols. Edited by G. Johannes Botterweck, Helmer Ringgren, and Heinz-Josef Fabry. Translated by David E. Green et al. Grand Rapids: Eerdmans, 1974–2006
TynB	*Tyndale Bulletin*
VT	*Vetus Testamentum*
VTSup	Supplements to Vetus Testamentum
ZAW	*Zeitschrift für die alttestamentliche Wissenschaft*

Introduction

Consider three of the Hebrew Bible's verses, each of them about worship, each occurring serendipitously in a different part of that Bible, the first in the book of Psalms, the second in the book of Isaiah, the third in the book of Leviticus.

First, a verse from Psalms, the most extensive book in the third part of the Old Testament, the Writings: Psalm 96 speaks of God's kingship, his greatness, such greatness that he is abundantly worthy of praise. Thus the psalmist exalts, "For great is the Lord, and greatly to be praised; he is to be revered above all gods" (Ps 96:4), and here the psalmist has employed two of the Hebrew Bible's characteristic words in its vocabulary of worship, words we shall consider below. Both of these are verbs, each giving expression to what should be the devotee's responses to their awareness of the greatness and the otherness of the Lord God of Israel; all that is indicated by the words "praise" and "revere, hold in awe."

The second biblical verse comes from the Prophets, Isa 6:3, "Holy, holy, holy is the Lord of hosts; the whole earth is full of his glory." This is part of the vision we are told the prophet-to-be Isaiah the son of Amoz was vouchsafed in the year that King Uzziah died, the cry of the seraphs in praise of their Lord—high and lofty as he was on his throne, the mere hem of his robe being sufficient to fill the temple. These words portray a scene permeated with the spirit of worship, a scene compellingly portrayed as inducing in Isaiah not only a sense of deepest awe but also a feeling of his own dreadful unworthiness. This is a vision of all that holy otherness that is God, that *mysterium* of which Rudolph Otto wrote in his book *The Idea of the Holy*, that *mysterium* that is both *tremendum* and also *fascinans*.[1] Further, that worshipful exclamation of the seraphs would be taken up into the Trisagion and the Sanctus in Christian worship, having already been used in Jewish worship in the Kedushoth.

Our third verse comes from the Torah, the Pentateuch, from Leviticus, occurring at the ending of the chapter that tells of the highly elaborate ritual of the Day of Atonement: "This shall be an everlasting statute for you, to

---

1. Otto, *The Idea of the Holy*.

make atonement for the people of Israel once in the year for all their sins. And Moses did as the Lord had commanded him." (Lev 16:34) This verse may be about what is for many people today more than likely a much less compelling, attractive, and exciting aspect of the worship about which the Hebrew Bible speaks. Yet it is one that is vital, for it is concerned with an indispensable aspect of that worship. It is to do with the forgiveness, and the assurance thereof, of the sins against the holy Lord God committed by his ever-sinful people, and the present study will give full attention to this aspect of the worship that is spoken about in the Hebrew Bible. Something of the importance and significance of this whole matter of how a person or a group could secure forgiveness, and be assured they had been forgiven their sins, can be seen in the reaction of Isaiah to his vision of the Lord when he said "Woe is me! I am lost, for I am a man of unclean lips, and I live among a people of unclean lips; yet my eyes have seen the King, the Lord of hosts!" (Isa 6:5). Or we may consider the the witness of the psalmist, "If you, O Lord, should mark iniquities, Lord, who could stand?" (Ps 130:3).

The subject of this book is worship, in particular the worship we read about in the Old Testament, that is in the Hebrew Bible,[2] and the above citations may serve by way of example and harbinger of all that material in the Old Testament not only about worship in general, but also about specific aspects and themes of worship. In these scriptures there is worship spoken about as coming from a variety of contexts and historical eras, worship that is deemed to be appropriate, equally, at times, what is judged inappropriate, while elsewhere we are given visionary expressions of ideals in worship.

But what is worship, and how is it to be described, if possible defined? According to Evelyn Underhill, in a work first published in 1936, "Worship, in all its grades and kinds, is the response of the creature to the Eternal . . . ," going on to say, "There is a sense in which we may think of the whole life of the Universe, seen and unseen, conscious and unconscious, as an act of worship, glorifying its Origin, Sustainer, and End."[3] A little later, Underhill says of worship: "That awed conviction of the reality of the Eternal over against us, that awareness of the Absolute, that sense of God, which in one form or another is the beginning of all worship, whether it seems to break in from without, or to arise within the soul, does not and cannot originate in man."[4] This "awareness of the Absolute" is present to a marked degree in the

---

2. In this work I use the titles "Old Testament" and "Hebrew Bible" indiscriminately in an attempt to be respectful to the different faith communities who regard these documents as their scriptures. However, to designate the eras I use BCE and CE rather than BC and AD.

3. Underhill, *Worship*, 3.

4. Ibid., 7.

Hebrew Bible. The mighty appearance of the Lord to Isaiah in what appears to be the Jerusalem temple has already been spoken about, yet it is there also in a number of similar occurrences, such as the incident when Moses was addressed by the Lord out of the burning bush on the mountain called Horeb (Exod 3:1–6), or the occasion when a similar experience on what is portrayed as the same mountain took place for the prophet Elijah (1 Kgs 19:9b–18). The book of the prophet Ezekiel begins with a not-dissimilar theophanic appearance to Ezekiel (Ezek 1:1—3:27), and the list could go on.

Also to be considered with profit is the Old Testament's language of the recording of and the response to such and other appearances of the Lord to individuals or groups. Frequent within such accounts are words to the effect that the individual, or the group "bowed down" in worship, more often than not this being rendered in the Hebrew by the verb š-ḥ-h, in the hithpaʻel form, and meaning "bow down, worship, prostrate oneself, make obeisance." This verbal form occurs frequently in the Hebrew Bible, a large number of these being about the worship of God, bowing down to the Lord.[5] A. S. Herbert observed that this verb "emphasizes the physical expression appropriate to one who comes into the presence of the holy majesty of God: he bows himself down, prostrates himself."[6]

In this regard we should also take notice of the word that, for example, occurs in the story of the encounter of Moses with the Lord on Mount Sinai where we are told there was a burning bush, out of which mysteriously Moses heard the Lord speaking to him. This was clearly something totally outside of normal life experiences, and we are not surprised to read that, in the words of the NRSV translation, "And Moses hid his face, for he was afraid to look at God." (Exod 3:6) Now the word there translated "afraid" is a Hebrew verb (y-r-ʼ) that can mean either being afraid, frightened, scared in a normal human sense, or—and indeed is found in this sense in the majority of occurrences in the Hebrew Bible—overcome with a sense of *awe*, perhaps we might say feeling a sense of *reverence*. This is the sense of holy awe that we have already observed being spoken about by Rudolph Otto in his justly famous study of the "numinous."[7] R.H. Pfeiffer went as far as saying that this "fear of God" may be the earliest term for religion in biblical Hebrew, and indeed in Semitic languages in general."[8]

---

5. It has to be said that there is an ongoing discussion about what is the grammatical root of the verb here, in particular as to whether it is š-ḥ-h, or whether ḥ-w-h. For details see, e.g., *DCH*, 8:316–19; and *TDOT*, 4:248–56. See also Emerton, "The Etymology of Hištaḥᵃwāh"; Davies, "A Note on the Etymology of hištaḥᵃwāh."

6. Herbert, *Worship in Ancient Israel*, 10.

7. On this important word, see Fuhs, "yārēʼ."

8. Quoted by Fuhs, "yārēʼ." 297.

We can go further than this and say that this word, and the associated concept, "fear" is part of the language of worship. Rudolph Otto in his study of these matters speaks of there being in those special moments a feeling of the sense of the holy, the numinous, along with the associated feeling of personal dependence, the creature-feeling of awe before and dependence upon the holy one, and that all this is akin to worshipping the deity thus revealed.[9] This sense of reverential awe may be experienced either within a holy building, as for example it was by Isaiah son of Amoz (Isa 6:1–8), or else away from such a building, as for example by Moses on a mountain (Exod 3:1–6). Further, such an experience may result in the human person, or persons, worshipping in the formal arrangements of the contemporary cult, or else in their own particular or chosen way.

Before we move on there are among the many words employed in the Hebrew Bible to express aspects of worship a number that we should consider briefly, as follows:

1. The Hebrew word *k-b-d* in general usage is to do with "weight," but when used of the Lord it indicates "glory." Thus in that vision Isaiah had of the Lord the seraphs were calling out "Holy, holy, holy is the Lord of hosts; the whole earth is full of his glory" (Isa 6:3). This "glory", or perhaps "effulgence," here and in other such Old Testament contexts, can indicate something of the revelation of the great holiness and otherness of the Lord. Hence there is the sense that the awesome and transcendent Lord reveals an immanence, a closeness of his divine presence. This is a word that we shall encounter again, a word that has a significant usage in the so-called Priestly writings, and in the book of the prophet Ezekiel.[10]

2. Another significant word in the Hebrew Bible as regards worship is the verb *'-b-d*, which is usually translated "work" or "serve", and in its *hipʿil* form can be employed in the religious sense of "make service," "make worship." There seems to be the thought here that the one who is the worshipper is without doubt the subject person to the great being to whom he or she is bringing their worship. Yet the parties seem to be envisaged as being in a covenant-like relationship, such that a crucial part of the service of the Lord is the making, the offering of worship. An example of such usage occurs in Ps 100:2 "*Serve* the Lord with gladness; come into his presence with singing," which NRSV

---

9. Otto, *The Idea of the Holy*. See also Mowinckel, *Religion and Cult*.
10. On the word *kābôd*, see Weinfeld, "*kābôd*."

(understandably) translates "*Worship* the Lord with gladness; come into his presence with singing."[11]

3. A further word associated with the realm of worship, and whose major usage occurs in the books of Psalms and Chronicles, is *h-l-l*, meaning "praise". Its occurrences in the Hebrew Bible number over 140, the majority of which refer to the praise of God, being found in the *pi'el* (intensive) form.[12] This verb expresses the praise of God on the part of an individual, a group, or a leader for the reason that the Lord "is good, his steadfast love endures forever" (Pss 100:5; 106:1; 107:1; 118:1, 2, 3, 4, 29; 136:1–26). Many other such references from both Psalms and Chronicles could be cited, including the one we considered above in Ps 96:4 "For great is the Lord, and greatly to be praised [*h-l-l*]."[13] An associated word, one that comes from the verbal form *h-l-l*, "praise", is the noun *tĕhillâ*, which speaks of the "praise," the "glory" that rightly is to be given to the Lord. Although the majority of its occurrences are in the Psalms (see, for example, Pss 9:14; 22:3, 25), they are not exclusively there. Two further matters are to be noted: First, what comes over as a liturgical cry, the *Hallelu-jah*, is literally "Praise Yahweh," "Praise the Lord" an expression which occurs some 24 times in the Hebrew Bible. Second, the title of the whole book of psalms is *Tĕhillîm*, literally "Praises."

4. We should also take note of the word "bless" (Hebrew *b-r-k*), which in regard to worship is used in two senses: not only does God bless individuals and groups, and thereby give something of himself to them for their ongoing lives in the world, so also people are spoken of blessing God, that is they give something of themselves in the expression of their worship of the Lord. A. S. Herbert, having said that throughout the Old Testament the humans bless God who is high above all blessing (Neh 9:5), continues "The worshipper gathers together all the energies of his life and directs them towards Him from whom all blessing flows (Ps 103:1, 22; 104:1. Cf Deut 8:10; Judg 5:2; 1 Chr 29:20, etc.)."[14]

5. Time would fail us to speak at this point about many more of the various Hebrew words employed in the Hebrew Bible's vocabulary of

---

11. On '-b-d see Herbert, *Worship in Ancient Israel*, 10–11; and Otzen, "'ābad."

12. There are two further Hebrew verbs *h-l-l*, meaning "shine" and "be foolish" respectively.

13. See further Ringgren, "hll".

14. Herbert, *Worship in Ancient Israel*, 12. See also Scharbert, "brk"; and Mitchell, *The Meaning of BRK*.

worship. Many of these will be spoken about in the pages that follow, but mention may perhaps be made of a few more that may serve by way of further introduction to this study of worship in the Old Testament. Not uncommon in the psalms, but also found elsewhere, is the verb *r-y-m*, meaning "exalt," as for example in Ps 34:3 "O *magnify* the Lord with me, / and let us *exalt* his name together." The verb that occurs at the beginning of that verse is another such word used to express something of the incomparable greatness of the Lord, "magnify, make great" (*g-d-l*). Or for two further characteristic Hebrew Bible words used to express the praise of the Lord consider two more psalms. In Ps 48:9 (Heb v. 10) we read "We ponder your *steadfast love* (*ḥ-s-d*) O God", and in Ps 57:5 (Heb v. 6) we have "Be *exalted*, (*r-y-m*, as in Ps 34:3 above) O God, above the heavens. Let your *glory* (*k-b-d*) be over all the earth." Or there is the word *tôdāh*, meaning "thanksgiving" whose main occurrences in the Hebrew Bible are in the books of Leviticus, Nehemiah, Chronicles, and Psalms, as for example in Ps 26:7, "singing aloud a song of *thanksgiving* (*tôdāh*)." Here then are just a few more of the words in the Old Testament speaking of the Lord's *exalted* nature, of his incomparable *greatness*, his abiding *steadfast love*, his otherness, that is his *glory*.

We may also appreciate something of the centrality of worship in the Hebrew Bible by recalling the fact that quite simply it is present there, running through so many of the various parts of this whole work. Ronald E. Clements, for example, has pointed out to us that there is a cultic dimension to the religious faith of the people of Israel as portrayed in the Old Testament, saying "what is of paramount importance in the Old Testament is the presence of God, rather than any doctrine of his existence. To seek God was to go up to see his face at a sanctuary, rather than to engage in an intellectual debate."[15] Thus there is much in the Old Testament about worship, about shrines, and festivals, and also about those people who were appointed to particular offices and roles in the worship life of ancient Israel. Nor should we forget those who in days of widespread slackness and carelessness as regards worship condemned, in some most outspoken words, what in their days passed for worship, not infrequently castigating it as a mockery of true worship, sometimes even a perpetuation of what should not even be taking place. Thus further, the Old Testament comes replete with various pictures and prescriptions of a life of renewed worship for a future age. Indeed, in some parts of the Hebrew Bible what we are reading about may not be so much what at one time in the past took place in worship, but what rather at

---

15. Clements, *Old Testament Theology*, 40.

some future time *should*, according to some individual or group, be taking place.

If doubts still remain regarding the centrality and importance for the Old Testament of the subject of worship, we may briefly consider its books in turn and note how in one way or another—either in what the text is plainly talking about or alternatively what we perceive lies there within the text, perhaps somewhat below the surface and yet bound into the very fabric of that writing—that in no small number of those books there is the matter of the worship of the Lord God.

Worship is there in the first book of the Hebrew Bible: before Genesis chapter 4 is complete we have Cain's prayer to God, something of a personal lament, "My punishment is greater than I can bear! Today you have driven me away from the soil, and I shall be hidden from your face; I shall be a fugitive and a wanderer on the earth, and anyone who meets me may kill me." (Gen 4:13–14) At the close of the account of the flood in Gen 7–9 we read that in thanksgiving for the deliverance of himself, his family, and all those who had been with him in the ark, Noah built an altar to the Lord and offered a series of burnt offerings to him upon it (Gen 8:20). When we turn to the second part of Genesis, chapters 12–36, we have a series of clear indications of worship. The patriarchs pray to God, have visions of God, set up pillars at places where they have received epiphanic experiences, and build altars to the Lord. Then in the third part of Genesis, in the chapters (37–50) that tell the long story about Joseph, about his being sold by his brothers and so eventually coming into the service of the Egyptian Pharaoh, and thus saving the Egyptian peoples—and others—from starvation, we have an account deftly written up as if so much is owing not only to human wisdom but also in fact to human mendacity and jealousy. Thus the elements of prayer and sacrifice are somewhat conspicuous by their absence, and yet at the end (perhaps indeed as its conclusion?) there is uttered that statement, put into the mouth of Joseph, that it was not so much the brothers who had brought Joseph to Egypt, but rather God himself and at that for the purpose of saving life. This indeed, says the text, "he is doing today" (Gen 50:20, and compare 45:5 and 8). Surely, in these statements we are not far from the realm of mystery, and the very spirit of worship—but rather, very near.[16]

The book of Exodus may be understood as being concerned with a number of themes, among which are deliverance, pilgrimage, and lawgiving. At the end of the material about the deliverance from Egypt we have in Exod 15:1–20 a song of Moses celebrating the fact that Israel has been delivered by the Lord from the oppression of the Pharaoh. "This",

---

16. For worship in Genesis, see below, 19–23.

says Walter Houston, "is a victory song, but the victor is God, so it is also a hymn of praise and thanksgiving."[17] The Song of Moses is followed in Exod 15:21 with the Song of Miriam, another song of praise to the Lord, "Sing to the Lord, for he has triumphed gloriously; horse and rider he has thrown into the sea." What is being spoken about here clearly is worship, and when the ongoing pilgrimage of the Israelites continues and they come to Sinai with its associated law-giving, the people's sin of the manufacture of the calf to which they bow down and worship, and at the same time to which they pray that it may lead them on their journey, we are still in a realm where matters of worship are of central importance. So too when we read of Moses' impassioned prayers for his people, and in all the details about the Tent of Meeting, the manufacture of the Tabernacle, and the place and theology of the ark of the covenant.[18] As regards the three remaining books of the Torah/Pentateuch—Leviticus, Numbers, Deuteronomy—it is abundantly clear that at the heart of each there are issues about worship, that it is to be done in correct ways, that it is to be properly led, and that the appropriate appointments of official personnel are made for its ongoing life and purposes.[19]

With the book of Joshua we are further confronted with an emphasis on worship: here it is insisted that Yahweh alone is to be worshipped, and at that in a single place of worship as specified in Deuteronomy; here it is said to be at Shiloh, but perhaps there is in these words a certain background thought that here is the central shrine, "The Place" for worship (Josh 18). In the book of Judges are references to issues of the Israelite monotheistic faith, condemnation of fertility rites and other unacceptable matters in worship. Here we read of sacrifices being offered (Judg 2:5; 13:16; 20:26), of people worshipping the Lord (7:15), of crying out to God (3:15; 6:6); yet at the same time the worship of Baal and Astarte is taking place (2:13; 3:7; 10:6). Bearing a certain similarity to the Songs of Moses and Miriam in Exod 15:1–21, we find in the book of Judges the Song of Deborah and Barak in which God as the Divine Warrior is praised for his defeat of his people's enemy (5:1–31). Moreover, altars to the Lord are built (Judg 6:24), while one to Baal is pulled down (6:28–32). On the one hand Gideon worships the Lord; on the other a man in the hill country of Ephraim named Micah was manufacturing an

---

17. Houston, "Exodus," 77.

18. In this regard see Davies, "The Theology of Exodus." On worship in the book of Exodus, see below, 23–25.

19. For Leviticus and Numbers, see below, 211–17; for Deuteronomy, see below, 218–20.

idol of cast metal, having a shrine, and later the addition of a Levite to serve as its priest (17:1—18:31).[20]

Thus we come to two large works, the books of Samuel and Kings, both of which ostensibly give the impression of being historical records, but which on the most perfunctory of investigations show themselves to be works primarily of theology. There is much about worship here, and further of worship in what are both ongoing and also developing historical and political situations. There is also the issue of the national leadership, and the matter of what sort of national leadership is required for these times. In a particular way the issue is whether a kingly rule is to be of a dynastic or non-dynastic kind. Thus, what will be the relationship between this leadership and the religious institutions of the nations of Israel and Judah, where and of what nature will be those nations' places of worship, and who will be the officials who are responsible for the worship in them? What, further, will happen about alternative forms of, and also alternative places of, worship?[21]

With the books of the prophets there is an ongoing interaction between the prophetic interventions and the worlds of political matters and, as ever, worship. This is to be seen, for example, in the Isaiah book where we have condemnation of worship that takes place in situations of anti-social behaviour and living (Isa 1:10–17), and also a vision of temple worship and leadership therein open to a vast host of people (Isa 56:6–8). Also here are songs of thanksgiving (Isa 12:1–6), doxological expressions, and visions of the Lord of all (Isa 19:16–25; 42:10–13; 49:13; 55:10–13). With Jeremiah we have a prophet who we are told came from a priestly family, but in which and with which his prophetic calling and his priestly relationships did not always co-mingle uneventfully. Jeremiah, presumably as prophet, was critical of a certain magical-like dependence of the people on the temple for their well-being. Further, the temple was the setting for some of Jeremiah's warnings of impending divine judgment. In the case of the book of the prophet Ezekiel we have an expansive section of the book devoted to what is portrayed as the prophet's vision for a rebuilt temple in Jerusalem, which will be considered later in this work.

When we turn to the Twelve (Amos to Malachi) prophets we find again no dearth of links with the world of worship. The prophet Hosea is portrayed as being scandalized by what he observes going on in the land of Israel that passes for worship. For him it is rank desertion of the people's true relationship with their God, and this is expressed in the bold metaphor of prostitution (Hos 1:2—3:5). Let these people return with deepest

20. On worship in Joshua and Judges, see below, 32–33.
21. On these issues, see below, 75–77.

humility to their God, for which the prophet gives them a prayer of confession to pray (Hos 14:1-3). The prophet Joel also speaks of the urgent need for heartfelt confession of sin on the part of his people, as in a spirit of worshipful contrition they make their return to the Lord (Joel 2:12-17). Amos inveighs against falsity of worship that is not accompanied by righteousness and justice in the lives of the worshippers (Amos 5:18-24), while in the book that bears his name there are a number of doxological expressions that give a marked worshipful aspect to the whole work. In Micah we have not only the passage, shared with the Isaiah book, that speaks of the prominence of the house of the Lord in future days (Mic 4:1-4; Isa 2:2-5), but also at its conclusion a passage about the divine forgiveness of sins with no mention of any liturgical means of either seeking or securing it (Mic 7:18-20). Nahum's book contains a powerful picture of a theophanic appearance of God, though to a certain extent problematic to us because in places it strikes a harshly vindictive note (Nah 1:3b-8; see v. 8b). The prophecy of Habakkuk appears to speak of contemplation of the things of God, waiting upon him, and the resolution of the problem of theodicy that the prophet has through the literary and theological medium of a psalmic construction (Hab 3:1-19). Among various other matters the prophecy of Zephaniah contains a call to repentance of sins, while Haggai is concerned with what comes over as a singularity of purpose, namely the urgent need to rebuild the then-present ruins of the temple in Jerusalem in the post-exilic period. The first part of Zechariah (chs 1-8) is also concerned with that restoration and rebuilding of the city and temple in the holy city. Finally among these books of the prophets is Malachi where we read of the condemnation of unfaithful priests (Mal 1:6—2:10).[22]

The third part of the Hebrew Bible, the Writings, opens with the book of Psalms, which clearly and unarguably takes us into the realm of worship. This book, if for this reason alone, demands its own chapter in what follows.[23] Yet the book of Job should not be neglected in this regard, for while so much of it is taken up with a somewhat intellectual approach to the deep and intractable problems that human beings, even those who apparently are being held in the care of God, have to endure large and unexplainable sufferings and problems in their lives, even so any theological resolutions to these matters are arrived at rather through a sense of wonder at the greatness of God, the mystery of his being, and the inscrutable nature of his ways. Any "solution" that this book can offer is in fact in language akin to that

---

22. For the prophets and worship, see below, 240-75.
23. For Psalms, see below, 119-61.

of worship (see Job 28:12, 20, 28; 38:1—40:1; 40:6—41:34; 42:5–6).[24] Then further: The book of Ruth contains a series of prayers of thanksgiving and intercession; Daniel has various prayers, affirmations of faith, and some (extended) confessions of sin. With Ezra and Nehemiah we are taken back into that world where there is urgent need to rebuild the city of Jerusalem and its temple in the post-exilic period, to make confession of sins for those things that it is believed brought about the judgment of the exile and for further sins committed since then. All in all, it may be argued that there is indeed a very great deal in the Old Testament about the subject of worship.[25]

Many Christians these days, particularly those who live in what is called the western world, seem not to be overly concerned about the Old Testament scriptures, frequently regarding a good deal of the material within them that deals with worship as having been made outdated, even now irrelevant, through the further revelation in Christ Jesus. Thus, while we do indeed still use the biblical psalms a good deal in Christian worship, there will at the same time be a temptation to dismiss the Hebrew Bible's talk of sacrifices as now meaningless and redundant. Nevertheless, it is surely only reasonable that we should be concerned to enquire as to why there were in ancient Israel all those sacrifices and offerings prescribed, and what it was that perhaps there was envisaged as happening when a sacrifice was offered. This I endeavour to do in the pages that follow.[26] I believe that there are matters here that will inform us, and enable Christians the more clearly to see deeper significance in what has been given in Christ: what, for example, it was, and what was the significance thereof, that led the writer of the Letter to the Hebrews to say that "he [Christ] did once for all when he offered himself" (Heb 7:27b). Thus I am concerned to make clear what is the great problem and burden that the Old Testament understands humanity is afflicted with in its sinfulness, its turning away from God's will and ways. This problem and burden of humanity is writ large in the Hebrew Bible's talk of sacrifices and offerings, in its records of humble prayers to God for his forgiveness, in its accounts of the Lord's gracious forgiveness of his people's sins. I submit that there is a very great deal in the Old Testament both to inform us in our discipleship in Christ, and also to contribute to the prayers and praises, ceremonies and sacraments of Christian worship.

It should be made clear at the outset that there are various necessary limitations upon the scope of this work: first what it cannot do; second,

---

24. See Thompson *"Where is the God of Justice?,"* 105–56. See also below, 234–35.

25. On the book of Ruth see below, 110; for Daniel, 67; for Ezra and Nehemiah, 85–86, 109–10.

26. On sacrifices, see below, 162–78.

what it does not try to do; third what it modestly seeks to do. First then, what it cannot do is to present what we might call a history of worship in the Old Testament. Some fifty or so years ago we might have been sufficiently confident as to our knowledge of the course of the history of ancient Israel, and about the dating of many parts of the Old Testament, to have reconstructed a history of the worship spoken about therein.[27] However, in more recent decades questions have been asked about the presuppositions on which such confidence in matters historical was based, and thus we have come to pay greater attention to the matter of what sort of documents we have in the Hebrew Bible, in particular that we are dealing here with writings whose main concern is with theological and religious matters, and only secondarily with historical issues. Further, we are less clear than we thought we were about the processes whereby the present Old Testament books came to be built up from earlier units and just when, and where, those units took their beginnings. This is not to say that we cannot do Old Testament history these days, but rather that what ancient Israelite history we do attempt, we do more cautiously than we did in the past. The history of the worship spoken of in the Hebrew Bible, then, will not be attempted in this work, apart from making what I feel may be some reasonable and modest generalizations. Further, as regards the historical span of the work I seek to study what is spoken about in the Hebrew Bible, with a few extensions into later periods so as to observe briefly what became of some earlier institutions, buildings, ways of worship.

Second, what is also not attempted in this work is the untangling of what are various knotty problems in our understanding of some institutions to do with Old Testament worship, in particular the course of their development over the changing conditions of time. The two main considerations here are priests and Levites, and the prescribed festivals and feasts. These matters will be spoken about in what follows, but I shall not presume upon the patience of my readers by seeking to set out the difficulties we have in reconstructing the *development* of the Old Testament priesthood, the relationship between priests and Levites, and what were the interrelationships between various lists of, and prescriptions for, the observance of the festivals. Rather, I shall present what in these matters appear to be likely answers, conclusions, at the same time indicating works that offer more details for those who have the enthusiasm along with the necessary stamina to pursue them in greater depth.

---

27. Thus see, e.g., the work of Rowley, *Worship in Ancient Israel*. See also in this regard the studies of Kraus, *Worship in Israel*, and Schramm, *The Opponents of Third Isaiah*.

Third then, what is it that I seek to do in this work? I seek to write for those in Academy or Church who are looking for a reasonably user-friendly survey of the worship the Hebrew Bible speaks of, presents, describes. It is for such readers that I seek to give reasonably full references in my footnotes to further works on the subject. I trust that those who do not need those footnotes can leave them on one side and read on in the main text. While I do not attempt to give detailed consideration to that above-mentioned development of the priestly office, or the changing regulations about sacrifices and offerings, I shall try to set out something of what I understand to be the heart of these matters. Thus I attempt to communicate something of the spirit of the prayers and praises, the rites and ceremonies of worship, of which we read in the Hebrew Bible.

The Hebrew Bible portrays the worship of Yahweh as taking place in a number of settings, such as in a place where the deity has made himself known, has appeared, to a certain person or group, or else in a place specifically set aside for worship, namely a temple or a particular sanctuary, or in a family home.[28] A further setting of worship that calls for at least some consideration is the institution of the synagogue which while it does not make any clear and unambiguous appearance in the Old Testament, is there in apparently considerable fullness by New Testament times.[29]

There are two further matters regarding the Hebrew Bible's recorded acts of worship that call for comment at this introductory stage. First there is the issue of a certain hiatus between what the Hebrew Bible regards as acceptable worship, and what it seems actually took place. For example, the deuteronomistic literature consistently condemns various manifestations of Israelites becoming involved in the religions of the Canaanites and in particular in the rites of that worship. The fact that the deuteronomistic literature so frequently and consistently condemns such Israelite practices suggests that the matter was truly ongoing. While there are those who argue that what might be labelled "non-Israelite practices" should be taken with seriousness in our studies, in this particular study I am concerned to highlight much more those rites, practices, and acts of worship that in general terms we might label as to do with the "official" religion of ancient Israel.[30]

Second, just what is there in the Old Testament about what we might call ordinary, everyday—or perhaps everyweek—worship? To be sure there is no shortage of material here about extra-ordinary happenings as when

---

28. On the home as a setting of worship, see below, 49–51.

29. On the Synagogue and its worship, see below, 51–53.

30. On this matter, see Stavrakopoulou, "'Popular' Religion and 'Official' Religion." See also below, 66–68.

for example Isaiah was confronted by the holy Lord God in what looks as if it is the Jerusalem temple (Isa 6:1–8), or when Moses was called to service by the Lord in a mighty epiphany on the mountain (Exod 3:1–6), about special occasions when people went on pilgrimage to Jerusalem, specific festivals about which there were abundant regulations, and so on. But what are we told about more routine, daily, weekly worship? This matter calls to be considered in view of the fact that so much that is presented to us as being worship material in the Hebrew Bible gives the distinct impression of being accounts of what we might call special worship events.

How then, does one organize the Old Testament's worship material? This is the ever-present problem for those who would seek to study a Hebrew Bible "theme," and it is problematic because manifestly these scriptures have not come down to us in any "thematic" form or arrangement, but rather as a varied and, particularly in some parts, disparate collection of documents, many of which appear to come with their individual historical developments, but which developments frequently we are not any longer able to reconstruct in detail. We might, of course, be able to write about worship in the Old Testament by going through the various books one at a time, but that would more than likely end as something of a dull catalog which displayed little sense of order. Or one could concentrate on certain of the books of the Hebrew Bible, such as Leviticus (the Levitical book), maybe Deuteronomy, certainly the psalms, undoubtedly some of the prophets. But then other books, where the references to worship are more perfunctory, even fleeting, would have to be included, so bringing us back to something of a dull catalog. Thus it is that for better or for worse I have chosen to set forth my work in four main parts, these leading towards something by way of a number of concluding reflections in the fifth part, namely: Part I, The Place of Worship; Part II, The People at Worship; Part III, The Liturgy of Worship; Part IV, Visions and Warnings; Part V, Concluding Reflections. Within each of these parts there is generally more than one chapter as the contents page makes clear, and it is to be hoped that the various forward and backward references in the footnotes to sundry matters and various aspects of worship will be found useful.

Something about the use of certain terms and titles in this work needs to be said at this introductory stage. There is, first of all, the word "cult" about which writes J. G. Davies: "Like the French *culte*, cult and cultus designate an act of religious worship."[31] The word is generally used to designate the rites and ceremonies of the worship of a system of religious belief, and

---

31. Davies, "Cult, Cultus," 202. Mowinckel pointed out that "Cultus is the Latin word for worship" (*Religion and Cult*, 5).

that is the sense in which it is employed in this study, that is of the whole set up of worship that the Hebrew Bible sets forth as the legitimate form in which the people of Israel should engage.[32]

Then there is the word "Ritual," a word that has been defined by one Hebrew Bible scholar thus: "'Ritual' as used here refers to a complex performance of symbolic acts, characterized by its formality, order, and sequence, which tends to take place in specific situations, and has as one of its central goals the regulation of the social order."[33] In popular parlance "ritualist" can be used in a somewhat disparaging sense of those who are believed to be addicted to ceremonial of an elaborate nature, and who thereby are further believed to have lost something of, or indeed much of, the essential nature of their religious faith. In this study of worship in the Old Testament by "ritual" is intended the use of human language, artefacts, actions, music, visual imagery, and so on, in order to make a worshipful expression of certain parts and aspects of the Hebrew religious faith, and as a way in which human beings may reach out to their God. In the Hebrew Bible perhaps the clearest manifestation of "ritual" and "rituals" is found in the contributions of the so-called Priestly writers which we shall be considering below.[34]

In the third place there is the word "liturgy," a word that is derived from the Greek *leitourgia*, which in Hellenistic Greek indicated an act of public service, and the discharge of such service, and used in at least two ways in regard to the worship of God. In the first place it may be used to indicate a complete, a *whole* act of worship, as it is used for example by Christian liturgists of the whole of the service of the Eucharist. I use the word in this sense as the title for Part III of this work, "The Liturgy of Worship," insofar as I wish in that section of the study to consider some of the various fundamental modes of human expression employed in the Hebrew Bible to set forth the approach of the worshippers to the Lord, that is in prayer, in psalms, through sacrifices, and by means of appointed feasts, festivals and religious calendars.

However, the last chapter (11) in Part III of the work "Evidences of Liturgies" uses the word "liturgy" in a second sense, namely of a particularly

---

32. In speaking of "cult" we should be aware of the fact that in modern parlance the word is commonly used to designate a religious group that frequently sets itself apart from other religious groupings and wider associations. On this usage see, e.g., Rambo, "Cult," 137.

33. Gorman, *Ideology of Ritual*, 19. Elsewhere Gorman says about ritual, "It is a means of 'doing theology' or of 'theological enactment' . . . Ritual is a means of engaging the self, the community, the world, and God. The meaning of ritual is found in the enactment of the ritual itself" (*Divine Presence and Community*, 6).

34. For the Priestly writings, see below, 162–78, 211–17.

worded *part* of an act of worship. The question that this chapter seeks to address is whether or not there are evidences of small, or even not so small, liturgical fragments, pieces to be found in the pages of Old Testament. In this search I am looking for texts where we might have actual *wording* of an element in an act of worship. In particular I am concerned in that chapter to give brief consideration to some of the many suggestions that over the years scholars have made about certain parts of the Hebrew Bible, claiming that that they were at one time used in the worship of the Jerusalem cult.

This mention of the Jerusalem cult usefully serves to lead us into the first main part of this work, namely The Place of Worship, with three chapters therein, to which we now turn.

PART I

The Place of Worship

I was glad when they said to me,
"Let us go to the house of the LORD!"

—PSALM 122:1

Fifteen psalms bear the title "A song of the ascents," and perhaps the "ascending" is the going up of the worshipper to the temple in Jerusalem. What joy indeed was experienced by the psalmist merely by the thought of making this ascent; perhaps this person was a pilgrim to Jerusalem, so that the going up was something special, in no way a routine experience. The psalm follows the worshipper's progress, and at v. 2 there is the realization, as if of a group of them, "Our feet are standing within your gates, O Jerusalem," which could mean either that they have just arrived, or else that they are about to depart. If the latter, then—so it has been suggested—vv. 6–9 could be the prayer the pilgrims make on their departure.

Yet temples are not the only places of worship spoken about in the Hebrew Bible. The book of Genesis speaks of worship taking place without temple or other building, though in Judges there is talk of shrines, and in Samuel of temples, but not yet in Jerusalem. The talk in the book of Exodus of tent and tabernacle in the wilderness requires particular treatment, for while tent is surely appropriate for desert conditions, tabernacle would seem to be in some manner a retrojection of the later Jerusalem temple.

Further, we must pay attention to family homes as places of worship, and for the period after the destruction of Solomon's temple, the rise of a later temple, the so-called Second Temple, and then also, and from a later and indeterminate period, the rise and ministry of the synagogue. These various and varied places of worship make up the subject of this part of the present study.

1

Holy Places

There are parts of the Hebrew Scriptures that portray the worship of God as taking place without the benefit of temple or formal priesthood. Thus it is in Genesis and in parts of Exodus. These books portray a series of historical events that will eventuate in the establishment of the people of Israel in the land of Canaan, and where in the fullness of time buildings will be established, buildings where in particular ways the Lord may be sought and worship be offered. There are in connection with both of these books serious questions that have been asked about their portrayed historical backgrounds, this being particularly the case with the book of Genesis, and to this we first turn.

While chapters 1–11 of Genesis speak of primeval times, and with one exception do not mention the matter of worship, they do not lend themselves to be treated as historical literature, but rather in terms of myth,[1] the historical background of Genesis 12–50 having in recent decades been much discussed with differing views being presented. On the one hand there are those who argue that what we read about Abraham, Isaac, Jacob, Joseph and others in Gen 12–50 reflects what was happening to the ancestors of Israel in antiquity, others argue that this is later material that has been given the form and appearance of coming from antiquity.[2] What, however, is clear is that within these chapters there is portrayed a religious belief and practice that in a number of ways is distinctively different from what we might call classical Yahwism, what we read in the Old Testament as prevailing from the time of the entry into the land of Canaan, and that developed there until the occurrence of the event that was so radically to change Israelite life and religious practices, the defeat of Judah and Jerusalem by the Babylonian army and the destruction and burning of the temple on Mount Zion.

---

1. It hardly needs saying that by "myth" I intend not what is fictional; rather my usage is to indicate material that is expressed in story form and intended to convey religious truth and to present certain religious facts. See Rogerson, "Myth."

2. The issue of matters historical in regard to Gen 12–50 is well set out by Moberly (*Genesis 12–50*, 75–87).

What is portrayed in Gen 12–50 as being that earlier period when the patriarchs, Abraham, Isaac, Jacob, and Joseph, were in the land, is a religion that had some distinctive characteristics. In the first place, there is what comes over as a real sense of openness in belief, and in particular towards other deities and the worship offered by their devotees. While the deity worshipped by the patriarchs appears to go by various names—for example, El, El Elyon, El Shaddai, El Bethel, El Roi, El Olam—equally other deities are mentioned (see for example Gen 31:42, 53) and there is no great concern expressed about this, but rather a real sense of tolerance. Such a level of tolerance is a far cry from what we find in, for example, Deuteronomy and the Deuteronomistic writings. Further, there seems to be no perceived problem with Canaanite religion, its followers and their worship practices, there being no hint of such non-Yahwistic worship rejection as we read about in the Deuteronomistic History and in the books of Hebrew prophets like Hosea.[3] Moreover, intermarriage seems to be acceptable with Canaanite people, there being no mention of issues that so agitated the authors involved in the books of Ezra and Nehemiah.[4]

So to the matter of worship, and first we must consider what is said in Gen 4:26, "At that time people began to invoke the name of the Lord." Similar statements regarding the patriarchs occur in Gen 12:8; 13:4; 21:33; 26:25, and the expression "call on the name of the Lord" could, in the words of Gordon Wenham, be "an umbrella phrase for worship, most obviously prayer and sacrifice. On this view Gen 4:26 is noting the origin of regular divine worship, just as the preceding verses have noted the origins of farming, music, and metallurgy."[5] This, however, leaves us with the statements in Exod 6:3 and 3:14–15 which say that this worship of the Lord (*yhwh*, Yahweh) did not take place until the days of Moses. Perhaps all that we can say with any measure of assurance is that in these early parts of the Hebrew Bible there are different understandings of when the worship of Israel's God Yahweh began. What nevertheless we can say is that whatever may be the historical facts of the matter, these particular traditions that came to be incorporated into the Old Testament were intended to affirm the early commencement of the worship of the Lord God of Israel.

Genesis 12–50 speak about the patriarchs building their altars in a wide range of places. Further, trees and pillars in connection with worship are mentioned, again without words of judgment. Nor do sabbath and

---

3. On these "stricter" approaches to the matter of worship on the part of the people of ancient Israel, see below, 218–23, 250–52.

4. On patriarchal religion, see McKane, *Studies in the Patriarchal Narratives*, 195–224.

5. Wenham, *Genesis 1–15*, p. 116. See also ibid., "The Religion of the Patriarchs."

food laws feature in instructions, nor circumcision receive much emphasis. Further, there is an emphasis on individual personal religion, as if each individual or group did what seemed appropriate and right for them, and we do not hear of the involvement in worship of prophets or even priests—with the exception of the few references to the rather mysterious Melchizedek, to whom later we must return.[6] Rather, the patriarchs themselves offer their sacrifices without the mediation of a priest. Some scholars have maintained that the element of holiness, the otherness, of deities is markedly absent in the stories of the patriarchs,[7] but it can be argued that this is true only to a certain extent. Surely there is communicated a real sense of the numinous in the words of Jacob after his night at Bethel, "Surely the Lord is in this place—and I did not know it!", and in what follows, "And he was afraid (*y-r-'*), and said, 'How awesome (*nora'*) is this place! This is none other than the house of God, and this is the gate of heaven" (Gen 28:16–17).[8] It is perhaps also present in those statements at the close of the Joseph story, reading as if uttered in something of a hushed awe that out of sinfulness and calamity there could be seen a mysterious, providential working of God and his purposes, "And now do not be distressed, or angry with yourselves, because you sold me here; for God sent me before you to preserve life" (Gen 45:5; see also 45:8 and 50:20)

Further, there is nothing in Gen 12–50 about the building of a temple, or a shrine, or some other sanctuary. What, however, we do read of is what appears to be the establishment of places where a significant event or happening of a religious nature has been experienced, and where the person concerned sets up a pillar either to mark that place, or, so it has been argued, to make some claim to that part of the land, or even to be in the nature of an altar. Thus at Luz Jacob, while on his flight from home and in particular from his brother Esau's wrath, after his dream of the ladder between that place and heaven, in the morning set up the stone that had in the night been his pillow, poured oil on it, and called the place Bethel, "House of God" (Gen 28:18–19). In view of the theophoric naming of the place, and the earlier portrayal of Jacob's dream and of his being joined in relationship with the heavenly realm, to which it may be added the pouring of oil on it which elsewhere in the Old Testament is associated with the consecration of cultic items and persons (see Exod 40:9–13; Lev 8:10–12; Num 7:1), it is perhaps not unreasonable to assume that we should understand that the pillar was intended to mark the

---

6. On Melchizedek, see below, 87–88, 97–98.

7. Thus, for example, Moberly, *Genesis*, 85–86; and Wenham, "Religion of the Patriarchs," 184.

8. On the Hebrew *y-r-'* (be afraid, be in awe), see above, 3–4.

place of a divine appearance. That is, here is an important locality, a place where spiritual intercourse between God and a human person had taken place.[9] However, at Bethel Abram is portrayed as having built an altar to the Lord and to have "invoked the name of the Lord" (Gen 12:8), and it would seem to be clear that in the historical period prior to the establishment of the monarchy, and also later, Bethel had a distinctive status as a holy place, for in that place there was domiciled the sacred ark of the covenant (Judg 20:27). Elsewhere in these chapters we read of prayers of intercession being made (Gen 18:23–33; 20:7), of calling on the Lord (13:4; 21:33; 28:20–22), of libations, tithes, vows being made (31:53–4; 32:29–31). Yet few details are given as to what may have been any understandings, perceptions on the part of those worshippers in and through their religious acts.[10]

Something needs to be said here about altars.[11] It is clear that altars are of ancient and widespread provenance in religions. However, whilst a goodly number have been uncovered by archaeologists, that does not necessarily help us in our understanding as to their ancient purpose or purposes. Various ancient altars have been discovered, such as the one from the Chalcolithic period (c. 3000–c. 4000 BCE) at En-gedi,[12] that have come in a variety of styles, some being little more than shelves in rock faces—as, for example, in the ruins of ancient Petra. It would seem that a principal employment of altars lay with being the place where sacrificial victims and offerings were made to a deity, and such is portrayed as being the case in the Old Testament's first reference to an altar in Gen 8:20–21. This, we are told, is the altar that Noah built and upon which he offered burnt offerings to the Lord after the waters of the flood had receded, and that "the Lord smelled the pleasing odor," saying in his heart "I will never again curse the ground because of humankind, for the inclination of the human heart is evil from youth; nor will I ever again destroy every living creature as I have done" (Gen 8:21) We shall return to the matter of what might have been the worshippers' perceptions about what happened when offerings were made to the Lord.[13]

However, in these Genesis stories of the patriarchs the significance of the altars appears to be as much with the marking of a place where some significant religious event or experience has taken place as with providing

9. For details of and discussion about other possible meaning of the "pillar," see Westermann, *Genesis 12-36*, pp. 457–58; Wenham, *Genesis 16-50*, pp. 223–24.

10. For details of these matters, see Wenham "The Religion of the Patriarchs," 162–64.

11. See Vaux, *Ancient Israel*, 406–14.

12. See Aharoni, *The Archaeology of the Land of Israel*, 43–47.

13. See below, 177–78.

an artefact where a sacrifice may be offered. An example of this is the altar we are told that Jacob raised up at Bethel following on from his night there when the Lord appeared to him in a dream (Gen 28:18–22).[14] Nevertheless, the story in Gen 22:1–14 is clearly about sacrifice, and I shall return to it later in this work.[15] In the meantime it should be observed that the matter of calling on the name of the Lord was generally at the place where an altar had been built. We read of this in Gen 12:8; 13:4; 26:25, but we may observe that in Gen 21:33 there is no note of an altar, but rather of Abraham having planted a tamarisk tree at Beersheba.

We now need to consider the book of Exodus, in particular that considerable part of it concerning matters of worship. For the book of Exodus, though it may be thought of as the story of how the Israelites escaped from their slave-existence in Egypt, is a remarkably rounded work displaying disparate materials. At its beginning it is about the plight of the Israelite captivity under a harsh Pharaoh and the successful escape into the desert (Exod 1:1—18:27), going on then to speak of the Lord's revelation to their leader Moses and of his making a covenant with them, complete with conditions by which they shall live in their relationship with the Lord and with one another (19:1—24:18). Finally in a large block of material (25:1—40:38) we are told about matters of worship, and in particular of places for worship, and what the people and their leaders are to do in the worship of the Lord who in his grace has brought them thus far and who promises to lead them on into the future. All this makes for a theologically interconnected presentation of a people loved and rescued by their Lord, brought into covenant relationship with him, he thereby becoming the focus of their ongoing life of worship. In these chapters we read about three "places" where worship is to take place.

The theme of the "holy place," unadorned with temple or any other building, is there in the book of Exodus, and occupies serious space within the total theological presentation of that book. The place is, of course, the mountain called Horeb (as it is named in Exod 3:1; 17:6; 33:6; generally in Deut; in 1 Kgs 8:9; 19:8; 2 Chr 5:10; Ps 106:19 and Mal 4:4) and which appears to be the same mountain, or at least to be in the same mountain range, as Sinai (which appears in Exodus 13 times; Leviticus 5 times; Numbers 12 times; Deuteronomy once; Judges and Nehemiah once each; Psalms twice). At any rate according to the record we have in Exod 3:1–15 it was at Horeb, the mountain of God (v. 1), that Moses is portrayed as having a profound experience of the mighty and mysterious God, to whom he feels

---

14. See below, 280–81, for more on such "non-verbal signs."
15. See below, 167–68.

compelled to approach, but then told to come no closer and to remove his sandals from his feet because the place where he is standing is "holy ground" (v. 5). The mysterious God introduces himself as the God of the ancestors, and says that he has heard the cry of his people who are suffering in Egypt and with the human assistance of Moses is going to lead his people out of Egypt into that good and broad land which flows with milk and honey (vv. 7–11). When his people are led out of Egypt they and Moses will come to this mountain to worship this God, the God who declines to give his name to Moses but who declares himself to be "I am that I am"—which could equally be translated "I will be what I will be" (vv. 12, 14). Undoubtedly this is a major "holy place" spoken about in the Hebrew Bible, and it is indeed what is portrayed in Exod 19 onwards (though there it is called Sinai) as being the setting for the making of a covenant relationship which includes the giving of the God's laws to his people. Once again, what will come to be regarded as a holy place is where a decisive encounter between God and his people takes place, and such will again take place when Elijah flees there on being threatened with death by Queen Jezebel (1 Kgs 19:8). Our records clearly indicate that sense of holiness, otherness, that sense of the numinous in the encounters with the Lord that these human individuals experienced, that experience which Otto described as "quite different from anything that can be exhaustively rendered in rational concepts, namely, on the sheer absolute wondrousness that transcends thought, on the *mysterium*, presented in its pure, non-rational form."[16]

Exodus also speaks about what we may call shrines, structures that are portrayed as having some sort of materialism, even permanence, that seem intended to be places where the presence of the Lord is expected to be encountered in worship. Two of these are to be dealt with in the following chapter of this work, for the fact is that one of them, the "tabernacle," is portrayed as being of such a degree of elaborateness, even of permanence, that it is difficult to believe that it had real, material existence in the desert, certainly of having been built by what are portrayed as a group of escaping slaves from Egypt who yet have a long way to go on their journey through the desert to the good and fertile land which they have been promised. Further, this portrayed tabernacle appears to reflect so many of the details and features of what we are told were found in the temple built by Solomon in Jerusalem. This surely indicates that what we are dealing with in the Exod 25—40 account of the building of the desert tabernacle is a retrojected account of the temple that in the days of Solomon was built in Jerusalem, but which is here portrayed as built to the divine specifications received by

---

16. Otto, *The Idea of the Holy*, 81 (his italics).

Moses "on the mountain." This tabernacle/temple matter will therefore be discussed in some detail in the chapter that follows this present one.[17]

What does need to be considered briefly here is what is called "the tent of meeting", spoken of in Exod 33:7–11. It reappears in Num 11:16–30 and 12:1–16, and in all these accounts it is Moses who "met" there with the Lord. Here, we are told, "the Lord used to speak to Moses face to face, as one speaks to a friend" (Exod 33:11). We hear nothing by way of sacrificial worship being made here, or offerings presented, but rather only an intimate meeting of the divine and human parties through the medium of prayer. Nor do we have here anything about either the construction or the dimensions of this "tent," but it certainly seems credible that something like this was a reality as a portable shrine for the life and wanderings in the desert.[18] We shall later in this work come across references to a tent as providing a house for the ark of the covenant until that came to a more permanent and, perhaps, more dignified setting in Solomon's temple. We should perhaps also take note of the fact that this "tent" tradition, at least in its desert setting gives a real emphasis to the place of prayer in worship, a matter to which we shall return.[19]

In the meantime we consider the various shrines and temples that came to be established in the land of Canaan, and elsewhere, and something of the Hebrew Bible's portrayed significance of these places for the faith and worship of the people of Israel. This is the subject of the chapter that now follows.

---

17. See below, 26–29, and further, 33–48.

18. For the "tent," see further Haran, *Temples and Temple-Service*, 260–75; Rowley, *Worship in Ancient Israel*, 79n.; Rad, "The Tent and the Ark."

19. For prayer, see below, 105–18, and further, 285–87.

2

Temples

There is a certain amount of groundwork that needs to be covered before we can come to the building of the temple in Jerusalem, it being necessary in the first place to return to the matter of the desert sanctuaries, and second to consider the various shrines we read of in Canaan in the period leading up to the great project of the Jerusalem temple.

Once Again, the Desert Sanctuaries

These have already been spoken about in the preceding chapter, but more now needs to be said about them, namely, the tent of meeting and the tabernacle. The second of these, is given the name "tabernacle," but as has already been observed there is high improbability that such an edifice could have been built by a community on an extended journey through desert areas. Rather what we have here seems to be material that is in fact about the temple that came to be built in Jerusalem in the days of the kingship of Solomon, but the account is presented as a retrospect of what had been divinely revealed to Moses "on the mountain," Horeb, during the days of the desert journey. The predominant word employed in the account in the book of Exodus that this sanctuary be built is *miškān*, a word that is frequently translated "tabernacle", and which comes from the root *š-k-n* meaning "dwell." As we shall come to see later this is a word used predominantly in the Hebrew Bible by the so-called priestly writers, who seem to have been the main contributors to Exod 25–40, and who perhaps intended it to carry the sense of the Lord's "dwelling place," namely, that it was by means of this sanctuary that the Lord remained with his people on their desert journey.[1] In other parts of the Hebrew Bible, in non-priestly writings, other words will be used of the Jerusalem temple, amongst which are *hêkāl* "temple," and also *bayit* "house", the latter often appearing as "house of God," or "house of the Lord," or even "house of Yahweh." But all these terms would seem to

---

1. On the so-called priestly writers and their particular approach to worship, see below, 211–17. For the symbolism of the desert tabernacle, see Jenson, *Graded Holiness*, 111–14.

be intended to indicate an edifice of greater permanence than the *miškān*, "tabernacle" language, as employed about the "temple" in the priestly material, and to this matter we shall return.

The desert tabernacle (*miškān*) which we read about in Exod 25 is portrayed as a highly elaborate structure for which the people were called to bring their offerings of "gold, silver, and bronze, blue, purple, and crimson yarns and fine linen, goats' hair, tanned rams' skins, fine leather, acacia wood, oil for the lamps, spices for the anointing oil and for the fragrant incense, onyx stones and gems to be set in the ephod and for the breastpiece" (Exod 25:3-7) All this, so the command of the Lord runs, "And have them make me a sanctuary [here called a *miqdāš*, sanctuary], so that I may dwell among them" (25:8). Further, this portrayed desert sanctuary is to be the setting and place of domicile for the ark of the covenant. That ark was to be made with overlays of gold inside and outside (25:10-16), with the mercy seat made of pure gold (25:17-22). Further, there was to be the table of acacia wood and gold (25:23-30), and the lampstand made, again, of pure gold (25:31-40). The sides of this sanctuary were to be made of curtains (26:1-6), the whole edifice being over-arched and covered by a great tent made of animal skins (26:7-14). So the account continues in much detail through the rest of Exod 26 and on into ch. 27. It is widely accepted that we have here a retrospected account of what came to be built in Jerusalem, but some have argued that this is rather someone's picture—vision perhaps—of some sort of ideal of a sanctuary.[2]

Then there is "the tent of meeting," spoken about briefly in Exod 33:7-11, a place for worship which gives all the appearances of being eminently suitable for such a purpose in the desert setting, and what was said earlier does not need to be repeated.[3]

What though we do need to consider here is the succeeding account in Exod 35:1—40:38 which details the construction of all that Moses had been commanded to make by the Lord, namely, tabernacle (*miškān*), tent (*'ōhel*), ark with poles, mercy seat, curtain for screens, table and the bread of the Presence, lamp stand, altar of incense, the altar of burnt offering, and a good deal else beside (35:10-19). We note here the mention of "tent of meeting" within this talk of the "tabernacle," and one conclusion about this might be that in this account two traditions have become conflated. However, there are manifold problems in understanding the literary relationship of what

---

2. For a small selection of a range of views on this, see, e.g., Haran, *Temples and Temple-Service*, 189-204; Clements, *God and Temple*, 114-15; Davies, "Tabernacle"; Friedman, "Tabernacle"; Barker, *The Gate of Heaven*, 137; Houston, "Exodus," 85-86; and Durham, *Exodus*, 352-53.

3. See above p. 25.

are presented as the giving of the divine command on the mountain, about what is to be built in the desert (Exod 25:1—31:17), and what we have in Exod 35:1—40:38 about the actual building thereof. About the relationship between these passages there is a dearth of scholarly agreement. Thus perhaps we have to leave the matter as it is. However, it can be restated that what we have here in these accounts appears to be something that belongs to settled days in the land, and not to the inevitable constrictions of the life of a people who have escaped from captivity and who are engaged on a long and arduous desert journey. It would therefore appear that what we have in both Exod 25:1—31:17 and 35:1—40:38 do have a relationship with what later came to be built for the days of settled life in the promised land, and especially in Jerusalem.[4] In all probability we should understand this material—and in particular the material here about the Tabernacle—as intended to speak of ideals of worship and of the relationship between the Israelite people and their God, that we should be understanding some deeper realities beneath the surface meaning of the words. Something of this is expressed by Coggins who says about Exod 39:43, "The Hebrew could be literally rendered 'Moses saw all the work and they had indeed done it as the Lord had commanded.' This is reminiscent of the work of creation described in Gen 1:1—2:3. The importance of the tabernacle is stressed by picturing it as a creation in little."[5] Further, both tent and tabernacle were intended to speak of the presence of God with his people, the tent for the desert days, the tabernacle for the settled days in the land, especially in the chosen city.

One of the principal religious artefacts that was to have its home in the tabernacle was the ark of the covenant, although both the beginning and the ending of this religious object are from the historical aspect unclear to us.[6] Yet the ark features in the stories of the desert-wandering days of the people of Israel, in this regard it being spoken of as having been made and installed in the tabernacle (Exod 25:10–16). Here is detailed the fact that it was constructed of acacia wood, that it was two and a half cubits long, a cubit and a half in both width and height, that the wood was overlaid with gold both inside and outside. But what did it represent? What was it intended to "say," to indicate to those who either saw it or knew of its presence? In the Exod 25 account, the ark has a cover, what has been translated as "mercy seat," at

---

4. On the matter of the relationship between these parts of the book of Exodus, see, e.g., Barker, *The Gate of Heaven*, 137–38.

5. Coggins, *Exodus*, 130. On the matter of parallels between the accounts of creation of the world and construction of the tabernacle, see also Barker, *Temple Theology*, 16–21.

6. For the possibilities for the historical demise of the ark, see the detailed study of Day, "Whatever Happened to the Ark of the Covenant?"

the ends of which were two golden cherubim (Exod 25:17–21), and within which was "the covenant" that the Lord would give to Moses (v. 21). These contents, in Hebrew "treaty, testimony" (*'ēdût*), would seem to indicate what we might call "covenant documents," that is the covenant stipulations for the people who have been brought into covenant relationship with God, namely the Ten Commandments. It was in this place that the Lord pronounced that he would meet with Moses:

> There I will meet you, and from above the mercy-seat ["cover"], from between the two cherubim that are on the ark of the covenant, I will deliver to you all my commands for the Israelites. (Exod 25:22)

This account, which as has already been noted is widely thought to come from the work of the so-called priestly writers, of the beginnings of the ark of the covenant would appear to picture it as representing both the presence of the Lord and also his commandments to them as to how they should live in relationship with him and with one another.

There is another understanding of the ark of the covenant in the Hebrew Bible. It occurs in the book of Deuteronomy, and this account takes a rather more muted approach to the matter of the ark representing the presence of God than does the priestly material. Deuteronomy, rather, regards the ark of the covenant as a container for the tablets of the law, as is made clear in the account in Deuteronomy of the making of the ark of the covenant (Deut 10:1–5), and while these writers are chary of speaking of the immediate presence of God on earth, so that they do not speak of God *dwelling* on earth, they can yet present the ark as in some way representing the Lord's gifts to and his expectations from his chosen people. Perhaps above all they were concerned to make the matter of the Lord's presence with his people a *spiritual* presence, a *spiritual* matter, and thus they speak of him "causing his name" to be in such and such a place. That is, while these writers wish to stress both the transcendence and immanence of God they do not go as far as making the immanence into a physical presence of God on earth (so in Deut 12:11; 14:23–24; 16:2, 6, 11; 26:2, etc.).[7]

---

7. I am aware of the contribution of Wilson, that in Deut 10:8 we do have the instruction of the Lord that the tribe of Levi is, "to carry the ark of the covenant of the Lord, to stand before the Lord to minister to him and to bless in his name . . ." ("Merely a Container?," 214). Wilson seems to me to make this one text go a long way in his argument that Deuteronomy does speak of the direct presence of the Lord through the ark, and does not take sufficiently seriously all the occurrences of the divine "causing his name" to be present in the place of worship.

Shrines in Canaan

In 1 Sam 3:1–3 we read of the ark of the covenant being in the temple at Shiloh, it having at that time a rather troubled involvement in the Israelite-Philistine disputes. Later it came to be located in Kiriath-jearim where it remained until the time when it was taken by King David to Jerusalem (2 Sam 6:1–19), later being installed in the Jerusalem temple that Solomon established. Yet further, 1 Sam 3:1–3 has the Old Testament's first mention of a "temple," and it is termed "the temple (*hêkāl*) of the Lord," and within it was housed the ark of the covenant. This was in the time when the boy Samuel was ministering to the Lord under the priest Eli, and such was the setting for the dramatic call of the Lord to Samuel (1 Sam 3:1–21). The ark, from this setting of the Shiloh temple became involved in some of the Israelite disputes with the Philistines (1 Sam 4:3–7), even being captured at one time by the Philistines, but the troubles and difficulties it brought upon its captors resulted in its soon being returned to the Israelites (1 Sam 4:12—7:2). Thus the ark came to be lodged at Kiriath-jearim, until the time when it was conveyed to King David's newly-acquired city of Jerusalem, where it was temporarily housed in a tent (2 Sam 6:1–19), until its permanent home was built—the Jerusalem temple (1 Kgs 8:1–9). Meanwhile Shiloh's importance as a place where there was a temple seems to have declined (see Ps 78:60–61; Jer 7:12–15), though just what were the historical circumstances that brought about its demise elude us.[8]

Another religious shrine we read about in what are portrayed as these early times was in Shechem. We are told that Abram built an altar there to the Lord who had appeared to him in that place (Gen 12:6–7). Now according to Judg 9:4, 27, 46 there was a temple there, in v. 4 called "the temple [literally "house" *bayit*] of Baal-berith," and in v. 46 "the temple [again *bayit*] of El-berith," which perhaps suggests that this was, or had earlier been, a place of Canaanite worship. At any rate by the time the northern tribes broke away from the Jerusalemite kingship of Rehoboam after the death of Solomon it was to Shechem they went and where they made Jeroboam the son of Nebat their ruler. Clearly in the eyes of some in those days Shechem was a place of certain significance.

Also significant for these northern tribes was the shrine at Dan which with the one at Bethel became something of the respectively northern and southern temples of the northern kingdom of Israel. The two became homes for the golden calves set up by Jeroboam (1 Kgs 12:28–29), animal symbols

---

8. It is possible that the decline of the Shiloh temple was dramatic, that it was destroyed by the Philistines c. 1050 BCE, and that this was the event alluded to in Jer 7:12, 14 and Ps 78:60–61. See Day, "The Destruction of the Shiloh Sanctuary."

that it seems came to be venerated as deities, but which, along with the molten calf made in the desert, being roundly condemned in the Old Testament (Hos 8:4–6; 10:5; Exod 32; Deut 9:8–21; Ps 106:19–23; Neh 9:18). Further, Bethel in Amos 7:13 is referred to as the "king's sanctuary [*miqdāš*]," "a temple [*bayit*] of the kingdom." Yet the roots of the cultic center of Dan appear to go back further than this, for we read of the town here, then known as Laish, being taken by the Danites, being renamed Dan, and of the establishment there of an idol of cast metal, an ephod and teraphim, all under the care of a priest (Judg 17:1—18:31).[9]

Other temples and shrines could be spoken of, but perhaps a general survey is sufficient for this brief consideration of shrines prior to the establishing of the temple in Jerusalem. According to Gen 13:18 Abraham built an altar at Hebron, and we are told that there was a shrine at Beersheba where the Lord had appeared to Isaac and where Isaac had built an altar (Gen 26:23–25), but which was destroyed in the religious reforms of King Josiah (2 Kgs 23:8); there were altars in Gilgal (1 Sam 11:14–15); and also in Mizpah where Jacob offered sacrifice (Gen 31:54), and where Samuel had a number of dealings (1 Sam 7:5–17).

What can be said about the religious rites carried out in these places? For much of the time, it has to be admitted, not a great deal. As far as the stories of the Patriarchs in the book of Genesis are concerned, we are told that sacrifices were offered, but no further details are given as to what it might have been believed were the results of so doing. Then further, we read that prayers were made to God, that libations were offered, and that tithes were given. There is here—apart from the talk in Gen 14 of Melchizedek, king of Salem, and "priest of God Most High" (Gen 14:18), to whom I shall return[10]—no talk of priestly involvement in worship. Each person, or each family head perhaps, seems to have been responsible for such matters. Nor is there any talk here of the ministry or the intervention of prophets; rather what is portrayed is God appearing directly to various individuals, and that in some cases various places came to gain a cultic status for the reason that they were settings where God had made his appearance to some human individual. An example of this is the appearance of God to Jacob at Bethel (Gen 28:10–17), which led, so we are told, in the fullness of time to the establishment there of a temple, this probably being intended to give at Bethel a like status and religious foundation to rival those of the Judean city and temple of Jerusalem. All this serves to raise the question about what in religious terms—rather than political—these temples, sanctuaries meant to the

---

9. On ephod, teraphim, etc., see below, 31–32, 49–50, 50n2.
10. On Melchizedek, see below, 87–88, 97–98.

peoples and leaders of their day. Yet we can hardly satisfactorily answer such questions as our sources are not sufficiently forthcoming about the issues.

Again, we have to admit to a limited knowledge of the sort of religious rites that took place in that general historical period leading up to the building and establishment of the Jerusalem temple, that is regarding what we read about in the biblical books of Joshua, Judges, 1 and 2 Samuel. Certainly there is talk here of priests, one of them being Eli (1 Sam 2:27-36). Here also there is talk of sacrifices and offerings (vv. 28-29), of the offering of incense, and of the wearing of the ephod (v. 28, Hebrew *'ēpōd*).[11] The ephod seems to have been a sleeveless yet ornate outer garment that was worn by an Israelite priest. This is spoken about at some length in Exod 28:15-28; 35:27; 39:1-26, and is also mentioned in 1 Sam 2:28; 22:18; 2 Sam 6:14, but we have to admit that its real significance eludes us. The word also seems to be used in a more general sense as a common garment that may be worn as David did when he danced before the ark on its journey into Jerusalem (2 Sam 6:14), or indeed as the boy Samuel did in the temple at Shiloh (1 Sam 2:18). Further, we read about an ephod being used in seeking guidance, and that sounds like a tangible object rather than as an item of clothing (1 Sam 14:3; 23:6, 9; 30:7). Finally in passages such as Judg 8:27 we have reference to what looks like being an idolatrous artefact; is it something like this that is intended in Isa 30:22, NRSV "images"? Thus while we have a goodly number of references to "ephod" in the Hebrew Bible we yet have to admit to our ignorance both of their significance and also of their relationships.[12]

We also read about teraphim (Hebrew *tĕrāpîm*) and these would appear to have been in the nature of idols. Sometimes, they are portrayed as being small and stealable (Gen 31:19, 34-35), perhaps almost "household gods" (Gen 31:30), but in 1 Sam 19:13, 16 there is a teraphim the size and shape of a man in the house of David and Michal. Clearly they were used in the cult, at least in the period portrayed as preceding the Hebrew kingdoms (Judg 17:5; 18:14, 17, 20), but they came to be roundly condemned (1 Sam 15:23; 2 Kgs 23:24).[13] We also read of terebinths (Hebrew *'ēlôn*), which were large trees, perhaps oak trees, and mentioned in Gen 12:6; 13:18; 14:13; 18:1; Deut 11:30. They come to be condemned in the Old Testament as associated with high places where unacceptable worship took place (Hos 4:13).[14]

11. On priests and priesthood, see below, 71-88; on incense, see below, 83-84.

12. On ephod, see below, 49-50, 82, 86. See also Meyers, "Ephod"; Haran, *Temples and Temple-Service*, 166-68; Davies, "Ephod"; and Eddinger, "Ephod."

13. On teraphim, see below, 31-32, 49-50. See also Eddinger, "Teraphim"; and Gordon, "Teraphim."

14. On terebinths, see, e.g., Moore and Younker, "Terebinth"; and Trever, "Terebinth." Also see below, 32.

We should also notice the occurrence in Judg 17:4-5 of what in NRSV is translated as "an idol of cast metal" (Hebrew *pesel*). Although in the Old Testament these are generally roundly condemned, usually because the religious use of them is associated with the religious ways of the surrounding nations, Susan Niditch makes a defence of them, arguing that such "hewn and cast objects are not idols but iconic representations that allow worshippers to focus upon the deity and upon his/her qualities." Whether the Hebrew Bible writers would have agreed is a moot point.[15]

Then there are "high places" (Hebrew *bāmâ*): these are commonly mentioned in the Old Testament, and seem to have been (originally) places of Canaanite worship, and Israelites either took some of them over for their worship or else established their own "high places." In times of religious reforms the reformers sought to remove them and to ban their use for Israelite worship.[16]

Temples

The whole matter of sanctuaries and shrines in the Hebrew Bible takes on a profound change with the accounts of the building and establishment of the Jerusalem temple. Jerusalem came into the cultic frame when the Jebusite stronghold of Zion was captured by David, and as a result of his establishment there of a royal palace and the bringing of the sacred ark of the covenant into the city and lodging it within a tent (2 Sam 5:7-11; 6:17). According to the Deuteronomistic Historian it was the wish of David to build in Jerusalem a house for the ark to be lodged in, but that by divine will was unable to do so, for we are told it was the Lord's purpose that he (the Lord) should give to David a "house," that is a dynasty, rather than David giving to the Lord a "house," that is a sanctuary, a place of worship (2 Sam 7:1-7). No doubt there were various political, economic—and doubtless practical—factors lying behind what is presented as this divine word, but about these we can no more than speculate. Perhaps we have simply to accept the fact that David did not build a temple in Jerusalem but that later his son and successor on the throne, Solomon, did.

Further, there was a particular political situation in Israelite Jerusalem of which notice should be taken. This Jebusite city was conquered by David and his own soldiers, thereby becoming David's own possession, and

---

15. Niditch, *Judges*, 181.

16. See Haran, *Temples and Temple-Service*, 18-25; Nakhai, "High Place"; Davies, "High Places"; Barrick, "High Place"; and Vaughan, *The Meaning of 'BAMA'*. See further below, 53-54.

so being referred to as city of David. Moreover, the city was geographically situated between Judah in the south and the northern Israelite tribes, and thus made the obvious center for government not only for that city but also for both the states of Israel and Judah. No doubt the enhancement of Jerusalem with royal palace and religious temple strengthened both of these political and religious dimensions of the city of David, and served to add to the strong possibility that the one king could rule Jerusalem, Judah and Israel—and also, it might have been hoped, could his kingly successors too. However, this present study is concerned with the worship of the Lord of all these peoples, and so with this background awareness of these military and political factors, we may turn to matters more specifically religious and cultic in Davidic Jerusalem.

We read in 1 Kgs 5:1–12 that King David's son Solomon made a treaty with king Hiram of Tyre for help with the construction of the Jerusalem temple; thus this project became something of an international enterprise. In particular, Hiram was to supply materials for the building of the temple, especially quantities of cedar wood. In 1 Kgs 5:1—8:61 there are no less than 18 references to cedar wood (though only three in the Chronicler's account, 2 Chr 2:1—8:16) being used in this building project. Presumably part of the significance of our being given these details is to indicate the quality of building materials used in this great project. In Israelite eyes the cedar stood for strength (Pss 29:5; 37:35; Isa 2:13; 9:10), for splendor (Song 1:17; Jer 22:14), possessed of a particular glory (Ps 80:10; Jer 22:7; Zech 11:1). Certainly what we are told about Solomon having to pay for the cedar and cypress woods (1 Kgs 5:11) does suggest considerable cost.

The actual building of the temple is detailed in 1 Kgs 6:1–38, but we have to admit that in many verses we do not know the meaning and intended significance of various words, in particular those concerned with architectural details. Further those responsible for the ancient Versions clearly had trouble with them, sometimes doing no more than transliterating them, as for example with the Hebrew word 'ûlām, "porch, vestibule" in v. 3 which in the LXX is simply transliterated into the Greek as *ailam*. Again, in v. 5 the Hebrew *děbîr* "inner sanctuary, holy of holies" appears in the Greek as *dabir*. Moreover, to add to our sense of ignorance there are details of which we are not told. Perhaps not too serious is that we are not told what the thicknesses of the various walls of the temple were, but more difficulties are posed by the fact that it is not clear just how much the vestibule, the 'ûlām mentioned above, was a part of the building, whether it made up the first part of a three-part building, or alternatively whether it was in the nature of a vestibule, a portico that one went through in order to enter the temple.

Such different understandings of these, and other matters in regard to the temple, inevitably lead to differing interpretations of the whole plan of the building. Thus it will be observed that those scholars who have been sufficiently bold to present plans and illustrations representing what they believe the temple looked like come up with some rather different arrangements.[17] Certainly, the Deuteronomistic Historian appears to give considerable detail of temple architecture and building,[18] but perhaps the real significance of all this information lies in the overall picture thus presented—maybe intended to convey a sense of the majesty, the glory of the temple, to make clear that "nothing was spared" in the building thereof, that no expense was too great for this mighty and important enterprise. Maybe Richard Nelson is on the right track when he says that "the narrator of this section wishes to impress, to awe, to fix in the reader's mind a general impression of this particular attraction."[19]

One such impression that we thus gain concerns the size of the building, which we are told was 60 cubits long, 20 cubits wide, and 30 cubits high. Assuming that the cubit was around 20 inches, that is around 500 mm, we are here reading about a building measuring approximately 100 feet (30.5 metres) in length and 33.5 feet (10 metres) wide. My reading of 1 Kgs 6:3 is that the "vestibule" (Hebrew *ûlām*) was *in addition to* this length, for we read that "The vestibule in front of [Hebrew *'al pĕnêy*] the nave [Hebrew *hêkal*] of the house [Hebrew *bayit*] was twenty cubits wide, across the width of the house."[20] Then the 60 cubits of the house proper was made up of two parts, the first part which NRSV translates as "nave" (Hebrew *hêkal*), the second being the "inner sanctuary" (Hebrew *dĕbîr*, perhaps "holy of holies") (v. 5). There were other rooms, what are described as "side chambers," around the outside of the building and built on three levels, and there were windows—though the note that they had "recessed frames" (so NRSV) is a detail about which it is difficult for us to be sure (1 Kgs 6:4-6). Further

---

17. For some such plans and illustrations, see, for example, Jones, *Old Testament Illustrations*, 158–61; Stinespring, "Temple, Jerusalem," esp. pp. 536–37; Quellette, "Temple of Solomon"; Meyers, "Temple, Jerusalem," esp. p. 356.

18. The question as to the historical vantage point of the author of 1 Kgs 6-8 is certainly pertinent, even though any proposed date must inevitably be no more than provisional. See the helpful article of Tomes, "'Our Holy and Beautiful House.'" The fact that there is a marked lack of any talk in 1 Kings 8 about sacrifices possibly suggests a time when Israelite worship was moving towards non-sacrificial worship, and that Tomes's suggestion of it coming from the period between 597 and 578 BCE is not unlikely.

19. Nelson, *Kings*, 43.

20. So also Meyers, "Temple, Jerusalem," 357.

these extra rooms were not around the vestibule, again suggesting that the vestibule was something of a projection onto the main part of the building.

The approach to the temple, then, was through this "vestibule", the *'ûlām*, and either side of the entrance to this were the pillars, Jachin and Boaz, (1 Kgs 7:15-22), which according to the Kings account were 18 cubits high, but with their elaborate capitals being made 5 cubits taller.[21] Their purpose and possible symbolism have been endlessly discussed without any clear and convincing answer being suggested. From a structural point of view the temple building does not seem to have depended on them, thus suggesting their purpose was symbolic.[22] As regards the vestibule beyond these great pillars we are given fewer details than we are for the other two parts of the temple, and this, along with the fact that we are given few details about its furnishings and decoration, perhaps suggests it was of lesser significance. Maybe it was in fact neither more nor less than a "vestibule", possibly a "forecourt," the area that prepared the way into the building proper, intended to prepare the worshipper's way, physically and spiritually, into the temple.

The second part of the building is in the Hebrew called *hêkal*, a term that NRSV translates "nave," but because that word has come to be used of and connected with certain styles of much later Christian architecture, it is perhaps better to call it the "sanctuary." This was the largest single part of the whole temple, and it was finished in cedar wood, as the Deuteronomistic Historian explains "the cedar . . . had carvings of gourds and open flowers; all was cedar, no stone was seen" (1 Kgs 6:18) Not surprisingly, it contained a number of furnishings appropriate to its religious purposes. Thus here it seems was the golden altar and the golden table for the bread of the Presence, the pure gold lampstands, cups, snuffers, basins, dishes for incense, firepans; in fact we are told that even "the sockets for the doors of the innermost part of the house . . . and for the doors of the nave" were of gold (1 Kgs 7:48-50).

Then the third, and most holy, part of the building was the *děbîr*, what NRSV translates as "inner sanctuary." At the end of 1 Kgs 6:16 this is called "holy of holies" (Hebrew *qōdeš haqŏdāšîm*), but in all probability that is a priestly term, one that is found in late books of the Hebrew Bible, that in its present setting is a gloss intended to clarify just which part of the temple is here being spoken about.[23] The *děbîr* was sumptuous indeed: here again

---

21. The Chronicler's version of these details increases the height of the pillars to no less than 35 cubits—plus 5 cubits for the capitals! See 2 Chr 3:15.

22. See, e.g., DeVries, "Jachin and Boaz"; Meyers, "Jachin and Boaz in Religious and Political Perspective"; and Meyers, "Jachin and Boaz."

23. For details, see Burney, *Notes on the Hebrew Text of the Books of Kings*, 71.

there was much gold, and here above all was the sacred ark of the covenant (1 Kgs 6:19). There were also two large golden cherubim, each with a wingspan of 10 cubits, and a height of 10 cubits. It seems clear that the perceived purpose of these cherubim was the protection of the ark of the covenant, the religious artefact that above all else represented the presence of the Lord God with his people. The way into this inner sanctuary was through doors made of olive wood which had carvings of cherubim, palm trees, and open flowers, all these being overlaid with yet more gold (1 Kgs 6:31–32).

There were also a number of artefacts outside the temple building, among them being a large basin, 5 cubits high and 10 cubits in diameter, and resting on four sets of three oxen. This was called either the "molten sea" (so 1 Kgs 7:23–26), or "the sea" (1 Kgs 7:24; 2 Kgs 16:17), or the "bronze sea" (2 Kgs 25:13; 1 Chr 18:8; Jer 52:17). The account in Kings does not tell us what was the purpose or symbolism of this sea. The usage spoken of in 2 Chr 4:6, for "the priests to wash in," sounds somewhat mundane for such an elaborate structure; perhaps it was one that had come to replace an earlier and more significant usage.[24] It is most likely that this "contained" sea was intended to represent that wild "natural" sea, and to represent it as having been conquered and "contained" by the Lord. However, for the Chronicler with his concern to establish clear links between the Jerusalem temple and the desert tabernacle, it is understandable that he should link the "sea" in the laver with what we read in Exod 30:18–19 about Moses being commanded to provide between the tent of meeting and the altar a bronze basin with a stand for water with which Aaron and his sons should wash their hands and their feet. Then in 1 Kgs 7:27–50 are set out a whole range of further objects and artefacts, the intended purposes in most cases eluding us, but again it would seem that little expense was spared. What NRSV translates as "stands" were certainly elaborate (1 Kgs 7:27–37) but their usage, of which we are not informed, remains unknown.[25]

There were further artefacts in this temple which should be considered. First, there were ten bronze basins (1 Kgs 7:38–39), five of which were set on each of the two sides of the temple. While we have a comparative wealth of information about their material and size, we are not told what they were intended to represent or what was their practical purpose. A likely purpose would have been to contain water for purification or for the making of libations.[26] Then there were the vessels about which we read in 1 Kgs 7:40–47,

---

24. Williamson says of the priests's use of the sea for washing: "By contrast with the original symbolism of the sea, this may represent an element of 'demythologisation'" (*1 and 2 Chronicles*, 211). See also the discussion in Japhet, *I & II Chronicles*, 565–66.

25. For a discussion, see Jones, *1 & 2 Kings*, 1:85.

26. See Sweeney, *1 & 2 Kings*, 122–23.

Hiram of Tyre having been responsible for their manufacture. Some of these we have already read about, but other items are spoken of here for the first time. Yet we can well understand that pots, shovels, and basins were all required for the smooth working of the temple services and ceremonies. No doubt the information imparted in 1 Kgs 7:47, that Solomon left the weight of the bronze vessels undetermined, is intended to invoke a sense of awe as to the magnificence of the temple and its artefacts within the mind of the reader.

Then there were the altars, a number of them, that had places and functions in Solomon's temple, though unfortunately the sources at our disposal are once again vague regarding the details. It would seem we should regard the significance of altars as being the meeting point with the divine realm, and upon which offerings were made to the Lord. Thus we read about altars at certain crucial moments for individuals and groups, such as the end of and deliverance from the flood (Gen 8:20-21), or at a locality where some particular person has encountered the Lord, experienced deliverance, or sought the help of God (Gen 12:7-8; 13:4; 22:9-13; 26:25; 33:20; 35:1, 7; Exod 17:15-16; Judg 6:24).[27]

Regarding Solomon's temple we read in 1 Kgs 6:20-22 that there was an altar, which we are informed was made of cedar and overlaid with gold, that was situated in the inner shrine, the *dĕbîr*, the inner sanctuary, the holy of holies, and it may have been before this altar that Solomon is spoken of as praying for his people (1 Kgs 8:22, 54), either standing (v. 22) or kneeling (v. 54). But it seems to be a different altar that is spoken about in 1 Kgs 8:62-64: this we are told was a large altar, larger than "the bronze altar," which in view of the fact that it is otherwise unmentioned, we may perhaps assume is one that stood in the court in front of the temple, and that maybe replaced the earlier altar made by David (2 Sam 24:25)[28]

In the days of king Ahaz, some two centuries after Solomon, we are told that another altar came to be added in the area at the front of the temple. This was after the style and design of the Assyrian altar that Ahaz had seen in Damascus to where he had been summoned by his new overlord Tiglath-pileser, the Assyrian ruler (2 Kgs 16:10-15).

These various altars seem in some way or other to have been intended for the offering of gifts and sacrifices to the Lord.[29] Yet although the common Hebrew word for altar is *mizbēaḥ*, a word apparently derived from the

---

27. For altars, see, e.g., Haak, "Altar"; Haran, *Temples and Temple-Service*; and Nakhai, "Altar."

28. So Jones, *1 & 2 Kings*, 1:207-8.

29. For the concept and meaning of sacrifice, see below, 162-78.

root *z-b-ḥ* "slaughter," it seems that the actual slaughtering of the sacrificial gifts took place elsewhere, in a place more suited to the requirements of handling the blood with much care, perhaps some distance away in the temple courtyard.

What we do not hear about in Kings is anything about an incense altar in Solomon's temple, though such is spoken of in Chronicles (1 Chr 28:18; 2 Chr 2:4; 13:11; 26:16, 19; 29:7) and elsewhere, as for example in the Priestly material in Exodus, Leviticus, Numbers, and in Ezekiel. In Isa 1:13 incense is apostrophized as an abomination to the Lord, and it does seem that in earlier times its use was condemned as an illicit import from false and foreign cults, which perhaps explains the silence about the matter in Deuteronomy and the Deuteronomistic History. We certainly have archaeological evidence from such places as Megiddo of incense altars.[30] Incense, a compound of gums and spices, seems to have been regarded as a suitable and worthy offering to have been made to the Lord. It constituted a costly offering (Song 3:6; 4:6, 14; Isa 60:6), and seems to have been used also in order to purify (in times of plague), and maybe also to overcome certain insanitary effects of the slaughter of sacrificial animals. Perhaps the fragrance of the incense offering was believed to have been well-pleasing to the Lord.

What then was this great and splendid temple for? What was its purpose, or more likely its purposes? Undoubtedly it had a political purpose, and we may conveniently deal with that first before going on to its more religious significance. Clearly the temple did have a purpose in the political sphere in that the city-state of Jerusalem, which had been conquered by King David was in the central place in David's kingdom, conveniently to the south of the northern kingdom of Israel and to the north of the southern kingdom of Judah. Politically speaking there can hardly have been a more obvious place in which the king of this "united" kingdom of Israel and Judah should establish his capital and place of government. Thus, in the great Jerusalem building project that had, for whatever reasons, to wait for the days of Solomon, immediately next to the temple there was established the king's palace, the building of which took thirteen years—as against seven for the temple (1 Kgs 6:38; 7:1). Once again costly materials were used in the construction of this large complex of palace buildings (1 Kgs 7:9–12), which was made up of the House of the Forest (7:2–5), the Hall of Pillars (v. 6), the Hall of the Throne (v. 7), and then Solomon's own house along with a further house for the Pharaoh's daughter whom Solomon had taken in marriage (v. 8). These buildings are portrayed as being elaborate and grandiose.

---

30. For a helpful treatment of incense and incense altars, see Haran, *Temples and Temple-Service*, 230–45. On incense, see below, 83–84.

We may take note of the fact that just one of these buildings in the palace complex was larger than the temple: the House of the Forest was, we are told, 100 cubits long, 50 cubits wide, and and 30 cubits high (v. 2), while the temple was 60 cubits long, 20 cubits wide, and 30 cubits high (1 Kgs 6:2). Surely, whatever else Solomon's Jerusalem temple and palace complex was intended to be, making a political statement was certainly among them.

Nevertheless the religious significance of the temple was profound, it being intended to speak of and represent the presence of the Lord with his people on earth. While Solomon's prayer at the dedication of the temple may have expressed in exalted tones the fact that the Lord cannot be contained even by "heaven and the highest heaven" (1 Kgs 8:27), and that thus the Deuteronomists could speak of the temple as being not a dwelling place of God, but rather "the place where he had caused his name to dwell" (Deut 12:5, 11, 14, 21, etc.),[31] even so Solomon's prayer employed the words, "I have built you an exalted house, a place for you to dwell in forever" (1 Kgs 8:13), and that would seem likely to be akin to the way most people of the day might have thought about the temple. Here was the place where in some manner God was believed to have his dwelling, in the sense that although God's greatness and otherness were such that on those occasions when human beings were confronted by him the setting was far more than merely worldly, but rather filled with a sense of the numinous, yet at the same time there seems also to have been a sense of the immanence, the closeness, proximity of God with his people. Indeed, such was this sense of the immanence of the divine that the Lord could be spoken of as *present* for his people, there in the temple. For indeed the Lord God of Israel was believed to be the God who is both far away and also near at hand, both transcendent and also immanent.[32] This sense of the immanence of God to his people is particularly emphasized within the *děbîr*, the inner sanctuary, that most holy part of the temple, where the sacred ark of the covenant was, that which was understood to be giving expression either to the presence of God in commitment to his people through his covenant relationship with them, represented through the depositing of the covenant treaty documents within it, or alternatively through understanding that this ark was in the nature of a divine throne for Israel's Lord God.

We may express the matter in another way, and say that the Jerusalem temple was understood to be the meeting point of the Lord and his people. Such thinking is made clear in the fact that certain religious rites took place here which were clearly intended either to strengthen the covenant

---

31. For a study of this formula, see Thelle, *Approaches to the "Chosen Place"*.
32. See Preuss, *Old Testament Theology*, 1:250–53.

relationship between God and his people, or else to repair it. This may be said to be a major understanding that the Deuteronomistic Historian lays before us through the long prayer of Solomon at the dedication of the temple (1 Kgs 8:22–53). The prayer is itself, in a manner of speaking, a treatise on prayer, above all a setting forth of belief about prayers of confession. The heart of this prayer is that when people pray within this temple, or failing that pray *towards* it, or failing that pray within their heart towards it, and confess their sins, then may God hear them and forgive them their sins. What is being presented here is the understanding that prayer to God may in a special and particular way be made in the Jerusalem temple, for the very reason that this temple is the meeting point of God and his people. This understanding is there in that post-exilic writing in Isa 56:7: "for my house shall be called a house of prayer for all peoples."[33]

A further sense in which the temple in Jerusalem was understood to be the meeting point of God and his people was in the fact that sacrifices were offered there, the Jerusalem temple becoming in at least some Israelite official thinking the only fit and acceptable place for these sacrificial offerings. It has to be said that in Solomon's prayer at the dedication of the temple there is a somewhat strange silence about the temple as a place where sacrifices are to be offered, but nevertheless there is no shortage of reference to sacrifices in the surrounding material. We read in 1 Kgs 8:5 of Solomon sacrificing so many sheep in the temple that they could neither be counted nor numbered. That is portrayed as being before the prayer of dedication, while after it we go on to read of the king offering sacrifices, of well-being no less than 22,000 oxen and 120,000 sheep. We are then told that because the "bronze altar that was before the Lord" was too small for what was required, burnt offerings, grain offerings, and the fat pieces of the sacrifices of well-being were offered in the newly consecrated "middle of the court" (1 Kgs 8:62–64).[34]

The third aspect in an understanding of the temple being a meeting point between God and his people is in the talk of its purity. Judging from the witness of the Hebrew Bible it would seem that ritual purity was an important issue in daily life in ancient Israel. It was clearly a most important matter for those of the priestly tradition, as we can see from the content of the priestly writings,[35] and it could be said in this regard that the heart of the matter is to be found in Lev 11–15, a series of chapters that sets out regulations concerning ritual purity and pollution. What, however, is dif-

---

33. See below, 105–18, for prayer in the Hebrew Bible.
34. See above, 31–32, and 162–78, below, for more about sacrifices.
35. On the priestly writings, see below, 211–17.

ficult for us to understand is the theological significance of these regulations and laws: are they about hygiene, or morality? Are they quite simply divine decrees, or are they decrees that come with traditional ways of ordering societies (for example as argued by Mary Douglas, in her study *Purity and Danger*)? Or are they regulations that are intended to protect and preserve life?[36] These questions continue to be debated, and a clear consensus of opinion is still awaited. What, however, we may say about the whole matter is that on the one hand there is Yahweh who is utter and complete holiness, while on the other the members of the human race who are mired in their sinful ways, their sheer sinfulness. This human sinfulness is what is being spoken about in the complex narrative of the great flood in Gen 6–9, and in particular in its two texts, "The Lord saw that the wickedness of humankind was great in the earth, and that every inclination of the thoughts of their hearts was only evil continually" (Gen 6:5), and "the Lord said in his heart, 'I will never again curse the ground because of humankind, for the inclination of the human heart is evil from youth.'" (Gen 8:21)

Yet this holiness of God and the sinfulness of his people come together in a particular way in the temple, and in this regard we may take note of the three parts of that building, which beginning with the *ʾûlām* and culminating in the *dĕbîr* are arranged in increasing realms of holiness. The particular holiness of the *dĕbîr* was represented, symbolized by the sacred ark of the covenant, portrayed as containing the tablets which were believed to set forth the divine demands, the moral imperatives (1 Kgs 8:9), laid upon those called to be the Lord's people in the world. Into this most holy place only the chief priest on his own entered, just once a year, and at that only after much preparation including ritual purification for his own sins, in order to fulfil the prescribed rituals by which it was believed forgiveness would by divine favor be granted to the sinful people.

This Jerusalem temple was, it seems, to become something of a place of pilgrimage. At the most basic level we can understand that in the context of its age and setting it was indeed a wonder of its world. What more grandiose set of buildings was there for the people of Israel to admire and wonder at in the days of the united monarchy, and the time of the independent states of Israel and Judah, than that mighty complex of temple and palace that Solomon had established in Jerusalem on Zion's hill? Yet at a deeper and more profound level there seems to have become established the tradition of making pilgrimages to Jerusalem, in particular to the temple. The words of Isa 30:29 would seem to suggest a background setting of preparation for

36. In this regard, see the summaries in Childs, *Old Testament Theology*, 84–91; Hartley, *Leviticus*, 140–47; Grabbe, *Leviticus*, 49–62; Jenson, *Graded Holiness*; Sklar, *Sin, Impurity, Sacrifice, Atonement*; and Blenkinsopp, *Wisdom and Law*, 108–13.

a pilgrimage to Jerusalem, while what is said in Ps 42:4 would seem to be reflecting the same activity. Then Pss 84 and 122 would seem to bear the hallmarks of pilgrimage to Zion, while the whole block of Pss 120–134 that have been called "Pilgrimage Psalms", the psalms of this group all having the heading "A Song of Ascents," the "ascents" widely believed to be referring to the "going up" of pilgrims to the temple. Further it has been noted that the names Zion and Jerusalem occur with some frequency in this group of psalms, along with "house of the Lord" in two of them, that various liturgical phrases and language are to be read in them, and that there is an overall tone that breathes a spirit of the piety of pilgrims.[37] Witness to the matter of pilgrimages to Jerusalem is also there in the requirement in Deut 16:16, "Three times a year all your males shall appear before the Lord your God at the place that he will choose: at the festival of unleavened bread, at the festival of weeks, and at the festival of booths."[38]

Something further needs to be said about the temples at Dan and Bethel, for it would seem that though their establishment may have been prior to that of Solomon's temple in Jerusalem, it was only after the last-named was built and had made its presence felt politically and religiously that the earlier places perhaps came to their *apogee*. After the death of Solomon his son Rehoboam ascended the throne of Judah, but the Israelite tribes chose for their leader—with the assurance that they would then be governed rather less firmly and more democratically—by the returned refugee Jeroboam the son of Nebat (1 Kgs 12:1–11). Henceforth the kingdoms of Israel and Judah became separate, and Jeroboam initiated developments at his rival sanctuaries, presumably seeking to "update" them in the light of the remarkable developments that had earlier taken place on Zion's hill. Thus Jeroboam, having taken counsel, made two calves of gold, saying to the people "You have gone up to Jerusalem long enough. Here are your gods, O Israel, who brought you up out of the land of Egypt." (1 Kgs 12:28) We must clearly make allowance for the fact that here is polemical talk on the part of the Judean-based Deuteronomistic Historian, and also see the relationship between this account and that of the wilderness itinerary account of what was adjudged to be the sinful manufacture of the golden calf and the people's bowing down to, worshipping, and seeking guidance from it for their onward journey. At any rate, according to the records that we have, Jeroboam placed one of these calves in Bethel and the other in Dan, and that the people did worship before them. Further, Jeroboam appointed

---

37. For these and other details, see Mays, *Psalm*, 385–87; and Day, *Psalms*, 61–66. On the biblical psalms and worship, see below, 119–61.

38. On these festivals, see below, 179–87.

priests who were not of the levitical families, established a religious festival to rival that of Jerusalem, and offered sacrifices to those golden calves (1 Kgs 12:29–33).[39]

About what happened to these temples at Dan and Bethel we cannot be sure. Of Dan we do not read anything after 2 Kgs 10:29, where we learn that the calves in Dan and Bethel were still being worshipped in the days of the kingship of Jehu the son of Nimshi. We gather from the prophecy of Amos that in the eighth century Bethel was deemed, at least by some, to be "the king's sanctuary, and it is a temple of the kingdom" (Amos 7:12), while in 2 Kgs 23:15-20 we read of the thorough destruction of the altar, the high place, and much else, at Bethel by Josiah in his religious reform.[40] The temple of Solomon on Zion, along with much else in Jerusalem came to an end in 587/6 BCE at the hands of the Babylonian army, and many of the inhabitants of Jerusalem were taken away to exile in Babylon, while others were able to make their escape to spend their times of exile elsewhere, such as in Egypt.

However, we are told in 2 Kgs 25:13-17 about what looks like the depredation of the Jerusalem temple and the associated carrying away of the sacred temple vessels by the Babylonians to Babylon, "They took away the pots, the shovels, the snuffers, the dishes for incense, and all the bronze vessels used in the temple service, as well as the firepans and the basins" (2 Kgs 25:14–15a; see also 2 Kgs 24:13; Jer 52:17–19; 2 Chr 36:7, 18). Now although we are told that it was for their silver and gold that the captors took away these vessels (2 Kgs 25:15b), yet in the account of what happened around half-a-century later we read that these temple vessels were brought back by some of the earliest returnees to Jerusalem following the edict of the new Persian ruler, Cyrus (Ezra 1:7–11; see also Ezra 5:14–15; 6:5). We further read about the restoration of these vessels in Jerusalem in Ezra 7:19; 8:26–28, 33–34; Neh 10:39; 13:5, 9, while we read similar material in Dan 1:2; 1 Esd 4:43–46, 57; 2 Esd 10:21–22; 1 Macc 1:23; 4:49; 14:15. See also 2 Macc 1–2 and Bar 1:8–9 for the same theme. It was Peter R. Ackroyd who in a stimulating article drew our attention to this theme that he labelled "Continuity," namely that while we cannot know, and in all probability never will know, the precise historical details concerning the Babylonian fate of these temple vessels, what is of greater importance is the sense and theme of continuity between the pre- and post-exilic religious communities. The community that sought to re-establish life and faith, belief and worship after

---

39. On the temples at Dan and Bethel, and their various religious artefacts, see Haran, *Temples and Temple-Service*, 28–31.

40. For Josiah's reform, see below, 100–102.

the years of exile are here portrayed as having a real continuity with those who went before them. Ackroyd ended his article by saying of the post-exilic Jewish community, "It is the same people of God which lives on in consciousness of its ancestry of faith."[41]

It was indeed the accession to power in Babylon of Cyrus the Persian ruler in 539 BCE that was the enabling factor in bringing about a return of some of the Jewish exiles to Judah and Jerusalem, who under various leaderships and encouragements set about establishing a new temple, one that would be the successor to that built by Solomon and apparently ruined beyond the possibility of being rebuilt. Thus various voices were heard at different times calling for work to be carried out that would result in the building of what has come to be known as the Second Temple.

However, the biblical sources that purport to speak of this period of Israelite history do not enable us to reconstruct with any sense of confidence the historical progression of various events and happenings, one of which was the building of the Second Temple in Jerusalem. The fact is that in no less than three different accounts we hear of this rebuilding, and yet, as Grabbe observes, "We are dealing not with historical narratives but with three theological accounts that, incidentally, contain some historical data."[42] In the first place, according to Ezra 5:13-16 Sheshbazzar was allowed by Cyrus to bring back from Babylon the temple vessels and to rebuild the temple; we are told that the foundations of the building were laid but that the work was not completed. With that this source of information runs out. Then second we read about Zerubbabel who worked at the project, though any relationship with the Sheshbazzar work is not spoken of, but whose work is interrupted (Ezra 4, 6). In the third place we read in the books of Haggai and Zechariah about Zerubbabel's successful attempt at the said rebuilding, here there being no mention of an interruption. To harmonize these various accounts is tempting, but perhaps better resisted, it being accepted that eventually a temple was completed, this being in the sixth year of the reign of King Darius (Ezra 6:15).[43]

Of this temple — commonly called Zerubbabel's temple — we know little as regards its dimensions and the materials used in its building. According to 1 Esd 4:57 those temple vessels, earlier taken away from Jerusalem by the Babylonians were restored to Jerusalem, "And he [King Darius] sent back from Babylon all the vessels that Cyrus had set apart; everything

---

41. Ackroyd, "The Temple Vessels," 60. See 2 Chr 36:7, 10, 18, 19 for the particular approach of the Chronicler to this matter of the temple vessels.

42. Grabbe, *Judaism from Cyrus to Hadrian*, 128.

43. See below, 268-70, for these post-exilic prophets and their call to rebuild the Jerusalem temple.

that Cyrus had ordered to be done, he also commanded to be done and to be sent to Jerusalem." Thus, as Ackroyd observed in his study, "The community which sought to re-establish itself after the exile, deeply conscious of its ancestry in faith, but also aware of the problem of continuity with that faith, made use of the theme of the vessels . . . to make good its claim to be the true successor . . . , to be directly linked with those who stood on the other side of the exilic gulf."[44] However, in the view of the prophet—or one of the prophets—of Isa 56–66 this temple was to be somewhat different from what had prevailed in times before the exile, namely that it was now to be a house of prayer for *all* peoples (Isa 56:7), though how many of the populace and their leaders would have agreed with that view, and how much it became a reality, is difficult to answer. No doubt there was ongoing debate in the post exilic community over the whole issue of how much in the new situation should be reflective of what prevailed in the past, or alternatively how much it should be a response to the new situation in which the Jewish people now found themselves. Then also, how much of that visionary material in Zech 1:7—6:15 perhaps reflects features of this temple is a matter about which it is difficult to be sure. Perhaps a window onto second temple life is opened for us through what we are told in Neh 10:32–39 and 12:44–47. No doubt a range of issues regarding both continuity and also contemporaneity were very much to the forefront in those post-exilic days, and perhaps something of that is to be seen in what we read in Neh 10:32–39 and 12:44–47, understanding it as possibly representing some modifications to earlier laws and regulations now to be found in the Pentateuch. There is some encroaching of these changes as regards worship: for example as seen in what is said in Neh 10:31 about work on the sabbath day, and in 10:32–33 about tax for the upkeep of the sanctuary. In both of these cases the later materials give a stricter ruling. Further, Neh 10:34 concerns the issue of the wood offering needed to keep the fire burning continuously on the altar. In this case there was now a law that all the people were to take a share in this task.[45]

A major development of the Jerusalem temple built in the days of Zerubbabel took place during the reign of the Roman ruler Herod; he was appointed King of the Jews and reigned from 37 BCE until his death in Jericho in 4 BCE. His temple rebuilding was referred to by Josephus as revealing "the grandeur of his [Herod's] conceptions,"[46] and took many years.

---

44. Ackroyd, "The Temple Vessels," 60.

45. On these matters, see Williamson, *Ezra, Nehemiah*, 334–36; and Clines, "Nehemiah 10 as an Example of Early Jewish Biblical Exegesis."

46. Josephus, *The Jewish War*, 301–6.

However, this is outside what we might call the Old Testament period, and what this present study seeks to set forth.[47]

In spite of the reforms of the Judean kings Hezekiah and Josiah both of which included the centralization of worship in the temple at Jerusalem, we do know of two temples that came to be established in other places. Though the details are unclear to us, it is evident that sometime between 170 and 150 BCE one of the high priests fled to Egypt and established a temple in Leontopolis where there was a large Jewish population. It appears to have been founded either by the high priest Onias III, or else by his son Onias IV.[48] Perhaps the most that we can say about this is that a certain Onias, a Zadokite priest, fled from Jerusalem and founded a temple in Egypt.[49]

We know of another temple, this being at Elephantine, again in Egypt, this time on an island in the Nile opposite Aswan (Syene), but earlier than the temple at Leontopolis. We hear about a Judean community at Elephantine in Egypt in Jer 43–44, and Aramaic documents were discovered there dating from the fifth century BCE. It seems that the Jewish refugees established a temple in that locality, but that the worship was hardly representative of pure Yahwism, for as well as Yhw (an abbreviation of YHWH) being worshipped, worship was also made to a female deity (Anath-yhw) alongside other Canaanite deities. We may also consider in this regard another Jewish sanctuary we know about, one that it has been suggested was in existence in the eighth century BCE situated at Kuntillet 'Ajrud. The Elephantine temple seems to have been destroyed by Egyptians in 410 BCE, and as things turned out was never rebuilt, for the Persian influence in Egypt came to an end, the Jewish garrison in Elephantine being moved out and the temple abandoned.[50]

The matter of the establishment of these temples far away from Jerusalem in plain contradiction of the Deuteronomic insistence on worship being centered upon the one place in Jerusalem, was probably due to the different situation that came to prevail after the various deportations and fleeings of Israelites and Judeans following on from their military defeats of the eighth and sixth centuries BCE. This is not the only example of changes coming into the Israelite worship-life in response to changes in the political

---

47. For the ruler Herod, see Richardson, *Herod*; Grabbe, *Judaism from Cyrus to Hadrian*; and Sanders, *Judaism: Practice and Belief*. About the life of Herod's temple, see Hayward, *The Jewish Temple*.

48. See Josephus, *The Jewish War*, 406–7; Josephus, *Jewish Antiquities: Books 12–14*, pp. 199–203 (12.9.7); and Hayward, "The Jewish Temple at Leontopolis."

49. See Grabbe, *Judaism from Cyrus to Hadrian*, 266–67; and Sanders, *Judaism: Practice and Belief*, 23–24.

50. See Rowley, "Papyri from Elephantine"; and Porten, "Elephantine Papyri."

situations in which they perforce found themselves.[51] At the same time, what we are told about the worship that prevailed at such places as Elephantine does it perhaps demonstrate a certain wisdom on the part of those who insisted on Yahwistic worship being offered only at the one central shrine?

Nevertheless there were yet more places of worship that call for some consideration, and they form the subject of the chapter that follows.

---

51. See above, 43–44, and below, 249–50.

3

Other Places of Worship

Clearly not all worship in ancient Israel took place in a shrine of some variety, or in a temple. There are portrayed in the Hebrew Bible a number of settings where it is clear that worship took place, some of these being acceptable to priests and other leaders, others that were deemed to be unacceptable.

The Home as Place of Worship

Rainer Albertz has made an attractive case for our taking seriously the element of Israelite religious observance in the people's homes, yet it has to be said that though it may well be likely, even highly probable, that acts of worship did take place in those settings, we can hardly be specific over details as our sources are not as forthcoming as we might have wished.[1] No doubt, there were those who in various periods of Israelite history wished these things to take place in the freedom of homes. But equally there were those who believed that emphasis on shrine- or temple-based worship was the more to be desired for the reason that there a check by those officially appointed could be kept on what took place, that the practices were acceptable.

Nevertheless in the material we have in Gen 12–50 about the patriarchs, material that gives the impression of representing what took place in what we might loosely call "early times," it is clear that there was scope for worship to take place in individual homes, not least for the reason that shrines had apparently not yet been established for the offering of worship by individuals or groups. Perhaps we may posit that while such things as sacrifices would have been offered at the various altars we read of being raised up (and does not the account in Gen 22 perhaps suggest that from time to time child sacrifice took place at these, or some altars?), yet we are also informed about such items as those teraphim which Rachel stole from her father Laban and which she was able to hide in the saddlebag of her camel (Gen 31:19, 34–35). Albertz suggests that these are "probably envisaged as

---

1. Albertz, *A History of Israelite Religion*.

small figurines of deities in the possession of the family, as they are called 'my' or 'your gods' . . . by the persons concerned."[2] While we should be careful not to build too many theories around very little evidence, nevertheless the scene presented to us in Judg 17:7-13 does seem to suggest a situation in which family, cult, and cult officials are all closely bound up together.[3]

The archaeological discovery at Megiddo of what appears to have been something in the nature of a "house chapel" in the antechamber or courtyard of a tenth century private house has suggested to some that we have evidence of a temple here, possibly dating from as early as 3000 BCE, along with other evidences of religious observance.[4] Whether we can really regard that as constituting evidence of the early existence of family worship must inevitably remain questionable. As also does the situation in the period Albertz designates "Late Monarchy."[5] However, we can well understand that in exilic days there were necessarily religious observances then taking place in individual homes including such rites as circumcision, dietry customs, sabbath observance, and passover—what Albertz referred to as "the most important element of the subsidiary family cult."[6] We may also assume that until a replacement temple for Solomon's was built in Jerusalem following the return there of at least some of the exiles, worship and other religious observances must perforce have continued to take place in individual homes. Was it because such worship was taking place in settings that were inevitably beyond the power and influence of priests to guide and superintend, and maybe even to control, that there were a number of calls to build a new temple? Nevertheless we should recall the strictures of Deuteronomy which surely if strictly obeyed and adhered to could have been understood and interpreted as worshipping the Lord in one's own home:

> Keep these words that I am commanding you today in your heart. Recite them to your children and talk about them when you are at home and when you are away, when you lie down and when you rise. Bind them as a sign on your hand, fix them as an emblem on your forehead, and write them on the doorposts of your house and on your gates. (Deut 6:6-9)

---

2. Albertz, *A History of Israelite Religion*, 1:37. On Teraphim, ephod, etc., see above, 31–32.

3. See the remarks of Niditch, *Judges,* 182; and Soggin, *Judges,* 266–70. See also Meyers, "Household Religion."

4. See Schofield, "Megiddo," 311.

5. Albertz, *A History of Israelite Religion*, 1:186–95.

6. Albertz, *History of Israelite Religion*, 2:410.

Thus Carol Meyers has suggested the likelihood of there having been a series of religious practices that took place in the setting of the home and household, at least because of the sheer distance of many homes from shrines, and later a temple. Meyers points to various archaeological discoveries, which though not numerically large, seem to be of artefacts looking as if they are to be associated with sundry household religious practices, such as incense burners, figurines, amulets, ceramic stands, and various vessels. Then it would seem that there were a number of household rituals that took place, such as those celebrated in connection with the natural seasons, in particular the feast of Passover, which for Deuteronomy is to be celebrated in the central sanctuary, but is envisaged in other parts of the Hebrew Bible as taking place in the home (see for example Exod 12). Perhaps the feasts of Weeks and Booths were originally celebrated in homes, and only later, like Passover, becoming pilgrimage feasts. Further, various sacrifices seem to be envisaged as taking place in individual homes (see for example Exod 20:24; Judg 13:19–23).[7]

Synagogues

The subject of the institution of the synagogue only indirectly impinges upon this particular study, but does at least call to be noticed. The facts briefly are: The institution of the synagogue comes right at the historical end of the whole period of time which gave birth to the Old Testament documents, yet there are no clear and unambiguous references to synagogues in the Hebrew Bible. However, references to the synagogue are common in the New Testament, giving the impression that the word indicates both a building and also the associated institution. Further, there is in the New Testament no suggestion that the buildings and the institution of the synagogue are new or recent additions to the Jewish religious scene, and both Josephus and Philo of Alexandria take them for granted, not giving us any indication when and for what reason they came to be established. Archaeological evidence points to the existence of at least some Palestinian synagogues from as early as the first century BCE, for example those at Gamla, Masada, and Herodium.[8]

What came to be the characteristic features of the life and worship of the synagogue—whatever may have been the specific reasons that lay behind its establishment—was worship centered around what we would call

---

7. For various religious rites that likely took place in homes, see below, 66–68.

8. A full treatment of these matters is to be found in Binder, *Into the Temple Courts*.

the scriptures. The so-called Theodotus inscription, which was discovered in Jerusalem and has been dated in the first century CE, a certain Jerusalem synagogue was founded as a place for "the reading of the law and the teaching of the precepts."[9] It is difficult not to compare this with what we read in Luke 4:16–20, an event portrayed as taking place in the first century CE in the synagogue in Nazareth. Further, what appears to be the general design and layout of the various Palestinian synagogues, with their benches along the walls, suggests an intended purpose of enabling a congregation to look towards a speaker; indeed, such a scene is reflected in some of the New Testament references to synagogue services (see Mark 6:1–5; Luke 4:16–30; Acts 13:13–16).

Bearing in mind this apparent nature and style of synagogue life and worship, there are two possible periods that have been suggested as times when the institution took its rise. The first is in the exilic period in Babylon, Egypt, and elsewhere, as a substitute for the loss of the temple and its associated sacrificial worship. It is certainly imaginable that in those difficult days there was a perceived need of opportunity for the meeting together of Jewish people both for fellowship and mutual support, and also for worship. Such worship is portrayed in the documents that have come down to us as being based upon a prayerful consideration of an emerging collection of religious texts, texts that in the fullness of time would become "scripture," the Jewish people's special, even normative, religious documents. The Achilles' heel of this theory of the genesis of the synagogue is that in the biblical documents that seem to come from post-exilic times there is no reference to what might appear to be the institution of the synagogue. The lack of any references in Isa 56–66, in the books of Ezra and Nehemiah, or in the work of the Chronicler, suggests that this institution must have come later than this historical period. Did it then come about in the difficult days of the Hellenistic rule in Palestine, from the same sort of setting from which the book of Daniel seems to come? Alas, until some definite evidence is found we can do no more than speculate in this matter.

Whatever may be the answer to such questions of a historical nature, there is yet an important observation to be made. In what we have come to know as the whole style of the synagogue worship with its reading of the words of scripture, its meditation upon them, and perhaps above all the exposition of that word by a leader, there is surely provided some significant stepping stones from the worship that in a predominant way the Old Testament sets forth, and which develops into a service centered more upon *word* than upon *sacrifice*. In the fullness of time such a style of worship would

---

9. On such inscriptions, see Binder, *Into the Temple Courts*, 82–86.

come to be witnessed in the Christian worship tradition of the reading and exposition of the scriptures. Such development is in particular to be observed in a further stage in the Protestant Christian tradition of the reverent reading of the scriptures accompanied by that centrality of the preached sermon. Indeed, something of that had surely been prefigured in the scene of rededication portrayed in those post-exilic days of Ezra and Nehemiah. Here we read of the day when Ezra was required to read from "the book of the law of Moses, which the Lord had given to Israel," and that "the Levites helped the people to understand the law, while the people remained in their places. So they read from the book, from the law of God, with interpretation. They gave the sense, so that the people understood the reading." (Neh 8:1-8, see vv. 1, 7b-8) It is not beyond the bounds of possibility that this talk of close attention being given to a written document in a worshipful setting is something by way of a reflection of the worship that came to take place in the synagogue.[10]

High Places

The Hebrew word *bāmāh*, "high place, ridge, high ground," occurs over one hundred times in the Old Testament, but its majority usage is "cultic high place," or even "cult place," as for example in 1 Sam 9:12; 1 Kgs 11:7; 2 Chr 33:17; Jer 48:35. In fact there are some 80 occurrences of the word apparently in this sense. It seems to have indicated a place for worship, de Vaux maintaining that the meaning that best satisfies all the occurrences being "a mound or knoll for the purposes of worship."[11] Archaeologists have uncovered evidences of such places, an example being the oval platform at Megiddo which seems to have been used for sacrificial worship; another being at Nahariya, near Haifa, with, again, a platform in a nearly circular space; and a further one at Hazor. There are others as well.[12]

But just what is being indicated in the Old Testament's approximately eighty references to a mound or knoll established for the purposes of worship? In particular, is the worship taking place here acceptable or unacceptable? Numbers 33:52 speaks of a high place that in the eyes of the Canaanites was acceptable, but that when the Israelites moved into the land

---

10. See the treatments of Williamson, *Ezra, Nehemiah*, 279-86; Blenkinsopp, *Ezra-Nehemiah*, 284-49. Also see below, 84-86.

11. Vaux, *Ancient Israel*, 284.

12. See further Schunk, "*bamah*," 141-42; Barrick, "High Place"; Nakhai, "High Place"; and Edelman, "Cultic Sites and Complexes." For archaeological details, see also Vaughan, *The Meaning of 'BAMA'*, 37-54.

the Israelites were commanded to destroy. Eryl Davies says, "The 'high places' . . . were a characteristic feature of Canaanite worship, and they were to prove a constant source of temptation to the Israelites."[13] Indeed, within the Old Testament there is a consistently negative assessment of the high places, they being regarded as places of Canaanite worship, at which any activity of worship in which Israelites engaged is to be condemned. Yet at the same time it has to be said that the clear witness of the Hebrew Bible is that Israelites in age after age *did* repair to and engage in worship at the high places. Further, we are told that when Jeroboam separated off the northern tribes from Judah and established places of worship at Dan and Bethel, he also established high places in his kingdom and further established within them non-levitical priests (1 Kgs 12:25–31). It is also clear that there were, at least in some periods of its history, high places in Judah which were attended, and at which worship took place, by some of the people of Judah—a practice that Josiah sought to end by means of his thoroughgoing religious reforms (2 Kgs 23:5).[14]

For the Deuteronomists, and some others in particular perhaps Jeremiah and Ezekiel, the worship of Israelite people at the high places is condemned in the strongest terms.[15] Nevertheless, it is clear that in spite of all the instructions that they received from priests, prophets and others the people continued to frequent them and engage in worship at them. The fact that the high places continue to be condemned would seem clearly to point to the fact that the strictures of priests and prophets were not taken as seriously as they would have wished, and that Israelite worship did continue to take place at them. Further, the fact that in certain times in Judah there was a call for the centralization of worship in the Jerusalem temple alone cannot have helped to keep worshippers away from the high places. Presumably there must have been practical difficulties for many a worshipper to get to Jerusalem in order to worship there. In that sense a nearby high place would be the rather obvious place to go to and there engage in worship—even in spite of the strictures of the religious leaders.

High Hills and Green Trees

There is in certain parts of the Hebrew Bible a condemnation of the making of offerings and the practicing of other religious rites on the hills and under

---

13. Davies, *Numbers*, 348.

14. On the reforms of Josiah, see below, 100–102.

15. See, e.g., 1 Kgs 14:23; 15:14; 22:43; 2 Kgs 12:3; 14:4; 15:4, 35; 16:4; 17:9, 11, 29, 32, etc. See further Amos 7:9; Jer 7:31; 17:3; 19:5; 32:35; 48:35; Ezek 6:3, 6; 16:16; 36:2.

green trees, this being found in the books of Deuteronomy, 1 and 2 Kings, 2 Chronicles, Isaiah, Jeremiah, Ezekiel and Hosea.[16] It would seem that on the "high hills" and under "green trees" were regarded by the Canaanites as suitable settings, localities at which to locate their shrines, though the evidence from various archaeological discoveries suggests that not all of them were in fact established on "high places" (*bāmāh*). It was perhaps at such shrines that there might have been a "pillar" (*maṣṣēbāh*), a standing stone, which might have been in the nature of a commemorative stele intended to indicate where divine help had been found, but that had become in other cases the symbol of a male deity. The female variety of this was the ʾ*ăšērāh*, the symbol of a female deity, though this same word seems also to have been the name of an actual female deity.[17]

Qumran

Although not strictly germane to our subject, nevertheless brief attention should be given to the Jewish community at Qumran near the Dead Sea, this in view of the considerable interest in and significance of the associated Dead Sea Scrolls. As far as we can judge the life of this religious community was from around 150 BCE to 68 CE, and though we do not have direct information as to the style and content of the communal and individual worship there, we have among the many scrolls the community prepared and preserved, both clearly with much care, in particular such varieties as the Psalm Scroll from Cave 11 and the Words of Blessing. About these documents Michael Knibb observes, "It is not clear whether the psalms in this collection were intended for private use or for use in the liturgical services of the community, but probably both should be envisaged."[18] These psalms are in the style of the biblical psalms, and there is a significant emphasis upon thanksgiving. There are also hymns for use at baptism, a liturgical rite that would come to be practiced in later times, but which is not spoken of in the Old Testament, along with other rites for maintaining ritual purity, and an emphasis on calendrical matters. Not surprisingly, sacrificial worship does *not* seem to have taken place at Qumran. Yet it could be, at least to judge

---

16. For lists of these occurrences, see Driver, *Deuteronomy*, 139; Holladay, "On Every High Hill."

17. See Braulik, "The Rejection of the Goddess Asherah"; Ackerman, *Under Every Green Tree*, 152-63; and Day, *Yahweh and the Gods and Goddesses of Canaan*, 2-67. See below, 61-66, for Israelite worship practices possibly influenced by Canaanite religious rites.

18. Knibb, *The Qumran Community*, 158.

from the evidence of the preserved psalms and hymns, that in the words of Eisenman and Wise, "The period of the Dead Sea Scrolls was apparently a time of extensive development in the area of liturgy."[19]

---

19. Eisenman and Wise, *The Dead Sea Scolls Uncovered*, 221. See in particular here "Hymns and Mysteries" (221–55), and "Calendrical Texts and Priestly Courses" (106–34). On the Dead Sea Scrolls, in particular regarding psalms, see Holladay, *The Psalms through Three Thousand Years*, 95–112; Gillingham, *A Journey of Two Psalms*, 17–22. See further Lim et al., *The Dead Sea Scrolls in their Historical Context*; Callaway, *The Dead Sea Scrolls for a New Millennium*; and Vermes, *The Dead Sea Scrolls in English*, esp. "Worship in the Community of the Covenant" (46–51).

PART II

The People at Worship

Hezekiah appointed the divisions of the priests and of the Levites, division by division, everyone according to his service, the priests and the Levites, for burnt offerings and offerings of well-being, to minister in the gates of the camp of the Lord and to give thanks and praise. The contribution of the king from his own possessions was for the burnt offerings: the burnt offerings of morning and evening, and the burnt offerings for the sabbaths, the new moons, and the appointed festivals, as it is written in the law of the Lord. He commanded the people who lived in Jerusalem to give the portion due to the priests and the Levites, so that they might devote themselves to the law of the Lord.

2 CHRONICLES 31:2–4

These three verses, however, their historical accuracy is assessed, conveniently summarize aspects of the roles and contributions of king, priests and Levites, and the worshipping people to the worship that took place in the Jerusalem temple. The verses come from the Chronicler's work, in particular being part of his account of the religious reform of King Hezekiah, more particularly where the writer sets out his vision of continuing and faithful worship in the temple. No doubt there is set out here and in the surrounding material a vision, an ideal of the worship that the Chronicler has for the future of his people. And though here particular and precise divisions of responsibility are allocated to king and people, to priests and Levites, no doubt such changed with the passing of the years and with the varying political and religious leaderships. What it is possible to reconstruct of these differing—and changing—responsibilities and privileges of king and people, of priest and Levite, makes up the subject of the next three chapters of this work.

4

The Worshipping People

Perhaps no literary document can ever be wholly free of the emphases, points of view, even biases, of its author or authors, and in this regard the various documents that make up the Hebrew Bible are no exception. Thus we search in vain for an unbiased account of what may have passed for regular worship of a normal or unexceptionable nature in some age or other in the period covered by the Old Testament documents. On the one hand we read about such matters in the deuteronomistic documents, or in the writings of the Chronicler, or in the Priestly writings, yet in all of these what we read will inevitably be through the lens of their particular theological approaches, their historical judgments, their various and distinctive partialities. On the other hand we can read about these matters in what are doubtless more idealized pictures and presentations in the book of psalms. Thus, if we wish to read about what may be thought of as deviations from what some deemed to be orthodoxy in worship, we should turn either to the books of Kings or else to the work of the Chronicler. If alternatively we wish to read about what was perhaps generally felt by various groups in ancient Israel to represent more normative and acceptable worship and devotion, then it is perhaps to the book of psalms that we should turn. This indeed we shall now do, and later move on to some of the matters that are presented by the Deuteronomistic Historian and the Chronicler.

Thus, for example, Ps 84 presents what looks like a series of pictures of the joyful experience of a worshipper, or group of worshippers, on the pilgrimage to and worship in the temple on Mount Zion. Here has the worshipper found a place where they feel accepted and welcome (Ps 84:3), and happy indeed are those who sing here the praises of their God (v. 4); even while they were but on the journey to the holy place they were filled with a sense of joy (vv. 1–2, 6–7). Here the pilgrims proclaim all the good things that God gives to those who seek them (vv. 10–11), and they bear witness to their joy in the Lord (v. 12).

We are given a series of similar experiences about and reactions to the involvement of those engaged in the worship of the Lord in the collection of psalms that each bear the title "A Song of Ascents," namely Pss 120–34.

Thus, for example, the glad opening of Ps 122 reads "I was glad when they said to me, 'Let us go to the house of the Lord!'" (Ps 122:1). There in the temple the worshippers pray about the things that at present trouble them in their lives (for example Ps 130:1–8), and give thanks and praise for deliverances from troubles and afflictions (for example Pss 126:1–6; 131:1–3).

Moreover there are clearly represented in the book of Psalms various other aspects of life in the world that the worshippers of ancient Israel might have been bringing to their worship. The opportunity to pour out before God the woes of life that may have been afflicting a worshipper is well represented in the frequent occurrence of the individual psalms of lament in the psalter. Alternatively if the mood of the worshipper is of thanksgiving, there is psalmic provision for the expression of that, or of confession of sins to God, or of the singing of praises, and various other matters and moods. There is more to be said about these matters in the chapter of this work about the biblical psalms.[1]

We should also take note of those, comparatively speaking, few depictions in the Old Testament of Israelites who joined in occasions of worship in the temple and elsewhere. In 1 Sam 1:1–28 we are afforded a glimpse into what are portrayed as some of the worship patterns of a devout couple, Elkanah and Hannah, being told about their offering sacrifices and worship at Shiloh. In particular we read of the prayers that Hannah made to the Lord that she might bear a child, and when a child was born the psalmic-like prayer of praise and thanksgiving that she made to the Lord, again in the shrine at Shiloh, this being accompanied by the giving of the boy to the service of the Lord in that place (1 Sam 2:1–11).

Again, we read that in pre-temple days when King David brought the ark of the covenant into Jerusalem "David and all the house of Israel were dancing before the Lord with all their might, with songs and lyres and harps and tambourines and castanets and cymbals" (2 Sam 6:5). It seems to be a large and representative group that is portrayed as taking part in the dedication of the recently completed Solomon's temple, heads of tribes, leaders of the ancestral houses, in fact, so we are told "all the people of Israel" (1 Kgs 8:1–2). Such verses as 2 Kgs 23:3; 2 Chr 7:4; Dan 6:10 speak of individual Israelites making their devotions. Further, the scene presented to us in Neh 9 suggests a large gathering of people in Jerusalem (see especially Neh 9:1–2). These are hardly normal, routine occasions, and we are given less information about the more routine events and other religious celebrations. Perhaps we just have to say that the Hebrew Bible is rather better and more

---

1. See below, 119–61. On the subject of Israelite personal piety see Albertz, "Personal Piety."

fulsome when speaking of, on the one hand the great and glorious religious occasions, and on the other about what are perceived to be irregularities in matters of worship, than about the routine (weekly? monthly? annual?) services, occasions of worship in temple and elsewhere.

Irregularities in Worship

Parts of the Hebrew Bible set before us severe judgments upon particular acts of worship, presenting what has taken place as being an irregularity in worship. Thus, for example, in the days of the Babylonian lordship and influence in Palestine we read in Jer 7:16-20 and 44:15-19, 25 of the worship of the "Queen of Heaven," which it is generally agreed was an importation from Mesopotamia concerned with the worship of the goddess Ishtar, a worship which, at least at some times, included the offering of special cakes. Leslie Allen suggests that "This cult is selected [for inclusion in the book of Jeremiah] as the most provocative instance of a number of pagan cults."[2] Then also, we read in Ezek 8:14 of the worship of Tammuz, who seems to have been a deity worshipped in both Mesopotamia and Canaan. Tammuz was a young fertility god who at the time that vegetation died was taken into the underworld and to whom his consort Ishtar subsequently descended in order to rescue him. Then through a sacred marriage fertility and thus vegetation returned, so it was believed, to the earth.[3]

Further in Isa 57:3-13 we have a complex and elaborate composition, capable of being read with a series of double meanings, and probably intended to be thus read.[4] The passage concerns a woman who combines sorcery with sexual transgressions, and in both of these matters she is followed by her children. In vv. 3-5 it is the children who are addressed and in vv. 6-13 the sorceress herself. There is also an adulterous father spoken about (v. 3), but no details are given. It is widely felt that what is being portrayed here is an idolatrous cult that could have been in existence in Palestine in both pre- and post-exilic times. What is involved appears to have been sexual rites ("you that burn with lust among the oaks, under every green tree" v. 5a), but there is also child sacrifice as is made clear in v. 5b, and from the reference to Molech in v. 9. All these practices are roundly condemned, and their practitioners are warned that on the day when these worshippers

---

2. Allen, *Jeremiah*, 98. See also Ackerman, *Under Every Green Tree*, 5-35.

3. See Ackerman, *Under Every Green Tree*, 37-93; Burnett, "Tammuz"; and Handy, "Tammuz."

4. For details, see Blenkinsopp, *Isaiah 56-66*, pp. 162-63.

cry out for help they will find no deliverance in their collection of idols, but that those who take refuge in the Lord "shall possess the land." (v. 13)[5]

There is a further Isaian chapter that calls for consideration, namely Isa 65:1–7, which speaks of further rites: here there is condemnation both of cults of the dead (v. 4) and also of fertility rites (v. 3), accompanied by the reminder that Yahweh will bring his judgment upon those who participate in such rites: "because they offered incense on the mountains and reviled me on the hills, I will measure into their laps full payment for their actions." (v. 7)[6]

This conveniently brings us to consider some of the worship practices which appear to have come to Israel and Judah from their inevitable contacts with their Canaanite neighbors.[7] For example there is that relatively common condemnation found in the Hebrew Bible that offerings have been made on the high places, on the hills, and under green trees.[8] Perhaps the most trenchant criticism in the Hebrew Bible of this slide into the worship practices of the Canaanites comes from the book of Hosea, where the indictment is that they have turned to the god named Baal, and where a wide range of terms is used to indicate idols, images, lovers, artefacts, all human-made. There is even talk of calves (Hos 8:5, 6; 13:2), no doubt intended to be connected with the story of the manufacture of the desert calf of Exod 32, and the calves that were set up in Bethel and Dan by Jeroboam (1 Kings 12:28–30).[9] At the same time as well as there being the worship of other gods, there is also the portrayal of false worship of the true God (see for example Hos 10:1–8).[10]

The profound illness of the people of Israel—and this is what is manifest so tragically in the worship they engage in—is what has been described by Macintosh in his commentary on Hosea as "surrender to a desire to accommodate themselves to the seductive charms of a religion so closely associated with the cultivated land (cf. Gilgal in [Hos] 9.15; 12.12 EVV11)."[11]

---

5. On Isa 57:3–13, see Ackerman, *Under Every Green Tree*, 101–63. See also above, 54–55, for Israelites worshipping under "green trees." For Molech, see below, 64.

6. On Isa 65:1–7, see Ackerman, *Under Every Green Tree*, 165–212.

7. For these Canaanite influences on Israel and Judah, see Albright, *Yahweh and the Gods of Canaan*; Day, *Yahweh and the Gods and Goddesses of Canaan*.

8. See above, 53–55, for consideration of high places, hills, and green trees as places of worship.

9. For full details of these and other false and pagan gods, and also other titles and epithets used in the book of Hosea, see the helpful appendix in Andersen and Freedman, *Hosea*, 649–50. Also, see below, 250–52.

10. See Ackerman, *Under Every Green Tree*, 3.

11. Macintosh, *Hosea*, xc. On cultic prostitution, see also Thelle, *Approaches to the*

That is to say, the Israelite worshippers had allowed themselves to become engaged in the feasting and drinking, and further in the sexual rites, associated with the religion of Baal (see Hos 4:10–19).

Within the pantheon of Canaanite gods the chief deity was El, itself a common term for "god" in the world of the Old Testament. For the Canaanites El appears to have presided and had authority over other deities. Another of the gods was Baal, this word meaning "master, lord," and it was applied not only to one particular god but also to a number of other deities to the extent that the name became to a large degree the generic name for a Canaanite god, and thus it is used in parts of the Old Testament. The god El had a consort, Asherah, whose name was also used of a female cult object, as is found, for example in Judg 6:25.

Among the literary finds at Ugarit was the "Baal Epic" (or "Epics," or "Myths") which tells of Baal's victory over the deity Mot (death), a story that reflected the cycle of rain and drought, seed time and harvest, death and life.[12] It was perhaps this aspect of Canaanite religious beliefs and rites that impinged the most closely upon the religious beliefs and rites of the peoples of Israel and Judah, this being particularly so in the northern kingdom of Israel where much crop-growing agriculture took place, and there was a somewhat perennial temptation for Israelites to adopt Canaanite ways either instead of, or else in addition to their own religious practices. Nevertheless, there were other Canaanite deities, Anat and Astarte, also various astral deities (Sun, Moon), as well as a number of deities of the underworld, Mot, Molech, and the Rephaim.[13] It should also be added that remains of Canaanite temples display a style of architecture similar to what read about in connection with the temple of Solomon in Jerusalem.

It can thus be seen that these religious shrines and practices of the Canaanites presented a serious temptation to their Israelite and Judean neighbors, perhaps in the first place because these various peoples lived in comparatively close proximity. Thus came about that understandably serious and ongoing temptation to the peoples of Israel and Judah probably to reflect some at least of the Canaanite rites for their own worship, which was to earn them censure from some of their leaders.

As well as these possible influences of Canaanite rites upon the Israelites in the sphere of agriculture, there is also the matter of sun worship—which seems clearly to have taken place not only in Canaan but also

---

"Chosen Place," 147–50.

12. See *ANET*, 129–42; and Thomas, *Documents*, 128–33.

13. For full details of these deities, see Day, *Yahweh and the Gods and Goddesses of Canaan*. See also Curtis, "Canaanite Gods and Religion"; and Curtis, *Ugarit: Ras Shamra*.

elsewhere in the ancient world. In both Egypt and Mesopotamia the sun was regarded as having divine powers. Further, in Palestine and Ugarit the sun god features in the cult, for as has been observed, "in Ugarit the sun deity plays only a modest role in cult and myth and is feminine. She is called Shapash or Shapshu, whereas in Palestine the masculine sun god Shamash is worshipped."[14] Moreover, there is evidence both in the biblical documents and from archaeological discoveries, of a certain prevalence of sun worship in Israel and Judah.[15] Although at one level such worship was forbidden (see Deut 4:19; 17:3), yet at the same time clearly it did take place (2 Kgs 21:3, 5; Jer 8:2; Ezek 8:16). While it was proscribed by Josiah in his religious reform of 621 BCE (2 Kgs 23:5), even so there was perhaps a more subtle way in which it still came into Israelite and Judean worship, in that its language seems to have been adopted to express certain aspects of the greatness of Yahweh. Thus, for example in Ps 19:4b–6 the sun is spoken of as displaying characteristics of the glory of the Lord.[16]

Another aspect of Canaanite religious practice that calls for comment is the offering of human sacrifices, even child sacrifices, in particular to the god Molech (Molek), or Moloch as it appears in the LXX. Molech, in Canaanite thought, seems to have been a ruler of the underworld, and we read about this deity in Lev 18:21; 20:2–5; 1 Kgs 11:7; 2 Kgs 23:10; Jer 32:35. The Deuteronomistic Historian roundly condemns all religious practices concerned with Molech, but it would seem that in certain times and circumstances such worship was practiced by Israelites and that certain of the Canaanite rites were adopted to some degree or other—see for example Judg 11:34–40; Josh 6:26; 2 Kgs 16:3. Whether or not this was a part of the cult of Molech, there seems to have been a certain tradition of participation in the sacrificial offering of a firstborn child (e.g., Gen 22:1–14; Exod 13:2, 12–13, 15; Mic 6:6–7), and it may be that a part of the significance of the story of Abraham's attempt to offer his son Isaac is about the fact that Yahweh does not require such sacrifices.[17]

It seems that in spite of the religious reforms initiated by various Israelite and Judean leaders over the centuries, the influences of other religious systems and their human leaders prevailed, in particular those connected

---

14. Bernhardt, "Ugaritic Texts," 188.

15. Taylor, *Yahweh and the Sun*. See also Gaster, "Sun"; Brady, "Sun"; Toorn, "Sun"; and Day, *Yahweh and the Gods and Goddesses of Canaan*, 151–63.

16. For this and further details, see Taylor, *Yahweh and the Sun*, 257–65; and Smith, "Solar Language for Yahweh."

17. See Levenson, *The Death and Resurrection of the Beloved Son*; Day, *Molech*; Day, *Yahweh and the Gods and Goddesses of Canaan*, 209–16; Heider, *The Cult of Molek*; and Andersen et al., *Micah*, 532–39.

with the religious rites we have considered, namely some of the religious rites of Canaanites, Assyrians, and Babylonians. The phenomenon of adhering to at least some degree to more than one religious belief system is known in our own age in certain parts of the world, and it is understandable that when one is dealing with beliefs rather than certainties there will be those who choose to spread their dependence upon more than only one system of belief. Thus perhaps it was that in certain periods of the different ages covered by various parts of the Hebrew Bible we read of these officially-forbidden practices being followed, even adopted, by at least some of the people of Israel and Judah.

Nevertheless what we might call normative Yahwism stressed the worship of one Lord and only one Lord, Yahweh the God of Israel, yet as has been said the evidence within the various parts of the Hebrew Bible does suggest the reality was something different, and various cults other than the strictly Yahwistic ones were practiced by at least some of the people for at least some of the time. To what extent this was so, and for how long, is beyond our knowing. We cannot be sure, for example, how many transgressors were being imagined, thought of by the Deuteronomistic Historian when writing about these matters, or by Isaiah, Jeremiah, and Ezekiel, and their editors, when their various documents were being compiled. Further, it has to be said that in the Hebrew Bible there are no unbiased accounts and assessments of these religious cults that came to the people of Israel and Judah through their (inevitable) contacts with the peoples and leaders of neighboring nations. Such non-Yahwistic cults are in the Hebrew Bible routinely condemned, for the reason that those who were responsible for passing on the Yahwistic traditions—who to a large extent came from the deuteronomistic tradition—were convinced that the influence of, and certainly any additions in the Yahwistic worship and beliefs from the various "foreign" cults, constituted a geat danger to the purity of the Yahwistic faith.

What is also condemned in the Hebrew Bible, in particular in the books of some of the prophets, is the worship of the Lord being accompanied by unrighteousness in the lives of the worshippers. The matter is there in the opening chapter of the Isaiah book, the complaint being that the human hands being lifted up to God in praise and prayer are "full of blood." The prophet avers that the Lord will hide his eyes from such "worshippers" (Isa 1:15). Rather, before praying what these people must do is to cease from evil ways, and adopt those that are good (Isa 1:16–17). The matter receives its most explicit condemnation in Amos where the prophet proclaims that worship coming from unworthy lives, in particular from lives where justice in personal relationships is not manifested, is nothing less than hateful to the holy Lord (Amos 5:21–24), and the theme is set forth with renewed vigour and cogency in Micah (Mic 6:6–8). What surely is being condemned here is not the practice of worship per se, as has in the past sometimes been argued,[18] but rather the worship of God that comes from the lives of individuals and groups that lack justice and righteousness. This for some of the prophets is the offering of the most unworthy worship.[19]

Household Religion

Another aspect of worship that took place in Ancient Israel calls for further consideration, namely the worship that took place in the family setting, in the home, in the family grouping.[20] The general subject of family, or household religion is one that has in recent years come to be studied as regards a number of ancient cultures and faiths. Indeed as Bodel and Olyan observe in their jointly edited volume *Household and Family Religion in Antiquity*, "Family and household religion is a cutting-edge topic in several of the fields represented here", that is in Second Millennium West Asia (including Ugarit), First Millennium West Asia (including Israel), Egypt, Greece, and Rome.[21] In this volume there is a contribution from Susan Ackerman on "Household Religion, Family Religion, and Women's Religion in Ancient Israel," while elsewhere the subject is dealt with by Carol Meyers, Rainer Albertz, and others.[22]

Our concern is the worship that took place in the family or household setting rather than in the large, official sanctuary of the nation, and the matter continues to be open to debate as to its nomenclature, the title "family" laying stress upon the people involved, "household" upon the setting.[23] In what follows I use both of these terms, and I proceed by considering what by way of worship might have taken place in the family residential setting, a matter that we can understand did in some regards change over the course of time. Judges 17–18 speaks of a certain Micah, and what is presented appears to be about worship taking place in a domestic setting, this one being complete with Levite/priest who served in a shrine which had an idol of cast

---

18. See, e.g., the classic survey of views in Rowley, "Ritual and the Hebrew Prophets."

19. See also below, 243–46, 252–55.

20. See above, 49–51.

21. Bodel and Olyan, *Household and Family Religion*, 1.

22. See Ackerman, "Household Religion"; Meyers, "Household Religion"; and Albertz, *A History of Israelite Religion*, 1:99–103, 186–95; 2:399–411. See also Toorn, *Family Religion in Babylonia, Syria and Israel*; Miller, *The Religion of Ancient Israel*, 62–76.

23. See the remarks of Ackerman, "Household Religion," 127–29.

metal, an ephod and teraphim (Judg 17:4–5).[24] It has been maintained that some of the furnishings in certain Israelite houses and compounds, such as narrow benches for offerings, offering stands, incense burners, discovered in archaeological activities suggest rooms that were intended for worship.[25]

What sort of religious practices might have taken place in such households, in such a bêt 'āb ("house of father")? It has been suggested that these may have been related to the natural or religious calendars, such as the feasts of Passover, Weeks, and Booths until they became festivals that were to be celebrated at the central shrine.[26] These festivals involved sacrifices, so it would appear that such took place, perhaps in those earlier times in the household setting, rather in the way we read about in stories of the ancestors in Genesis (for example Gen 13:3–4, 18; 26:25; 33:19–20; 35:1, and compare Judg 13:19–23). It is likely that monthly feasts were celebrated in the home, such as new moon (see Num 28:11–15), and sabbath observance.

Another group of household-based religious observances might have been those concerned with recurring activities in the human life cycle, such as marking the beginning and the end of life; prayer and offerings for human conception (see Gen 25:21; Judg 13:2–24; 1 Sam 1:1–20; though we are told that worship at a shrine was also involved in this matter); circumcision of male infants (Gen 17:23; Lev 12:3); acceptable mourning customs (Gen 50:10; 2 Sam 1:11–12; 3:31; Jer 6:26; 9:17–20);[27] procedures to ensure purification in various situations (Lev 11:24–40; 12:2–8; 14:34–53; 15:1–33; Num 19:1–22); the seeking of help for various bodily problems (1 Kgs 17:17–24; 2 Kgs 4:32–37; 20:7/Isa 38:21); expressions of distress (2 Kgs 20:1–3); fasting perhaps; and no doubt others of which we do not read.[28] Does not what we are told Daniel did when commanded *not* to pray to his own God, namely, to pray to his God three times a day in his house (Dan 6:10), suggest a tradition of prayer in the home?

No doubt there were various religious practices taking place in the household setting that were deemed to be—or came to be regarded as—irregular, so that it was stipulated that they were to take place at the central shrine, presumably so that those having responsibilities in these matters

---

24. See above, 49–51.

25. See Ackerman, "Household Religion," 132–40; and Meyers, "Household Religion," 119–23.

26. See below, 179–87.

27. It should be noted that there were a number of mourning rites practiced by Israel's neighbors that the Hebrew Bible regards as unacceptable. See, e.g., Lev 21:5; Deut 14:1.

28. On these household matters, see Meyers, "Household Religion"; Ackerman, "Household Religion"; and Olyan, *Biblical Mourning*.

could make sure that such rites were carried out correctly and regularly. Thus for example in Jer 7:16-20 and 44:15-25, 29 we have the prophet's condemnation of the cult of the Queen of Heaven, which with its offerings of cakes would suggest a setting in the home. Another aspect of such varieties of worship that earned condemnation was rites in connection with ancestors, the offerings of food to them (Deut 26:14; Tob 4:17; Sir 30:18), or even consulting them (1 Sam 28:8-19).

Women in the Israelite Cultus

This is another subject that in recent years has received scholarly attention, and what is said here is influenced in particular by the writings of Phyllis Bird and Patrick Miller.[29] Bird has suggested that while the leadership of the Israelite cult was at all times under male control, women were not excluded either from sacred space or from cultic service. Nevertheless with time the responsibilities of women in this regard did not increase, and males continued to occupy the positions of greatest authority, sanctity, and honor. Rather, women's cultic service was largely centered upon weaving, sewing, preparation of cultic meals, and of food used in the ritual, and the cleaning of cultic vessels, the furniture, and premises. Further, women were involved as singers and dancers, and in earlier times as musicians (on these see Exod 15:20-21; Judg 4:4; 5:1; 21:19, 21; 1 Sam 1:3; Ps 68:25-26).

We also read of women praying (1 Sam 1:10-16); seeking oracles (1 Kgs 14:2-5; 2 Kgs 4:22-23); making vows (Num 30:3-15; 1 Sam 1:11, 24-28); pronouncing blessings (Ruth 2:20; 4:14); participating in festivals (Num 6:2; Deut 16:1-22; 29:10-11; 31:12; Neh 8:2; 10:29-30; 12:43; Ezra 10:1). Bird has also suggested that in the ceremony at the time of purification following birth of a child, while the priest *offered* the animal, the woman had *presented* it (Lev 12:6-7).[30] There are also references in the Hebrew Bible to women who "served" (Exod 38:8), but just what was intended, and what the task was, we have to admit ignorance.

Personal Piety and Devotion

Parts of the Hebrew Bible appear to suggest that personal piety must have been known of in Ancient Israel; but to what extent that led to the practising

---

29. See Bird, "The Place of Women in the Israelite Cultus"; and Miller, *The Religion of Ancient Israel*, 201-6. See also Toorn, *From Her Cradle to Her Grave*; Vos, *Woman in Old Testament Worship*.

30. See Bird, "The Place of Women in the Israelite Cultus," 415-16, n.34.

of personal devotions we do not know. Certainly, some references appear to suggest there were worshippers who sought God and worshipped as individuals; or even if certain individuals were part of a larger assembly they were at the same time making their own devotions, expressing their own praise and thanksgiving, making their own prayers of petition and intercession. Thus, for example a goodly number of psalms read as if it is an individual who is thus praying; this we find in the psalms of individual lament and individual thanksgiving.[31] But have such psalms been expressed in the singular so that they might be suitable to help an individual who is praying on their own to do so? Or did this actually happen, to some degree or other? We have to confess our lack of knowledge and thus of certainty. Yet one way or another it does appear that there would have been individuals who engaged in worship and who made their personal approach to God.

Certainly, there is a significant number of psalms that resound with the confidence of a personal faith, such as Ps 23, a psalm of confidence, "The Lord is my shepherd, I shall not want" (Ps 23:1); or Ps 25, a psalm of lament, "To you, O Lord, I lift up my soul" (Ps 25:1). Psalm 51 although clearly applicable to any number of people using it, yet in the manner of its presentation looks like a composition for use by an individual making their confession of sin, thus, "Have mercy on me, O God, according to your steadfast love; according to your abundant mercy blot out my transgressions" (Ps 51:1). Similar observations may be made about other psalms, for example Ps 73, in particular with its, "Whom have I in heaven but you? And there is nothing on earth that I desire other than you. My flesh and my heart may fail, but God is the strength of my heart, and my portion forever" (Ps 73:25–26), and see also, Pss 22, 84, 130, 139. Further, note also the singular suffixes in the Hebrew in Isa 43:1; 44:2, 24, and also that while Deut 6:4–9 is presented as being addressed to all the people of Israel, the instructions are expressed in the singular, as if being enjoined upon each individual person. Thus it may be said that we can speak of an expressed individual piety in the Old Testament in which individuals made their own thanksgivings and petitions, their own praises and confessions, but that we are not told on what sort of basis, regular or not, individuals made such expressions of worship.[32]

---

31. For the psalms of individual lament and the individual thanksgiving psalms see below, 124–39.

32. On this subject, see Albertz, "Personal Piety"; and Anderson, "'Sicut cervus.'"

Corporate and Individual Worship

There is a certain lack in the Old Testament of pictures and insights into what we might call normal worship, that is ordinary worship that took place in times of quiet and peace, without celebration of some particular occasion or special happening. About what we might call the special event we are given a numbers of descriptions in the Hebrew Bible, but it is probable that on the part of some writers there is an element of exaggeration in the spirit of worship, the people's hearty and earnest responses, the numbers in attendance. Examples of such occasions might be, for instance, the dedication of the first Jerusalem temple (1 Kgs 8.1–61; 2 Chr 6:1–42), or Ezra's promulgation of the law of the Lord (Neh 7:73b—8:18).

Nevertheless it is perhaps in the book of psalms that we may be best able to appreciate the sense of joy, devoutness, seriousness about worship, maybe a spirit of worship that was not only present on the special occasion, and the particularly high occasion of celebration, but also—and perhaps above all—in ordinary times, and in the lives of ordinary yet devout peoples. The matter has been well expressed in what William P. Brown says at the conclusion of his helpful study of the psalter:

> Whereas other books of the Bible contain God's words and the narratives of God's work, both in history and creation, the Psalter conveys something of Israel's vociferous response to God— the community's cries and acclamations, its proclamations and discursive reflections. The Psalms present, in short, a sanctuary of shouting and singing.[33]

And on that note we move on to consider those who it seems were appointed in ancient Israel to particular responsibilities in the leadership of worship, namely the priests and the Levites. This is the subject of the following chapter.

---

33. Brown, *Psalms*, 160.

5

Priests and Levites

Much as we might wish to present a reconstruction of the history of the Israelite priesthood, we must accept that we do not have the literary resources to do so. It is as Blenkinsopp expressed it: "The problems besetting the history of the priesthood in Israel explain why no one has attempted to write such a history since Aelred Cody."[1] Thus the procedure followed here is first to take in turn each part of the Old Testament where extended reference is made to priests and Levites, that is the books of Leviticus, Numbers, and Deuteronomy, and after that to make some more generalized comments about what are presented as the callings and duties of priests and Levites in certain historical periods. And in view of the fact that the book of Leviticus contains by far the largest number of references to priests in any part of the Hebrew Bible, it is with this book that we may begin.

Leviticus

The book of Leviticus appears to make the assumption that there is a temple in existence, and further what we read about this temple in a variety of ways reflects what we read about the tabernacle of Exod 25–30. As has already been observed we may perhaps say that the description of the desert tabernacle is likely to be a reflection of one of the Jerusalem temples, either the pre-exilic Solomonic temple, or perhaps more likely the second temple, that of Zerubbabel. Further, in all probability there is a distinct element here of the idealization of temple worship, and that the description of the wilderness tabernacle is itself something of an imaginary projection back into the wilderness period of what was later known in the settled land.[2] Moreover, what we are told about the priests and their duties in Leviticus is again likely to be something of a statement of the ideal. That is, what is spoken about here is what the authors of Leviticus believed was intended to take place,

---

1. The work to which Blenkinsopp in his *Sage, Priest, Prophet* referred (p. 185) was Cody, *A History of Old Testament Priesthood*. On the approach to matters historical in the Hebrew Bible followed in this present work, see above, 12.

2. On the wilderness tabernacle, see above, 26–29, and also below, 213–15.

what should ideally take place. We have not been given here a picture of worship, and the priestly and levitical offices and responsibilities therein, "warts and all," but rather what was intended to be in the nature of an *ideal* which at least some in ancient Israel held in their religious imagination.

The central aspect of the priestly ministry in Leviticus is to do with the altar and the offering of sacrifices. Further the particular contribution which the priests made in the matter of sacrificing could only be done by the priests. When the sacrificial animal—unless it was a bird, which the priest himself killed (Lev 1:14-17)—had been slain, the priests were responsible for the sprinkling of the blood (see, for example, Lev 1:5, 12; 3:2, 8, 13; 4:6-7, 17, 25, 30, 34). For these duties the priest wore distinctive clothing, vestments, in Leviticus sometimes literally "holy vestments" (for example Lev 16:32). Another priestly responsibility was to ensure that the fire on the altar never went out (Lev 6:12-13), while other duties were with the incense offering (Lev 16:12); with the "waving" or "lifting" of offerings towards the altar (Lev 7:14, 30); and with the bread of the Presence on the Sabbath (Lev 24:8). Yet we should not think that these were in any way meaningless actions: rather, as Lester Grabbe expresses the matter, "These workaday activities were invested with complex symbolism and filled with deep meaning. The actions of cutting, slicing, sprinkling and burning had no intrinsic value, but God had invested them with religious significance. The priests were holy, and what they did was holy work."[3] Another cultic duty that fell to the priests was the ceremony of the Day of Atonement, set out in much detail in Lev 16.[4]

According to Leviticus the priests were also responsible for aspects of religious teaching, like, the appropriateness and efficacy of various sacrifices for particular settings and situations (Lev 7:11-21); the conditions regarding admission to the cult (Lev 15:28); when payment was to be made instead of an offering (Lev 27:8, 12, 18); how to distinguish between what was clean and what was unclean in daily life, whether in diet (Lev 11), or in illness (Lev 13), or in sexual intercourse (Lev 12).

The reference above to payment being made to priests in certain circumstances instead of making an offering raises the whole issue of the

---

3. Grabbe, *Leviticus*, 65. Elsewhere in this work Grabbe says, "it would be a mistake to assume that the priests were only repetitively going through empty rituals. On the contrary, there is reason to believe that the rites had considerable spiritual meaning for the priests and for the ordinary Israelites. One may only guess at this meaning, but it is certain that it was there. The priests were probably the first theologians in ancient Israel" (75).

4. Concerning the Day of Atonement and its rites and ceremonies, see below, 170-75.

financial support of, and other provision for the ancient Israelite priesthood. Leviticus 6 and 7 specifies that whereas in the case of the whole burnt offerings all the offering was burned upon the altar, with most other offerings only part of the offering went to the altar, while some portions went back to the one who was making the offering, and other portions to the priests. In some sacrifices all of what was not consumed upon the altar went to the priests. Leviticus 7:28-36 sets out some of these matters in detail. Thus, for example in the sacrifice of well-being (*zebaḥ šâlôm*) it is stipulated that the breast belongs to the priests ("Aaron and his sons", v. 31), and the right thigh also for the priests (7:32-33, see also vv. 34-36).[5] These portions which were to go to the priests, we are told in v. 34, were "a perpetual due", literally "a perpetual ordinance [*lĕḥāq ʿôlām*]".

A further matter concerning priests is their genealogy. In Exodus, Leviticus, and Numbers, along with 1 and 2 Chronicles the priestly line is consistently spoken of as being made up of those who are descended from Aaron. This suggests that in these documents there is a perceived importance attached to the sense of continuity with the traditions about Moses and his assistant Aaron. In documents that purport to speak of monarchical times the predominant priestly line is portrayed as the one descended from Zadok, and this is a matter to which we shall return.[6]

As far as the Levites are concerned the book of Leviticus is (somewhat surprisingly) muted, only mentioning them four times, and at that twice each in just two verses, Lev 25:32, 33. Further the subject here is the provision of places of ongoing dwelling for the Levites, the background being that apart from this provision the Levites were not given any possession of land of their own. Thus we may say that the book of Leviticus does not have anything specific to say about the cultic or other religious duties of the Levites. Yet it appears to assume their existence, which here seems to have been a subservient one to the priests; the Levites' particular responsibilities lay with the care of the tabernacle and assisting the priests in their duties.

Numbers

In the book of Numbers we *do* hear a good deal about the Levites, they being portrayed as cultic servants, clergy who are in a defined subservient role to the priests. Nevertheless, Levites are set-apart for service in the place of

---

5. For discussion of what is meant by *tĕnûpāh* ("an elevated offering") in Lev 7:30 and *tĕrûmāh* ("a present") in 7:32, see, e.g., Hartley, *Leviticus*, 101; and Wenham, *Leviticus*, 126.

6. See below, 77-78.

worship, and thus not only are they to be exempt from military service, but are also to be numbered separately from other Israelite tribes (Num 4:1–49). They were responsible for the fabric of the place of worship, in particular being charged with the taking down, transporting, and re-erecting the desert tabernacle (Num 1:48–54). Further, their subservient status vis-à-vis the priests is again evident in the place where they are to be domiciled in the camp on the desert march (Num 3:38). While the priests were responsible for the sanctuary rituals, the Levites were to serve as their assistants; it would seem that the Levites had to share a portion of their tithe with the priests (Num 18:26). Perhaps not altogether surprising was what looks like something of a rebellion on the part of some of the Levites over the issue of their terms of employment (Num 16:1–11). Nevertheless, the Levites were seen to have important, even religiously vital, duties in the sanctuary (Num 1:53; 3:1–13; 8:14–19), and the Israelites were commanded that they had responsibility for the financial support of the Levites (Num 31:25–31).

Then, Numbers, like Leviticus, emphasizes the responsibilities of the priests at the altar—with the Levites as their assistants—and with due rewards for the services they rendered (Num 18:1–32). The priests were also responsible for consulting the sacred lot, Urim (Num 27:18–21) and to accompany the troops on military campaigns, taking sanctuary vessels—not forgetting the trumpets (Num 31:6). We also get here in Numbers references to the high priest, or chief priest (Num 35:25, 28, 32), and judging by other references to such a person, probably an office that historically belonged to later times (see Lev 21:10; 2 Kgs 12:10; 22:4, 8; Hag 1:1; Zech 3:1; Neh 3:1).[7]

Deuteronomy

The references in Deuteronomy to priests and Levites are less clear than we might wish, resulting in a division of scholarly views on the subject. The fact is that the title Levite appears to mean something different in at least some of the places where it occurs in Deuteronomy from what it means in the Priestly material in Leviticus and Numbers. Sometimes in Deuteronomy there is talk simply of Levites, as in, for example, Deut 12:12, 18–19; 14:27–29; 16:11, 13–14; 18:6–7; 26:11, 12. Usually here there is talk of Israelites providing some help for Levites, in particular for reasons along the lines of "because he has no portion or inheritance with his brothers/with you" (10:9; 12:12; 14:27–29; 18:1).

Yet in other places the reference is to Levitical priests (17:9, 18; 18:1–2; 24:8; 27:9), and there are further instances where there are not dissimilar

7. On the matter of the office of the high priest, see below, 80, 270.

references, as for example in 10:8–9; 17:12; 21:5; 26:3–4; 31:9; 33:8–11. The question is this: is Deuteronomy speaking about two groups of people, or is it using different titles for what was intended to indicate one group? Both points of view have their champions, the former, that there were two distinct groups, is held, for example, by John R. Spencer in his contribution to the *Anchor Bible Dictionary*,[8] the latter, that there was essentially one group, being held for example, by Lester L. Grabbe in his study *Priests, Prophets, Diviners, Sages*.[9] Nevertheless, however, they were described or denominated, the priests/Levites/levitical priests were, according to the Deuteronomists responsible for a variety of duties, whether those were concerned with the altar (thus 10:8–9; 18:6–8; 33:10); teaching the law (33:10); caring for the written law and proclaiming it (31:9–13, 24–26); giving help if needed to judges in deciding difficult legal cases (17:8–13; 19:17; 21:5); or consulting the divine lots, Urim and Thummim in an attempt to ascertain the will of God (33:8).

Priests and Levites in the Tribal Period

By this I intend what we read in the Hebrew Bible purporting as coming from the tribal period, which may or may not entirely accurately reflect what was going on in those times. At any rate in the book of Joshua we find the Deuteronomic language of "levitical priests" being employed. Thus we read of "levitical priests" carrying the sacred ark across the Jordan (Josh 3:3); but when we come to Josh 6 it is "priests" who carry the ark around the perimeter walls of Jericho—which may or may not be intended to indicate the same group. When it comes to the reading of the law at Mounts Ebal and Gerizim, however, it is again the levitical priests who are carrying the ark (Josh 8:30–35).

Joshua 13:14 notes that the Levites were the one group who did not receive an inheritance of land. Rather their "inheritance" was their work in connection with the burnt offerings, and further, in this book we are also told that they received a number of cities in which they might live (Josh 21), a provision that is widely thought likely to come from a later time than the tribal period. Joshua 21 goes into detail about the three-fold division of the families of the Levites, and it is in this same chapter that we have mention of the sole-named priest in this book, Eleazar, who is said to have been

---

8. Spencer, "Levites and Priests," esp. pp. 303–5. See also Abba, "Priests and Levites in Deuteronomy," and "Priests and Levites."

9. Grabbe, *Priests, Prophets, Diviners, Sages*, 42–43; and Emerton, "Priests and Levites in Deuteronomy."

involved at Shiloh in the matter of the levitical cities (21:1). Eleazar, we are told, was involved again at Shiloh with Joshua and the heads of the families of the Israelite tribes in the distribution of the land of Canaan (Josh 21:1-2).

Judges 17 and 18 are instructive for here we read of a certain Micah, a man we are told who was of the hill country of Ephraim (Judg 17:1), who made an idol of cast metal, established a shrine, made an ephod and teraphim, and installed one of his sons as his priest (Judg 17:4-5). Judges 17:7-13 goes on to speak of a Levite from Bethlehem coming to Ephraim and making an agreement with Micah to serve as a "father" and as a "priest" at Micah's shrine (17:10-13). Later in this story we are told that the Danites took over what Micah had established, conquering and destroying the city and people of Laish, then rebuilding it and renaming it Dan (18:27-29). They established Micah's idol as their own, retaining the services of the Levite whose name was Jonathan son of Gershom, son of Moses; we are told that his sons were priests to the tribes of the Danites until the time the land went into captivity (18:30-31).

What is this story about and what does it tell us about priests and Levites? There is little general agreement about the significance of Judg 17–18: are they intended to be about the foundation myth of the Israelite city of Dan?[10] Or are they about changes that took place in the structures of the Israelite tribes' political organization, either to justify the Israelite kingship, to provide something by way of an "apologia" for kingship (note the comment in 17:6; 18:1) and perhaps for its necessary expenses? Or was the purpose of this story to speak of the corruption and venality of priests and Levites? What is perhaps of particular interest to us is the relationship between priests and Levites spoken about in these chapters, and the fact that a member of the community of the Levites could be appointed to the office and duties of a priest in a shrine.

In the books of Samuel we find remarkably few references to Levites: in fact there are only two, 1 Sam 6:15 and 2 Sam 15:24, and both are about the Levites removing the ark of the covenant to another place. There are considerably more references to priests, especially in 1 Samuel. Further, Shiloh seems at that time—that is until its unrecorded demise—to have been a significant shrine, and it was here that Eli and his two sons, Hophni and Phinehas, served as priests (1 Sam 1:1-13). It was at Shiloh also that the boy Samuel served (as an assistant to Eli?) and where the call of the Lord came to him (1 Sam 3:1-13, 15-16), a call which in the fullness of time he fulfilled in a variety of ways, as seer, as prophet, as judge, as well as in

---

10. This is argued by Niditch in her contributions, "Judges"; and *Judges*, 172–85, esp. p. 180. Other possibilities are set out by McMillion, "Worship in Judges 17–18."

being a priest, and these responsibilities in various settings, Bethel, Gilgal, Mizpah, Ramah. See, for example, 1 Sam 7:13-17; 9:3-20; 10:1; 13; 15. It also appears from what we are told in 1 Sam 14:3 and 18 that another priest at this time was Ahijah son of Ahitub, Ichabod's brother, and no doubt there were others. Perhaps we do not hear of such others, or anything about their priestly ministries, because the great matter of the day that First Samuel is concerned about is the question, what sort of leader the Israelites tribes are to have? Should they continue with the leadership of the judges, or should they have a king? Samuel is portrayed as first favoring the former option, but later coming to see the point of view of others that a king was needed (1 Sam 8:1-22). Thus came about monarchy in ancient Israel, first, in a modest way in the kingship of Saul the son of Kish, and later in what would turn out to be a much more radical way in the kingship of David the son of Jesse. Moreover, with the capture of Jerusalem, and the establishment there of the religious and political capital of the people of Israel, and later with the building of a temple in that city, considerable further changes took place in cultic personnel. And it is to such matters that we now turn.

Priests and Levites in the Monarchical Period

King David's priests, we are told in 2 Sam 8:17-18, were Zadok son of Ahitub, Ahimelek son of Abiathar, and two unnamed sons of David. However, elsewhere in 2 Sam mention is made of Abiathar son of Ahimelek, and it is widely thought likely that is what we should read in 2 Sam 8:17.[11] Now Abiathar son of Ahimelek is known to us through his being mentioned in 1 Sam 22:20 as one of the priests who survived Saul's purge of those close to him and who transferred their loyalty to David on his rise to power. Thus we can see that Abiathar came to David as one who had served in the earlier political order.

But from where did Zadok come? The Chronicler has him descended from the priestly line of Eliazar and Aaron (1 Chr 6:3-8), but it is slightly puzzling that he is not mentioned in the account of Saul's destruction of Nob, from which we are told that only Abiathar the son of Ahimelech escaped (1 Sam 22:20). Thus it has been suggested that Zadok was priest in Jerusalem prior to David's capture of the city, that the words in 1 Chr 6:3-8 about his lineage are an attempt at an Israelite—and perhaps even more important, *priestly* descent from Aaron—legitimization. For, so it has been pointed out, the name *Zadok* is reminiscent of parts of the names of two

---

11. See, e.g., Gordon, *1 & 2 Samuel*, 246; and Mauchline, *1 and 2 Samuel*, 237.

early Jerusalemite kings, Melchi*zedek* (Gen 14:18) and Adoni*zedek* (Josh 10:1).[12]

It seems that both Zadok and Abiathar served David as his priests in Jerusalem (2 Sam 15:24–37), but that later Abiathar, by backing Adonijah rather than Solomon, was dismissed by David, who then made Zadok what looks like the leader of the priests in Jerusalem (1 Kgs 2:35). Zadok's son Azariah became that Jerusalem priest in the days of the kingship of Solomon, David's son (1 Kgs 4:2).

After the death of Solomon and the accession of Rehoboam in Jerusalem, Jeroboam took the northern tribes on an independent course, making himself their king (1 Kgs 12:1–24), and establishing two cultic centers, Dan in the north and Bethel in the south, between them intending to provide rival places of worship to that of Jerusalem (1 Kgs 12:25–29). The account in the Deuteronomistic History displays considerable antipathy to Dan and Bethel, in particular to the calves of gold that they present as having been established by Jeroboam. Yet these were places of ancient provenance for Israelite worship, Dan having been the setting for the exploits recounted in Judg 17–18, while Bethel had the tradition of having been the geographical setting for Jacob's dream (Gen 28:10–22). We are told that the people went to worship at these places, that moreover Jeroboam established what appear to have been places of worship on high places,[13] and that he also appointed priests "from among all the people, who were not Levites" (1 Kgs 12:31). He further established a religious festival on the fifteenth day of the eighth month (that "he alone had devised," 1 Kgs 12:33), at which he presided at the altar to offer incense. We also hear of Jeroboam presiding at the altar in 1 Kgs 13:1–6.[14]

The books of Hosea and Amos speak of these northern sanctuaries and their priests, Hos 10:5 having the prophet of that name speaking of "idolatrous priests" at Bethel, in particular over "its glory that has departed from it." Hosea also castigates the priests in 5:1–2 and 10:15, and elsewhere (see Hos 4:4–6, 9; 6:9), while in Amos 7:10–17 is the account of the Bethel priest Amaziah's dismissal of Amos because of his harsh words of judgment upon King Jeroboam. In neither of these two prophetical books do we read of Levites—nor, it has to be said, any positive words about priests.

---

12. For succinct treatments of these matters, see, e.g., Ramsey, "Zadok"; Schley and Spence, "Zadok"; Bartlett, "Zadok and His Successors at Jerusalem"; Cross, *Canaanite Myth and Hebrew Epic*, 209–15; Rehm, "Levites and Priests"; Vaux, *Ancient Israel*, 372–74, 394–97.

13. On "high places," see above, 53–54.

14. On kings acting as priests, see below, 97–98.

With the book of Micah, it is probable that we have words addressed to the southern kingdom of Judah and Jerusalem. Again, there is expressed dissatisfaction with the priests—along with rulers and prophets! (Mic 3:11). Within the book of Jeremiah too, there is a good deal of criticism of priests; see, for example, Jer 5:31; 6:13–14; 8:10–11; 14:18. We are told that Jeremiah himself belonged to a priestly family in Anathoth in the land of Benjamin (Jer 1:1), and the fact that the prophet was so critical of priests must have at least contributed to the troubles and unpopularity, even hatred, that he experienced (see, e.g., Jer 11:21, 23). We also read of the priest Pashur, "the chief officer in the house of the Lord", striking Jeremiah and putting him in the stocks for a night (Jer 20:1–3). Yet it does seem that priesthood is there in the thought of this book for the future life of the nation, including mention of levitical priests no less than three times in Jer 33 (vv. 18, 21, 22). Thus to that later time we now turn.[15]

Priesthood in Post-exilic Times

The leaders Ezra and Nehemiah are portrayed in the Hebrew Bible as being active in Jerusalem in the time of Persian rule. Those must have been very different times from the period prior to the conquests of the Babylonians in Jerusalem and the surrounding towns and countryside. Now Jerusalem and its environs were in a Persian province, certainly no longer able to have their own king. Yet judging from what we read in various documents that appear to emanate from this period, both priests and Levites seem to have a place in the life of the restored community. There are extended genealogies in Ezra 2 and Neh 7, and in these we read of various personnel of the cult, Levites, singers, gatekeepers, temple servants, and priests (Ezra 2:36–63; Neh 7:39–60, 72–73). Ezra 3–6 speaks of the re-establishment of the temple and its worship, the priests being assisted by *other* priests (3:2), and with a larger group for the celebrations on the occasion of the laying of the foundations of the new temple—not to mention those who continued to mourn the passing of the old temple (Ezra 3:10–13).

However, Ezra is portrayed here as being as well as a priest (Ezra 7:11, 12, 21; 10:10, 16; Neh 8:9; 12:26), also as a scribe (Neh 8:1, 4, 9, 13; 12:26, 36); in Ezra 7:12 being called "the scribe of the law of the God of heaven." We also read of Ezra's involvement with issues of marriages of some Israelites with the peoples of the land, some of these Israelites being priests and Levites (Ezra 9–10). It should also be noted that in Isa 56–66, chapters that appear also to reflect this historical period, there is a more inclusive thought

---

15. See below, 240–75, for further on prophets and worship.

and approach regarding the place of priests and Levites in the temple cult, in Isa 66:21 having talk of the Lord's acceptance of some members of other nations to serve as priests and Levites. Further, the promise here is also that "From new moon to new moon, and from sabbath to sabbath, all flesh shall come to worship before me, says the Lord" (Isa 66:23), and "my house shall be called a house of prayer for all peoples" (Isa 56:7).

All three of the books of the prophets Haggai, Zechariah, and Malachi are portrayed as coming from the post-exilic period. In the short book of Haggai there is comparatively large mention of "Joshua son of Jehozadak, the high priest" (Hag 1:1, 12, 14; 2:2, 4), who also appears in Zech 3:1, 3, 6, 8, 9; 6:11. What are we to say about the office of the high priest? Deborah Rooke argues that what we read about the high priest in the prophecies of Haggai and Zechariah 1–8 represents the beginning of any influence such a person may have had in Israel, and that at this stage that person had no jurisdiction outside the sphere of the temple, nor do these books portray him acquiring any.[16] There is nothing in Malachi about a high priest, yet what we do have in Mal 1:6—2:9 is a sustained criticism of and attack upon the priests for their failure to offer correct sacrifices in the prescribed manner and in the right spirit. In all probability any power that the High Priests had was acquired in post-exilic times, and that in the absence of kings certain of the old kingly responsibilities began to devolve upon the High Priest. Yet it was a responsibility based upon, and no doubt drawing authority from, the Jerusalem temple, and when that was destroyed by the Roman leader Titus in 70 CE, that was the end of what had been an influential institution of the post-exilic era.

In the books of Chronicles we find a detailed treatment of priests and Levites, particularly in 1 Chr 23–26. Although these books are late, apparently coming from a time after the exile, it is not always easy to be sure when they are reflecting the situation in pre-exilic times or in the post-exilic age. It could be that what we read here concerning the cult bears a relationship with what prevailed in the days of the Second Temple.[17] At any rate, after 1 Chr 21–22 has set out the details of David's census and purchase of a site for the temple, chs 23–26 detail the cultic personnel who will serve therein. Thus 1 Chr 23 speaks of the divisions and duties of the Levites, and ch. 24 about the organization of the priests (vv. 1–19), and (this possibly being the

---

16. Rooke, *Zadok's Heirs*, 151. On the subject of the high priest, see Bartlett, "Zadok and His Successors at Jerusalem," 11–15; Boccaccini, "High Priest"; and Vaux, *Ancient Israel*, 397–403.

17. On this see, e.g., Grabbe, *Priests, Prophets, Diviners, Sages*, 51; Williamson, *1 and 2 Chronicles*, 157–78; and Williamson, "The Origins of the Twenty-Four Priestly Courses," 251–68.

work of a reviser) again of the organization of the Levites (vv. 20-31). Then ch. 25 is about musicians and their temple duties: these all being "under the direction of their father for the music in the house of the Lord with cymbals, harps, and lyres for the service of the house of God" (1 Chr 25:6) Chapter 26:1-19 gives details of the gatekeepers, and in vv. 20-32 of various further duties of the Levites.

What about priests and Levites in the Ezekiel book? Ezekiel, as well as being a prophet, is also a priest (Ezek 1:3), the sins of the priests are spoken of along with those of the prophets and others (22:23-31). In Ezekiel's vision of the new temple in chs 40-48, it is the Zadokite priests who are to minister at the altar (40:45-46); in 43:19 these are referred to as "levitical priests of the family of Zadok." Their duties are further spoken about in 44:15-21, where we are told about their prescribed linen vestments, about who they are allowed to marry, about the fact that they are to teach people the difference between the holy and the common, between what is clean and what is unclean. Further, they are to give judgments in lawsuits, and to ensure that appointed festivals and sabbaths are kept holy. As they do not have their own inheritance, they are to receive portions of sacrifices and other sacred offerings, and they have their own special quarters in the temple for the consumption of their food (42:13; 46:19-20).[18]

What Were the Callings of the Levites and Priests?

We have seen that the history of priesthood and levitical service in ancient Israel was complex, and further observed that in view of the nature of the documents we have at our disposal it is unlikely that we can now reconstruct the details of the historical development of those institutions. What perhaps we can more realistically attempt is an outline of what appear to have been the principal duties of those Levites and priests and what was involved in their special callings to these offices.

According to the author of the Letter to the Hebrews, "Every high priest chosen from among mortals is put in charge of things pertaining to God on their behalf, to offer gifts and sacrifices for sins" (Heb 5:1). While we do perhaps have to understand and accept that this reflects what in Hebrew Bible terms is a statement of a view held in an historically much later period, even so it does set before us the common understanding of the calling of the Old Testament priesthood, namely their ministry at the altar of offering gifts and sacrifices. Blenkinsopp characterizes this by saying that the "priest . . .

---

18. See further below, 256-64, for Ezek 40-48.

exists in the first place to *facilitate* the carrying out of ritual."[19] We understand that the priest did not do all of the actions in this regard, for we read that the actual immolation of the sacrificial animal was the responsibility of the offerer (Lev 1:5; 3:2, 8, 13; 4:24, 29, 33), yet the crucial part of the ceremony, that concerning the blood, was the special responsibility of the priest, presumably because not only was the blood the holiest part of the victim (Lev 17:11, 14), but also because the offering of this was upon the altar and immediate contact with that could only be undertaken by the religious specialist, one who was fully cognizant of the precise regulations regarding the holy acts of making sacrifices. For we should understand that it was believed that continuing life for the offerer depended upon the correct carrying out of those sacrificial regulations. The belief was held (see Lev 1–7) that it was through this means that the forgiveness of a range of unwitting, involuntary sins was to be gained, and thereby ongoing life secured. The centrality and importance of this priestly ministry at the altar is expressed in what was said about those priests of the high places who in the religious reform of Josiah were deposed for their unfaithfulness, and of whom the Deuteronomistic Historian observed "The priests of the high places, however, did not come up to the altar of the Lord in Jerusalem" (2 Kgs 23:9).

According to what we understand as some of the Priestly writings, the priests wore particular items of clothing, vestments, in the carrying-out of their priestly duties. According to Exod 28:6–12 and 39:2–7 they wore an ephod, a garment that was around the body from the loins downward, and held there by shoulder-pieces, and gold, woollen, and linen threads were used in the making thereof. To cover the priest's body higher than the ephod was the breastplate (*ḥōšen*), into which were worked twelve precious stones, each bearing the name of one of the Israelite tribes. Exodus 39:27 also speaks of a tunic (*kutōnet*), with a girdle, while linen breeches (Exod 28:42; 39:28), which seem to be undergarments, were to be worn for reasons of modesty, lest the wearer expose themself (see Ezek 44:18). We are also told that Aaron had a turban, that his sons had what looks like more modest head dress (Exod 28:39–40), while Aaron himself had a golden diadem, upon which was a rosette of pure gold engraved with the words "Holy to the Lord" (Exod 28:36–38; 39:30–31). Further, we are told that the theological thought behind the rosette was that it should be "on Aaron's forehead, and Aaron shall take on himself any guilt incurred in the holy offering that the Israelites consecrate as their sacred donations; it shall always be on his forehead, in order that they may find favor before the Lord" (Exod 28:38).[20]

---

19. Blenkinsopp, *Sage, Priest, Prophet*, 80 (his italics).

20. For full details of these and other priestly vestments, see Haran, *Temples and*

There were some further responsibilities that fell to the lot of the priests. In the first place they were responsible for the acts to do with incense, and such is spoken of in the Blessing of Moses in Deut 33:1-29 (see v. 10), though the main references to it in the Hebrew Bible are in the so-called Priestly parts and in the Chronicler. Incense is a compound of gums and spices which when burned produces a perfumed smoke. Closely related to incense (Heb *qĕṭōret*) is frankincense (*lĕbônāh*), and we read of the use of incense by a wide range of the peoples of the ancient Middle East, in connection with funerals, divine worship, magic rituals, and for both cosmetic and medicinal applications. The Old Testament speaks of incense altars, and in various texts we read of the burning of incense, not only in worship (see for example Exod 30:1-10; Lev 10:1; 16:12-13) but also for cosmetic and medical use as in the Song of Songs. Exodus 30:7-8 speaks of the regular morning and evening offerings of incense on the incense altar in front of the holy of holies in the tabernacle, and perhaps the envisaged purpose of the incense was to carry up the prayers to the Lord. The use of incense in the ritual of the Day of Atonement has some prominence (Lev 16:12-13), and is portrayed as providing protection for Aaron as he fufils his ministry in the most holy part of the holy sanctuary. It would seem that in Lev 16:2 the cloud in which the Lord appeared to Moses is envisaged as being that of the burned incense. In a similar way the reference to the house being "filled with smoke" in the call narrative in Isa 6:4 is probably to the smoke of incense.

Kjeld Nielsen in his helpful article about incense observes that the Old Testament does not reflect much upon the origin of the employment of incense, and that its use is simply based on the divine commandment in Exod 30, adding that unlike the mythological literature of the surrounding peoples the Hebrew Bible has no such speculation as to why God wants incense to be used.[21] It is not easy to give reasons and explanations for the use of incense in worship, and perhaps Nielsen goes as far as it is possible for us to go in this regard when he says,

> The ritual use of incense is an expression of man in an emotional state. It is a call upon the gods expressing helplessness, happiness, or gratitude. The basic role of incense is to persuade, to threaten, to remedy, to cure, to reveal, to defend, to please, to seduce. In other words, incense is always used with a purpose, be it the substance, its odor, or its smoke. The use of incense is a symbolic expression of man's yearning to understand himself

---

Temple-Service, 165-74; and Jenson, *Graded Holiness*, 124-28.

21. Nielsen, "Incense," 407.

in a dramatic world where odoriferous ritual is an indispensable part of the drama.[22]

In not dissimilar tones, but in reference to Christian worship, W. Jardine Grisbrooke observes that among various uses of incense in divine worship one is "simply to create a worshipful atmosphere."[23]

Another responsibility of the priests, as well as burning incense before the Lord, and offering sacrifices was to be teachers, that is "They teach Jacob your ordinances, and Israel your law" (Deut 33:10) This aspect of the priestly ministry is set forth in Deut 31:9-13, 24-26, in particular that what is spoken of as the law Moses had written is to be heard by the people, "so that they may hear and learn to fear [y-r-'] the Lord your God and to observe diligently all the words of this law" (Deut 31:12). We gain some information about this priestly function in such texts as Hos 4:6; Jer 2:8. However, while the matter of the people knowing and obeying the law of the Lord is emphasized in Isa 2:3 (=Mic 4:2), we are not told there whose responsibility it was to do the vital work of teaching that.

Significant in this regard would seem to be all that we read about the proclamation made by Ezra and recorded for us in Neh 8:1-18.[24] Here we read of Ezra proclaiming what was in "the book [sēper] of the law of Moses, which the Lord had given to Israel" (Neh 8:1). We go on to read about Ezra standing on a wooden platform that had been made for this purpose (v. 4), and opening the book with a good deal of solemnity, accompanied by his audience standing, responding to his expression of praise, lifting their hands, bowing their heads and worshipping, and how he read from his podium ("pulpit" might we say?) the words of the book (vv. 5-7a). Further, we are told "the Levites helped the people to understand the law, while the people remained in their places" (v. 7b).[25]

---

22. Nielsen, "Incense," 405; and ibid., *Incense in Ancient Israel*.

23. Grisbrooke, "Incense," 265. On incense and incense altars, see also Haran, *Temples and Temple-Service*, 230-45; and Jenson, *Graded Holiness*, 109-11.

24. There continue to be many questions unresolved in regard to the authorship of the books of Ezra and Nehemiah and the sources that lie behind the texts that we now have. The view taken in this work is that with the books of Ezra and Nehemiah we have different authorship from that of the books of Chronicles. See in this regard Williamson, *Israel in the Books of Chronicles*, 5-82. As far as the sources that lie behind the Ezra and Nehemiah books are concerned, it is widely agreed that one of these is what has been called "The Ezra Memoir" comprising Ezra 7-10 and Neh 8, with some adding Neh 9-10. Less completely agreed, but accepted in this work, is that this document does come from Ezra. See, e.g., Williamson, *Ezra, Nehemiah*, xxviii-xxxii; and Clines, *Ezra, Nehemiah, Esther*, 6-8.

25. I follow NRSV's "the Levites" rather than the Hebrew text's (MT) "and the Levites," along with Blenkinsopp, *Ezra-Nehemiah*, 284; and Williamson. *Ezra, Nehemiah*,

What appears to be taking place here is a written document being accorded a significant religious place, that further, its reading is accompanied by a real sense of devoutness, that its reading and being heard are felt to be serious religious acts, and that what it has to say to the people assembled is to be taken with such seriousness that the Levites are in attendance to help the people understand what was being read to them. We gain the impression that Ezra must have read a portion of the text of the book of the law of Moses, and that then the Levites would have helped the people to understand something of the significance for themselves of what they had just heard.

Two questions are thus presented to us. First, what was the precise role of Ezra in all this? And, was what we are reading about here something in the nature of an early stage in the development of the sermon?

First, the role of Ezra in all this: In the Hebrew Bible Ezra is only spoken about in the books of Ezra and Nehemiah, in particular in Ezra 7 and 10, and in Neh. 8 and 12. Within these chapters it is said ten times that Ezra was a scribe, and eight times that he was a priest. Does this indicate that Ezra worked and was active in both of these spheres, and if so when he was reading to the people from the book of the law of Moses was he acting in his role as a scribe, or in his role as a priest? It does have to be said that we do not otherwise read of priests being involved in such a ministry,[26] and yet I would suggest that for at least a provisional conclusion we may accept that it was in the role of a priest that he was acting. In that way he would have had a particular status in that post-exilic community where he was speaking. As regards Ezra in his acting as scribe we may suggest that this was where his authority came from in his use of and proclamation from what was a comparatively new form of religious communication, namely what is here called "the book of the law of Moses, which the Lord had given to Israel." This, presumably, must have been a written document that came out of the work of scribes in the years of exile, a part of what would eventuate as the Torah, or in the language that the Christians would use, the Pentateuch.

Then second, we may perhaps be permitted to say that this does look like an aspect of the beginnings of a ministry of preaching, and that what we seem to have here is talk of a sermon. This is a subject to which we shall return in our consideration of what the Chronicler has to say on the matter of worship. [27] Yet for the time being we need to note, further, the role of the Levites in all this, namely their responsibility to interpret for the people what Ezra was reading. That is, the Levites were to help the people under-

---

26. In this regard, see the remarks of Blenkinsopp, *Sage, Priest, Prophet*, 82–83.
27. See below, 223–31.

stand what the written document perhaps had to say to them in their lives in a new and different setting.

All this is to say that we may understand that Ezra and his assisting Levites were in the nature of religious officials who were being called to engage in new activities in a new situation. A written document was being given prominent religious status, it was being accepted as containing a serious "word" for the people, and that there were the emerging roles of those who would read, even perhaps we may say "proclaim", and those who would interpret. Further, as a part of this, but not specifically spoken about here, is the matter of what would come to be known as the sermon, a part of worship that would come to a certain prominence for Judaism after the destruction of the Second Temple, in the Jewish synagogue, and also in the even later Christian Church. It further warrants mention that the Old Testament records considerable changes in the roles and works of the Levites. Whereas in the desert days with its portable shrine the Levites were literally and physically those who fetched and carried, yet by the stage we have reached here in the restored Jerusalem community after the years of exile they are being thought of as having a role in the matter of the interpretation of a religious document. We may further observe that in comparison the priests did not perhaps experience quite such a range of changing roles.[28]

A final area of work the priests engaged in should also be mentioned, namely divination, though what we read about in the Old Testament does not make the situation particularly clear to us. There is talk in various parts of the Hebrew Bible about ephod, these in the main coming from Exod 25–39, from Judges and 1 Sam, clearly a garment and which we have already considered.[29] However, there is in Exod 28:15, 30 an item which is referred to as "breastpiece of judgment," which is to be made in the style of an ephod, and which would appear to be that priestly garment, but which not only bore twelve stones to represent the Israelite tribes, also had a pocket in which were kept Urim and Thummim, (Exod 28:15–35). About the last-named we also read in Deut 33:8, and a use they were put to is recorded in Num 27:12–23. This was the matter of who was to succeed Moses after his death.[30] It would seem that Urim and Thummim were in all probability divining stones, artefacts that were used in the seeking of judgments in sundry matters. It should also be borne in mind that as regards the ephod there are references in the Hebrew Bible to an idolatrous ephod: see Judg 8:27, and in particular Judg 17–18, this last in the house shrine where there

---

28. In this regard, see the last paragraph of Vaux's treatment of "the priest as teacher" (*Ancient Israel*, 353–55).

29. See above, 31–32, 82.

30. For Urim and Thummim, see also Lev 8:8; 1 Sam 28:6; Ezra 2:63; Neh 7:65, and see Dozeman, "Urim and Thumim."

was appointed the Levite as the priest of Micah. It looks likely that after these comparatively early times the roles of priests and Levites in the arena of giving oracles declined considerably, and perhaps we need to take note of what is said in one text of the Talmud, namely that since the time of the deaths of the "first prophets," that is Samuel, David, and Solomon, there had been no Urim and Thummim.[31]

Summary

What then by way of summary can we say about the roles of priests and Levites as they are spoken of in the Hebrew Bible? One way or another they stood between the people and God, which is perhaps to say that they were mediators, whether they were officiating at the altar, whether teaching or instructing, or whether seeking a ruling on some difficult or disputed matter. Not surprisingly they were frequently open to criticism for having failed in their appointed duties, or for being too much concerned with their own welfare and not sufficiently about those human beings to whom they were called to mediate holy things, and on whose behalf they offered the gifts their people wished to give to their Lord. Perhaps the author of the Christian Epistle to the Hebrews sums the matter up as well as we can express it when he said,

> Every high priest chosen from among mortals is put in charge of things pertaining to God on their behalf, to offer gifts and sacrifices for sins. He is able to deal gently with the ignorant and wayward, since he himself is subject to weakness; and because of this he must offer sacrifice for his own sins as well as for those of the people. And one does not presume to take this honor, but takes it only when called by God, just as Aaron was. (Heb 5:1-4)

What Can We Say about Melchizedek?

In truth, remarkably little. Although over many years much scholarly energy has been devoted to the subject of Melchizedek, it has to be said that we know little about this figure.[32] In the Old Testament he is spoken of in just two places: Gen 14:19-20 and Ps 110:4, while in the New there are references to him a number of times in the Letter to the Hebrews (Heb 5:6,

---

31. See *Sota* 48a.

32. For a very brief selection of the large mass of secondary literature on Melchizedek in the Hebrew Bible, I suggest: Emerton, "The Riddle of Genesis xiv"; Wenham, *Genesis 1-15*, pp. 301-22; Westermann, *Genesis 12-50*, pp. 182-208; and Astour, "Melchizedek (Person)."

10; 6:10—7:19). There are also references to him in the Qumran documents, in 11Qmelch.

In Gen 14:18 Melchizedek, whose name means either "King of Righteousness" or perhaps "My King is Righteous," is said to be "king of Salem" and "priest of God Most High" (*'ēl 'elyôn*). It is widely thought that Gen 14:18-20 are verses coming from a later time than the surrounding material in Gen 14, having been inserted into that earlier material. Equally, many would regard the verses that speak of Melchizedek here as representing an ancient tradition, but in the context of this study the real question is when Melchizedek offered gifts of bread and wine to Abraham was he acting as a king or as a priest? Undoubtedly the language sounds cultic, as if from the realm of worship, and the actions as those of a priest. Yet any such cultic offering and act would be totally different from any acts in the world of worship that we read about in other parts of the patriarchal narratives (Gen 12–50), thus suggesting that Melchizedek appears here to be acting in his capacity as a king, as "King Melchizedek."

Further, the reference to Melchizedek in Ps 110:4 comes in what is generally regarded as a Royal Psalm, this being one that gives large significance to the attributes, position, role of the Israelite king. We may therefore not unreasonably suggest that in the references to Melchizedek in both of the books of Genesis and Psalms we have references to kings rather than to priests. That is, in Gen 14:18-20 we have Abraham being lauded by the *king* Melchizedek for his, Abraham's, success in battle over Chedorlaomer and the kings who were with him (v. 17), and that the gifts of bread and wine are celebratory offerings from one king to another: not what might be called the standard fare of bread and water, but rather royal gifts of bread and *wine*. This conclusion, that we should regard Melchizedek primarily as a king who also acts in the cultic setting, is in line with conclusions of Deborah Rooke in her recent study that in these texts, "Melchizedek's significance . . . is that he is first and foremost a king who is also a priest, not a priest who is also a king."[33] Thus I suggest we too should regard Melchizedek first and foremost as a king, who in that kingly capacity acted as a priest, a situation we find prevailing in the reigns of many of the kings in ancient Israel, and in the contemporary surrounding cultures.[34] And this issue of the involvement of the Israelite king in the national cult is the subject of the following chapter.

---

33. Rooke, *Zadok's Heirs*, 102. For her treatment of Melchizedek, see pp. 80–103.
34. See below, 97–98.

6

The King and Worship

There are a number of aspects of the involvement and responsibility of the ancient Israelite king in worship that call for treatment, namely: the rite of worship when the king assumed his kingship; the king as a priest; the influence of the king upon the nation's worship; the place and significance of the so-called royal psalms.

However, before embarking upon a consideration of these matters the familiar caveat should be noted concerning our limited knowledge of certain of these issues. Our main sources of information are in the works of the Deuteronomistic Historians and the Chronicler, all of whom present understandings of worship taking place in Israel in terms dictated by their own distinctive theological approaches, and within such parameters each individual king is assessed. Thus we have in the Deuteronomistic History and the writings of the Chronicler no unbiased assessments of the kings of either Judah or Israel. With the kings of the northern kingdom of Israel this is particularly so, for not only does the Chronicler choose to omit treatment of the reigns of these northern kings, but also what is presented in Kings as taking place in the northern kingdom has come down to us through the lenses and theological understandings of those in Judah, most likely in Jerusalem, whose approach seems to have been somewhat different. Thus we cannot claim to have dispassionate accounts of the place of the kings in the worship of their nations, this being particularly so in the case of the northern kingdom. We must once again accept the Hebrew Bible on its own terms, and by reading with a certain critical judgment seek to answer some of our questions about what were the beliefs and practices in those now long-past times.[1]

The Accession of the King

Many years ago Gerhard von Rad made a study of what he called "The Royal Ritual in Judah," a consideration of the accounts in 1 Kgs 1:38–39 and 2 Kgs

---

1. On these matters see, e.g., Vaux, *Ancient Israel*, 100–14; and Miller, *The Religion of Ancient Israel*, 194–97.

11:12 of the accession ceremonies of kings Solomon and Joash respectively.[2] With Solomon's accession there was anointing at the spring Gihon by the priest Zadok, this being accompanied by the blowing of the trumpet and the people saying, "Long live King Solomon." In the case of Joash the ceremony seems to have taken place in the by-then established temple (2 Kgs 11:11) where there was the placing of a crown (*nēzer*) upon him, the presenting of "the testimony" (*'ēdût*, NRSV "the covenant"), what would appear to be a written statement of divine promises and requirements,[3] and the proclamation that he was king, accompanied by anointing, clapping, and the calling "Long live the king!"

Apart from these brief accounts of what took place in the accessions of these two kings, in all other cases—and this includes the accounts of all the accessions in the northern kingdom of Israel—there are no details of rituals accompanying their accessions. That could be because such rituals as we read of in the accessions of Solomon and Joash were regarded by the historians as having taken place, because quite simply, such rituals as these *did* take place on these momentous occasions. Alternatively, it could be that such rituals did *not* take place normally. However, it would seem more likely than not that at such a crucial juncture of life for both the nation and the incoming king we would expect something by way of religious ceremony to have taken place. But that, it has to be said, can be no more than a speculation. Nicolas Wyatt in a contribution "Royal Religion in Ancient Judah" points to a number of texts from ancient Ugarit that speak of ritual practices for the accession of Ugaritic kings that are not totally dissimilar to those in the Hebrew Bible concerning the accessions of Solomon and Joash. However, whether such texts from Ugarit really help us to understand what might have normally taken place in Jerusalem must remain something of a moot point.[4] As far as possible initiation ceremonies taking place in the making of a new king in the northern kingdom of Israel we have to confess even greater ignorance.

A further matter open to question in this regard concerns to what extent these ceremonies may be said to have constituted worship. We may accept that they would have been understood as solemn ceremonies for crucial historical moments in the life of the nation, and that when later there was a temple they took place within its walls. Moreover, the mention in the case of the accession of Solomon of the *'ēdût* ("testimony, royal protocol")

---

2. Rad, "The Royal Ritual in Judah." See also Vaux, *Ancient Israel*, 102–7.

3. For a full discussion of views about *'ēdût*, "testimony, covenant," see, e.g., Jones, *1 and 2 Kings*, 2:481.

4. Wyatt, "Royal Religion in Ancient Judah," esp. pp. 70–71.

seems to indicate that some faithfulness to the will and perceived purposes of Yahweh was being sought. While undoubtedly there probably was the propaganda factor, and what we might call a political edge to these matters, yet it would seem that in this solemn national moment these high matters of the relationship between the nation and its God, and in particular the special and individual place within that relationship now being occupied by a new king, would likely have been given prominence and focus in worship. We can imagine that an accession ceremony of a king would be an occasion for prayer, prayer for both the nation as a whole and also for the individual who was becoming king. We can further imagine that this was a moment when the king would be prayerfully reminded of his new and high responsibilities, both matters that are given focus and prominence in some of the Old Testament psalms that have been called coronation psalms, and more particularly those that have been called by the more general designation royal psalms, and to these we now turn.

The Royal Psalms and Possible Coronation Psalms

Hermann Gunkel (1862–1932) in his studies of the biblical psalms set forth the thesis that there is in the Psalter a group of psalms concerned with the Israelite king, and which he called royal psalms.[5] Gunkel regarded Pss 2, 18, 20, 21, 45, 72, 89, 101, 110, 132, 144:1–11 as royal psalms, these being psalms that set forth some aspects of what appear to be ideals of kingship[6]. From what we have in the Hebrew Bible it would seem that rarely was this ideal lived up to, but such does not detract from the setting forth of the ideal, and at that in material that has to do with the cult and national worship. It has also been suggested that some of the royal psalms were perhaps used in the coronation ceremonies of the Israelite kings, maybe Pss 2 and 110, and possibly also 72 and 101, and thus they have been designated coronation psalms. Our present concern is with the possible use of at least some of the royal psalms in the ongoing life and work of the Israelite king.

Further, in the past various scholars have set forth theories about the use of some of the royal psalms in elaborate rituals about the Israelite king in his relationships with Yahweh, the people he was appointed to lead and

---

5. On the royal psalms, see, e.g., Day, *Psalms*, 88–108; Gillingham, *The Poems and Psalms of the Hebrew Bible*, 220–22; Westermann, *The Living Psalms*, 56–64; and Grant, "The Psalms and the King."

6. It has been argued by various scholars that there are in the Hebrew Bible a greater number of royal psalms than this, but such views have failed to receive majority agreement. See, e.g., Eaton, *Kingship and the Psalms*; and Eaton, "The Psalms and Israelite Worship."

govern, and himself as an individual. However, the fundamental problem with such theories is that there is no clear evidence in the Old Testament that any of them did actually take place, and thus they are not further considered in this present work.

Nevertheless some further consideration of the issues of kingship, the royal psalms, and worship is necessary, for the royal psalms have been perceived as concerned not merely with Israelite kingship, but also, being psalms, are understood as having a definite relationship with the world of worship and the cult, in all probability with the national manifestation and expression of that cult. Thus to at least some extent the royal psalms do hold in relationship the Hebrew Bible's book of Psalms and the historic Israelite kingship.

The royal psalms set forth a vision of kingship for the life of the people of God in the world, a life that is envisaged as being the living-out of a covenant relationship with their God, Yahweh. Further, within that covenant relationship the nation's king is envisaged as having a crucial role, both in his leadership of his people *and* also in his own faithfulness to the revealed will of Yahweh. Above all, the king's nation was to be seen and understood as being different from other nations, for the reason that the Israelites believed themselves to be in a close and all-encompassing covenant relationship with a deity. For the royal psalms do not set forth a vision of the ideal of Israelite kingship in terms of, say, a charter of kingship, some agreement that worldly parties might draw up, but rather in the language of worship, in particular in a series of psalms that come from and relate as psalms do, to the activity of worship. Other nations might set up an inscribed stone to celebrate kingship, but the Hebrew Bible preserves for us a series of psalms that were used in its most holy shrine. What then, are some of the issues that the so-called royal psalms set forth about the Israelite king in his relationships with Yahweh, the people of Israel, and the peoples and leaders of the neighboring nations?

The first of the royal psalms is Ps 2, a psalm that emphasizes the divine appointment of the king to his kingship, his closeness of relationship with the Lord (v. 7), the blessedness of those who live under his rule (v. 12b), and the care that other nations should take of the people blessed with this divine oversight and leadership (vv. 1–6). Overall the psalm gives a very exalted place to what is believed to be a nexus of divine purposes regarding the king who reigns in (presumably) Jerusalem, for here in Ps 2 the king is portrayed in exalted language, he being described as no less than "son of Yahweh." This sounds like the expression of the king's divine appointment to his office, and thus other worldly rulers should take notice of this and serve the Lord with "fear and trembling" (v. 11), remembering that "Happy are all who take refuge in him" (v. 12). Here are grounds indeed for the worship of the Lord for his beneficent provision for life for his people in the world.

Further, while inevitably speculative, it is not beyond the bounds of possibility that Ps 2 did have an application as a coronation psalm. This is suggested by the reference to foreign kings (vv. 1–3), in response to which is the divine statement that on the holy hill of Zion, that is Jerusalem, the Lord has placed his own nominee, "my king" (v. 6), thereby conveying a certain suggestion of usage at the accession of a king in Jerusalem. Further, the reference to "decree" (*ḥōq*) has frequently been associated with the reference to the '*ēdût* ("testimony, royal protocol") in the account of Joash's accession ritual in 2 Kgs 11:12.

The second Royal Psalm is Ps 18, an extended song of thanksgiving after a victorious battle. It is the king who is the speaker in this psalm; in tones of exaltation, he rejoices that in faithfulness to God he has been enabled to defeat his enemies. Thus he gives praise to God. Second Samuel 22 is in general terms a parallel text to this psalm, giving a presentation of extended thanksgiving to the Lord by King David at the close of his life. The psalm affirms that God in his heavenly abode heard the cry of his servant (vv. 6, 25), who intervened and by unleashing divine power took the king out of danger (vv. 4, 5, 9–19). Thus this psalm affirms not only that the Lord is the rock and God of the king's salvation (vv. 46–48, 50), but also the one whom the king extols "among the nations, and sing(s) praises to your name" (v. 49)

Both Pss 20 and 21 are royal psalms, the first appearing to be a prayer for the king either when troubles have come, or else as prayerful preparation for their coming, while the second is perhaps about thanksgiving that a time of crisis is past, that deliverance has been experienced. Once more the king has experienced the delivering will and power of God. To say that there is an intended relationship between these two psalms would perhaps be going further than the evidence suggests, yet the predominant theme of Ps 20 is the king asking the Lord for strength so that he is enabled to have success in battle, while Ps 21 looks remarkably like a thanksgiving for just such a deliverance. Thus while Ps 20:4 asks for the king ("his anointed", v. 6) "May he grant you your heart's desire," Ps 21:2 sets forth concerning the king (v. 1) "You have given him his heart's desire." That is, we see in the first of these psalms (Ps 20), vv. 1–5 making a prayer of intercession, while vv. 6–9 are about confidence in God's help; in Ps 21, vv. 1–7 are about the blessings that the nation's king is able to gain for his people, while vv. 8–12 are about the great power and might that God has, and thus praise is given to him, "Be exalted, O Lord, in your strength! We will sing and praise your power." (v. 13)

Then Ps 45: "Psalm 45 is a song for the marriage of the king," says Kraus.[7] Its original composition could possibly have been for the marriage of King Ahab to Jezebel, the Phoenician princess, this being suggested by the reference to Tyre in v. 12. Others argue that the psalm could equally have come from a variety of different occasions, but most likely within the period of the Hebrew monarchy. Naturally, such a marriage would take place at the national sanctuary, and here thanksgivings are offered and prayers made that the king may "ride on victoriously for the cause of truth and to defend the right" (v. 4).

Psalm 72 is another of the royal psalms, one that might have been used at the worship in the accession ritual for the Judean king, for here there is essentially a prayer for the king.[8] The prayer is that the Lord may give to the king a sense of the divine justice in the execution of his responsibilities among his people (vv. 1–4); that the divine life may be passed to the people and the land through him (vv. 5–8); that the nation's enemies may yield to him (vv. 9–11); (once again) that the king may be compassionate to his people, and especially to the poor and needy (vv. 12–14); and finally that the king may have long life and be enabled to lead his people to enjoy prosperity (vv. 15–17). Can one imagine there being a more appropriate prayer than this in the ritual of worship at a new king's accession?

It does have to be said that this is an idealized picture of the Israelite kingship, one that judging by the documents we have seems to have been rarely attained, and that there are considerably different assessments of the historical kingship between what we read on the one hand in the Deuteronomistic History, in the Chronicler, and also in the books of the prophets, and on the other hand what we have in this psalm. Nevertheless what is set forth here in Ps 72 is undoubtedly a fine vision—indeed an ideal—of a national leader, which continues to have a deeply significant relevance. Further, this idealized picture is set out in the psalm in the form of prayerful desire that these ideals may be better known in the contemporary life of Israel. The association of the psalm with the world of worship and cult is re-emphasized by the presence of the doxology in vv. 18–19, which has the added effect of orientating this particular part of the book of psalms to the realm of worship and adoration of the Lord God.

A further Royal Psalm is Ps 89, one that encompasses something of a gamut of themes and emotions, but all appear to be connected in the treatment here of the subject of Israelite kingship. Thus vv. 1–18 make up a hymn

---

7. Kraus, *Psalms 1–59*, pp. 453.

8. On Ps 72, see Johnson, *Sacral Kingship in Ancient Israel*, 7–13; and Hossfeld and Zenger, *Psalms 2*, pp. 201–20.

of praise to God, the divine covenant with (the house of) David being spoken of in vv. 3-4. Then vv. 19-37 make up an oracle about David, remarkable in the affinity of its contents with those of Nathan's oracle to David in 2 Sam 7:4-17. The third part of the psalm is vv. 38-51, an extended lament about the fact that the Lord seems to have rejected David and the line of kings that descended from him. Thus the totality of the psalm expresses praise for the workings of the purposes of God through David and his descendants, and at the same time prays for the latter member of this dynastic line who is experiencing in his time of kingship such difficulties, and who cries out to God, "Lord, where is your steadfast love of old, which by your faithfulness you swore to David?" (v. 49). Thus in this Royal Psalm there is both thanksgiving for the Davidic kingship, and also intercessory prayer for the current ruling member of the dynasty.

So we come to Ps 101, another of the royal psalms, one that reads like a series of vows made by the ruling Davidic monarch, and whose setting could have been that of his accession, but other possibilities have been suggested.[9] The king offers himself in loyalty to the Lord with commitment to study the way that is blameless (vv. 1-2), and that he will separate himself from those whose way of life is base, perverse, evil, slanderous, or arrogant (vv. 3-5). Rather, this new king will "look with favor on the faithful in the land" (v. 6), and rid himself and his nation of those who are wicked (vv. 7-8). The psalm is about loving kindness or loyalty (*ḥesed*) and justice (*mišpāṭ*) (v. 1), and though it could be argued that this could have had wide possibilities of application, at the same time it is not improbable that in the days of the Jerusalem kingship it had a particular place in the ritual when another king was enthroned and thus entered upon his high responsibilities.[10]

Then there is Ps 110, which may or may not have been used on the occasion of the accession of a Judean king. We should heed the warning of Kraus, "No other psalm has in research evoked so many hypotheses and discussions as Psalm 110."[11] Leslie C. Allen in his commentary on this part of the Psalter helpfully sets out some of the principal suggestions as to dating and original setting of this psalm, and about these he observes, "The most popular setting of the psalm is a royal coronation at the temple in Jerusalem."[12] This, then, being a likely early usage of Ps 110, we may observe that expressed within it is the close relationship between the earthly king and his heavenly Lord, "Sit at my right hand until I make your enemies

---

9. See, e.g., Hossfeld and Zenger, *Psalms 3*, pp. 12-13.
10. See the comments of Kraus, *Psalms 60-150*, p. 280.
11. Kraus, *Psalms 60-150*, p. 345.
12. Allen, *Psalms 101-150*, p. 83.

your footstool," (v. 1), and further the promise that the king will be given daily strength for his task (v. 3). In a second divine speech (vv. 4-7) there is again the emphasis on the defeat of the earthly enemies, and the promise of the strength of the Lord for the task, this being followed by the divine pronouncement that the king is a "priest forever according to the order of Melchizedek," a matter that is considered elsewhere in this work.[13]

Psalm 132 as well as being a Royal Psalm is also one of another group of the biblical psalms, the Songs of Ascents (Pss 120-134).[14] The "Ascents" may perhaps refer to the going-up of pilgrims to the temple on Mount Zion, and the psalm reads as if this particular ascent is for liturgical reasons, maybe in connection with the kingship, though just what that might be is difficult to know. What, however, is clearer is that there is being celebrated not only the Davidic dynasty (see esp. vv. 11-12), what David had done in particular in securing an appropriate resting place for the ark of the covenant, but also that this kingship should be prayed for, that its rule may go on in the city of Jerusalem (esp. vv. 10, 17-18). Thus may the Lord be acknowledged as the God of Zion (vv. 1-5, 13-16).

Psalm 144:1-11 makes up the last of Gunkel's list of royal psalms. Verses 12-15 of this psalm are rather different, being expressed in the first person plural, and perhaps intended to take up the thought of the Royal Psalm in vv. 1-11, adapting it for later and more communal usage. At any rate Ps 144:1-11 reads as though the speaker is the king who here is praying for God's blessing upon him and further, divine help for himself, the reigning king, in his present difficulties. For the king has in the past experienced the help of God (vv. 1-2), and in spite of the comparative insignificance of human beings (vv. 3-4), even so God's help is prayed for again (vv. 5-8). Thus may this one who is at present praying to God come to the moment when he can once again sing God's praises (vv. 9-11).

What can be said in summary of the above treatment of the so-called royal psalms in the particular setting of this study of worship in the Hebrew Bible? The point has already been made that in the royal psalms we are being given words expressing ideals of the kingship in Ancient Israel; of these particular kings we are not being given "warts and all" pictures and portraits. Those "warts and all" are there in full measure in other parts of the Old Testament. Further, what we have in the royal psalms is material that has its setting in the nation's worship of its God; such is clearly indicated by the setting in material of worship, the psalms. Further, this is material that has a relationship with the Jerusalem cult; here in clear lines are set forth the

---

13. See above, 87-88, and below, 97-98.
14. On the "Psalms of Ascents," see below, 123, 154, 156.

themes of worship and praise of the Lord who has given to his people their kings, along with prayers for the king, and also for the people of the day. Here is a vision expressed in terms of worship setting forth the dedicated life of the Israelite king, in particular that it may be a life that begins in faithfulness and that continues in care that there may be justice and peace for all.

Was the King a Priest?

This question is presented to us because in the Hebrew Bible's historical books we read in a significant number of places of the involvement of the king as the leader of acts of worship, and of his participation in other aspects of the cultic life of the nation. Thus it was King David who set up the first altar in Jerusalem (2 Sam 24:25), and the same David who expressed the wish to built a place to house the ark of God (2 Sam 7:2-3), and who further, according to the Chronicler, did much of the preliminary planning for the building of the temple, the house of the Lord (1 Chr 22-29). This was the temple that in the fullness of time Solomon would build and over its dedication would preside (1 Kgs 5-8). Later, following the death of Solomon, when the northern tribes separated themselves from Judah and Jerusalem, their king, Jeroboam, founded sanctuaries in Dan and Bethel (1 Kgs 12:26-33). No doubt these northern sanctuaries were intended to fulfil in their kingdom similar state functions to those carried out in the Jerusalem temple in the southern kingdom. Moreover, when there were priests to be appointed those appointments could be made by the king (2 Sam 8:17; 20:25; 1 Kgs 2:26-27; 4:2). Perhaps even further to the point is the consideration that we have no shortage of references to kings offering sacrifices (1 Sam 13:9-10; 2 Sam 6:13, 17-18; 24:25; 1 Kgs 3:4, 5; 8:5, 62-64; 9:25; 12:33; 13:1-2; 2 Kgs 16:12-15). Yet at the same time there is no mention of the king actually being a priest, nor is there anything about a ceremony in which a king is appointed, consecrated as, a priest. Rather the evidence we have before us would seem to suggest, and this I think is a commonly held view,[15] that the king was not in any formal sense a priest, but that as king he was able to, was perhaps entitled to, fulfil priestly functions. Thus on certain occasions the king did act as a priest, and perhaps this was particularly so on the great national and religious occasions.

This brings us, once again, to the somewhat mysterious figure of Melchizedek, who, as has been seen, in the account in Gen 14:18-20 did seem to act as if he were a king, but who also engaged in what appear to be

---

15. See, e.g., Rooke, *Zadok's Heirs*, 80-103, esp. pp. 101-3; Rooke, "Kingship as Priesthood"; and Wyatt, "Royal Ritual in Ancient Judah," 65-70.

priestly tasks. We concluded earlier that it was *as a king* that he so acted, that it was the one who was king who was entitled to fulfill at least some of the priestly functions.[16] And that would seem to be the way to deal with the Hebrew Bible's other reference to Melchizedek, that in Ps 110:4,[17] to understand that in its context of inclusion in one of the so-called royal psalms as referring in the first place to Melchizedek as *king*, but as a king who was also able to act in at least certain ways as a priest.

Thus, in answer to the question "Was the king a priest?" we may answer in the negative, yet with the qualification that kings did at times assume the priestly role. This appears to be a role that the king was entitled to fulfil—and perhaps even expected to do so.

The King as Religious Leader

According to the Old Testament's historical books what we might call the religious lives of both nations, Israel and Judah, was to a large degree dependent upon the reigning kings. That is, both the deuteronomistic books of Kings, and also the Chronicler in his account of his people's history, judge each king in turn in terms of that leadership which enabled his people to live and worship in the ways of the Lord God of Israel, and in the associated proscribing of what were perceived to be unacceptable religious practices, in the main learned from their Canaanite neighbors. We have already given attention to what the Deuteronomistic Historian and the Chronicler both regarded as corrupt, evil, and faithless practices in worship, but the point now needs to be made that the historians fairly and squarely put the responsibility for this evil upon the kings. So very often when we are informed about the accession of a new king, whether that be in Jerusalem or whether in Samaria, it is followed by a summarizing statement about what particular worship was encouraged and allowed in the land. The fact is that the reigning kings were, not unreasonably, judged by what they had done, and in particular what they had achieved, in their time of kingship, and that prominent in these accounts is what they had done about *worship*. Thus, for example, King Omri in his reign over the northern kingdom of Israel established the capital city of Samaria, but at the same time was censured that "he walked in all the ways of Jeroboam son of Nebat, and in the sins that he caused Israel to commit, provoking the Lord, the God of Israel, to anger by their idols." (1 Kgs 16:26)

---

16. See above, 87–88.
17. See above, 87–88, and below, 154–55.

Omri's son Ahab, who we are told reigned for no less than twenty-two years, was for the Deuteronomistic Historian an even worse king than his father, for not only did he marry Jezebel, the daughter of King Ethbaal of the Sidonians, a woman who the Deuteronomistic Historian presents as something of a zealot for her own native religious ways, but who also erected an altar for Baal in Samaria. Further, Ahab also made a sacred pole (Asherah), and "did more to provoke the anger of the Lord, the God of Israel, than had all the kings of Israel who were before him." (1 Kgs 16:29–34)

The situation is hardly different in what is said about the kings in the southern kingdom of Judah. Thus, for example, we read in 2 Kgs 15 of the long reign of fifty-two years of King Azariah the son of Amaziah that "He did what was right in the sight of the Lord, just as his father Amaziah had done. Nevertheless the high places were not taken away; the people still sacrificed and made offerings on the high places" (vv. 3–4). The Deuteronomistic Historian clearly put the responsibility for the continuance of what appear to be religious rites of the Canaanites within or alongside the Yahwistic worship in Jerusalem upon this king. That this happened was due, according to the historian, to king Azariah.

However, when we read about king Azariah in the Chronicler's history (2 Chr 26:1–23) here named Uzziah, there are significant differences from what we read in Kings. The Chronicler gives greater emphasis to and details about what he lists as Uzziah/Azariah doing for the good of Judah, in particular to strengthening the defences of the country and the possibilities of developing trading links (vv. 6–15). But later "when he had become strong he grew proud, to his destruction" (v. 16), and the particular sin that the Chronicler speaks about is Uzziah's making an offering on the altar of incense in the temple. This was the particular sin also of Jeroboam, which he committed in Bethel (1 Kgs 12:33—13:2); it would seem that doing this constituted a stepping beyond what was regarded as the responsibility of the king in the arena of worship.

Then there was Ahaz who according to the Deuteronomistic Historian, "even made his son pass through fire, according to the abominable practices of the nations whom the Lord drove out before the people of Israel. He sacrificed and made offerings on the high places, on the hills, and under every green tree" (2 Kgs 16:3b–4). In 2 Kgs 16:10–18 we are told of further changes in the Jerusalem temple effected by Ahaz "because of the king of Assyria" (v. 18), such as the making of a new altar like the one that Ahaz had seen in Damascus when he met the king of Assyria there, and establishing and using it in worship in the Jerusalem temple (vv. 10–16). We also read that Ahaz removed the laver from the frames and the sea from the bronze oxen (vv. 17-18), but we cannot be sure as to the significance of these further items.

Another Judean king we may usefully consider in this regard is Manasseh, about whom we read in 2 Kgs 21:1-18 and 2 Chr 33:1-20. For the Deuteronomistic Historian there was hardly a worse king than Manasseh, for here he is regarded as responsible for rebuilding high places in Judah, erecting altars for Baal, making a sacred pole (Asherah), worshipping, and building altars in the temple for, the host of heaven (2 Kgs 21:3-5). He went further, engaging in child sacrifice; practising soothsaying and augury; dealing with mediums and wizards (v. 6). For this historian it is clearly king Manasseh who was responsible for this deleterious situation of temple worship in Jerusalem. The Chronicler in his account of Manasseh does not disagree, setting out details in 2 Chr 33:2-9, but adding material about the king's repentance which led to his subsequent acts of taking away the foreign gods, idols, altars from the temple, and in their place restoring the Yahwisticly acceptable artefacts (2 Chr 33:10-16). But we should take note of what the Chronicler says in 2 Chr 33:17, for it speaks of a matter to which we shall return:[18] "The people, however, still sacrificed at the high places, but only to the Lord their God" (2 Chr 33:17).

Yet in marked contrast to such Judean kings as Azariah/Uzziah and Manasseh, the two religiously most faithful kings according to both our historians were Hezekiah (2 Kgs 18:1—20:21; 2 Chr 29:1—32:33) and Josiah (2 Kgs 22:1—23:30; 2 Chr 34:1—35:27), both of whom purged Judah and Jerusalem of what these historians regarded as unacceptable foreign cults, who sought to re-establish acceptable Yahwistic worship, and who moreover sought to centralize worship in the temple in Jerusalem, presumably thus to ensure its rectitude and purity. Once again, we can see the crucial role accorded by those who were responsible for passing on the traditions of the people of Israel in the days of the kingships to the whole matter of the worship that took place in Israel and Judah, and that it was owing to the will and decisions of the reigning monarchs what of Yahwistic worship, and what of non-Yahwistic practices would be allowed, even tolerated, in particular in the central sanctuaries in Israel and Judah, especially in the national shrines.[19]

In the Deuteronomistic History there is a good deal of material about the kings of Israel and Judah and the issue of worship: to a considerable

---

18. See above 53-55, and below 101-102.

19. On the reforms of kings Hezekiah and Josiah, see Haran, *Temples and Temple-Service in Ancient Israel*, 132-48; Lowery, *The Reforming Kings*; McKay, *Religion in Judah under the Assyrians*, 13-19, 28-44; Finkelstein and Silberman, "Temple and Dynasty"; and Edelman, "Hezekiah's Alleged Cultic Centralization."

extent the kings are judged in terms of what they did, or did not do, about the worship that took place in their realms. It does perhaps therefore seem strange that there is no mention in Deuteronomy's law of the kingship (Deut 17:14–20) concerning the matter of worship, in particular there being nothing in this passage stipulating the purity of Yahwistic worship that is to be offered. For while this subject of worship may not be mentioned in Deut 17:14–20 there is yet a good deal on the subject of worship in the book of Deuteronomy, with its stipulations that worship shall be centered on the central sanctuary (Deut 12:5–14). Further, the teaching of Deuteronomy about sacrificial worship emphasizes the inner and spiritual aspects (Deut 14:22–27), and that the festivals are to be kept (Deut 16:1–7). Moreover, the worship of deities other than Yahweh is to be strictly avoided; such practices are offensive to the Lord God (Deut 13:1–8; 17:2–7), and they and their associated artefacts of worship are to be eliminated (7:1–5, 25–26; 12:2–4, 29–31; 16:21—17:1; 18:9–14).

Nevertheless, we continue to read of the ongoing life and influence of the high places. This prevailed in the kingship of Rehoboam (1 Kgs 14:23–24; 2 Chr 11:15). Also Asa, we are told, put away male prostitutes and idols, but *left* the high places (1 Kgs 15:12–16; cf 2 Chr 14:3–5; 15:8–17); Jehoshaphat, according to the Deuteronomistic Historian, exterminated the male prostitutes but left the high places (1 Kgs 22:41–50); according to the Chronicler, he *did* remove the high places (2 Chr 17:6). Indeed the situation is rather as Lowery expressed it, that between the Judean kings Rehoboam and Ahaz those who were adjudged in the books of Kings to be good kings even so failed to abolish the high places.[20] How could it be deemed acceptable to retain the high places, when elsewhere their presence is so roundly condemned? Might the answer lie in the fact that there was something impractical for certain people in that the journey to Jerusalem was not possible for them to make, as is acknowledged in those regulations concerning the tithe set out in Deut 14:24–26? Perhaps the plain and practical consideration was that for at least some people it was, let us say, helpful, even perhaps necessary, that there was the provision of a series of more local places for worship in addition to the temple, and other shrines, where they could worship. That is, maybe at a "high place" certain peoples, even groups, on a regular basis offered their Yahwistic sacrifices and offerings. Is this the situation that is perhaps envisaged by the Chronicler in his account of the centralization of the cult in Jerusalem in the days of Hezekiah, when he adds, "The people, however, still sacrificed at the high places, but only to the Lord their God" (2 Chr 33:17)? A stage beyond this might have been that

---

20. See Lowery, *The Reforming Kings*, 62–65.

in actual practice there were those who did make their prayers, sacrifices, and offerings to the Canaanite deities—*as well as* making their Yahwistic devotions in the central sanctuary, a practice that not improbably lies behind the polemic of the book of Hosea and elsewhere in the Hebrew Bible.

By Way of Summary

A central part of the material considered in this chapter on the Israelite king and worship has been the so-called royal psalms, a group of psalms in the Hebrew Bible that are particularly concerned with the Israelite king. Among other things this group of psalms presents us with the Old Testament's most extravagant assessment of the institution of monarchy, one in which the king holds a place in what are portrayed as being the purposes of God whereby the king is in a special relationship with the Lord. This is a place of high responsibility in which the king is called upon to defend his people from their enemies, and also to ensure that conditions of justice abound among the people of the nation.

By way of contrast those who passed on to us their theological-historical writings in the books of Deuteronomy, Kings and Chronicles present us with what we feel are rather less exalted pictures of the kings, less idealistic, no doubt rather more realistic and down-to-earth. Very likely these latter documents are truer to historical reality, but even so they make it clear that what sort of worship was presented in the days of the individual kingships was very much owing to the individual devotions of particular kings in their kingly responsibilities and to the execution of their high offices. These kings were indeed those who had great responsibilities, and it was clearly within their power to do a good deal to ensure that worthy worship of the Lord took place in their realms. A few of the Judean kings, perhaps in fact just two of them, Hezekiah and Josiah, came up to and satisfied the historians' standards in this regard, whereas for both the Deuteronomistic Historian and the Chronicler the rest of the kings in both Israel and Judah fell woefully short of the expected standards in regard to the Yahwistic purity of the cult. Is it perhaps partly for such reasons that in the material we have in the Hebrew Bible there is no talk after the time of the exile about the nation once again having a king?

PART III

The Liturgy of Worship

> O come, let us worship and bow down,
> let us kneel before the Lord, our Maker!
> For he is our God,
> and we are the people of his pasture,
> and the sheep of his hand.
>
> PSALM 95:6–7a

In considering v. 6 of Ps 95 there is profit in attending to the verbs, and in v. 7a to the personal prepositions. Thus: In v. 6 the verbs speak of the call, or perhaps the invitation, to *come* and to *worship* the Lord. The psalmist then uses the word *kneel*, very possibly intending to mean the same as was earlier indicated through the (in the Hebrew) one word *let us worship*. Yet already by the end of v. 6 we are invited to attend to the significant use of the prepositions; we wish to, are called to, worship the Lord God for the reason that he is *our* God, and we are the people of *his* pasture, and the sheep of *his* hand.

This is to say that the worship of God is intended to be taking place within the setting, the framework, the firm assurance of a real relationship between the worshipper and the Lord. Further what is envisioned here is worship of the God who has, so to speak, gone on *before* his people so that he may provide for them and protect them: the statements that the worshippers are the people of the Lord's pasture, the sheep of his hand, are expressions of the belief that the Lord is the one who both *provides for* and also *protects* his people. Truly, as another of the psalmists expressed the matter,

> I will give to the Lord the thanks due to his righteousness,
> and sing praise to the name of the Lord, the Most High. (Ps 7:17)

Our concern in this third part of our study is with the liturgy of the worship about which we read in the Hebrew Bible, in particular its content. Thus we consider what the Old Testament has to tell us about prayers, psalms, sacrifices, feasts, festivals, calendars, and discuss evidences of possible liturgical pieces—prayers, thanksgivings, confessions of faith.

7

Prayers

The prevalence of prayer is widespread among the religions of the world, the Yahwistic faith being no exception. Friedrich Heiler began his study of prayer with the words, "Religious people, students of religion, theologians of all creeds and tendencies, agree in thinking that prayer is the central phenomenon of religion, the very hearthstone of all piety."[1] More recently, in a study of the Ugaritic ritual text *KTU* 1.119 Patrick D. Miller concluded: "So it is that this unique text from Ugarit reminds us again of the continuities in the religious practices of people and groups within Syria-Palestine, continuities that neither obscure the complexity and particularity of any single unity nor are confined to the rituals of Ugarit and Israel."[2]

There is a notable number of prayers and references to prayer in the Hebrew Bible: according to Moshe Greenberg forty-three passages in which ad hoc prayer is mentioned, and no less than ninety-seven in which the wording of ad hoc prayers appears.[3] Further there are prayers that are made to God by individual believers who are either at worship or else going about their lives in the world, and there are also those more formal prayers that are offered by a leader, a priest or a Levite, maybe a prophet, even a king, maybe or maybe not in the official cultic life of the nation. What, however, all have in common is motivation on the part of an individual or group to offer prayers in confidence that they can indeed make such prayers to the Lord, whatever be the content of the prayer.[4]

---

1. Heiler, *Prayer*, xiii.

2. Miller, "Prayer and Sacrifice," 100. See also ibid., *They Cried to the Lord*, 5–31; and Singer, *Hittite Prayers*.

3. Greenberg, *Biblical Prose Prayer*, 59–60.

4. In this regard, Miller says, "Prayer was the point at which the human creature dared to approach the transcendent, holy deity with no restrictions on what could be expressed; thus the human was free not only to cry out in rage, anger, despair, and hate, as in the lament part of the prayer, but also to beseech, urge, and persuade" ("Prayer as Persuasion," 343).

The Vocabulary of Prayer

There is a varied vocabulary used in the Hebrew Bible concerning prayer, various Hebrew words being used to express different aspects of, various intensities or nuances of, the many prayers we are told were prayed. Briefly expressed these may be set out in the following way.[5]

1. Many of the formal prayers in the Hebrew Bible, like Pss 17, 86, 90, 102, 142, or Jonah's prayer in Jon 2:2–9 are called in the Hebrew *tĕpillâ*, "prayer." The verbal form is *hitpallēl*, "pray." Further these forms can be used to describe various kinds and types of prayers, such as confession, thanksgiving, praying for oneself, praying for others.[6]

2. Then there is the Hebrew word *rinnâ*, again indicating "prayer", but this more in the sense of "shout," "cry out," "call out." It occurs with some regularity in the Psalms to indicate what is being said to the Lord with a degree of passion, concern, either of joy or of lamentation.[7]

3. Then the verb *p-g-ʿ* in the *hipʿil* form can indicate "urge strongly," that is "pray, plead for, intercede for," but it has to be said that this does not occur commonly in the Hebrew Bible (however, see Gen 23:8; Jer 7:16; 27:18; Job 21:15; Ruth 1:16).[8]

4. There is further the verb *ḥ-l-h* which is used in the Old Testament in the sense of "pleading, entreating," even perhaps we should express it "quiet pleading," as in the intercession of Moses in Exod 32:11.

5. Another word for praying is *ʿ-t-r*, and it means "pray, plead, intercede." It is a word that occurs in relationship with cultic ritual—but not, however, in the Psalms. It is there, for example, in Exod 8:8 (Heb 8:4) and in the following verses when the Pharaoh calls upon Moses and Aaron to pray to God for the cessation of the plague of frogs.[9]

6. Finally, there is a series of words that come from the Hebrew verb *ḥ-n-n*, for example *hitḥannēn* meaning "entreat," but this is employed in cases of definitely polite address to God. It tends to be used for prayers of petition and intercession, and it has two noun forms, namely *tĕḥinnâ*

---

5. For more about these Hebrew words for prayer, see Sawyer, "Types of Prayer in the Old Testament." See also the older work of Ap-Thomas, "Some Notes on the Old Testament Attitude to Prayer"; and ibid., "Notes on Some Terms Relating to Prayer."

6. On the Hebrew *pll*, see *TDOT*, 11:567–78.

7. For further details, see the entry *rānan* in *TDOT*, 13:515–22.

8. For details of *pgʿ*, see *TDOT*, 11:470–6.

9. For details about the Hebrew verb *ʿ-t-r*, see *TDOT*, 11:458–60.

(prayer), or in more liturgical situations with the same (gentle and polite) meaning and nuance "prayer," *taḥănûnîm*.[10]

7. It should also be added that at times the normal Hebrew verb for "say" is used to indicate prayer, as in "and he [the one praying] *said* [that is, to God/the Lord] . . ." Further, there are other situations that clearly speak about praying, but where there is no use of any particular word for "prayer." This can be observed in, for example, Ruth 1:9; 2:12; 3:10; 4:11-12 and elsewhere. Perhaps we may say that in such references what we might call a "prayerful wish" is being expressed. Moreover in this regard we should take note of the Hebrew particle *nāʾ*, which is perhaps to be translated "please" or even "I/we ask." It only occurs in reported speech, and is usually expressed by an inferior person when addressing a superior, and thus does appear in words in which a human addresses the Lord. It may have been added to express the sense either of politeness or entreaty, and at times in translation it is simply not translated.[11]

Prayers of Petition

We can now consider the types of situations and attendant circumstances in which we read of individuals and peoples praying to the Lord. For the first few of these examples which of the various Hebrew words for "prayer" and "pray" will be indicated, but this will not then be continued.

First there are those prayers that individual people make to the Lord, and frequently these come from the setting of their daily lives—and not all of these come from some great or momentous phase of life. An example of such a prayer is that prayed by King Hezekiah, not about some great or troublesome matter of state, but because of a personal matter, his boil. Yet this situation was not without seriousness, for the king had been warned of the gravity of his state of health by the prophet Isaiah who advised him to take steps to set his house in order. Thus we are told, "Then Hezekiah turned his face to the wall and prayed[12] to the Lord: 'Remember now, O Lord, I implore you,[13] how I have walked before you in faithfulness with a whole heart, and have done what is good in your sight'" (Isa 38:2-3). Out

---

10. For these words, see *TDOT*, 5:22-36; Ap-Thomas, "Some Aspects of the Root HNN."

11. For *nāʾ* is, expressed grammatically, an enclitic particle of urgency, politeness, or entreaty.

12. The word for prayer here is number 1. above, *hitpallēl*.

13. The word here is number 7. above, *nāʾ*.

of this situation there was indeed a satisfactory conclusion, for the king did experience healing.

Another example of an individual person praying to the Lord as he went about his life in the world is that of Abraham's servant who was sent on an important and delicate mission, that of finding a suitable wife for Abraham's son Isaac upon whom such large hopes rested for the continuation of those divine purposes entrusted to Abraham and his descendants. Thus as the servant went about his task, from time to time, and in particular at crucial moments in the venture, he prayed to God for the good outcome of his endeavours (Gen 24:1-67).[14] We may call these prayers of petition, both those of Hezekiah and those of Abraham's servant, that is, prayers in which the pray-ers pray for themselves. The traditions about Nehemiah are particularly rich in such prayers of petition (see for example Neh 5:19; 6:14; 13:14, 22b, 29, 31b).[15]

Prayers of Intercession

Then as well as such prayers of petition there is a series of intercessory prayers made by various people, some being offered by an individual on behalf of a larger and wider group who for some reason or another find themselves in a parlous situation. I shall return to these prayers below, in particular to the matter of whether or not the pray-er achieves for their people what it is that they are asking. Certainly in this group of prayers are the intercessions of Moses which he made to the Lord on behalf of his people who had sinned so grievously in their manufacture of, and then praying to a golden calf in the desert (Exod 32:11-14, 31-32).[16]

Further, in Amos 7:1-3, 4-6 we read of the prophet praying for his people when they are under threat of what appears to be immediate divine judgment. The prophet appeals to the mercy of God on the grounds of these people being so "small" (Amos 7:2, 5), and we are told that after each prayer the Lord relented, resolving not to effect the punishment. The matter of a prophet interceding for a people under divine judgment for their sinfulness is also spoken about in the Hebrew Bible in the book of Jeremiah. However, in this case it is in a negative sense, for Jeremiah is portrayed as having been commanded by God *not* to pray for this people (Jer 7:16; 11:14; 14:11, 13,

---

14. Gen 24:12, 27 and 42 each have "and he said"; v. 45 "speaking in my heart."

15. In each of these verses God is asked to "remember for their good" either Nehemiah, the pray-er, or those for whom he is praying.

16. In Exod 32:11, the verb for praying is number 4. above, ḥ-l-h to express quiet pleading, the imploring of the Lord.

and see also 15:1). This command to Jeremiah *not* to pray for his people carries within it a certain suggestion that Jeremiah might normally have been expected *to* pray, to intercede for his people. It would seem that the likely significance of the command to Jeremiah *not* to pray for these people is because their sin is so great that it cannot be forgiven and that therefore any prayers for them would be in the nature of a "waste of breath" on the part of the prophet.

At one time there was considerable speculation and discussion as to whether or not the Hebrew prophets had a particular ministry of intercession, but it does have to be said that the evidence within the prophetical books of the Old Testament is hardly sufficient for us to be dogmatic either way about the matter. Perhaps we may say that while the probability is that the canonical prophets were not expected as a part of their prophetic calling to pray for their people, yet at the same time some of them as well as announcing to their people the coming judgment of God upon them for their sins, did also make intercession for them, and on behalf of them did plead for the mercy and compassion of the Lord.[17]

The Old Testament's prayers of petition and intercession are portrayed as sometimes being accompanied by human endeavours of one kind or another in an attempt to retrieve, rectify—or even merely to accept—a troublesome situation. For example, the prophet Isaiah, according to the account in Kings, is portrayed as ministering to king Hezekiah when the latter was troubled by his boil. The prophet advised the king to pray to the Lord and at the same time as well as suggesting that the king should face up to the possibility of the worst case scenario—namely death—also prescribed the application of a poultice to the boil (2 Kgs 20:1-7). This is an example of prayer being accompanied by human activity; what we might call prayer and work. However, in the parallel account of this incident in the book of Isaiah (Isa 38:1-6) there is no mention of the application of the poultice to the boil; that is to say, while in the Kings account as well as prayer there is some human action, healing in the Isaiah book account is portrayed as having been achieved by prayer alone, without human activity.

Another example in the Hebrew Bible of prayer being accompanied by some human activity intended to redeem a troublesome situation is in the account of Nehemiah's rebuilding of the Jerusalem walls following his gaining permission to return there from his exile in Susa. In the face of the hostile plottings of "Sanballat and Tobiah and the Arabs and the Ammonites and the Ashdodites," Nehemiah and his associates responded, "So

---

17. On the subject of this possible intercessory ministry of the Hebrew prophets, see below, 240-75, esp. p. 274.

we prayed to our God, and set a guard as a protection against them day and night" (Neh 4:7, 9). In the book of Ruth there is a series of prayers of intercession (Ruth 1:8-9; 2:12; 3:10; 4:11-12) and as I have shown elsewhere each of these is accompanied by some human action (Ruth 1:6-18; 2:1-17; 3:6-15; 4:1-12).[18]

Moses' impassioned pleas for his people in the wake of their grave sin in making the golden calf in the desert contain words whose full import is not clear to us, but which yet call for consideration. According to Exod 32:11-14, after Moses had first prayed to the Lord, he then we are told in vv. 31-32 said to the Lord "Alas, this people has sinned a great sin; they have made for themselves gods of gold. But now, if you will only forgive their sin—but if not, blot me out of the book that you have written." Now the question is, what is intended by the words "blot me out of the book that you have written"? Does it mean that if God is going to leave these people unforgiven then Moses does not any longer wish to have a part in the service of God, and in particular in this mission of rescuing them from Egypt and leading them through the desert? Or is it rather intended to mean that Moses is offering to give his life that the sinners may receive forgiveness and thus their lives? We cannot be sure which of these is intended, or indeed some other possibility, for the text is far from being clear and straightforward.[19]

There are other prayers in the Hebrew Bible, where impassioned prayers to God, intended to avert divine judgment are made, but in which it is prayer alone, with no accompanying action. Thus in Gen 18:23-33 we read of the intercession of Abraham for the people of Sodom. This indeed is prayer alone, indeed something of a bargaining with the Lord over a series of hypothetical numbers of righteous people the Lord might find in this sinful city. But then, it could be added, what else was there in that situation that Abraham could have done? What is being portrayed here is one of those situations in life for which all that can be done is to pray for those who are involved, for the reason that the situation is so grave, far beyond human ability to change.[20]

Further, in 1 Sam 7:5-9 is a prayer of Samuel for the people of Israel who had sinned through their failure fully to trust the Lord, due to their attempted reliance on foreign deities. Here Samuel intercedes for the people, and at the same time there is fasting and the offering of sacrifice. In 1 Sam

---

18. See Thompson, "New Life Amid the Alien Corn," esp. pp. 204-9; and ibid., *I Have Heard Your Prayer*, 89-93.

19. For further details, see Thompson, *I Have Heard Your Prayer*, 103-10.

20. On such prayers, see, e.g., ibid., 1 and n.1 therein.

12:17–23 the issue is the sin of the people who wished to have a human king rather than putting their trust completely in the Lord. Here Samuel prays for them, and there is no mention of any sacrifices accompanying the prayers.

Prayers of Thanksgiving

Also in the Old Testament are prayers of thanksgiving, as for example the one uttered by the servant of Abraham upon the successful completion of his task of finding a suitable wife for Isaac (Gen 24:26–27). Further, among the biblical Psalms are many thanksgivings, some of individual people (for example Pss 30; 32; 34; 41; 116; 138), others of a more communal nature such as Pss 66:8–12; 67; 124; 129.[21] Further, there is also Ps 107, a psalm of thanksgiving in a class all of its own, for something of a group of people make their "general thanksgiving" for the Lord's deliverance from a range of difficulties and distresses: hunger and thirst in desert conditions (vv. 4–9); being in prison (vv. 10–16); experiencing illness (vv. 17–22); sailors in a storm (vv. 23–32). In each of these situations the sufferers in their crises, "cried to the Lord in their trouble, and he delivered them from their distress" (vv. 6, 13, 19, 28), which leads to these various erstwhile-sufferers' expressions of thanksgiving, "Let them thank the Lord for his steadfast love, and for his wonderful works to humankind" (vv. 8, 15, 21, 31).

Prayers of Confession

Confession of sin to God makes another type of prayer in the Hebrew Bible. There are both the remorseful expressions of individuals, such as that of king David for his indiscretion in taking a census of his people (2 Sam 24:10); or all that is expressed in Ps 51 over a psalmist's conviction of human sinfulness; and there are also corporate expressions of sin. These expressions of corporate sin become more prevalent in written materials that appear to come from exilic and post-exilic times, no doubt as a response to the common perception that the experience of the exile came about as a result of the national sinfulness. At any rate in no small detail there is poured out to God in, for example, Ezra 9:5–15 and Neh 9:1–37 the sins that are believed to have brought leaders and people to their present circumscribed situation.[22]

---

21. However, it should be noted that some scholars understand there to be fewer communal thanksgiving psalms in the Old Testament than are listed here. For details see, Day, *Psalms*, 48–50.

22. See Boda et al., *Seeking the Favour of God*, vol. 1.

Prayers of Lament

Prayers of lament have a prominent place in the Old Testament, and call to be considered with some seriousness. In these so-called "laments" a particularly characteristic feature is the outspokenness of the one praying to the Lord. There is a real sense of the pray-er laying aside any attempt at politeness in their address to God, but rather expressing with much outspokenness to the Lord how things have been for him or her in their life. It is a matter of telling how it is for the lamenting one, in particular that life has not been proceeding well for them, and there is further a sense of an implied criticism of the Lord for allowing such a bad situation to prevail. This lament-praying is to be found in some profusion in the book of Psalms where there are both individual and corporate laments. The former are more numerous than the latter,[23] and are to be found in greater numbers in the earlier part of the book of psalms than in the later. What is particularly important about the lament style of praying is that it betokens a person hanging on to God in the face of difficulties and disappointments, in no way giving up on God as the ultimate source of strength and well-being, but rather nagging at, prevailing on, even berating the Lord for the things that that person is having to go through and, more, endure. Such prayers do surely demonstrate a real sense of faith and trust in the Lord and in his will and power to change the sufferer's situation on the part of the one who is praying. Thus the pray-er does not give up on God even though their troubles still prevail.

This style of individual lament-praying is found also in other parts of the Old Testament than the psalms. An example of such is those intense outpourings of the prophet Jeremiah about the difficulties he encountered in his attempt to be faithful as the Lord's prophet. These have been called the "Confessions" of Jeremiah and are to be found in Jer 11:18–23; 12:1–6; 15:15–21; 17:14–18; 18:19–23; 20:7–18. In these "Confessions" Jeremiah is portrayed as using extremely strong language in his address to the Lord, perhaps no more so than when he accuses the Lord of having "enticed" him, "overpowered" him (Jer 20:7), been to him, "like a deceitful brook, like waters that fail" (Jer 15:18). This style and manner of praying is also there in parts of the book of Job, among some of those speeches of the grievously-suffering Job who instead of addressing his so-called friends has turned to address God as in, for example Job 13:24, "Why do you hide your face, and count me as your enemy?" Once again we observe the pray-er determined

---

23. The following psalms would generally be regarded as individual laments: Pss 3–7; 9/10; 13; 17; 22; 25–28; 31; 35; 38–39; 40:13–17 (=70); 42/43; 51–52; 54–57; 59; 61; 64; 69–71; 77; 86; 88; 94:16–23; 102; 109; 120; 130; 139–143.

to cling on to the Lord, yet equally determined to be assured of the Lord's continued care and provision for him or her.

There are some psalms that read as if we are hearing the communal prayer of a whole nation, of a people who are pouring out their prayers to God about their present distresses, and seeking assurance that the Lord will aid them in their present trouble and strife. It would be generally agreed that the following are among these Old Testament so-called communal lament psalms: Pss 12; 44; 60; 74; 79; 80; 83; 85; 94:1–11; 126 and 137. Psalms 58 and 90 also have some of the characteristics of the communal laments, as also do the following passages in other parts of the Hebrew Bible, Isa 63:7—64:11; Jer 14:2-9, 19-22; Lam 5:1-22. The issue that appears to draw forth these laments looks like national disasters, political and/or military, it having been suggested that perhaps they were used on days designated as special times of national lamentation in the temple. The laments in Jer 14 and Joel 1–2 suggest that there could also have been days of corporate lamentation, days for prayers in times of other crises such as droughts and locusts.[24]

Some Formal Prayers

Then there is a series of prayers that are set out in more formalized ways, those that give the impression of coming from what are portrayed as formal cultic settings rather than the private devotions of an individual person. An example of this is the extended prayer that Solomon is portrayed as praying at the dedication of the Jerusalem temple. The Deuteronomistic Historian's account of this is to be found in 1 Kgs 8:14–53, while the Chronicler's account, which in parts is somewhat different, is in 2 Chr 6:3–42.[25] It would seem that this long prayer is intended to be something in the nature of a treatise on prayer rather than an account of what went on in the temple, either routinely or else on a special occasion. For example, it is at first sight strange that there is no mention in this "prayer" of sacrifices and offerings, when we would expect that Solomon would go on to pray that they too may be acceptable to the Lord and yield their promised and expected results and benefits. That is, although sacrifices are spoken about as being offered in profusion in what follows the "prayer" (1 Kgs 8:62-64; 2 Chr 7:4-5), yet they do not feature in the prayer itself. Rather, what is presented as the

---

24. On these psalms and prayers of lamentation, see Thompson, *I Have Heard Your Prayer*, 39–56; and ibid., "*Where is the God of Justice?*," 31–57.

25. On Solomon's prayer, see Thompson, *I Have Heard Your Prayer*, 179-96; and Talstra, *Solomon's Prayer*.

prayer in 1 Kgs 8:22–53 and 2 Chr 6:12–42 is in fact something in the nature of a theological disquisition on prayer. In particular here is the request to the Lord that when in a variety of situations God's people sin, when they pray to the Lord towards the temple, may they be granted the divine forgiveness. We may note, in passing, the emphasis here on forgiveness of sins being found through prayer—with no mention of this taking place through the sacrificial system.

Also worthy of note about the prayer of Solomon is that it is offered by a national leader on behalf of all the people. In this case it is the king who leads his people. Not dissimilar examples are those in Ezra 9 that record the scribe Ezra leading the people in a great corporate prayer of confession. Another is when Nehemiah does the same (Neh 9), and perhaps most memorably the account of Moses interceding for the people after the incident of the manufacture of the golden calf in the wilderness (Exod 32:11–14, 31–34).[26]

These then are some examples of corporate prayer being offered in more formal cultic situations than when individual people were making their own personal prayers to God. Further, we must surely reckon on the biblical Psalms, whatever their individual origins may have been, in the form in which they have come down to us are presented as formalized prayers which could be used by groups of people, perhaps in the worship of the temple.

In the prayer of Solomon in 1 Kgs 8 we have one of the Hebrew Bible's most formalized prayers, and what is of further interest to us lies in its being a composition that is rich in theological thought about issues to do with prayer. In this prayer the thought is expressed that the Lord far transcends any—indeed all—earthly places of worship, but yet does have a real relationship with his people on earth. Further, this great Lord is envisaged as having a presence on earth, particularly so in the Jerusalem temple—the temple is the place where he has decreed, "My name shall be there" (v. 29) even though the Lord is *not* envisaged as actually dwelling there (v. 27). Towards this holy place, God's people are able, and privileged, to pray, and here their prayers will be heard; in particular their penitential entreaties for the forgiveness of their sins will be heard and granted (vv. 30–45).[27] Indeed, here, in these is expressed the wonder that a person, whether an individual (v. 31), or a people (vv. 33, 35, 37), or a foreigner (v. 41), may pray to God

---

26. See Thompson, *I Have Heard Your Prayer*, 103–8, for further details about this prayer, and 108–10 for the Deuteronomist's account of this praying (Deut 9:25–29), and further the matter of God "changing his mind" (Exod 32:14).

27. See Tomes, "'Our Holy and Beautiful House'"; and Levenson, "From Temple to Synagogue: 1 Kings 8."

in the expectation that their prayer will be heard by the Lord who occupies the highest and most exalted place in the whole of creation (vv. 34, 36, 39, 43, 45). Further, the belief that such prayer may bring about change in the situation in which the individual or the community finds themselves (vv. 30, 32, 34, 36, 39, 43, 45).[28]

Thus while the Old Testament portrays individuals as being enabled—even perhaps invited?—to make their prayers to God, at the same time within its pages are recounted occasions when prayers are offered by an individual leader, either by a priest or else a Levite, a king (as in the case outlined above), or a prophet, or some other leader of the people. The setting portrayed in 1 Kgs 8 is of an important and significant moment in the national life of the people of Israel with the completion of the temple in Jerusalem. We can believe that there may be some historical truth behind the talk of the leadership of Solomon on that occasion.

The Old Testament and Prayer

In the Old Testament not only is there a large number of prayers, but also those prayers occur in a variety of themes, being concerned with various cares and other matters. Further, they are prayed by a wide range of peoples from individuals to leaders, royal, national, and religious. Something of this wide range and variety in prayers are represented in the biblical psalms, many of which are indeed prayers of one sort or another. Nevertheless it does have to be said that in certain parts of the Hebrew Bible there is something of a silence about prayer. Thus, for example, prayer seems strangely muted in the so-called Joseph Narrative in Gen 37–50, the only three prayers within it being of praise and blessing (Gen 43:14; 48:15–16; 48:20), and there are no prayers of petition and intercession. This could be because the author of this work was convinced that within the varied circumstances about which he was writing the Lord would bring about a satisfactory deliverance of Joseph and the fulfillment of higher purposes, without any need of the prayers of the human servants involved.[29]

Further, we do not have in the Hebrew Bible any statements about what prayer is, and how it may be understood to operate, work, be effective; when it is appropriate; even what should be its content and concern. Here in the Old Testament there is nothing to compare with the Lord's Prayer in the New, and the possible teaching about prayer that represented. Yet it seems

---

28. See further, Thompson, "What Happens When We Pray?"

29. On these accounts of happenings not accompanied by prayer, see Miller, "Prayer and Divine Action," 461–62; and Thompson, *I Have Heard Your Prayer*, 215.

that in the lives of the people spoken about in the Old Testament, prayer is a natural and widespread activity, an activity moreover widespread among so many religious people. As the people of Israel prayed to their God, so too did Israel's neighbors pray to their own gods. It would seem, moreover, that for the people of ancient Israel to pray to the Lord was a perfectly natural activity, a natural part of daily life for individuals, for groups, even for nations. Just as the Lord is portrayed in the book of Exodus (Exod 33:11) as speaking with Moses in the Tent of Meeting "as one speaks to a friend," presumably there was something in the nature of the other side of the activity of praying in which the human party was believed to be able to speak easily and naturally with the Lord, albeit with due regard for the divine nature of the one being spoken to, and the sinful nature of the one praying. Yet, as already observed, some of the prayers to God, especially those of complaint, can be expressed in seriously outspoken ways to God, which do at times suggest that the one praying feels some sense of having been abandoned by God and his care. Even so God can still be addressed personally as "my God," as in Ps 22:1 "*My* God, *my* God, why have you *forsaken* me?" There is within the covenant relationship of the Israelite people with their God a sense of freedom to speak openly and in a manner that cannot but appear to be challenging to the Lord, even somewhat confrontational.[30]

What then may have been thought to happen when a person in ancient Israel prayed? If the prayer were one of thanksgiving, then it would surely have been thought of as the glad expression of emotions at a time of deliverance or blessing. But what would have been the thinking about prayers of petition and intercession, either of such prayers as these having been addressed perhaps calmly, or maybe with crying out to God, even with anger? Could such prayers change the situation for the pray-er, or the situation for the one or many for whom the prayer was being prayed? Perhaps in some situations there came about a change in the emotional life of the pray-er once the deeply troublesome matter had been entrusted to the Lord. Thus, perhaps, in such settings the one who had prayed did feel a sense of greater confidence about their troublesome circumstances as a result of their having made their prayer(s) to God.

Yet there are other situations in which as a result of prayer having been made the Lord is said to have changed his mind about certain actions he had earlier announced. Thus Ps 106:23 in speaking about the result of the intercessory ministry of Moses—who is portrayed in his praying as standing in the breach between his people and their God—can speak of the Lord having been induced "to turn away his wrath from destroying them." There

---

30. See the study of Boyce, *The Cry to God in the Old Testament*.

is in the Hebrew Bible this thought about a "change of mind," or as we might express it a "change of heart," on the part of God as a result of his having been implored in prayer. This, we have to say, confronts us with the great mystery of the Lord who is portrayed as, and believed to be, unchangeable, who yet can be portrayed as at times changing his mind (thus Exod 32:14), while at other times appears *not* to change his mind. However, at other times God can be entreated yet when eventually the Lord does speak to the sufferer it may not be in the desired way. Such was the experience of Job in the book that bears his name: when eventually in Job 38:1—40:2 the Lord is portrayed as responding to and speaking to this suffering man and all his prayers and expostulations it is in no way to answer Job's many questions and complaints about the sufferings he has experienced, but rather to challenge Job over what of the wonders of the creation he understands.[31]

Patrick D. Miller has pointed out that in various trying circumstances in which the suffering one makes their prayer to God they might appeal to the compassion of God, that he will act according to his steadfast love, or to his mercy.[32] There are, however, in the Hebrew Bible incidents recounted in which the element of the miraculous is pronounced, as for example in the story of Elisha in 2 Kgs 6:15-20 in which in a battle situation with the Syrian army the Israelite prophet is portrayed as praying in rapid succession three different prayers that will affect the outcome of the battle. Further, in rapid succession thus it was, and thus were the Syrians defeated. I suggest that in stories of this nature the Old Testament is not being at its most helpful to us as to the mystery of prayer.[33]

Perhaps we should say that the prayers of petition and intercession in the Old Testament are in essence about appealing to the compassion of God, a pleading that the Lord will act in compassion towards this pray-er, or pray-ers. It is perhaps not without significance that the account in Exodus of the impassioned pleas of Moses for the Lord's forgiveness of his people with the golden calf are so soon followed with the first occurrence of a formula, portrayed as having been spoken by the Lord himself to Moses, which will

---

31. On the prayers of Job in the book that bears his name, and the eventual responses of the Lord, see my *"Where is the God of Justice?,"* 105-56.

32. See, for example, Pss 6:4; 25:7; 31:16; 44:26; 51:1; 69:13, 16; 86:5, 15; 109:21, 26; 143:12. Miller in this regard also points to Ps 79:9 with its "deliver us, and forgive our sins, for your name's sake," and also to the fact that if he does not help his suffering ones then God will appear either to be uncaring or to lack the necessary strength. Miller, "Prayer as Persuasion," 339-41.

33. On the account of this incident, see my article, "What Happens When We Pray?," 371.

recur in the Hebrew Bible about the mercy and compassion of the Lord. Thus:

> The Lord, the Lord,
> a God merciful and gracious,
> slow to anger,
> and abounding in steadfast love and faithfulness,
> keeping steadfast love for the thousandth generation,
> forgiving iniquity and transgression and sin,
> yet by no means clearing the guilty,
> but visiting the iniquity of the parents
> upon the children
> and the children's children,
> to the third and fourth generation. (Exod 34:6–7)[34]

Thus whether it was in praise or in thanksgiving, whether in intercession or petition, whether in complaint or in searching, the Old Testament speaks of prayer as divine gift whereby an individual or group, or even nation, could speak to its Lord and God, and thereby perhaps receive his word for them. It has been said that "Prayer was the point at which the human creature dared to approach the transcendent, holy deity with no restrictions on what could be expressed; the human was free not only to cry out in rage, anger, despair, and hate, as in the lament part of the prayer, but also to beseech, urge, and persuade."[35] And that varied spirit of worship and approach to God is also to be observed in the biblical psalms, to which we now turn.

---

34. This formula, with variations, is also to be found in Num 14:18; Pss 86:15; 103:8; 145:8; Jonah 4:2; Joel 2:13; Nah 1:3; Neh 9:17. See below, 192–95.

35. Miller, "Prayer as Persuasion," 343.

8

Psalms

The Hebrew title for the book of Psalms is *tĕhillîm*, meaning "praises." While this may not appear to us to be a strictly accurate statement of fact, in that manifestly not all of the psalms are expressions of praise but on the contrary many of them give voice to a wide range of different moods and life-experiences of the worshippers, yet we can surely acknowledge with a sense of some wonder that such a variety of utterances and moods are offered in a spirit of prayer and praise to the Lord. For in the book of Psalms, as well as expressions of praise the notes of confession to God are to be found, and so too, as we have already seen, laments both of individuals and of communities, in which are revealed the urgent asking questions of God as to troubles and difficulties in life, questions about the supposed guidance of God in the world.[1] There are other psalms, again that we have already observed, that focus on the institution of kingship,[2] while others express a sense of deep trust and confidence in the Lord, others that are nothing less than bold and unequivocal hymns of praise. Indeed, overall there breathes through this biblical book the spirit of seeking God either to express worship of him or else to ask deep questions about his plan and purpose for those whose lives appear to be taking unexpected turns.[3]

What, however, we do not have is what we might regard as sufficient indication of the settings in life of individual psalms. On what particular occasions and in what possible circumstances might individual psalms have been used in ancient times? We are not given such information, and in that void in our knowledge it is all too easy to resort to theories, educated guesses as to what such particular or typical backgrounds might be. Further, while individual psalms have words we assume were used in worship, they are not specific about the particular services in which such words were used. In other parts of the Hebrew Bible we are given abundant instructions about what is to happen in certain of the cultic rites, but there is a silence about what words might have been employed in those rites.

1. On the psalms of lament, see above, 112–13.
2. On the so-called royal psalms, see above, 91–97.
3. See Goldingay, "The Dynamic Cycle of Praise and Prayer."

Another aspect of the use of the Old Testament psalms in worship concerns their musical accompaniment. "Music and its tools of production, musical instruments, as mentioned in the Bible," it has been observed, "are among the most perplexing phenomena of the past."[4] As far as the Psalter is concerned we appear to have musical references in at least some of the headings to individual psalms. Occurring some 55 times in psalm headings, and also in Hab 3, is the expression "For the Choirmaster" (*laměnaṣṣēaḥ*) which may perhaps indicate instructions for the musical leader. The Hebrew *mizmôr*, occurring 57 times in the psalms, is thought to indicate singing with musical instruments. In the LXX it is translated *psalmos*, meaning "song" or "hymn to music." Yet when we come to such expressions as found in the heading of Ps 46 "According to Alamoth" (*'al-'ălāmôt*), we have to confess our ignorance: it has been suggested that this may indicate singing with instrumental accompaniment, or possibly "drum", or even "on the eighth (tone or mode)". Nevertheless, what we read about in Ps 150 sounds as if a good number of musical instruments are intended to join in the great chorus of praise with which the Psalter comes to its triumphal and joyful conclusion. Other expressions may be intended to indicate tunes for the singing of some of the psalms, such as "the Gittith", perhaps meaning "winepress"? (Pss 8; 81; 84); "Do not destroy" (Pss 57; 58; 59; 75); "To the lilies" (Pss 45; 60; 69; 80); "On the hind of the dawn" (Ps 22); "To the dove on far-off Terebinths" (Ps 56).

The evidence we have in the Hebrew Bible suggests that singing in praise of God (or indeed of other gods) was not uncommon, whether that was by one person (2 Sam 23:1), or by a group (Exod 15:1; 32:18–19; 2 Chr 20:21), with accompaniment of musical instruments (Exod 15:20–21; Ps 149:1–3), responsively (1 Sam 29:5; Ezra 3:10–11), or antiphonally (1 Sam 18:6–7). Further we hear at times of musical accompaniment, and we do find mention in the Old Testament of a range of such instruments, though just what such instruments are we cannot be sure of, and there are inevitably questions about how the various Hebrew words for them are to be translated. Perhaps the most that can be said is that in all probability such instruments were either of the string, or wind, or percussion varieties.

Mention should be made also of the ubiquitous yet at the same time still mysterious term "Selah," which occurs no less than seventy-one times in thirty-nine psalms. This does not occur at the beginning of verses, but rather in the middle or the end. Not infrequently it occurs after a refrain (see Pss 24:6, 10; 46:7, 11; 52:3, 5). Various suggestions as to its meaning

---

4. Braun, "Music, Musical Instruments." For further details, see ibid., *Music in Ancient Israel/Palestine*; Mitchell, "Resinging the Temple Psalmody"; Dell, "'A Time to Dance'"; Rogerson, "Music"; and Barker, *Temple Theology*, 15.

have been suggested: perhaps it is related to the Hebrew verbal root *s-l-l* and intended to indicate the raising of hands, or eyes, or voices. The LXX translated "Selah" as *diapsalma*, meaning pause: was that intended to indicate an interlude in the recitation or the singing of a psalm? What, however, is much clearer is the frequency of references to singing in the Psalter: there are no less that twenty-four references in the Psalms to the verb *š-y-r*, "sing", ten to the verb *z-m-r* (sing); seven to the verb *r-n-n* (sing aloud). Surely the Psalter is in at least some senses a book of songs.[5]

The Psalter is the part of the Old Testament the Christians were able most easily to take into their distinctive worship and use in their liturgies,[6] as clearly this material had earlier been used in Ancient Israel's and then in Judaism's liturgies. Again and again, in the book of psalms are words directed *to* God, rather than words *about* God. Moreover where in the psalms there are words about God, more often than not such portrayals are to the effect that therefore this mighty Lord is to be worshipped, or implored, supplicated, if necessary harangued. Further, these various aspects of human speech to God found in the psalms are but the various aspects of the whole movement of the people's worship of their Lord, that is, their praises, their confessions, their thanksgivings, their asking anguished questions, their prayers for the spread and prevalence of justice and peace in their land.

Before we consider the book of psalms as comprising words both for worship and also of worship, we need to be aware of two main directions in which the scholarly study of the psalms has in recent decades been directed. The first of these was what has been called the liturgical approach, and it owed much to the insights and studies of Gunkel and Mowinckel,[7] the first of a form-critical nature into the "types," or genre, of psalms—laments, thanksgivings, hymns, Royal psalms, wisdom psalms, Torah psalms, pilgrimage, entrance liturgies, and some other smaller groups. The gain to scholarly study of the psalms through Gunkel's insights has been great indeed. A further development of this came from Mowinckel, who argued that the psalms were cultic hymns, and who sought to reconstruct various liturgies employing these "hymns." More recently the legitimacy of the attempt to reconstruct such a series of entirely hypothetical festivals from

---

5. On psalm superscriptions, Selah, etc., see, e.g., Holladay, *The Psalms through Three Thousand Years*, 69–76; and Gillingham, *The Poems and Psalms*, 245–51.

6. See, e.g., Gillingham, *Poems and Psalms*, 264–69; *Psalms Through the Centuries*, vol. 1; *A Journey of Two Psalms*; Holladay, *The Psalms through Three Thousand Years*, 161–284; Maher, "The Psalms in Jewish Worship"; Pajunen, "Perspectives on the Existence"; and Lamb, *The Psalms in Christian Worship*.

7. For a summary of all this scholarship, see, e.g., Eaton, "The Psalms and Israelite Worship"; and Gillingham, "Studies of the Psalms."

what, hypothetically, might have been uttered and/or sung at them, has been questioned.[8]

The second of these two main directions in recent psalm studies has been of a more literary nature and has concerned the shape and order of the psalter. Questions have been asked about the significance of the five "books" into which the psalter is divided (Pss 1–41, 42–72, 73–89, 90–106, 107–150), the associated dispositions of certain types of psalms within those books, and other groupings of the psalms in terms of their headings, certain vocabulary usages within them, and so on. Whether this type of work can lead to fresh understandings of how the book of Psalms came to assume its present shape remains an unresolved question.[9]

The approach that will be followed in this present work as regards the biblical psalms and worship is to employ aspects of both of these approaches. The basic plan of what follows owes to the more recent approach of Wilson and others, and at the same time takes seriously earlier insights into the biblical psalms, in particular those of Hermann Gunkel. Thus I shall attempt a reading of the book of psalms, that understands them as expressions of worship in its various aspects. I shall be seeking to take due notice of the beginnings and endings of the five books of the whole Psalter, in particular noting the presence of doxological endings for each of those books. In my discussion of the psalms I shall be pausing for a longer discussion of the first appearance of each of the distinctive types of psalm.[10]

There are other groupings of the psalms of which we should to take notice, namely what have been called "clusters," these being indicated by a series of headings.[11] Thus most of Pss 3–41 bear the title "Of David," the exceptions being Ps 10—but perhaps that was originally the continuation of Ps 9 (see below)—and Ps 33. This looks as if Pss 3–41 may have been something of an already existing collection of psalms before the work eventually developed—perhaps through a series of stages?—into the psalter we know today. Then there are Pss 42–89 in which there is a predominance in the usage of the word Elohim (God) for the deity, some two hundred and forty

---

8. See, e.g., the comments of Kraus, *Worship in Israel*, 208–29. For similar reasons, I do not in this work make use of Eaton, *Vision in Worship*.

9. In this regard, see, e.g., Wilson, *The Editing of the Hebrew Psalter*; McCann, *The Shape and Shaping of the Psalter*; Whybray, *Reading the Psalms as a Book*; DeClaissé-Walford, *Reading from the Beginning*; and Brown, *Psalms*, 109–33.

10. The exception are the so-called royal psalms, which have been discussed earlier in this work in the chapter dealing with the Israelite king and worship. See above, 91–97.

11. On this, see, e.g., Gillingham, *Poems and Psalms*, 238–45; and Brown, *Psalms*, 85–107.

occurrences against only forty to Yahweh. Thus Pss 42–83 have been called the "Elohistic Psalter." However, there are further divisions to be noted here, for Pss 51–72 are in a Davidic collection, while Pss 84–85 and 87–88 have Korahite attribution. Psalms 73–83 bear the title "A psalm of Asaph."

Other collections of psalms seem to be based on thematic principles, such as Enthronement Psalms (Pss 47; 93; 95–99), Songs of Ascents (Pss 120–134), Hallelujah psalms (Pss 111–117, 146–150). Then there are the psalms somewhat on their own, like Ps 89 "A Maskil of Ethan the Ezrahite"; Ps 92 "A Psalm. A Song for the Sabbath Day"; and not forgetting Ps 102 "A Prayer of One Afflicted, when faint and pleading before the Lord." Clearly, a number of historical circumstances and stages in the collecting of groups of psalms lies behind the completed Psalter, and in all probability the historical reconstruction of those stages is not possible. What this means is that when we read and study the psalms we are dealing with materials that come from far-away times, that perhaps have undergone some adaptation for newer settings, possibly such processes taking place a number of times. Further, when we read them in yet another age, under very different social, religious, political conditions, we are having to make in one way or another, a yet further stage in the ongoing process of adaptation and accommodation. Moreover, such considerations render dating of individual psalms difficult, for where a reference to temple might indicate a time in the era of Solomon's temple; yet it might also be a reference to the later temple, or even to a possible (idealized) future temple. The same perhaps goes for references to a king in some of the so-called royal psalms; are the references to a historical personage, or alternatively to a vision of a future hoped-for king?[12]

It is widely agreed that Pss 1 and 150 provide respectively an introduction and a conclusion to the whole collection of the five books. Psalm 1 is generally classified as a "Torah Psalm", by content it having kinship with Ps 19:7–14 and Ps 119, in that they are concerned to express praise of the Lord who in "speaking" to his people gave them, it was believed, his instruction, law, "Torah," and to which in prayer and praise his people respond. Blessed indeed are those who shun the advices of the wicked and instead set their minds on the law of the Lord, seeking to meditate upon it constantly (Ps 1:1–2). Thus they are the ones who are prosperous and successful in their lives (v. 3), whereas the wicked find themselves in all manner of problems and distresses (vv. 4–5). Further, very different fates await these two contrasting groups (v. 6).[13] Hence, the book of Psalms may be said to open with

12. On the matter of the historical dating of psalms, see, e.g., Gillingham, *Poems and Psalms*, 253–5; and Day, "How many Pre-exilic Psalms are there?"

13. It must be said that experience of life cannot but suggest that the righteous do not always prosper, nor that the lives of the wicked are always blighted. As we shall see

an expression of praise that the Lord has revealed his will in his law (Torah, instruction) and that his people will find fullness of life in their living in obedience to that holy law.

The First Book of the Psalter

This comprises Psalms 2-41: many of these psalms are attributed to David, and while it has been suggested that this is the oldest of the psalm collections, this is hardly demonstrable. Some scholars are of the opinion that Ps 2 should be regarded as being part, with Ps 1, of an introduction to the whole psalter, but we cannot be sure about this, and I prefer to take it as the opening psalm of Book One of the psalter.[14]

Psalm 2 is the first of a group of psalms that Gunkel called "royal psalms." The others are Pss 18; 20; 21; 45; 72; 89; 101; 110; 132; 144:1–11, and these have already been considered, and will not therefore be further treated here.[15]

Psalm 3 introduces us to another of Gunkel's types of psalms, namely the individual laments. This is by far the commonest type of psalm in the psalter, making up almost a third of the whole book. The following would generally be regarded as individual laments: Psalms 3–7; 9/10, 13; 17; 22; 25–28; 31; 35; 38–39; 40:13–7=70; 42/43; 51–52; 54–57; 59; 61; 64; 69–71; 77; 86; 88; 94:16–23; 102; 109; 120; 130; 139–143. In these psalms we are hearing, as it were, an individual's outspokenness to God about the difficulties in life that he or she is having to face up to and deal with. It is noticeable, both in Ps 3 and also in others of the individual laments, that we are not told what the particular problem is that the psalmist was experiencing and complaining about to God. We may posit the strong possibility that originally there was a definite experience and associated complaint, but that at some later stage this was made into a psalm having as its background an unspecified and generalized problem, or problems, so making it useable and useful for a wide range of individuals who were experiencing sufferings.

The individual lament psalms are nothing less than outspoken complaints to God, and they make up a type of prayer that is by no means always

---

below, Pss 37, 49, 73 call these assumptions into question, as also does the book of Job and a good deal else in the Hebrew Bible. See Thompson, "Where is the God of Justice?"

14. Nevertheless, it should be bourne in mind that over the years various suggestions have been made about a relationship between Pss 1 and 2. See, e.g., Auffret, *The Literary Structure of Psalm 2*, pp. 31–34; Whybray, *Reading the Psalms as a Book*, 78–81; and Gillingham, *A Journey of Two Psalms*.

15. On the royal psalms see above, 91–97.

polite to God. Rather, the psalmists make their point, sometimes in the strongest possible terms, the worshipper feeling that in their moment of crisis God has been absent, that as their God he has failed this individual. Thus, in the usage of these psalms in worship there is the opportunity for the individual to be outspoken to God over matters that are causing the worshipper angst, unhappiness, even anger. Yet, usually with these psalms—more often than not at the end though it may occur earlier—there can be an abrupt change of mood and associated speech with, apparently, the psalmist coming to a sense of peace, the feeling that God is indeed there and that he has truly heard the suffering person's anguished prayer. Various explanations have been offered for this dramatic change of mood on the part of the suffering psalmist, the most likely being that the psalmist having entrusted the matter that has been troubling them to God is thereby enabled to find a sense of peace.[16]

Psalm 3 opens with the appeal of an unknown person to God about what are called his or her "foes" (NRSV), and "foes" here could refer to human beings, or else to forces, issues, circumstances. Perhaps it is more likely that individuals are being spoken about for it is claimed that they are mocking the psalmist, averring that there is no help to be found in the Lord (vv. 1–2). Nevertheless, the psalmist is sure that the Lord is his "shield," his "glory," indeed "the one who lifts up my head," that is enables him to stand anew in his life (v. 3). For not only does the psalmist call out to the Lord, but also the Lord answers from "his holy hill," perhaps indicating that the psalmist found help and assurance in the Jerusalem temple worship (v. 4). This sense of confidence in the Lord's care of this person is further made clear through what we are told in vv. 5 and 6, which affirm the psalmist's deep trust in the Lord so that he can sleep peacefully at night. The psalmist can even speak in terms of the Lord using physical violence in order to restrain the psalmist's "enemies," which can cause some difficulty for latter-day readers. About these words Peter Craigie says, "The words of v. 8cd seem at first vindictive and harsh, with respect to the enemy. Yet . . . it is not that one prays for God's action against the enemy as such, but against the evil which

---

16. Such compositions as these psalms are also to be found in the book of Jeremiah, where the prophet is portrayed as crying out to God over all the sufferings that he is experiencing in fulfilling his (undesired) ministry of being the Lord's prophet. See Thompson, "*Where is the God of Justice?*," 35–57. For the Individual Psalms of lament see, amongst a considerable amount of literature: Day, *Psalms*, 19–38; Thompson, "*Where is the God of Justice?*," 31–34; Thompson, *I Have Heard Your Prayer*, 41–56, 210–12; Anderson, "Enemies and Evildoers in the Book of Psalms," 18–29; Broyles, *The Conflict of Faith and Experience in the Psalms*; Gillingham, *Poems and Psalms*, 153–56, 216–19; Westermann, *The Living Psalms*, 65–122; and Johnston, "The Psalms and Distress."

they speak and do."[17] With the words of v. 8 "Deliverance belongs to our God" we have what Kraus calls "a closing statement (epiphonema) added for liturgical use."[18] Here indeed is the affirmation made in the psalmist's and others' worship, accompanied as it is by the humble prayer, "may your blessing be on your people!" Thus the psalmist moves from his statements of distress, to his expressions of confidence in the Lord' power and will to deliver, and the prayer that the divine blessing may be upon God's people.

Further individual laments follow in Pss 4, 5, 6 and 7. Psalm 4 reads like an evening psalm (see v. 8), and so it has been used in Christian liturgies, in particular in orders of service for Compline. Again it speaks of various disturbances that the psalmist has experienced, but the counsel here is that the sufferer should be careful of any (hasty?) words he may utter about such things, but rather maintain his giving of the appropriate sacrifices and the putting of his trust in the Lord (vv. 4–5). There is the prayer that sufferers may see better things in their lives, and that the light of the Lord may shine on them (v. 6). The psalm ends on the note of calm confidence, for the Lord has put a gladness into the sufferer's heart far greater in worth than much grain and wine (food and drink, v. 7), and thus can the psalmist both lie down and also sleep in peace, for the reason that—and here is the motive for worship—"for you alone, O Lord, make me lie down in safety" (v. 8).

Psalm 5 also speaks of the troubles of the psalmist, and these are poured out to God in prayer in the morning (vv. 1–3). Yet how confident this psalmist becomes as he contemplates the care of the Lord for his faithful people. Thus does he speak of his coming into the temple in a spirit of awe in order to worship and pray:

> But I, through the abundance of your steadfast love,
> will enter your house,
> I will bow down towards your holy temple
> in awe of you.
> Lead me, O Lord, in your righteousness
> because of my enemies;
> make your way straight before me. (Ps 5:7–8)

With Ps 6 we again hear a psalmist crying out to God over things in life that are causing the pray-er to "languish" (v. 2), but soon there are the notes of assurance for the reason that "The Lord has heard my supplication; the Lord accepts my prayer" (v. 9). Psalm 7 seems to be speaking of a psalmist suffering trouble and distress, yet also here is the confident faith that the

---

17. Craigie, *Psalms 1–50*, p. 75. Craigie's reference is to Ps 3:8 in the Hebrew, which in EVV is 3:7.

18. Kraus, *Psalms 1–59*, p. 141.

Lord is this sufferer's shield (v. 10) and righteous judge (v. 11), so that the psalm can end on the worshipful notes of thanks and praise: "I will give to the Lord the thanks due to his righteousness, and sing praise to the name of the Lord, the Most High" (v. 17).

Psalm 8, it is very generally agreed, should be classified as a general hymn of praise. These hymns comprise a large group within the biblical psalter, and most scholars would include the following in this category: Pss 8; 19:1–6; 29; 33; 46–48; 65; 66:1–7; 68; 76; 84; 87; 93; 95–100; 103; 104; (105?); 111; 113; 114; 117; 122; 134–136; 145–150.[19] Psalm 8 is an expression of unbounded praise of God, the composition being framed between the identical opening and closing statements, "O Lord, our Sovereign, how majestic is your name in all the earth!" (vv. 1a, 8). Between these statements, two matters are presented as giving rise to praise, the first being the wonders of the creation (1b–2). There are textual problems with these one-and-a-half verses, in particular about whether we take the phrase "from the mouths of babes and infants" with what precedes it or whether we take it with what follows. NRSV takes it with what follows, and that is here followed, being understood in the sense that even for the most infant and unlearned ones of earth the glories of the heavens and the general glory of the natural world are obvious. The infants even in their weakness, and presumably other limitations as well, are enabled to perceive the strength of the Lord's creation, and thus silence God's enemies and any who would oppose his works of creating and creation.

This leads onto the second cause for wonder and praise spoken about in the psalm: as the psalmist surveys the Lord's creation of the celestial range (heavens, moon, and stars), the question is inevitably raised in the beholder's mind, "what are human beings that you are mindful of them, mortals that you care for them?" (v. 4). The more so that they have been so fashioned that they have some sort of kinship and relationship with the creator and Lord of these things. Who are the humans that they have been made only a little "diminished" from a god, or gods—or even God?[20] For, more even than this, the humans have been crowned with "glory and honor"—as if they were royalty (v. 5)—and such responsibilities have been vested in them, namely dominion in the world over the animals of the lands and the fish of the seas (v. 6–8). What a remarkable place has been given in the created world to the human beings! For indeed so much and so many beings have been put "under their feet" (v. 6); this reads like a reference to what is perceived as the

19. For these hymns in the psalter, see Day, *Psalms*, 40–43; Gillingham, *Poems and Psalms*, 208–14; Brown, *Psalms*, 150–55; and Hutchinson, "The Psalms and Praise."

20. Perhaps it was because this seemed to be such a bold thought that for the LXX translators this became "angels" (*aggelous*).

intended mastery of the human race over living beings. Such thoughts and understandings lead the psalmist to his concluding paean of praise, an echo of that with which his composition began.

Our consideration of this particular psalm, and the further consideration that this is certainly a numerous group of psalms, perhaps serves to make us aware of the note of praise, adoration, worship that occupies a prominent place in the biblical psalter, and which it would appear, making use of psalms, must have made itself heard in the worship of the people of ancient Israel. At the same time Ps 8 reminds us of the particular and privileged place of the human beings in the world, but that yet they must be recognized as small indeed when viewed and contemplated alongside that surpassing greatness and glory of the Lord. As James Mays observes, "The recognition is evoked here by contemplation of the vast depth of the night sky with its moon and myriad mysterious stars, an experience to which people of many times and places have testified. The experience is not, however, that of being 'lost in the cosmos'; rather it is of awe and wonder at the marvelous majesty of God, who can make and has made a royal regent of this mere mortal. The question is asked in the psalm to serve the purpose of the hymn, praise of the Lord."[21] And so too do the many other hymns in the psalter add their own particular notes of praise to the Lord.

Psalms 9 and 10 seem originally to have been one psalm. Not only do they appear together in the LXX, also in the Vulgate, and in some Hebrew manuscripts, but further they are in a partial acrostic form going through what are now two psalms.[22] Once again we are reading a lament psalm of an individual, a psalm which is punctuated with expressions of distress, yet which also displays confidence that God hears the cry of the distressed (9:12–13, 18; 10:17–18), and that thus the psalmist can indeed "Sing praises to the Lord, who dwells in Zion" (9:11), and that "The Lord is king forever and ever" (10:16).

With Ps 11 we are introduced to a further group of psalms, what have been called psalms of confidence, sometimes psalms of trust. Most critics would agree that Pss 11; 16; 23; 27:1–6; 62 and 131 should be counted within this group. As the name of the group implies these psalms set forth the confidence the believer has in God, that the Lord is believed to be trustworthy. While this aspect of confidence and trust in God is to be observed in many other psalms, as for example, as we have seen in the individual lament

---

21. Mays, *Psalms*, 68.

22. It has to be admitted that the acrostic arrangement of Pss 9 and 10 into one psalm is neither complete nor perfect. Strong cumulative arguments for regarding them as originally one psalm are set forth by Kraus, *Psalms 1–59*, pp. 191–3, and such is followed in this present work.

psalms, the characteristic feature of the so-called psalms of confidence is that this is the sole subject of the psalm, and there is not the element of stress on the troubles, or the enemies, and so on that we read about in the lament psalms. There is indeed a relationship in content between the psalms of confidence and the psalms of thanksgiving, and there may be some discussion as to which group certain of the psalms are to be assigned.[23]

In Ps 11 the source of the psalmist's confidence is expressed above all in the words of the fourth verse, "The Lord is in his holy temple; the Lord's throne is in heaven. His eyes behold, his gaze examines humankind," and the worshipper gives expression to that sense of deep trust in the Lord, "For the Lord is righteous; he loves righteous deeds; the upright shall behold his face" (Ps 11:4 and 7). Given here in a short psalm are the words for worshippers' heartfelt and thankful profession that the Lord does indeed protect and help his people. Thus can they sing in their worship of their confident faith in God.

Psalm 12 brings before us another group of psalms, namely the psalms of communal laments. As the name implies here is a whole community lamenting its problematic and suffering situation. This group of psalms, much fewer in number than the individual laments, would frequently include Pss 12; 44; 60; 74; 79; 80; 83; 85; 94:1-11; 126. Perhaps Pss 58 and 90 should also be included within this group, for they do display features in common. Further, we also read such "communal laments" in Isa 63:7—64:11; Jer 14:2-9, 19—22; Lam 5. More often than not these communal laments are concerned with political and military disasters that have befallen the nation, and it has been suggested that perhaps they were used on certain special days of national lamentation, such occasions as those we read about in, for example, Josh 7:5-9; Judg 20:23, 26; 1 Sam 7:6; 2 Chr 20:3-12; Jer 14; Joel 1-2; Zech 7:3, 5; 8:19; Jdt 4:9-15. Here is another aspect of worship expressed in a number of psalms, when a nation, or at least some part or parts of it, make their agonized prayer to God, "You, O Lord, will protect us; you will guard us from this generation forever" (Ps 12:7).[24]

Psalm 13 is another of the numerous individual lament psalms, in which, characteristically, there are set out the reasons why the psalmist is lamenting his apparently having been forgotten by God, and when the psalmist asks "how long" this negative situation will prevail (Ps 13:1-4). As occurs frequently (as a result of the psalmist having in prayer entrusted the

---

23. On the psalms of confidence, see, e.g., Day, *Psalms*, 52-4; and Gillingham, *Poems and Psalms*, 219, 224-5.

24. On the communal laments, see, e.g., Day, *Psalms*, 33-36; Gillingham, *Poems and Psalms*, 214-19; Westermann, *The Living Psalms*, 21-41; Brown, *Psalms*, 46-52; and Johnston, "The Psalms and Distress."

matter to the Lord?) the psalm ends on the notes of peace and confidence: "But I trusted in your steadfast love; my heart shall rejoice in your salvation. I will sing to the Lord, because he has dealt bountifully with me." (Ps 13:5–6)

Psalm 14, it has to be admitted, rather defeats the scholarly enterprise of endeavoring to understand each psalm as belonging to a particular type. Psalm 14 does not fit into any one category, but rather exhibits characteristics of a number of psalm types. Perhaps we have to leave it at that, saying that with its talk of the "fool" expressing (surely, practical rather than theoretical) atheism (vv. 1–6) we seem to be in what we might call a "wisdom" emphasis, while v. 7 looks rather like the talk of an individual lament, in particular with its confident expression of divine deliverance.[25] Yet we may say that the overall spirit of the psalm reflects that of an individual lament, such that an individual can go as far as saying that there is no God (Ps 14:1). Further, the characteristic confident ending of a lament psalm is there in the second part of the last verse, "When the Lord restores the fortunes of his people, Jacob will rejoice; Israel will be glad" (Ps 14:7b).

With Psalm 15 we come to the first example of another of Gunkel's psalm types, though here the present psalm is nearly on its own. This psalm is very generally known as an "entrance liturgy", but similar wording is to be found in Ps 24:3–6, and also in Isa 33:14–16. All these compositions are divided into three parts: (a) The question is posed concerning who may be admitted to the temple (Pss 15:1; 24:3; Isa 33:14); (b) An answer is given couched in terms of ethical requirements (Pss 15:2–5b; 24:4–5; Isa 33:15); (c) A blessing is assured for those who may enter the temple (Pss 15:5c; 24:6; Isa 33:16.[26] The question being asked here concerns worthiness to enter the temple, and presumably we should think of it as setting before the worshipper an inward, spiritual examination of themselves, associated perhaps by a confession of sin for perceived lapses. However, the whole tenor of the requirements set out for the worshipper to consider are noteworthy for their being seemingly "acultic," there being nothing here about levitical purity, cultic worthiness: rather the whole emphasis is upon conduct in the world and relationship with neighbors.[27] Thus doing what is right and speaking

---

25. Another aspect of Ps 14 that should be noted is its close parallel with Ps 53. Further, in 14:2 and 53:2, the divine address is different—in the former (as in the so-called Davidic Psalter) to "the Lord," in the latter (as in the so-called Elohistic psalter) as "God."

26. On the entrance liturgy psalms, see, e.g., Day, *Psalms*, 60–61; and Gillingham, *Poems and Psalms*, 225–26.

27. Robert Alter says, "The answer to the opening question is a catalog of moral attributes. It is noteworthy that these are presented as an objective list of items without figurative elaboration; there is not a single metaphor in the poem. The enumerated virtuous acts all pertain to a person's moral obligations to others. Neither cult nor

the truth is featured (v. 2), so also slandering, doing evil to friends, taking up reproaches against neighbors (v. 3), honoring those who fear (reverence) the Lord, keeping oaths (v. 4), not lending money at interest, nor taking bribes against the innocent (v. 5a). In these conditions we seem to be in a different world from that of the priestly writers, yet here being clearly told that those who keep such standards shall never be moved (v. 5b). These, apparently, are the ones here judged worthy to abide in the Lord's tent (presumably a deliberately archaic way of speaking about the temple), that is dwell on the hill of Zion (v. 1).[28]

Psalm 16 expresses feelings of great confidence on the part of the psalmist, and thus it is generally agreed that we have a psalm of confidence. There are various textual problems in vv. 2–4a,[29] but overall the message is clear that the psalmist is possessed of a great sense of confidence and trust in the Lord. Yet what is the psalmist saying in the words of v. 10: "For you do not give me up to Sheol, or let your faithful one see the Pit"? Is he speaking of the hope for life after death, or is he referring to an experience when he was, as we might say, "at death's door," or perhaps when he had been grievously ill? We have to say we do not know, and scholars are much divided over the issue, so perhaps we do well to heed the words of Rowley when he said "that no clear doctrine is here enunciated, and it is unwise to press the interpretation on either side."[30] We shall return to this issue of a possible belief in life after death when we consider Pss 49 and 73, but it would be generally agreed that it is not until the book of Daniel (see Dan 12:2–3) that the Hebrew Bible can present us with unambiguous belief in a post-mortem existence.[31]

Psalm 17 is another of the individual lament psalms. Here the psalmist is sure that it is a just cause he is bringing to the Lord, and so he makes his prayer (v. 1). Thus Anderson calls this psalm "The Innocent Man's Cry for Help."[32] At the same time it has to be said that there is expansive confidence expressed by the psalmist about the Lord, that ultimately this worshipper is safe indeed living his life in trust in the Lord. Nevertheless, the psalmist asks for the Lord's protection in the face of his problems, yet seems sure that as another day dawns he will behold God's face in righteousness—that

---

covenant is involved" (*The Book of Psalms*, 43).

28. On Ps 15, see, among other contributions, Clements, "Worship and Ethics." On Isa 33, see Thompson, "Vision, Reality and Worship."

29. The textual problems in Ps 16 and the various options for dealing with them are set out in Anderson, *The Book of Psalms*, 1:142–43.

30. Rowley, *The Faith of Israel*, 175 n.2.

31. See Thompson, "Where is the God of Justice?," 168–73.

32. Anderson, *The Book of Psalms*, 1:147.

is, maybe, the psalmist will awake in the presence of the God who will be regarding him (the psalmist) as righteous (v. 15).

With Psalm 18 we have another of the royal psalms, which we have already considered.[33] Here we note that the king makes his profession of righteousness and loyalty; as we might put it, in worship he commits himself again to the tasks of his high calling as the king, confident that any victories he may win are really victories of the Lord his God (vv. 20–30).

Psalm 19 is a hymn of praise to God, and although it is in two parts they interlock satisfyingly. Verses 1–6 make up a hymn of praise to God for the wonders of the world of nature, such wonder that it reflects powerfully the greatness of the creator. In fact through this wonderful creation there is a silent and yet powerful speech going out proclaiming both the glory of God and God's handiwork seen in the firmament. The second part of the psalm, in vv. 7–13, expresses praise for the law that God has given to his people for their guidance. More, to obey the Torah ("law, instruction") of the Lord is a delight in itself, so this psalm avers: the ordinances of the Lord as well as being true and righteous, also "More to be desired are they than gold, even much fine gold; sweeter also than honey, and drippings of the honeycomb" (v. 10). This law warns the one who would be faithful to God, and hopefully keeps them free of great transgressions (vv. 11–13). The final verse has a humble prayer that the words and thoughts of the worshipper may be acceptable to God:

> Let the words of my mouth and the meditation of my heart
> be acceptable to you,
> O Lord, my rock and my redeemer. (Ps 19:14)

With the praise and the prayer set forth in this memorable psalm we are clearly in the realm of worship, the fact that the psalmist must come before the Lord in praise, openness, and humility being clearly expressed.

Psalms 20 and 21 are both royal psalms, which are considered above.[34] We have see that while we cannot be sure what particular events or cultic occasions drew forth the usage of these two psalms, it is clear that through the words of both of them there is portrayed a bringing into the arena and realm of worship the people's prayers of intercession and thanksgiving for their national leader. Here are prayers of the people in intercession and thanksgiving for the king, their national leader.

Psalm 22 brings us to another, and for Christians no doubt well-known example, of the individual lament psalms. A greatly-suffering individual

---

33. See above, 91–97.
34. See above, 91–97.

cries out to God for what appears to be the Lord's forsaking of him, in spite of his ongoing—daily and nightly—words, groans, and cries (vv. 1-2). Thus this heartfelt psalm goes on, speaking about the psalmist's sufferings (vv. 3-21a). Nevertheless there is, once again, a dramatic change of mood recorded in vv. 21b-31, verses that exude hope in the Lord. Is this once again the hope that is found in God when once more the deeply troublesome matter has been entrusted to him—in all probability through worship?

For many people Ps 23 is special. "The Psalm is unrivalled for calm serenity and perfect faith," said Kirkpatrick.[35] This is one of the psalms of confidence, and through its profound and moving words it sets out the sure grounds for hope on the part of an individual who has put trust in the Lord for all eventualities of life, including (perhaps) even death itself. Whatever may happen to the believer, the Lord—likened here in this psalm to a good shepherd—will ever be present, and thus the believer can be sure that he will always be a member of the household of faith, of the household of the Lord, "my whole life long" (v. 6).[36] This psalm is a statement of faith that has been used over many centuries in people's worship of God. Clearly this is so in Judaism and Christianity, and we may be sure that this happened for the people of Old Testament times.[37]

Psalm 24, it is widely agreed, is a liturgy,[38] though just what liturgy we should see it as a part of is more open to question. Certainly its middle part in vv. 3-6 is reminiscent of Ps 15, and sets out the desired inner attitude of the worshipper if their worship is to be acceptable to the Lord. We should perhaps call what precedes it in 24:1-2 a hymn of praise to the Lord which extols him for his creation of, and lordship over, the whole world. The closing verses, 7-10, make up a song of praise at the entrance of the temple, this being expressed in an antiphonal arrangement. Clearly this whole composition is a reminder to worshippers both of their Lord's power, might and wisdom, and also of their fundamental unworthiness to come before him with their song of praise.

Psalm 25 brings us to another individual lament, this one having been written in acrostic form. The psalmist speaks of being surrounded by enemies, who look set to overwhelm him, but who—or even what—"my enemies" are we are not told. Rather, the psalmist's "troubles" are here expressed in a generalized way, no doubt purposely in order that the psalm

---

35. Kirkpatrick, *The Book of Psalms (1-41)*, p. 124.

36. See, e.g., Johnson, "Psalm 23 and the Household of Faith."

37. See Holladay, *The Psalms Through Three Thousand Years*; Gillingham, *Psalms Through the Centuries*, vol. 1, ad loc.; and Westermann, *The Living Psalms*, 127-32.

38. See both above, 15-16, and also below, 191-207.

may become applicable to a wide constituency in future times. Thus sundry trials and enemies are spoken about, not least the sins of the psalmist himself. Yet the will of the Lord to lead the psalmist aright is also expressed (vv. 8–10, 13–15), and the psalmist petitions him that he will truly care for this worshipper, guard his life and deliver him from his troubles (vv. 16–18), ever being aware that the psalmist is in the midst of demanding circumstances.

Psalm 26 is another individual lament; here the psalmist protests his innocence, and asks that God will be gracious to him and redeem him. We should take notice in the context of this study that there is emphasis here on the psalmist's love of worship, delighting to "sing aloud a song of thanksgiving" (v. 7), going on to say, "O Lord, I love the house in which you dwell, and the place where your glory abides" (v. 8), ending the psalm with the words "in the great congregation I will bless the Lord" (v. 12).

We have to say about Psalm 27, that it displays two parts and two psalmic emphases, vv. 1–6 making a psalm of confidence, vv. 7–14 another individual lament. Yet, as Curtis observes, apropos this psalm, "Confidence and uncertainty can often go hand in hand in the experience of the worshipper."[39] We may take note of the fact that in this particular manifestation of an individual lament there is at the end the characteristic statement of confidence and hope in the Lord:

> I believe that I shall see the goodness of the Lord
> in the land of the living.
> Wait for the Lord;
> be strong, and let your heart take courage;
> wait for the Lord! (Ps 27:13–14)

Thus considered as a whole we observe that this mixed psalm displays a palistrophic structure: confidence (vv. 1–6), lament (vv. 7–12), confidence (vv. 13–14). One of the characteristic features of faith in the Lord is this close relationship for the worshipper of feelings both of trust and of need.[40]

Psalm 28 sets before us another individual lament, one which clearly falls into three parts. The first part, in vv. 1–5, sets out the lament in which the sufferer cries out to God in a characteristic way, though here, it has to be said, with a somewhat vindictive spirit towards those individuals who are causing him problems, while the second, in vv. 6–7, is the statement that subsequently the psalmist has come to a sense of peace, being confident that the Lord has heard his cries. Thus the psalmist has had his trust and confidence in God restored. The final part in vv. 8–9 is a prayerful expression of

---

39. Curtis, *Psalms*, 59.
40. See the remarks of Mays, *Psalms*, 132–33.

praise. The Lord is praised for his delivering mercies (v. 8), and interceded that such mercies may be extended to the Lord's people in general, that he may "be their shepherd, and carry them forever" (v. 9).

Psalm 29 is a hymn, and the psalm reads as if its background is a storm, with waters, even floods (vv. 3, 10), thunder (v. 3, which is also expressed as the voice of the Lord, vv. 3, 4, 5, 7, 8, 9), and lightning (v. 7). Or is this "storm background" rather material from an original Baal hymn? Is this a polemic against other beings, rather than Yahweh, being in charge of storms?[41] All this is a mighty display of the greatness and power of God, this being acknowledged in vv. 1–3, drawing from worshippers (who seem to be in the temple) the expressive word "Glory!" (v. 9). Here is a hymn of praise to God, also having the note of petition.

Psalm 30 is the first of five thanksgiving psalms, the others being 32, 34, 40 and 41.[42] In fact, the last two psalms of this first book of the Psalter are thanksgiving psalms, thus giving the distinct impression that in the arrangement of the so-called Davidic Psalter there is a clear progression towards, and emphasis upon, an ending bearing the message of thanksgiving. This observation is given added point when it is recalled that this particular collection of psalms does contain a comparatively large number of laments, especially individual laments.

The specific thanksgiving that appears to lie behind Ps 30 is deliverance from death (vv. 2–3, 8–10), and that thus mourning has been turned into dancing, and the wearing of sackcloth can cease (v. 11). Now the psalmist gives praise and thanks to God (v. 12), for the truth about life in the world under God is like this:

> For his anger is but for a moment;
> his favor is for a lifetime.
> Weeping may linger for the night,
> but joy comes with the morning. (Ps 30:5)

Psalm 31 takes us back to the individual lament theme—and after this individual lament there are yet four more of this type of psalm before the end of the first book of the psalter, namely Pss 35, 36, 38, 39. It has to be said that Ps 31 is an extensive psalm bearing the predictable aspects of an individual lament—that is prayer, lament, expression of trust, thanksgiving—and

---

41. See Craigie, *Psalms 1–50*, pp. 243–45; Rodd, "Psalms," 376; Curtis, *Psalms*, 63–64.

42. On the thanksgiving psalms, see, e.g., Day, *Psalms*, 44–5; Brown, *Psalms*, 54–55, 144–47; and Gillingham, *Poems and Psalms*, 222–24.

Craigie could well be correct in his insight that these have been arranged so as to give the psalm a chiastic structure.[43] Thus:

I Prayer
   (1) prayer (vv. 1–5) A
   (2) trust (vv. 6–8) B
   (3) lament (vv. 9–13) C
   (4) trust (v. 14) B'
   (5) prayer (vv. 15–18) A'
II Thanksgiving and praise (vv. 19–24)

One way or another, whether composed as one psalm, or else drawn together from various sources, here again are some of the familiar expressions of worship found in the book of psalms, namely, prayer and lament, along with expressions of trust, praise, and thanksgiving.

Psalm 32 is a thanksgiving psalm, as we have observed one of the compositions of this type that occur in something of a small clutch towards the close of the first book of the psalter. The source of the thanksgiving here is the reality of the divine forgiveness of sins, transgressions, guilt, for "Many are the torments of the wicked, but steadfast love [*hesed*] surrounds those who trust in the Lord" (v. 10).

The next psalm, 33, is one of confidence in the Lord, and in the reality of this there is a call to praise the Lord with the help of lyre, harp, and not forgetting to use a loud voice (v. 1–3). The psalmist then calls people to praise the Lord (vv. 4–5), setting out various reasons for this confident, thankful worship of the Lord: this is for the reason that the Lord has demonstrated his great power in the creation (vv. 6–9); for he directs the ways of humanity (vv. 10–15); he is the one who has the real power and ability in all things (vv. 16–19). This is why his people have confidence in him, so that as well as praising him they should pray for the continued gift of these things (vv. 20–22).

Psalm 34 is another of the thanksgiving psalms, this one being expressed in acrostic form, thus making it, as we might express the matter, an "a to z" of reasons why thanksgiving should be made to God. In the 17th century Nahum Tate and Nicholas Brady composed a paraphrase on this psalm for Christians to sing, "Through all the changing scenes of life." The psalmist here also points to the fact that the way to receiving the Lord's blessings is through the "fear" of the Lord, that is by reverencing him, being

---

43. See Craigie, *Psalms 1–50*, pp. 259–60. Others, however, have questioned this understanding of the psalm, pointing out that there are problems to accepting its unity. See, e.g., Kraus, *Psalms 1–59*, pp. 360–61. See also the discussion in Anderson, *The Book of Psalms*, 1:245–46.

in awe of him (vv. 7, 9, 11), and that at least part of the way to the "fear" of the Lord is through departing from evil and doing good, seeking peace and pursuing it (v. 14).

Psalms 35 and 36 are two further individual laments. The first speaks either of a number of individuals or groups, or else the same person/people who is/are variously described, who cause grief to the psalmist—at least to those for whom the psalmist has prepared this psalm. Again there are the statements of confidence in the Lord's rescue and deliverance of his suffering servant (vv. 9-10, 18, 27-28). In the second, Ps 36, we hear of wicked people, people of iniquity, mischief and deceit, people set on a way that has nothing good in it (36:1-4), but also of the greatness of the steadfast love (*ḥesed*) of the Lord, and the preciousness of the worshipper's relationship with him (vv. 5-8), for above all "For with you is the fountain of life; in your light we see light" (v. 9). The psalm ends with the prayer that this steadfast love and protective presence of the Lord may continue to be given to his faithful people (vv. 10-12).

With Ps 37 we have something different. This is what has been called a Wisdom Psalm, the others being 49; 73; 112; 127; 128; 133; 139.[44] These psalms present something of an intellectual approach—hence the name that they have been given by scholars—whereby they ask questions about particularly difficult problems of life. In each of Pss 37, 49 and 73 the issue is suffering, in particular the sufferings of apparently righteous people, with questions about what is God doing, if he—so-surely possessed of love and strength—is not rescuing those who are suffering?[45] Here in Ps 37 the specific issue concerns what appears to be the prosperity of the wicked. It has to be said that the psalmist does not come up with any solution to this (theodicy) problem, but he has at least aired the matter by posing the question. What, however, he counsels is waiting upon God, maintaining trust in him, and, to express the matter briefly, exercising patience in the face of this problem. As we shall come to see, Pss 49 and 73 do have rather more to say about these very serious theological matters, Ps 73 in particular linking the issue with that of worship.

Psalms 38 and 39 are both individual laments. Psalm 38 reads as if the psalmist's problems are to do with health, and these in a whole variety of ways. He is much stricken, and he interprets this as the judgment of God

---

44. The number of the so-called Wisdom Psalms is variously assessed. See the contribution of Whybray, *Reading the Psalms as a Book*, 36–87. See also Whybray, "The Wisdom Psalms"; Gillingham, *Poems and Psalms*, 228–9; Day, *Psalms*, 54–6; and Brown, *Psalms*, 58, 147–50.

45. For Pss 37, 49, and 73, see Thompson, "*Where is the God of Justice?*," 58–61, 81–84, 100–104.

upon him.[46] Alternatively, it could be that the language of the psalm is intended to be understood in more figurative sense, to indicate great suffering and distress. The psalmist prays for God's presence and help in his plight,

> Do not forsake me, O Lord;
> O my God, do not be far from me;
> make haste to help me,
> O Lord, my salvation. (Ps 38:21–22)

Yet in this individual lament psalm there is no expression of confidence such as is normally present in this type of psalm.

Psalm 39, says Mays, "is a strange prayer."[47] This is because although the language of the psalm is that of the individual lament, the issue at its heart seems to be a general one about the human predicament, here made the greater because of the present sufferings of the psalmist. This, for example, is expressed in v. 6 with its, "Surely everyone goes about like a shadow. Surely for nothing they are in turmoil; they heap up, and do not know who will gather." So Curtis says, "Not surprisingly, this psalm has been classified as a Lament, but in part it would perhaps be more accurately described as a meditation on the transitoriness of human existence and so it has affinities with the Wisdom Literature."[48] The closing words of this psalm have the psalmist pleading with God to hear his cry, but they can hardly be said to brim with confidence:

> Hear my prayer, O Lord,
> and give ear to my cry;
> do not hold your peace at my tears.
> For I am your passing guest,
> an alien, like all my forebears.
> Turn your gaze away from me, that I may smile again,
> before I depart and am no more. (Ps 39:12–13)

The last two psalms in the first of the Psalter's five books, Pss 40 and 41, are both thanksgivings. In Ps 40, vv. 1–10 read rather like a hymn of praise and thanksgiving, what Kraus calls a song of thanksgiving of one who has been rescued, and which he thinks extends to v. 11.[49] But what are we to make of the psalmist's words about sacrifices and offerings in v. 6, and what follows in v. 8 about this worshipper's delight in doing God's will, and that

---

46. On this understanding of suffering as having been caused by human sinfulness see Thompson, "Where is the God of Justice?," 7–21.

47. Mays, *Psalms*, 165.

48. Curtis, *Psalms*, 87–88.

49. Kraus, *Psalms 1–59*, pp. 421–23.

God's law is within his heart? Some would argue that what is being said here makes something of an anti-sacrificial worship argument, and to that it may be observed that there are other psalms that appear to have such an emphasis (e.g. Pss 50:13; 51:6). The issue about whether this is anti-sacrificial talk, or whether it is speaking about offering sacrifice by those who do not have the correct orientation in their hearts and minds, or whether even it is intended to be speaking of a different kind of worship than offering sacrifices, a worship maybe that comes out of the historical setting when there was no temple in which sacrifices could be offered, is one that is subject to ongoing debate.[50]

The second part of Ps 40, vv. 11–17, gives a certain impression of being a lament, and so it is understood by some. Equally, others—and this is the approach taken in the present work—regard this second part of the psalm as expressing the prayer of the psalmist that the Lord may keep him safe from harm and distress. The closing words of the psalm speak of the psalmist's confidence in, and also continuing need of the Lord's help:

> As for me, I am poor and needy,
> but the Lord takes thought for me.
> You are my help and my deliverer;
> do not delay, O my God. (Ps 40:17)

Psalm 41, another thanksgiving, again acknowledges the psalmist's continuing need of the Lord, yet is redolent with the note of thanksgiving that the Lord has delivered him from his problems (vv. 4–12). Indeed, the psalmist avers that those who live lives of similar caring for their neighbors will indeed know for themselves, in their own lives, the protecting and delivering presence of the Lord (vv. 1–3).

After Ps 41 comes a doxology which seems intended to conclude the first book of the psalter (v. 13). It is surely of some significance that this concluding word is one of doxology, rather than being of, for example, a gnomic nature, something let us say from the Hebrew Bible's wisdom tradition. Surely the presence and the usage of a doxology here—and also at the ends of the other books of the psalms—does something to establishing and making clear the relationship of the books of the psalms with the world of worship, the world of the cult. The book of Psalms is surely above all a worship book.

---

50. On this, see Kraus, *Psalms 1–59*, pp. 426–27; Curtis, *Psalms*, 90–91; Anderson, *The Book of Psalms*, 1:316–8; Rowley, "The Meaning of Sacrifice in the Old Testament"; and Whybray, "The Interpretation of Ritual Sacrifice," in *Reading the Psalms as a Book*, 100–117.

The Second Book of the Psalter

This comprises Pss 42–72, and like the First Book (Pss 2–41), many of these psalms are attributed to David. Further, at the conclusion of the last psalm here (72) there is, once again, an extended doxology, this one finishing with the words "The prayers of David son of Jesse are ended." Once more, it is the individual laments that are by far the most numerous of the psalm types in this Second Book of the Psalter. Counting Pss 42 and 43 as one psalm, there are 13 individual laments in this book, 2 communal laments, 2 royal psalms, 3 hymns, 1 wisdom psalm, 4 thanksgivings, 1 confidence psalm, and 4 others. We should also notice that these Pss 42–72, along with Pss 73–83 together make up what has been called the Elohistic Psalter, this from the fact that in Pss 42–83 there is a predominant usage of "God" (Elohim)—in fact over 240 times against around just 40 occurrences of "the Lord" (Yahweh).[51]

As has already been indicated I now follow a different procedure in this part of the study of the psalms and worship: whereas for Pss 1–41 I proceeded a psalm at a time, now, having introduced a majority of the main types of psalms, I shall proceed more synoptically, considering first the individual laments, then the communal laments, and so on until all the types of psalms in this particular book of the psalter have briefly been considered.

First then, the numerous individual laments that occur in this Second Book of the Psalter. There are no less than 13 of these (counting Pss 42 and 43 as one psalm), namely, Pss 42+43, 51, 54, 55, 56, 57, 59, 61, 63, 64, 69, 70, 71. We have already seen that these individual lament psalms are numerous in the First Book of the Psalter, and this continues to be so here in the Second. That is, there continues that strong emphasis on these compositions where an individual is portrayed as crying out to God because of their current distressing experiences of life, frequently speaking too of the deliverance they have experienced, and so witnessing to delivering mercies of the Lord. Further, this would seem to be indicative of the fact that for those who were responsible for the compilation and present arrangement of the various psalms there was serious provision made for this aspect of an individual worshipper crying out to God and thereby seeking help, comfort, and strength. The sheer size of the provision of this particular material for worship demonstrates what must surely have been its perceived importance and significance in the estimation of at least some of those responsible for passing on these writings for later generations of worshippers. It may be noted in passing that in the Third, Fourth, and Fifth Books of the Psalter the number of individual laments reduces dramatically. As we have paid

---

51. In Pss 3–41 there are over 270 references to God as "Yahweh" (the Lord), while there are less than 50 instances of "Elohim" (God, or gods).

considerable attention to examples of this type of psalm, accordingly the treatment now can be brief, and it will be sufficient to take note of Pss 42 and 43, and also 51.

Although Pss 42 and 43 have come down to us in the Hebrew—and also in the Septuagint and the Vulgate—as two distinct psalms, there are factors that suggest we should consider them as one. Not only are they both individual laments, but they also have a common refrain (42:5, 11; 43:5). Further, Ps 43 does *not* have a title, whereas most of the psalms in the Second Book of the Psalter do have titles. Moreover, not only do the two psalms exhibit the same sort of language, but they are also in the same Hebrew poetic meter. The thought of the combined psalm is straightforward in that the psalmist is apparently passing through difficult times in which things for him do not seem to be going as they used to (42:4, 6–10; 43:1–2), and this is why the psalmist is so "cast down" (42:5a, 11a; 43:5a), yet he continues to hope in God (42:5b, 11b; 43:5b). Thus the psalmist makes his plea, doing so in a real sense of confidence and hope:

> O send out your light and your truth;
> let them lead me;
> let them bring me to your holy hill
> and to your dwelling.
> Then I will go to the altar of God,
> to God my exceeding joy;
> and I will praise you with the harp,
> O God, my God. (Ps 43:3–4)

So continues the Psalter's strong tradition of setting out these prayers of crying out to God in the face of suffering and distress, and so passing them on for the use of future generations of worshippers.

Then there is Ps 51, a psalm that is generally regarded as being an individual lament, but in which the lamentation concerns the psalmist's deep sense of unworthiness and sinfulness. In the part of the psalm where normally the psalmist's lament would be spelled out, here it is replaced by the psalmist's confession of sin (vv. 10–17), this having been preceded in vv. 1–9 by an agonized statement by the psalmist of his sinful condition. It is a psalm that is reckoned as being one of the Christian Church's Penitential Psalms, the others being Pss 6, 32, 38, 102, 130, and 143. The last two verses of the psalm (vv. 18–19) give the impression that they are something of an addition to what precedes: they plead for a renewal of Jerusalem, not only of religious observances and rites there (v. 19), but also (v. 18) in regard to the rebuilding of its walls! This is a remarkable and important psalm that makes a particular contribution to what the Hebrew Bible has to say about worship in times past—perhaps in the days of Nehemiah?[52]—but also what it has to contribute to the worship of the Lord since then. As Zenger expresses the matter, "With its dialectic of radical knowledge/acknowledgement of sin and new creation, by the merciful God, Psalm 51, which has enjoyed a significant reception in both Jewish and Christian liturgy (including the Yom Kippur liturgy, and as an ecclesial penitential psalm par excellence), is one of the 'peak texts' in biblical tradition. . . . [T]he principal statement of the psalm is the confidence in a gracious God that is expressed in its opening words."[53]

Psalms 44 and 60 make up the two communal laments in this part of the psalter, in the first of these the complaint being that while God in past times appears to have cared for and rescued his people (44:1–8), latterly he seems to have afflicted them (44:9–16), even of apparently selling his "people for a trifle" (v. 12), rather as if they were of little worth. Verses 17–22 have the people maintaining their innocence, and then calling upon God to rise up and help them (vv. 23–26). Thus this psalm, although setting forth a nation's expression of complaint and distress, does not have any expression of actual, even anticipated, deliverance.

Nor does the other communal lament in this part of the psalter, Ps 60, have an unambiguous expression of the removal of distress—which is hardly surprising when the nation seems to be overwhelmed with various enemies. This psalm is noteworthy for its extended title, and at the same time it has a certain notoriety for modern readers through its presentation of the Lord as domineering, and at times of a somewhat martial nature. After all, this is the psalm that has God saying, "Moab is my washbasin; on Edom I hurl my shoe; over Philistia I shout in triumph" (Ps 60:8).[54]

There are two royal psalms in the Second Book of the Psalter, Pss 45 and 72, the first of these most likely being, as Kraus entitles it, "A Song for the Marriage of the King".[55] The second is Ps 72, and it certainly presents a picture of the ideal Israelite kingship. Alas that for so much of the time the reality in ancient Israel fell well short of this ideal.[56]

---

52. For a brief discussion as to a possible date of this psalm's composition, see, e.g., Anderson, *The Book of Psalms*, 1:390; Hossfeld and Zenger, *Psalms 2*, p. 18; and Kraus, *Psalms 1–59*, p. 501.

53. Hossfeld and Zenger, *Psalms 2*, p. 25.

54. Hossfeld and Zenger, *Psalms 2*, p. 94, say "Psalm 60 is a 'political' psalm. As such it presents numerous problems to the interpreter, both from a historical and from a theological point of view."

55. Kraus, *Psalms 1–59*, p. 450.

56. For further consideration of these two psalms, see above, 91–97.

There is just one confidence psalm in this part of the Psalter, Ps 62. It speaks of God alone being the psalmist's rock, salvation, fortress (vv. 2, 6), and that thus all should put their trust in him, pouring out their hearts (presumably in prayer) to him, for he is "a refuge for us" (v. 8). Here indeed is surely a call to worship the Lord God of Israel and to trust in him.

Psalms 46, 47, and 48 make up three hymns, all of which extol and glorify the Lord, and it is arguable that there is a relationship between them: there seems to be a link between them through the city of Jerusalem and the temple. Perhaps it is going too far to regard them as a trilogy that was intended to celebrate the remarkable deliverance of the city from the Assyrian threat, when during the reign of Hezekiah, Sennacherib laid siege to Jerusalem but did not succeed in his conquest of it, yet the theme of these three psalms *is* the greatness and the trustworthiness of the Lord for the welfare of his people and the city of Jerusalem. "God is our refuge and strength, a very present help in trouble" affirms Ps 46:1, while in Ps 47:7 there are the words, "For God is the king of all the earth; sing praises with a psalm", and in Ps 48:1 "Great is the Lord and greatly to be praised in the city of our God." This trio of psalms ends in 48:14 with the affirmation that "this is our God, our God forever and ever. He will be our guide forever." Here again in these three psalms is praise of God set forth clearly.

The following psalm, 49, is another of the so-called Wisdom Psalms and, as with Ps 37, deals with the subject of the suffering of those who appear to be righteous. If Ps 37 has begun to open up this subject for discussion, we may say that Ps 49 has rather more to say about the topic than the first. There is an emphasis in Ps 49 on the transitoriness of earthly life, that "Mortals cannot abide in their pomp; they are like the animals that perish" (Ps 49:12 and compare v. 20). Rather, any hope that the people of earth may have must be in the Lord, and it does seem that in this psalm there is some advance taking place in the direction of a belief in a life after death. This is expressed in v. 15 with its "But God will ransom my soul from the power of Sheol, for he will receive me." Perhaps this is not (yet) a belief in life after death, but it would certainly seem to be a move in that direction.[57]

We now need to consider three psalms which are somewhat different, and not amenable to the categories we have been using hitherto. However, a feature held in common by Pss 50, 52, and 58 is that their style and content are reminiscent of the sort of material that we find in the prophetical material in the Hebrew Bible. Thus they are described by some scholars as prophetic exhortations or prophetic liturgies.[58] In Ps 50, for example, the

---

57. For a fuller treatment of Ps 49 see my *"Where is the God of Justice?,"* 81–84.

58. On these psalms of prophetic exhortation see, Gillingham, *Poems and Psalms,*

issue appears to be to do with correct sacrifices, and the literary form of the psalm is that of a word spoken by God to his people. Certain parts of this psalm—see especially vv. 7–15—may give the impression that it is against the whole sacrificial system, but it could be that what is being called for here is the right attitude to making sacrificial offerings, such as we find in the prophetic books of Isaiah, Amos, Micah, Jeremiah.[59] Rather, let sacrifice be accompanied by thankful hearts on the part of the worshippers, for then will come to them the blessings of God: "Those who bring thanksgiving as their sacrifice honor me; to those who go the right way I will show the salvation of God" (Ps 50:23). There is certainly a word here for both leaders of worship and the worshippers themselves about correct attitudes towards what it is they lead and in which they engage.[60]

Psalm 52 in parts displays features of a prophetic exhortation, but the matter is not straightforward, in that while vv. 1–5 do indeed read like words of prophetic judgment, and are frequently likened to the judgment in Isa 22:15–18, at the same time it has been argued that vv. 6–7 have a "wisdom" feel about them and have been associated with Pss 37, 49, and 73, and further that vv. 8–9 with their confident tone of trust in the Lord look rather like the ending of a psalm of individual lament. We perhaps have to say that this is a mixed psalm, but that its first five verses do display like features to the thought of Ps 50.[61]

We have already observed the similarity of Pss 14 and 53.[62] Thus we can go on to Ps 58 which it is argued should be regarded as a prophetic exhortation. Here there is an emphasis upon justice, in particular that so many go astray from the ways of justice, and an assurance that in the end "People will say, 'Surely there is a reward for the righteous; surely there is a God who judges on earth'" (Ps 58:11). Once again, we have the suggestion that this note of justice, and the talk of the presence of the God of justice on earth (cf. Mal 2:17), was intended by at least some of those responsible for the book of psalms to be sounded and heard in the Jerusalem temple cult.[63]

226–7.

59. See below, 240–75 for the prophets and worship.

60. On Ps 50 see also Whybray, *Reading the Psalms as a Book*, 103–4; Craigie, *Psalms 1–50*, pp. 361–67.

61. For a full consideration see the detailed treatment of Hossfeld and Zenger, *Psalms 2*, pp. 26–34.

62. See above, 130, 130n25. For a thorough examination of the literary relationship between Pss 14 and 53, see Hossfeld and Zenger, *Psalms 2*, pp. 35–44.

63. On these aspects of Ps 58 see Tate, *Psalms 51–100*, pp. 84–85; but cf. Hossfeld and Zenger, *Psalms 2*, p. 79.

Before we come to the end of the Second Book of the Psalter (Pss 42–72) we should pay attention to four thanksgiving psalms, namely Pss 65, 66, 67, and 68. These make up a distinctive small group of psalms that, as it were, break into their surrounding psalms, those being psalms of individual lament (Pss 63, 64 and 69, 70, and 71), surely giving the impression of deliberate design in the arrangement. The distinctive words in the four thanksgiving psalms are clearly "praise," either in the grammatical form of a noun or a verb (65:1; 66:2, 4; 67:3 (twice), 5 (twice); 68:4, 32), or in the word "sing" (65:13; 66:2, 4; 67:4; 68:4, 32). The reasons for these outpourings of thanksgiving to God are for what he has done and still *is* doing for his people by forgiving them their sins (65:1–3), for his might and wisdom in creation (65:5–8), for his provision for his people (65:9–13), indeed for all that God has done for his people (66:1–20 and 67:1–7), for being the Lord who so wondrously has led his people through their historical pilgrimage, in particular all the way from Sinai to Zion, from the wilderness to the promised land and its city of Jerusalem (68:1–35). As Hossfeld and Zenger observe, "For a long time now the Psalm group 65–68 has stood out in relation to its neighboring psalms. It constitutes a cluster of hymns/songs of thanksgiving and, unlike the overwhelmingly individual lament in its context, it speaks in the 'we' of prayer."[64] Perhaps the theme of all four of these psalms is encapsulated in the closing words of the last of them:

> Ascribe power to God,
> whose majesty is over Israel;
> and whose power is in the skies.
> Awesome is God in his sanctuary,
> the God of Israel;
> he gives power and strength to his people.
> Blessed be God! (Ps 68:34–35)

Here are further notes that it would appear were sounded in the worship of the people of Israel—or at least it was believed *should* be sounded in that worship.

The Third Book of the Psalter

This book runs from Ps 73 to Ps 89, a total of 17 psalms, the largest single type found here being the 7 corporate laments (74, 77, 79, 80, 82, 83, 85). Then, and in decreasing order of frequency, there are 3 hymns, 2 prophetical

---

64. Hossfeld and Zenger, *Psalms 2*, p. 141.

exhortations, 2 individual laments, 1 wisdom psalm, 1 historical psalm, 1 royal psalm.

There is, however, what appears to be a certain emphasis in this book of the psalter, not only in there being no less than 7 psalms (out of a total of only 17 in this book) of corporate lament, but also in that it begins with another of the wisdom psalms in which the equation of the devout life and success in worldly life is questioned (Ps 73), and also at the end another of the royal psalms, but the one in particular that agonizes over what appears to be the demise of the Davidic kingship in Jerusalem.

But first, Ps 73 which continues a theme already introduced in Pss 37 and 49,[65] concerning the theological problem occasioned by the prosperity of apparently sinful people and at the same time the sufferings of the apparently righteous. We should take note of the fact that it has been suggested, in particular by Brueggemann, that Ps 73 occupies theologically a significant place here at around the mid-point of the Psalter. Brueggemann has argued that Pss 1 and 150 set the boundaries for faith in the book of psalms, this being in terms of obedience (Ps 1) and praise (Ps 150). While he understands Pss 25 and 103 as representing a movement beyond torah-piety, he also suggests that Ps 73 occupies "a peculiar and crucial position in the larger drama of protest and affirmation."[66] It is indeed true that within the Psalter there is a general movement towards praise and affirmation, this being from the theme of obedience as expressed in Ps 1, and in the widespread presence of the lament psalms in the earlier parts of the Psalter. Yet towards the end of the Psalter the hymns appear to have a dominant place. Further, it can be argued that at the mid-point of the psalter there is Ps 73 which in its context in the psalter, as it were, looks both backward and also forward. For Ps 73 begins by affirming the doctrine of the goodness of God to the upright and pure in heart (Ps 73:1), going on to ask questions about the justice of God in the world in the light of the perceived prosperity of the wicked (vv. 3–9), and yet ending with the affirmation that despite everything the psalmist has confidence in the ongoing love, care and provision of the Lord for himself (vv. 21–26). Thus the psalmist of Ps 73 does present a renewed sense of praiseful affirmation. Nevertheless, this psalmist has not been able to put forward any intellectual solution to the problem of the prosperity of the wicked, but yet in moving terms and tones he speaks of his conviction concerning the preciousness and abiding worth for himself of his relationship with the Lord. This leads him to declare:

> Whom have I in heaven but you?

---

65. See above, 137, 143.
66. Brueggemann, "Bounded by Obedience and Praise," 92.

And there is nothing on earth that I desire other than you.
My flesh and my heart may fail,
but God is the strength of my heart and my portion forever.
(Ps 73:25–26)

The psalmist also speaks positively about God guiding him with his (God's) counsel (v. 24a), but when he goes on to say that "afterward you [God] will receive me with honor" though he uses few words, each of them comes replete with problems of translation and understanding, that we cannot be sure just what meaning is intended.[67] Yet in the context of this particular study what should be noted is the fact that for the psalmist, grappling as he is with the problem of the justice of God, his great moment of change comes as he turns to the realm of worship and cult, "until I went into the sanctuary of God; then I perceived their end" (v. 17). If it is really so that Ps 73 does stand at this crucial place in the drama of protest and affirmation, it also witnesses to the psalmist's understanding of the centrality and importance of worship in the living of, and the possible beginnings of some understanding of, the meaning of earthly life.

With Ps 74 we come to the first of the seven communal laments that might be said to make up something like the backbone of this Third Book of the Psalter. It appears to be a difficult situation that lies behind this psalm. There is talk of foes, enemies (vv. 4–8, 18–19, 23), and of the ruins of Zion and other places (vv. 2–8), and it is probable that the situation spoken about is that following the Babylonian destruction of Jerusalem and other places in the land of Judah in 586/7 BCE. Thus the people ask "why" this can be so, and "how long" this suffering and abasement must endure (vv. 9–11). Not surprisingly, God is implored by his people to act for the good, in particular the rescue, of his people, above all to use again his power that has been seen in the past (vv. 12–17), to have regard for the covenant that he made with them (vv. 20–22), and not to ignore that "uproar of [his] adversaries that goes up continually" (v. 23). It has to be said that this psalm lacks a clear statement and expression of hope for a different sort of future for the city and people of God. There are further expressions of corporate lament in Ps 77, a psalm in which God is reminded about what powers he wrought against evil forces in the exodus events (Ps 77:11–20), and again in Ps 79, this latter most likely coming from the national situation after 586/7 BCE (see especially vv. 1–4). Psalm 80 is perhaps of northern Israelite provenance to judge from the references to Ephraim, Benjamin, and Manasseh in v. 2, but just what was the particular catastrophe being spoken about we cannot

---

67. The details are in the standard commentaries and also in my *"Where is the God of Justice?,"* 100–4.

be sure. In all of such psalms we have to bear in mind that some of their more precise details about sufferings being endured have most likely been generalized to various extents in order to be useful for future generation of sufferers in *their* seeking of and worshipping the Lord.

Psalm 82, though another of the corporate laments, is rather different. The picture is here presented of God presiding over a council of the gods, these gods being envisaged as the deities of other nations (v. 1), and challenging them about "How long will you judge unjustly and show partiality to the wicked?" (v. 2). God, that is the true God, Israel's God, challenges the other gods to give justice to the weak and orphans, to maintain the right of the lowly and destitute, to rescue the weak and needy from the grasp of the wicked (vv. 3-4). Then comes the truth of the matter: these are useless gods, having neither knowledge nor understanding (v. 5), who while they may be gods are not in fact immortal, and will die—just as mortals do, even princes (vv. 6-7). Thus the community—and this is where the communal lament makes itself heard—cries out to God "Rise up, O God, judge the earth; for all the nations belong to you!" (v. 8). This is a prayer that justice may be known in the world.

The theme of Ps 83 is the apparent threat by a number of enemies against the Lord's people, who wish to defeat Israel (vv. 1-8). Therefore the psalmist implores God to do something about redressing this desperate situation, and it has to be said does this in extremely harsh language (vv. 9-17) that causes difficulties for Christians (so also Pss 58 and 109). This is another communal lament in which the nation cries out to God, here addressed as "the Lord," and "the Most High," to act with justice and might for his own people (v. 18).

How different is the style and language of Ps 85, the last of the corporate laments in the Third Book in the Psalter. Its language is moderate, so different from what appears in Ps 83. Here the Lord is reminded of his acts of mercy and forgiveness to his people in times past (vv. 1-3). God is asked to act once again in this way (vv. 4-6); may he show steadfast love to his people, granting them his salvation (v. 7). The psalmist speaks as in a quiet, yet firm, confidence that the Lord will do this (vv. 8-9). Thus he can end his psalm on a calm and peaceful note:

> Steadfast love and faithfulness will meet;
> righteousness and peace will kiss each other.
> Faithfulness will spring up from the ground,
> and righteousness will look down from the sky.
> The Lord will give what is good,
> and our land will yield its increase.

> Righteousness will go before him,
> and will make a path for his steps. (Ps 85:10-13)

There are in this part of the Psalter, as well as these seven psalms of corporate lament just two individual laments, Pss 86 and 88. The first of these speaks of the psalmist crying out to God to hear his prayer for he is "poor and needy" (Ps 86:1), and moves along predictable lines for this type of psalm. Here, as well as there being the expressed complaint of an individual person (vv. 1-7), there is also an extended statement of the psalmist's confidence in God, which in v. 15 includes the words "But you, O Lord, are a God merciful and gracious, slow to anger and abounding in steadfast love and faithfulness." This description of God is found in a number of places in the Hebrew Bible, and in all three parts of it, in the Torah, in the Prophets, and in the Writings, and will be considered further below.[68] Then there is Ps 88, what Tate describes as "A Bitter Prayer of Distress,"[69] and indeed it is, for this individual lament is taken up completely with the psalmist's distress, and there is no appearance here of the customary expression of confidence in the Lord.

In the Third Book of the Psalter there are two psalms of Prophetic Exhortation, Pss 75 and 81. Psalm 75 exalts in the wondrous deeds of the Lord, and expresses a great sense of confidence that this might of God will be known again in the world and will right many wrongs, and that thus God will cut off "the horns of the wicked" and exalt the horns (used again as a symbol of strength) of the righteous (v. 10). Psalm 81 speaks expansively of offering much and varied praise to God, for he is indeed the God who does such great things for his people; this is what the "voice" of the psalm is proclaiming, what is regarded in this work as the prophetic exhortation that is being uttered in the name of the Lord. This is the God, this psalm affirms, who desires for his people:

> I would feed you with the finest of the wheat,
> and with honey from the rock I would satisfy you. (Ps 81:16)

Then to be considered are the three hymns found in the Third Book of the Psalter, Pss 76, 84, and 87. We have already come across this type of psalm, in particular in the case of Ps 8. Psalm 76 is a hymn of praise uttered about the greatness of God, in particular for the victory he has wrought over his enemies, that is, over the enemies of the people of the psalmist! God is envisaged in this psalm as dwelling on Mount Zion (vv. 1-2), and as defending the city from enemy attack (v. 3). Thus there is great cause to praise this

---

68. See below, 192-95.
69. Tate, *Psalms 51-100*, p. 393.

mighty and caring Lord (vv. 4–9), and to bring gifts and make vows to him (vv. 10–12), and for all to be in awe of him (v. 7).

The envisaged scene in Ps 84 is very different. Here there is no clash of armies, yet what is presented is an equal enthusiasm to worship the Lord in the temple on Zion. The psalm speaks movingly of the joy of anticipated worship in the temple even as the worshippers make their journey, indeed their pilgrimage, to Zion (vv. 5–7), for in that setting of dedication to worship and the seeking of the Lord in the holy place, there is provision for all manner of people, even more, a place for the smallest of the birds (vv. 3–4). Indeed, how great is the joy of the worshippers in that holy place (vv. 10–12)!

Then Ps 87, with its tremendous affirmations of praise that Zion is the city of God, of which glorious things are spoken (vv. 1–3). Alas that there are so many textual and interpretive problems in this psalm. What is the meaning of the talk about Rahab and Babylon, Philistia, Tyre and Ethiopia in v. 4? Are there Jewish proselytes in these countries that are being envisaged, or are they (imagined?) Gentile countries looking to Zion as the religious center of the world? Or are these nations being pictured as making their way in great pilgrimage to Jerusalem? For a recent discussion see for example the commentary by Hossfeld and Zenger, who lay emphasis on the privilege and joy of citizenship in Zion, and who aver that v. 7 is a picture of "the time when . . . the nations, together with Israel, learn and live the order of law and peace willed by YHWH, then and there truly paradisiacal times will begin . . . The psalm clings to this utopia—in a contemporary context full of hostile unrest and in which Jerusalem was anything but a peaceful place."[70]

Now a psalm with a difference, and a long psalm at that. This is Ps 78, which reads like a historical narrative, but which also sounds hymnic notes. Thus Mowinckel described it as "a synopsis of sacred history in the style of a hymn."[71] Arnold Anderson gave this psalm the title, "Praise to the Lord of History", while Marvin Tate had "The Riddle of God and Israel from Zoan to Zion."[72] For thus indeed does this (long) psalm, after introducing its subject in somewhat wisdom-like language (vv. 1–7), trace the story of Israel under the guidance and strength of the Lord from Zoan in Egypt (vv. 12, 43), through the wilderness, and in spite of much sinfulness and fickleness until they came at last to Zion. The psalm speaks of the Lord choosing Judah as his people rather than Ephraim (vv. 67–69), and of his giving them David,

---

70. See Hossfeld and Zenger, *Psalms 2*, pp. 379–82, and 385 for the quotation.
71. Mowinckel, *The Psalms in Israel's Worship*, 2:112.
72. Anderson, *The Book of Psalms*, 2:561; and Tate, *Psalms 51–100*, p. 277.

an erstwhile shepherd of sheep, to be the shepherd of the Lord's people, here called Jacob (vv. 70-72). This appropriately-called historical psalm makes the point that "no matter how heinous the infidelity, God stands ready to begin again."[73] This too would seem to be an aspect of Israel's faith that had a place in temple worship on Mount Zion, that is, an honest confession of human sinfulness along with a sense of wonder at the even greater measure of divine forgiveness for the chosen people. It is further worthy of note that all this historical account, both the Lord's provisions for and deliverances of his people, and at the same time the people's suffering and strife, all are here set out that they may be both rejoiced and grieved over in the worship of the Lord. Finally in Book Three of the Psalter is a Royal Psalm, Ps 89, a psalm that has already been considered.[74]

Thus ends the Third Book of the Psalter, a Book we may recall that began with Ps 73 asking questions about the fate of the faithful and the prosperity of the wicked, continuing with a certain concentration of psalms of corporate lament (Pss 74, 77, 79, 80, 82, 83, 85), and with three interspersed hymns (76, 84, 87), two prophetical exhortations (75, 81), two individual laments (86, 88), one historical psalm (78), and coming to its conclusion with the end of the Israelite monarchy in Jerusalem (89). Whatever may be the possible dating of the individual psalms in this Book, and whatever may be the date to be assigned to the completed Book Three of the Psalter, it certainly ends by bringing us in thought to the Babylonian destruction of Jerusalem in 586/7 BCE, and perhaps also during the course of our reading it to a sense of tragedy and impending tragedy. There are here indeed weighty matters that make up the content of these psalms and so also of the national worship for which they were presumably intended.

The Fourth Book of the Psalter

This runs from Ps 90 to Ps 106, as with the Third Book (Pss 73 to 89) a total of seventeen psalms. Yet the balance of the different types of psalms is changed once again between Books Three and Four of the Psalter. The number of laments is down, only one individual lament against the earlier two, and only three communal laments against the earlier seven. The significant difference is that whereas in Book Three there were no psalms of confidence, now there is one, and whereas there were only three hymns now in the Fourth Book there are no less than eight.

---

73. Clifford, "In Zion and David a New Beginning," see p. 138.
74. On Psalm 89, see above, 94-95.

We should perhaps begin with the three corporate laments: this Book both begins and ends with corporate laments, Ps 90 at the beginning, 94 coming a few psalms later, and the Book ending with the third, 106. Thus there is a certain continuity here with that aura of suffering and strife that we noted in Book Three of the Psalter, and also indeed in the two earlier Books. Psalm 90 speaks about the eternity of the Lord and about, in marked contrast, the shortness of the human span of life. The opening verses of the psalm speak of the eternity of God (vv. 1–2), with a return to this theme in v. 4, while between in vv. 3, 5–6 there is talk again about God's eternity. Then in vv. 7–11 human sinfulness and frailty is spoken about, which leads to the plea that the Lord will teach the humans to number their (few) days (v. 12). So (vv. 13–17), may the Lord favorably remember these short-lived and fallible human beings.

Thus this corporate lament (Ps 90) is rather different from those we have come across earlier in the psalter, insofar as it is not concerned with the problems posed by superior human foes, but rather by a more general human condition, the human shortness of life (and no doubt the generally accepted understanding of there being little hope of life after death), and human sinfulness. We shall return to this theme when we consider Ps 106. Meanwhile there is Ps 94, a more familiar example of corporate lament, where the people's plight lies in seeking to deal with superior enemies, and where the question is asked about the presence of God with those who suffer in these ways. Yet here is the familiar reassuring and confident word about the Lord's presence with his suffering people (Ps 94:22–23).[75]

With Psalm 106, however, we are back to the theme of Israel's inveterate sinfulness, and the difficulties into which that has brought the nation. Some argue that this is another historical psalm, like Pss 78 and 105, in that there is a recital of historical events in the life of the people of Israel. Yet the theme here is not so much the Lord's guidance of his people through history, rather that their history has been one of gross and frequent sinfulness and wrongdoing. It thus seems better to regard it as a corporate lament, and then that we should take cognizance of the fact that the two corporate laments that top and tail this particular book of the Psalter are both laments over the sad and inveterate sinfulness of the chosen people of God.

---

75. The point is frequently made that the second part of this psalm reads like an individual lament, and thus some read the whole psalm as made up of a communal lament in vv. 1–7, and an individual lament in vv. 16–23, with material in vv. 8–15 common to both parts. Others regard it as a single, and communal, lament, as I do. For consideration of the question, see Tate, *Psalms 51–100*, pp. 485–90; and Hossfeld and Zenger, *Psalms 2*, pp. 452–53.

There is then a series of once-occurring types of psalms in this Book, all these types being those we have met earlier. Psalm 91 is a psalm of confidence in which the psalmist says he will address the Lord as, "My refuge and my fortress; my God, in whom I trust." The following psalm, 92, is one of thanksgiving, in which the psalmist speaks of praising God morning and evening, upon various musical instruments, and with singing (vv. 1–4). Psalm 95 is another of what have been called prophetic exhortations (see above on Pss 50; 52; 58): this begins with a call to worship, and it then exhorts the worshippers to learn from the experiences of their ancestors in times past. Then Ps 101 is a royal psalm, which with its talk of the king's determination to maintain justice (v. 1) reminds us of Ps 72, another royal psalm, and of the royal vow to root out the wicked in the land, to cut off evildoers from the city of the Lord (v. 8).[76]

Psalm 102 is an individual lament which runs along predictable lines with an extended complaint section in vv. 1–24, followed by words of hope and assurance in vv. 25–28. Psalm 105 is a so-called historical psalm which, like the earlier Ps 78, gives a recital of the saving activity of God through his people's history. The beginning of the psalm speaks of giving thanks to God (v. 1), and the ending has "Praise the Lord!" (v. 45).

Thus we come to what we might call—to use an earlier image—the backbone of this particular book of the Psalter. For here in the Fourth Book we have no less than eight hymns, the greatest concentration of this type of psalm that is to be found in the Psalter,[77] these being Pss 93, 96, 97, 98, 99, 100, 103, 104. The first of these, Ps 93, is a brief psalm, one with no title, but full of a spirit of praise that expresses the majesty and glory of God, in particular speaking of his divine kingship over the world. While not wishing to subscribe to the theory that there was in Jerusalem an annual ceremony of Yahweh's kingship, we can see that divine kingship is the emphasis here, and that thus Ps 93, along with Pss 47, 96, 97, 98, 99, has been called an Enthronement Psalm. Certainly these psalms make up a powerful group of hymns of praise to the divine king of all the earth, and they not only call upon all people to join in praise of him, but also provide words for their worship. Thus, for example:

76. On Ps 101, see above, 95.

77. There are indeed a further thirteen hymns to be found in the Fifth Book of the Psalter (Pss 107–150), but in the total of 44 psalms that is a lower concentration than the earlier eight hymns out of a total of seventeen psalms in Book Four (Pss 90–106). On the other hand there is a different sort of concentration of the hymns in Book Five in that the last six psalms of the whole book of psalms are all hymns. It is certainly correct to observe that while there is a certain concentration of laments, and in particular the individual laments, at the beginning of the whole book, they do give way to an emphasis on hymns at and by the end.

> Ascribe to the Lord, O families of the peoples,
> ascribe to the Lord glory and strength.
> Ascribe to the Lord the glory due his name;
> bring an offering, and come into his courts.
> Worship the Lord in holy splendor;
> tremble before him, all the earth. (Ps 96:7–9)

Thus the make-up of the fourth book of the Psalter suggests that the fullness of worship not only acknowledges the problems and difficulties experienced by those who would worship the Lord, but includes exalted thoughts and words about the mighty and mysterious Lord of the covenant and the world.

The Fifth Book of the Psalter

This runs from Ps 107 to Ps 150, and is by far the largest Book in the Psalter. In ascending order of frequency it is made up of the following numbers of the psalm types we have been using: liturgy 1; Psalm 119, a psalm all on its own; royal psalms 3; communal laments 4; psalms of confidence 4; Wisdom 5; thanksgivings 6; individual laments 7; hymns 13.

The sole so-called liturgy psalm here is Ps 134, and it invites worshippers to bless the Lord.[78] We should note that this is the last of a total of fifteen psalms that bear the title "A Song of Ascents", this group beginning with Ps 120 and including all the psalms between that and Ps 134. This title may indeed indicate ascending, going up, to the temple in Jerusalem. The grouping is made up of a mixture of psalm types, and it is nearly the same grouping as the Great Hallel (Pss 120–136). Once again it is clear that within the psalter there are various different groupings of the psalms, perhaps coming from different times in the growth of the psalter and from different concerns for groups and arrangements of individual psalms.

Then there is Ps 119, a psalm that is different from anything else in the psalter, and moreover on a scale all of its own. With its extensive and highly elaborate acrostic arrangement, with reference one way or another to God in every verse, it looks like a compositional virtue performance on the part of an individual or a group who wished to stress the importance and significance of the Torah in the life and worship of Israel.

There are then three royal psalms in this book of the Psalter, Pss 110, 132, 144, where once again—and in spite of what has been said earlier in Ps 89—it is emphasized that the earthly king had a vital role to play in securing

---

78. On the matter of liturgy, see Gillingham, *Poems and Psalms*, 225–26; and see below, 191–207.

good life for his people; how much in need of the Lord's help was this king; how blessed were the people under his beneficent reign.[79]

Here, too, are communal laments, four of them, namely Pss 108, 123, 126, 137. These exhibit the familiar notes of this psalm type, the last, Ps 137, clearly coming from the bitter experience of exile in Babylon, and haunting in its lamenting. Psalm 137:8 would seem to be referring to Edomite incursions into the near-deserted Jerusalem in exilic times, while it is widely agreed in both Jewish and Christian circles that v. 9 has extremely harsh imprecatory words.

There are also the four confidence psalms, Pss 115, 121, 125, and 131. Psalm 115 is part of the Egyptian Hallel (see below on Ps 113), while Ps 121 is famous for its deep assurance of the help from the Lord there is for people: "The Lord will keep your going out and your coming in from this time on and forevermore" (v. 8). Then Ps 125 begins with the words, "Those who trust in the Lord are like Mount Zion, which cannot be moved, but abides forever" (v. 1), while Ps 131 ends on the note "O Israel, hope in the Lord from this time on and forevermore" (v. 3).

So to the Wisdom Psalms in this part of the Psalter, Pss 112, 127, 128, 133, 139, two of these it will be noticed occurring consecutively, namely 127 and 128. There would seem to be a certain relationship between Ps 111 (a hymn) and the Wisdom Psalm, 112. Both are in acrostic form, and both begin with the words "Praise the Lord!". Further, compare 111:3b with 112:3b, and 111:4b with 112:4b. Yet the main theme of Ps 111 may be said to be praise to the Lord for his gracious provision to humanity, while that of 112 is more about the wisdom of the humans who embrace this care of the Lord and entrust to him their present and future lives: "For the righteous will never be moved; they will be remembered forever" (Ps 112:6). The same theme is there in Ps 127, "Unless the Lord builds the house, those who build it labor in vain" (v. 1), in Ps 128 "Blessed is everyone who fears the Lord, who walks in his ways" (v. 1), while in Ps 139 there is a representative of the so-called Wisdom tradition musing upon the inscrutability and wonder of the ways of the Lord.

Then there are the six thanksgiving psalms (107, 116, 118, 124, 129, 138). Psalm 107 is something of a portmanteau thanksgiving, which after the introduction (vv. 1–3), sets out a series of situations in which people were in difficulties, out of which they cried to the Lord, and from which they were rescued: desert places (vv. 4–9); prison (vv. 10–16); sickness (vv. 17–22); storms at sea (vv. 23–32); all of these with the regular refrain, "Then they cried to the Lord in their trouble, and he delivered them from

---

79. On the royal psalms, see above, 91–97.

their distress" (Ps 107:6, 13, 19, 28), and the exhortation, "Let them thank the Lord for his steadfast love, for his wonderful works to humankind" (Ps 107:8, 15, 21, 31).

Psalm 116 reads as if the distress being spoken about is illness, but the psalm could also apply to other problems. Whatever was intended, the psalmist makes his witness to the deliverance of God (vv. 8–11), going on to ask what suitable response he can make to the Lord (vv. 12–19). Psalm 118 also sets out thanksgiving to God for deliverance from troubles. Weiser called this psalm "A Liturgy of Thanksgiving," adding that "This psalm was Luther's favourite psalm. He said of it: 'This is my psalm which I love—for truly it has deserved well of me many a time and has delivered me from many a sore affliction when neither the Emperor nor kings nor the wise nor the cunning nor the saints were able or willing to help me.'"[80] Then at 124 and 129 are further psalms of thanksgiving, both of these being in the block of twenty psalms (Pss 120-134) called Songs of Ascents. So to the last of the thanksgiving psalms in the Psalter, Ps 138, which fittingly ends with the words,

> Though I walk in the midst of trouble,
> you preserve me against the wrath of my enemies;
> you stretch out your hand,
> and your right hand delivers me.
> The Lord will fulfill his purpose for me;
> your steadfast love, O Lord, endures forever.
> Do not forsake the work of your hands. (Ps 138:7–8)

So we come to the most numerous group of psalms in the Fifth Book of the Psalter, six of which form a block of psalms bringing the whole composition to a finale of hymnic praise. These are the hymns and in Book Five there are no less than thirteen of them (Pss 111; 113; 114; 117; 122; 135; 136, and as the final group 145–50). Thus, whereas the Psalter in its earlier parts had lament, both individual and corporate as its predominant note, so here at the end the predominant note is of hymnic praise to God. In the acrostic psalm, 111, this series begins with the words, "Praise the Lord! I will give thanks to the Lord with my whole heart, in the company of the upright, in the congregation" (Ps 111:1), and the paean of praise comes to its climax in the Psalter's final psalm:

> Praise the Lord!
> Praise God in his sanctuary;
> praise him in his mighty firmament!

80. Weiser, *Psalms*, 723–24.

> Praise him for his mighty deeds;
> praise him according to his surpassing greatness!
> Praise him with trumpet sound;
> praise him with lute and harp!
> Praise him with tambourine and dance;
> praise him with strings and pipe!
> Praise him with clanging cymbals;
> praise him with loud clashing cymbals!
> Let everything that breathes praise the Lord!
> Praise the Lord! (Ps 150:1–6)

Thus the fifth and last book of psalms makes its distinctive witness to the content of true worship of the Lord with this grand finale of hymnic praise.

The Book of Psalms and Worship

What, we may begin by asking, what sort of book is the Book of Psalms? Is it a literary work? I am thinking of the comment by Gerald Wilson that although it has become popular in many circles to refer to the Psalter as a "hymnbook," he does not favor this characterization, for the primary reason that "the hymnbook analogy ignores the fact that, in the final analysis, the canonical Psalter has become a book to be read and meditated upon (Psalm 1), rather than music to be sung."[81] Now I think that one can make an argument that the Psalter is to be seen, in part, as a literary work, a book to be read, but at the same time I think that the "hymnbook" nomenclature is still appropriate. There is surely evidence in the fact that both the Jewish communities and the Christian churches have found the psalms to have provided useful and appropriate material for their worship. Surely the reason for this is because what we have in the Book of Psalms is in the first place worship material. Undoubtedly this psalmic material has been found to have various other usages, yet the most likely primary purpose of the collection would seem to have been for use in worship.

---

81. See Wilson, "Shaping the Psalter," 72. Wilson's second reason for questioning calling the Book of Psalms a hymnbook is that it "evidences our tendency over the last 150 years of Psalms study to focus almost exclusively on individual psalms to the neglect of the whole ensemble." I find myself largely unpersuaded by this second reason because I find few convincing arguments for seeing order and logic in the final arrangement of the Book of Psalms into its various five books. It seems to me that in this regard, Wilson and others seek to build considerable theories on rather slender evidences, as in, for example, the arguments centered on the observation of a certain, but by no means regular, occurrence of the royal psalms at the "seams" between the five books of the Psalter.

Further, it has frequently been pointed out that the headings, the superscriptions to the individual psalms all seem to point to the use of the psalms in worship. For example, the heading of Ps 30 reads, "A Psalm. A Song at the dedication of the temple," while Ps 38 has "for the memorial offering," and Ps 92 has "A Song for the Sabbath Day." The group of psalms from 120–134 all have "A Song of Ascents" and our best supposition about this term is that it refers to the the going up to Jerusalem and the temple for those on pilgrimage to the holy city. Moreover, all these titles suggest that the intended purpose of these psalms has been perceived by those who added these titles to be that of worship. Though we cannot be sure as to the significance of a further set of psalm titles, they would seem on balance to be indicating use of the psalms for worship. Thus: "with stringed instruments" (Pss 4; 6; 54; 55; 61; 67; 76). Would those be needed for the *reading* of the book of psalms? So too "for the flutes" (Ps 5); and also that series: "according to The Deer of the Dawn" (Ps 22), "according to Lilies" (Pss 45; 69), "The Dove on Far-off Terebinths" (Ps 56).

Apart from these considerations—and it is admitted that about some of these psalm headings there is a certain doubt concerning their full significance—there is an inner spirit in the contents of the psalter that clearly seems to suggest its purpose lying in worship rather than in reading. Would there be the references to singing (Pss 81:1–2; 144:9), or to the playing of musical instruments (Pss 81:2–3; 144:9; 147:7; 149:3; 150:3–5) for reading material? Would it not seem more likely that the intended usage was in worship? What about the various calls to worship God/the Lord in the psalms (Pss 47:1; 95:1–2; 96:1–3; 98:1; 100:1; 105:1–2; 113:1; 134:1–2), or those instructions "O give thanks to the Lord, for he is good" (Ps 118:1a), followed by what looks suspiciously like congregational response "his steadfast love endures forever" (v. 1b, 2b, 3b, 4b), or more elaborately all the repeated "for his steadfast love endures forever" in Ps 136, no less than twenty-six times in the same number of verses? Surely this is for the arena of worship, and surely at least for the main part of it we are dealing with what has been called a "hymnbook" rather than a "book for reading." See also the whole block of hymns that end the psalter (Pss 145–150), a block of psalms that is undoubtedly material intended for the activity of worship. Westermann makes the point that in the psalms the words are directed to God, "they are prayers and appeals to Him", saying that this is the reason for the continued vitality of the psalms for both Jewish and Christian worship. [82]

---

82. Westermann, *The Living Psalms*, 1. On the Psalms and worship, see the comments of Brown, *Psalms*, 78–79; and Whybray, *Reading the Psalms as a Book.*

If then, we consider the psalter as intended for use in worship, as an aid in the nature of what we might call a "hymnbook," what, we may go on to ask, are the "notes" that are being struck in these "hymns"? The themes for worship that the psalms offer are there in the various types of psalms that Gunkel so perceptively characterized those many years ago in his analysis of the psalms into groups, indeed "types." Thus here in the psalms is the theme of praise and adoration of God. It makes its first appearance early in the psalter at Ps 8, and it is there in abundance at the end with Pss 111; 113; 114; 117; 135; 136; 145–150, and throughout these hymns of praise there resound the notes of awe and wonder at the greatness and majesty of God, his sureness and wisdom in all his works, his goodness and loving kindness to his people. Further, God is trustworthy, and this note is sounded in the psalms of confidence (Pss 11; 16; 23; 27:1–6; 62; 131), perhaps above all in the words of Ps 23, "Surely goodness and mercy shall follow me all the days of my life" (v. 6a). Among the psalms are Entrance Liturgies (Pss 15, 24), material sometimes appearing to have been arranged in forms suitable for antiphonal use (see Ps 24), and not infrequently the expressed joy to be found in the singing aloud about the Lord and all he does for his people (see Ps 33). Here also are presented materials to assist worshippers to offer their thanksgiving to God: this is to be seen especially in that small clutch of Psalms that comes near the end of the Second Book of the Psalter, Pss 65–68. Yet the psalter does not presume, as it were, that in any easy way such blessings can be expected to continue being showered upon these people, these worshippers. Thus not infrequently there are the prayers for the continuing gifts and mercies of the Lord, as for example in the words, "Let your steadfast love, O Lord, be upon us, even as we hope in you" (Ps 33:22).[83]

Further the psalter shows itself to be a very realistic and down to earth sort of devotional aid, for it acknowledges that both individuals, and also whole communities may go through troubled and troubling times which may be sufficient to raise questions in the minds of worshippers concerning a contemporary presence of God with his people. As Brueggemann expresses it, "The Psalter is not a book of easy religion in which the settled practices of obedience and praise characterize Israel's life, but a literature which looks unflinchingly into the face of reality."[84] Thus beginning with Ps 3 there are the individual lament psalms, and beginning with Ps 12 the corporate lament psalms, each of them both bewailing and cataloging present

---

83. In this regard, see Goldingay, "The Dynamic Cycle of Praise and Prayer."

84. Brueggemann, "Bounded by Obedience and Praise," 89. See also Brueggemann's earlier contribution, "Psalms and the Life of Faith."

difficulties and distresses being experienced, usually, though not always, also speaking of the Lord's delivering mercies.

There is a certain sense in which the Psalter presents a religious devotion that does not seem to have any central place within it for the institution of sacrifice. Certainly there are a number of psalms (Pss 40; 50) that can be read as if they are speaking out against the sacrificial institutions, but perhaps it is preferable to understand them as setting forth certain dangers with forms of religious devotion that are maybe sometimes devoid of inward feelings of sinfulness and guilt, and that harbor the understanding that a person can all too easily be forgiven at least certain sins by recourse to the appropriate religious rites. That is, it would appear that the psalter that has come down to us is hardly one that places any great importance on the institution of the sacrificial system of the temple. Perhaps the book of psalms was intended to set forth an alternative series of approaches to God, perhaps what its editors felt was a more spiritual approach, not only of troubled people, but also of those who were convicted of their sins, as well as those who had much cause for rejoicing and thanksgiving.[85] Moreover, we should take note of the fact that some sins, such as those committed deliberately, "committed with a high hand," were not forgivable through the medium of the sacrificial system, whereas forgiveness for such sins seems to have been possible by means of prayers of confession and contrition, and perhaps something of this being expressed in such psalms as Ps 51.

Further, the religion of the psalms gave full place to those who were suffering bad experiences in life, who found themselves having to question the ways of God with them and perhaps also with others. Not only did the psalter provide for such people the large numbers of both individual and also corporate laments, but also a series of what have been called Wisdom Psalms, some of which have appropriately been called theodicy psalms, psalms which raise questions concerning the apparent justice of the Lord in his dealings with his people. While such psalms may not come forth with any convincing solution to these deep and perplexing theodicy problems, at least one of them can speak of the experience of one suffering psalmist who in continued engagement in worship in the temple came to make what was in fact the far greater discovery—or rediscovery?—namely:

> Whom have I heaven but you?
> And there is nothing on earth that I desire other than you.
> My flesh and my heart may fail,
> but God is the strength of my heart and my portion forever.
> (Ps 73:25–26)

---

85. On the attitude of the psalmists to the sacrificial cult, see Brown, *Psalms*, 71–74.

By whom and in what historical period might the psalter have been used in worship? The answer to that must surely be that the psalter we have before us can only have been completed by second temple days, and that its usage must in the main have been in that place in those times. Surely in earlier times some of the psalms must have been used in Solomon's temple, and maybe also in the temples in the northern kingdom of Israel such as Bethel and Dan. There is a good possibility that they would have been used also by groups such as Deuteronomists inveighed against, those who practiced worship at various shrines outside such religious centers in the Israelite and Judean countrysides. If they were not so used by such groups then why were there the strictures against them as for example in 1 Kgs 14:23; 15:14; 22:43 and in many other references?[86] On the whole it is hardly likely that psalms will have been used in personal worship in homes, as we cannot imagine there being many copies of psalms, even less of only modest collections of them, available apart from those that were prepared for temple usage.

Yet what is also borne out through the experiences of many worshippers in subsequent ages is the abiding worth of this psalmic material for the ongoing praise of and search for God. Such has been the experience of multitudes over many centuries, whether they have been worshippers in Second Temple times, or in later times in Jerusalem and Israel, in Jewish diasporas, in communities in such places as Qumran, or in the worship of the Christians.

---

86. On this, see above, 61–66.

9

Sacrifices

The presence of a significant number of texts dealing with sacrifices, and the various regulations pertaining to them, constitute one of the principal problems for some readers, in particular Christian readers, of the Hebrew Bible. There are at least two reasons for this, the first being that the talk and the associated thought-world of sacrifice is more often than not alien to many people in the Western world, those living in societies and cultures where religious sacrifices are not offered in their contemporary situations. What is going on in ceremonies and services when sacrifices are offered is to many a witness and onlooker an exceedingly strange and alien procedure, the significance of which in all probability eludes them—indeed much the same may hold when it is simply a matter of sacrifices being spoken about. The second reason for the strangeness of the world of sacrifice for many Christian people in the contemporary world is the fact that the New Testament Letter to the Hebrews specifically speaks about the temple sacrifices of old having been made outdated and redundant through the once and for all sacrifice of Christ. Thus the author of the Letter to the Hebrews writes:

> For if the blood of goats and bulls, with the sprinkling of the ashes of a heifer, sanctifies those who have been defiled so that their flesh is purified, how much more will the blood of Christ, who through the eternal Spirit offered himself without blemish to God, purify our conscience from dead works to worship the living God! (Heb 9:13–14)

Yet the fact is that in the Old Testament there is a good deal about sacrifices being offered to God, and also, apart from these accounts there are sundry references both to the institution of sacrifice and also to the concept of religious sacrifice. Further, it is to be noted that in the attempt to explain the work of Christ the author of the Letter to the Hebrews does use the institution of the sacrificial system, thus surely suggesting certain continuities of theological thought between the old and the new. This demands that we give due attention to this aspect of the worship spoken about in the Hebrew Bible. Nevertheless, a caveat should be entered at this point, namely that a good number of the features and details of the sacrificial system we read about in the Old Testament continue to elude our full understanding, and among these the following two features warrant attention at this stage.

In the first place, while in such books as Leviticus there is a good deal of text and detail about the ritual of a series of sacrifices, it has to be admitted that we do not have sure knowledge as to the historical setting, or settings, of such sacrifices. That is, we cannot for certain link up such rituals with definite historical settings and times. Certainly, there is no dearth of suggestions about possible historical settings, but in truth these are inevitably speculative, and need to be regarded as such.

In the second place it may be thought that we are able to be sure about what it was believed "happened" when a person, or group, or family, or priest, or some other offered a sacrifice, and perhaps in particular what happened as regards the relationship between the sacrificial offerer and the deity to whom the sacrifice was being offered. No doubt an "original" and primitive understanding of sacrifice was that here was food being offered to a deity, but in the accounts that we have in the Hebrew Bible the talk is of the end result of such offering, and we lack explanation *how* such end result comes about. It may be that those whose writings have been recorded in what has come down to us as the Hebrew Bible believed that they knew such things, and that those for whom they were writing also knew—and maybe understood—such things. Yet equally it could have been that the institution of sacrificing to the deity was accepted as a gift to the people in the maintenance of their relationships both with one another and also with their God, but that at the same time there was not understanding about how it "worked." In this situation of what we might call a void in our own knowledge and understanding Old Testament scholars have resorted to the understandings of anthropologists as to the meaning of sacrifices, but not infrequently we have gained somewhat conflicting information from such sources.[1]

The approach here will be to consider the principal sacrifices we read about in the Hebrew Bible and in each case seek to understand, if we are able to do so, what was believed to happen when such sacrifices were offered. That is, what was believed to be the resulting effect, blessing for the offerer when she or he made the sacrifice? And as Lev 1-16 provides the most sustained account that the Hebrew Bible gives us of sacrifices, we shall consider in turn the sacrifices spoken about in those chapters.

---

1. For a recent sample of such views and understandings, see Watts, *Ritual and Rhetoric in Leviticus*, 176–80; Carter, *Understanding Religious Sacrifice*; and Douglas, *Purity and Danger*.

However, before we can begin on this quest, we need to take note of the form in which the material in Leviticus has come down to us. It would be generally agreed by Old Testament scholars that the vast majority of what we have in the book of Leviticus comes from what have been called priestly writers. That is, the concern is with cultic matters, with priestly concerns that the things of the cult are carried out decently and in order, that sins are taken with real seriousness, and that the due rituals are carried out so that divine forgiveness may be granted to those individuals, or communities, who have sinned. Probably these so-called Priestly writings came from the time of the Babylonian exile, or even the time after the return from exile, no doubt incorporating older material from times past, times about which we are not able to be precise.[2]

The manner in which this material is presented is the setting of the Israelites coming out of Egypt, in particular at the point where Exodus leaves off. Thus in Leviticus there are the references to doing and making things as it was shown on the mountain, on Mount Sinai (Lev 7:38; 25:1; 26:46; 27:34), that is, as it was revealed to Moses following on from his having received the commandments and much else. Further, in Leviticus it is assumed that the instruction and regulations for worship will be carried out in the (desert) tabernacle, the details of which are given in Exod 25-30. It has already been noted that the details given about the desert tabernacle in Exodus look remarkably like what we are told was built as Solomon's temple in Jerusalem.[3] Undoubtedly the Jerusalem temple is the envisaged setting of the worship we read about in Leviticus, this being read back as if taking place in the desert setting. Perhaps further we may say that the primary purpose of the material we shall now be looking at in Lev 1-7 was to assure God's people that here was vital material to guide them in their worship, their lives and their pilgrimage. Here are matters being spoken about that must be taken seriously by the following generations.[4]

Burnt Offerings

Leviticus ch. 1 is about Burnt Offerings (*'ōlāh*), and in these sacrifices almost all the offering was burnt on the altar, the only part not burnt being the skin which was to be given to the priests, presumably by way of

---

2. For full details of these matters about the book of Leviticus, see Grabbe, *Leviticus*, 11-28. See also below, 211-17, and further, Jenson, *Graded Holiness*, for the particular theological point of view of the so-called priestly writers.

3. See above, 26-27.

4. On this, see Watts, *Ritual and Rhetoric in Leviticus,* esp. pp. 37-62.

maintenance, payment for their important services to the people in this and in other regards. What is offered in this sacrifice varied, most likely in accordance with the wealth or otherwise of the offerer, but certainly what is portrayed was for the particular offerer—whether it was an unblemished offering from the flock or else turtle doves or pigeons—the giving of an expensive gift. Further, the clear suggestion in Lev 1 is that the offering is pleasing to the Lord, this being spoken of a number of times in the wording, "an offering by fire of pleasing odor to the Lord" (Lev 1:9, 13, 17). How are we to understand such words? No doubt to contemporary Western minds they perhaps suggest a somewhat crude understanding of the nature of deity, a being who has a human sense of smell, even a being having a distinct appreciation of certain smells over against others. It might be suggested that this represents an "early" understanding of the nature of God. Yet we perhaps do better to understand that this is simply language being employed to express the pleasure of the Lord that the offerer has made this costly offering to him. We might, using contemporary language, speak of pleasant odors to God being a metaphor for what is pleasing to God.[5]

The first of the possible offerings for the making of this sacrifice is an animal from the flock of cattle (Lev 1:3–9), this no doubt being the most valuable and costly animal that could be brought. The costliness of the offering is emphasized in that it must be male and without blemish. Then there is the matter of the instruction being given by the Lord—for all the instructions regarding these sacrifices are presented and portrayed as coming from the Lord—that as the animal is being brought to the tent of meeting to be sacrificed there is the command, "You shall lay your hand on the head of the burnt offering, and it shall be acceptable in your behalf as atonement for you" (Lev 1:4). There are two matters that call for particular consideration here, the laying on of the hand, and what is translated here (so, among others, NRSV) "atonement."

First then is the command to the offerer to lay a hand upon the animal as it is brought to be sacrificed, in particular that it is only one hand that is specified (and we may reasonably believe that this must have been the right hand), whereas in the ceremony outlined in Lev 16 (the Day of Atonement) two hands are used, and the text there does clearly say that this is to be regarded as laying the sins of all the people on the head of the goat by the high priest. Is there any significance in that the instruction here in Lev 1:4

---

5. Hartley also uses the word *metaphor*, saying, "The pleasant, soothing odor of the sacrifice that ascends toward heaven pleases God. While this metaphor is anthropomorphic, it is no more so than numerous phrases in the OT, such as 'the hand of God'" (*Leviticus*, 22). It is the issue of the use of human language in seeking to express matters of religious belief that Williams helpfully deals with in his book, *The Edge of Words*.

is a stipulation about the use of one hand, whereas that in the Day of Atonement ritual in Lev 16:21 has an instruction about both hands? The matter has been considerably studied,⁶ and while certainty cannot be achieved it seems likely that the application of the one hand, as in the case of the burnt offering, was an act of the offerer whose intention was to associate himself or herself with the offering, "as a sign of confession, of a broken and a contrite heart . . . an attestation (as much to the priest as to God) that the victim comes from this particular individual or group, that it is offered in his or their name, and that the fruit shall be his."⁷

Then second, in Lev 1:4 it is said that this sacrifice of the burnt offering shall be acceptable, presumably to God, on the offerer's behalf as (in the translation of NRSV) "atonement for you." The verb behind this translation is the Hebrew *k-p-r*, expressed in the *piʿel* form. This verb appears in the Hebrew Bible predominantly in the book of Leviticus, and most frequently in the *piʿel* form, occasionally in the passive *puʿal*, only once in the *qal* (Gen 6:14), where it is usually translated "cover." Which is indeed how the verb is usually translated, the predominant view being held is that we should look to an Arabic root behind it meaning "cover," and this is accepted in a number of recent Hebrew lexicons.⁸ A somewhat less-widely accepted view is that we should understand the Hebrew verb *k-p-r* in terms of an Akkadian cognate term meaning "wipe off". In most of its occurrences in the Hebrew Bible the *piʿel* form of this verb is customarily translated into English as "atone" or "make atonement." In the Septuagint translation (LXX) of the Hebrew, the Greek word used consistently comes from *hilaskomai*, "propitiate, appease," while Jerome's Vulgate has *expiatio*, "atonement." The English word "atonement" made its appearance in the early sixteenth century to indicate "at-one-ment," in particular to speak of the restoration of relationships between the holy God and his sinful people. It is this sort of restoration of relationships that is spoken of in Lev 1:4 as having been brought about through the costly sacrifice of a burnt offering to the Lord. Leviticus 1 does not explain *how* this can take place, but it affirms that something significant (mysteriously) *is* happening, in particular that there occurs a "covering" of sins committed—and this from God. What takes place is portrayed as a "de-sinning" rite, one given to his people as a gracious gift of the Lord, whereby sinful people come to be regarded by the Lord as "sinless."

---

6. See in particular Sansom, "Laying On of Hands"; Hartley, *Leviticus*, 19–21; and Budd, *Leviticus*, 47–48. On Lev 1:4, see Milgrom, *Leviticus 1–16*, pp. 150–54.

7. Sansom, "Laying On of Hands," 325.

8. See, e.g., *DCH*, *KB*, and *BDB*.

Leviticus 1:5-9 gives detailed instructions as to how the whole of the burnt offering rite is to be carried out, what is to be done with the blood and the various parts of the animal, with the result that the correct and acceptable offering is made to the Lord, one that through the burning is "of pleasing odor to the Lord" (v. 9). Following on from this, detailed instructions are set forth about the burnt offering sacrifices that are to be given by those whose resources do not stretch to the, no doubt, expensive offering of an unblemished ox. Verses 10-13 set out what is to be done in the ceremony when the most a person is able to afford is the offering of a sheep or a goat, though again the stipulation is that this must be an offering without blemish (v. 10); verses 14-17 lay down what shall be done when the offering is a turtle dove or a pigeon. Yet in both of these possibilities the result is "an offering by fire of pleasing odor to the Lord" (vv. 13, 17).

In what situations and circumstances were burnt offering sacrifices made, and wherein lay the distinction between them and other expiatory sacrifices, like for example the sin offerings of Lev 4:1—5:13? From what we can glean in the pages of the Old Testament the burnt offerings seem to have been presented on days of particular moment either religiously or nationally. Thus we read of them being presented when the great flood was over, the waters having subsided, and Noah, his family, and his varied company were safely back on dry land (Gen 8:20); when the ark of the covenant was restored to Israel (1 Sam 6:14; 7:9); when the ark was brought into Jerusalem (2 Sam 6:17); at the dedication of the temple in Jerusalem (1 Kgs 8:64), and so on. But then, it may be observed that Job is portrayed as offering on a regular basis burnt offerings for the possible sins of his children (Job 1:5); possibly that is to emphasize the sheer goodness and pious devotion of Job, and thus to highlight further the mystery of the depths of his forthcoming sufferings. The great folly and general misguidedness of Job's friends, Eliphaz, Bildad and Zophar, is perhaps similarly emphasized at the end of that book in the command that they offer no less than seven bulls and seven rams as burnt offerings—as well as needing Job's prayers that their exceeding great folly may be forgiven (Job 42:8).

What are we to say about the account in Gen 22:1-19 of the attempt on the part of Abraham to offer his son Isaac as a "burnt offering" ('ōlāh, v. 2) in the land of Moriah? We read about such human sacrifices in times of extreme crisis (Judg 11:31-40; 2 Kgs 3:27; 17:17), but the prophet Micah's question in Mic 6:7 "Shall I give my firstborn for my transgression?" seems to be expecting the answer "No," and indeed it seems unlikely that this was ever a normal part of the Israelite sacrificial cult. There might have been, however, a Canaanite god named Molech (Hebrew *Mōlek*; LXX *Moloch*), to whom human sacrifices *might* have been made, but such practices for

Israelite people were roundly condemned in the Hebrew Bible (Lev 18:21; 20:2-5; 1 Kgs 11:7; 2 Kgs 23:10; Jer 32:35; Hos 13:2; Isa 66:3). Such a practice is sometimes referred to as causing someone, usually a son, to "pass through fire" (2 Kgs 16:3; 17:17; 21:6; 23:10). This is consistently presented in a condemnatory sense, and it may be that the story of Abraham's attempt to thus sacrifice his son Isaac in Gen 22:1-19 should be understood as an etiological explanation of why child sacrifice was not to take place in Israel. Perhaps the crucial words are those of v. 8 "God himself will provide the lamb for a burnt offering, my son."[9]

Other Expiatory Sacrifices

The book of Leviticus speaks of two further expiatory sacrifices: in 4:1—5:13 about what is called the "sin offering" (*ḥaṭṭā'ṭ*), and in 5:14-16 and 7:1-6 the "guilt offering" (*'āšām*), the latter otherwise known as the "sacrifice of reparation". These are for sins committed unintentionally (Lev 4:2, 13, 22, 27; 5:14-18), and a number of hypothetical settings where such sins might be committed are presented, along with the appropriate sacrifices to be presented in order that the priest may make atonement on behalf of the person, or group, that has committed the sin, and that the sinner(s) may be forgiven (Lev 4:20, 26, 31, 35; 5:6, 10, 13, 16). Thus in Lev 4:3-12 it is the case of the priest who having sinned unintentionally, and who thereby has inevitably brought guilt upon the people, is to bring an unblemished bull as a sin offering (*ḥaṭṭā'ṭ*) (v. 3). Full details are given regarding just what it is that the priest must do, in particular with the blood, the fat, kidneys and liver, what shall be turned into smoke on the altar of burnt offering and what shall be burned in a clean place outside the camp (Lev 4:4-12).

The second hypothetical situation requiring a sin offering is set out in Lev 4:13-21 and is for the time when the whole congregation of Israel has sinned unintentionally. Here the offering is a bull of the herd, and through sacrificing it the priest thus made atonement for the people and hence secured their forgiveness (v. 20). Then there is the instance of a ruler who sins (Lev 4:22-26): here the offering is a male goat without blemish. Further, there is the case of "anyone of the ordinary people among you" (v. 27) who has sinned unintentionally (Lev 4:27-35): here the offering is a female goat

---

9. On the subject of this paragraph, see, e.g., Levenson, *The Death and Resurrection of the Beloved Son*; Rowley, *Worship in Ancient Israel*, 25, 64-65; Vaux, *Ancient Israel*, 441-46; Westermann, *Genesis 12-36*, pp. 351-65; Rad, *Genesis*, 232-40; Wenham, *Genesis 16-50*, pp. 96-118; and Coats, "Abraham's Sacrifice of Faith," 389-400. See also, Day, *Molech*; Heider, *The Cult of Molek*; Heider "Molek"; Alexander, "Aqedah"; Noort, "Genesis 22"; and Kierkegaard, *Fear and Trembling*.

or sheep without blemish, which when it is turned into fire on the altar brings about atonement for the sin committed, and thus is the person believed to be forgiven. The last of the cited examples of sin that calls for the sacrifice of sin offering is that occasioned by silence in a legal matter when a person should be speaking as a witness, and the instance when a person becomes contaminated through contact with the carcass of an unclean animal or insects (Lev 5:1–13). The stipulated gift to be offered is a female goat or sheep (v. 6), or two turtle doves or two pigeons (v. 11), but if even those are more than the person can afford then some choice flour will suffice, and thus shall atonement be made for the sins committed and the person concerned be forgiven (v. 13).

Further, Lev 5:14–16 and 7:1–6 speak about the "guilt offering" (*'āšām*) which is portrayed as being offered only in instances when individuals rather than groups or communities have sinned. Again, this is for an unintentional trespass, and in each case the offering is a ram without blemish, which when offered will bring about forgiveness. According to Lev 5:15 the unblemished ram is "convertible into silver by the sanctuary shekel:" this is a phrase whose meaning and significance continue to elude us, though a possibility is that it, "reflects older custom in which guilt offerings were essentially a financial offering (reparation)."[10] Once again we note, first, that through this means the forgiveness for the unintentional sinner is secured (Lev 5:16), and second, that full details are given as to the manner in which the offering is to be made (Lev 7:2–5), with the additional instruction that all the male priests, presumably thereby excluding female members of priestly families, were to eat of it, that eating to be in the holy place, for "it is most holy" (Lev 7:6). Presumably the significance of this is that not only is there stated here something about the privileges enjoyed by the priests, but also about the sheer holiness of the place where all this is taking place—literally "holy of holies it [is]."

We are not told what it was that distinguished the guilt offering from the sin offering. Thus, as J. E. Hartley observes, "Many proposals have been put forth throughout the ages,"[11] and some of them are rehearsed by commentators.[12] Perhaps the most succinct, but which yet fails to come to any real solution to the problem, is that by Grabbe who says, "The notion common to all offences which call for the guilt sacrifice is that they are all cases

---

10. So Budd, *Leviticus*, 103. However, see also, by way of example of the range of views here, the comments of Gerstenberger, *Leviticus*, 68; and Noth, *Leviticus*, 47.

11. Hartley, *Leviticus*, 78.

12. Grabbe, *Leviticus*, 36–37; Vaux, *Studies in Old Testament Sacrifice*, 98–102; and Snaith, "The Sin Offering and the Guilt Offering."

of sacrilege against God, either by an infringement of holy things or by a trespass against the name of God."[13]

The Day of Atonement

Leviticus 16 sets out in detail the ceremonies of the Day of Atonement.[14] Nevertheless, as the commentators point out, Lev 16 presents us with a range of questions about both critical matters and issues of interpretation. As far as the former are concerned the reader is referred to the various commentaries on the book of Leviticus, while a number of the latter must inevitably be discussed in what follows.

Leviticus 16 should be read and understood in its relationship with some passages that precede and others that follow it in the Hebrew Bible, "preceding" and "following" being understood in the sense of how the Old Testament is arranged in the form that has come down to us. In this form, the crucial preceding material is, once again, all that mass of detail we find in Exod 25:1 to 40:38 where the arrangement of the desert tabernacle is set out, an arrangement which, as we have seen,[15] reflects what came to be built as the temple in Jerusalem. The following material is in the book of Leviticus where chs 1–15 are taken up with the Israelite sacrificial system (Lev 1–3); the various offerings and the laws about those offerings (Lev 4–7); the consecration and initiation of the priesthood (Lev 8–10); and matters of purity and pollution (Lev 11–15).

The ritual of the Day of Atonement is set out in detail in Lev 16. It is portrayed as a most solemn day in the Israelite liturgical calendar, in which human sinfulness is taken with the utmost seriousness, and where there is commanded the enactment of two great ceremonies for dealing with that sinfulness, and the stain and pollution, that in the thought of the Hebrew Bible, it brings upon things, people and even communities. Many procedural details are given with some precision, in particular considerable emphasis being laid upon the role of the community's religious leader, here the priest Aaron. Amongst much else Aaron must exercise great care with his clothes, not only being dressed appropriately and correctly for the solemnities of the day, but also in afterwards divesting himself of the clothes he has worn in the de-sinning rites, for the reason that through his engagement in those rites his clothes have become, so it is believed, contaminated and polluted

---

13. Grabbe, *Leviticus*, 37.

14. For the further account of the Day of Atonement in Lev 23:26–32, see below, 174.

15. See above, 26–27.

through the sinfulness with which he has been dealing; thus Aaron must undergo ritual bathing both before and after the ceremonies of this day (Lev 16:4, 23, 24, 26, 28, 32).

The first of the two particular rites that it is commanded must take place on this day is the offering of two sacrifices, both of them expiatory sacrifices, a ram as a burnt offering (*'ōlāh*), and a young bull as a sin offering (*ḥaṭṭā't*) (v. 3).[16] The particular place to which Aaron is to come is closely specified here: he was to come inside the curtain before the ark of the covenant, specifically it is said before the "*kappōret* that is upon the ark". Now at one level it could be said that this is saying that Aaron is to come "in front of the ark," for the text goes on to say that the Lord would appear "in the cloud upon the *kappōret*" (v. 2). We have already discussed the verb *k-p-r* observing that it is best translated "cover,"[17] and that therefore here the text would *appear* to be indicating the top (that is, "the cover") of the ark of the covenant. However, it does seem that something more than merely a "lid" to the sacred ark is being spoken about, and judging from other applications we have already come across of the verb *k-p-r*, namely that it is employed to indicate the place particularly concerned with the "covering of sin," suggests that what we are dealing with here is a particular and special "place of atonement." Thus it was that Luther translated the two occurrences of the Hebrew *kappōret* in v. 2 as *Gnadenthron*, "mercy seat."[18]

Thus Aaron was instructed to offer the bull as a sin offering for himself, in this way seeking to make atonement for himself and his family (v. 6). Aaron then turned his attention to the two goats, deciding by means of casting lots which of the two should be offered as a sin offering to the Lord, and which should be "to Azazel," or "for Azazel." The crucial words about this latter goat, the one "to/for Azazel," are in v. 10, which in NRSV read as follows:

> [B]ut the goat on which the lot fell for Azazel shall be presented alive before the Lord to make atonement over it, so that it may be sent away into the wilderness to Azazel. (Lev 16:10)

The major problem for us is that we do not know what is intended by the word—very possibly a name?—Azazel. The fact is that the word occurs only in the Hebrew Bible in ch. 16 of Leviticus, and it is clear that for a long

---

16. However, see Lev 16:5 where the offering for the sin offering has become two male goats. As Snaith observed of Lev 16, "This chapter is certainly composite" (*Leviticus and Numbers*, 109). On Lev 16, see Milgrom, *Leviticus 1–16*, pp. 1009–84.

17. See above, 166.

18. The French Jerusalem Bible renders the Hebrew *kappōret*, "le propitiatoire." See also Hartley, *Leviticus*, 220, 235, who adopts the translation "Atonement Slate."

time it has constituted a problem. The earliest translation of the Hebrew scriptures, that into Greek (LXX), had the rendering "for sending away," and so also Jerome's Latin translation (*caper emissarius*, "sent-away-goat"). Various modern translations of the Hebrew ʿăzāʾzēl (Azazel) have been offered: "jagged rocks," "precipice," "entire removal," "scapegoat" (the last of which is how Tyndale rendered the word), or else regarding it as a proper noun, the name of a certain being, "Azazel." This last is the one adopted in most modern translations and in view of our general lack of knowledge regarding who or what is being spoken about here is perhaps the one that is best adopted. Further, it would seem likely that William Tyndale was on to something significant when he used the word "scapegoat," for we know of many traditions from both antiquity and also from more modern times of the enacting of ceremonies where a "scapegoat" is sent away into the wilderness bearing, it is believed, the sins of those whose representative person has laid hands on its head.[19] We may take note of the fact that in the Leviticus account of this ceremony it is not one hand that is laid upon the goat "for Azazel," but rather:

> Then Aaron shall lay both his hands on the head of the live goat, and confess over it all the iniquities of the people of Israel, and all their transgressions, all their sins, putting them on the head of the goat, and sending it away into the wilderness by means of someone designated for the task. (Lev 16:21)

It would seem that here there is an intended emphasis on the fact that the goat is intended to be bearing not just one person's, or of some reasonably finite group's, sins, but rather the sins of the many, the multitude—even as the text affirms, the nation's.[20]

Meanwhile, earlier the other goat had been offered by Aaron as a sin offering not only for all the sins, transgressions and uncleanness of the people of Israel, but also for the uncleanness that by the sinful people's very presence had been brought into the sanctuary, thus causing it to become defiled. This was effected by a rite centered upon what has come to be called the "mercy seat" and also at the altar (Lev 16:15–19). Thus, in this day that is given such an expansive account in the book of Leviticus, there are these

---

19. See, for examples of this, Frazer, *The Golden Bough*, 736–68; Parrinder, *West African Religion*, 71–72, 102; Gerstenberger, *Leviticus*, 221–22; Wright, *The Disposal of Impurity*, 15–74; and Hieke and Nicklas, *The Day of Atonement*.

20. Thus, it may be added, the goat's "minder," the one spoken about in Lev 16:22, the person "appointed" (so NRSV), or even "available," thus becomes thoroughly polluted through their bearing of all these sins that afterwards must therefore go through a serious de-polluting rite (Lev 16:26).

two most serious and elaborate ceremonies for an annual expiation, "covering" we may perhaps say, of the sins of the whole nation, both the sins that individuals had committed and also those of the whole people.[21]

We may yet pursue further the matter of what it was believed happened in this elaborate ceremony. We are told that the goal of the total ceremony was the forgiveness of sins, this as we have seen being mentioned no small number of times, and further being achieved through the two individual parts of the ceremony. The first part was a sacrificial ceremony, the complete offering and immolation of an unblemished animal. It would seem that we should accept, as has already been argued, that the frequent and consistent usage of the Hebrew verb *k-p-r* indicates "covering," in particular the covering of sins. That is, through this religious act there is granted by the deity what has come to be called "atonement," "expiation." This, of course, is not a provable, verifiable matter for twenty-first century Western minds, with their approach of supposedly enlightened rationality, but is clearly something encompassed in the minds of ancient people, namely that the opportunity to sacrifice a valuable animal to the deity was a gracious and divine gift of that deity to those devotees who had sinned.

Something needs also to be said about the place and emphasis of blood in this and other Old Testament sacrificial rites. Once again we are in the realm of early religious beliefs and practices, and as far as those beliefs are concerned no doubt beyond our contemporary Western ways of thinking, beyond our abilities logically to fathom. It is certainly not in any way that the Hebrew Bible understands the Lord wishing to receive blood for food (see, for example Isa 1:11; Ps 50:13). Equally, the human beings are forbidden themselves to eat blood (see, for example, Lev 3:17; 7:26; 17:12 and so on), but paradoxically the humans are called to offer blood to the Lord, and through this offering there proceeds, so it was believed, the mystery of forgiveness of sins, of the "covering" of the iniquities of those who had unwittingly sinned. What is perhaps the Old Testament's classic statement of this is in Lev 17:11, "For the life of the flesh is in the blood; and I have given it [the blood] for you upon the altar for making atonement [*k-p-r*] for your lives, for it is the blood that makes atonement in the life."[22] What

21. Gerstenberger says about the account of this in Lev 16, "Two weighty atonement rites thus occupy the center of the early Jewish day of penance: a blood ceremony intended to purify the priests, people, and sanctuary, and to place them in a new condition of grace; and the dispatching of a scapegoat that carries away the entire load of guilt in a physical-symbolic fashion. . . . The main concern of this day of penance . . . is clear: the annual expiation of the congregation" (*Leviticus*, 222).

22. The translation of this verse is beset with a number of grammatical problems. The rendering I have presented above is somewhat different from that of NRSV. The whole issue receives a full treatment in Hartley, *Leviticus*, 273–77; and Milgrom,

this appears to be saying is that blood was believed to have been a sacred gift to humanity. It sustains life, as we all well know, and there is something precious in this gift to humanity, the more so in that it is acceptable to God and brings about forgiveness, the covering of sins, for in the mystery of these matters the ongoing forgiveness and life of humanity is "in the blood" (*badām*), and also, paradoxically, that same blood makes atonement "in the life" (*banepeš*) of humanity (Lev 17:11).

It also calls for mention that in the instructions for the observance of the Day of Atonement that it is also to be a day of fasting (Lev 16:29, 31; 23:27, 32; Num 29:7). Fasting is a penitential act, one we read about elsewhere in the Hebrew Bible that individuals or communities engaged in when convicted of their sinfulness or who wished to mourn, or to add support to their prayers, or for other reasons (Ps 35:13; 1 Kgs 21:27; Num 30:13; Deut 9:9–10; Dan 9:3). In the post-exilic period there seems to have been a certain increase in the religious employment of fasting (Ezra 8:21–23; Neh 9:1; Zech 8:19; Isa 58:3–9; Joel 2:12–13), but we can hardly claim that the practice has any great emphasis in the Old Testament.[23]

When we are to place historically the beginnings of the Day of Atonement is a question more easily asked than answered. On the one hand we have remarkably few references to it in the parts of the Hebrew Bible that purport to deal with the pre-exilic period, thus suggesting that this was not an "early" festival. We read about it in its major coverage in Lev 16, and then also in Lev 23:29–32; 25:9 and Num 29:7–11, yet it receives no mention in either the former prophets or the latter prophets,[24] or even in the Psalms. Further, the ark of the covenant, portrayed as an important artefact in the whole procedure disappears from our view with the exile, after that period it not being heard of again, and perhaps until some further light is shed upon the matter we do well to accept that the ark was destroyed along with the Jerusalem temple in 586/7 BCE.[25] Nevertheless, the Day of Atonement ceremonies could possibly have still been observed under rather different conditions and circumstances. As indeed it perhaps did, for we have full treatment of it in the Mishnah's document *Yoma*, while it is generally agreed that the references in Sir 50:5–7 and Acts 27:9 are indeed to the Day of

---

Leviticus 17–22, pp. 1469–79.

23. On religious fasting, see Muddiman, "Fast, Fasting"; Smith-Christopher, "Fasting"; and Vaux, *Ancient Israel*, 59–61, 75, 262, 265, 387, 507, 514.

24. The reference in Ezek 45:18–20 is widely thought to be referring to a ceremony other than the Day of Atonement. See, e.g., Joyce, *Ezekiel*, 234.

25. This, as we have seen, is the conclusion of John Day, after his careful consideration of a range of views and suggestions, in his article, "Whatever Happened to the Ark of the Covenant." See above, 28–30.

Atonement.[26] Such considerations perhaps tend to the conclusion that in the form of which we read about it in the Hebrew Bible, the Day of Atonement was a post-exilic festival. Such is certainly understandable when we consider the tendency to lay considerable emphasis upon long and elaborate prayers of confession in exilic and post-exilic times, such as we find in the books of Ezra and Nehemiah.[27]

At the same time we may say that the Day seems to have at least some ancient roots, for the talk of sending the goat away into the wilderness, and that it is to be "for Azazel" does suggest to us that we are dealing with an ancient rite, one of whose parts had a ceremony whose full meaning and significance over the course of time appears to have become lost to later generations. Further, what comes through to us with pellucid clearness is that this great Day of Atonement is portrayed as being a reassuring day for all those individuals and groups who were conscious of their sins, and who genuinely regretted, bewailed them. For here on this most sacred day there was not just one major assurance of sins forgiven, but rather two. Not only was there the assurance of sins forgiven through those most elaborate sacrificial ceremonies that Aaron is spoken of as conducting in the most holy part of the tabernacle, but there was also the whole ritual of what we may call the scapegoat in which the goat designated "for Azazel," with the sins of all the people symbolically laid upon its head, was sent away into the wilderness, thus taking away—indeed far away—the sins of all the people. And while Hebrew Bible scholars may quite justifiably ask questions about when such a day may historically have taken place—even asking if indeed it ever did historically take place—yet what is remarkable has been the importance of its ongoing life as a festival of later and contemporary Judaism.

The Grain Offering and the Well-Being Offering

In the Hebrew Bible we also read of these two sacrifices, the grain offering in Lev 2, and the well-being offering in Lev 3. We consider them in turn.

The grain offering (*minḥāh*) is in the Hebrew Bible something of a catch-all term, being used in rather general ways for a gift that a person may give to another, perhaps with the intention of winning some favor (as for example in Gen 43:11), or even as tribute to an overlord as in 1 Kgs 4:21 (Heb 5:1). Further, though this offering may be presented in various kinds (as for example in Gen 4:3–5), yet there is a more specific cultic application of the

---

26. See, Danby, *The Mishnah*, 162–72; Skehan and Di Lella, *The Wisdom of Ben Sira*, 550; and Barrett, *Acts 15–28*, p. 1188. See also Hieke and Nicklas, *The Day of Atonement*.

27. For further on this tendency, see above, 111.

term, namely a grain offering, in particular as it is set out in Leviticus. In this setting "the offering shall be of choice flour; the worshiper shall pour oil on it, and put frankincense on it" (Lev 2:1), a portion of this being burnt on the altar as a pleasing offering to the Lord, and what is left over being for Aaron and his sons, that is to say for the priests and their families (Lev 2:2–3). Sometimes this offering is presented along with another offering, not infrequently this being a burnt offering (as in Judg 13:19), or a peace offering (as in 1 Sam 2:29), but at other times being offered on its own, as for example in Judg 6:18. Our accounts of the sacrifice of the grain offering do not make it clear for what purpose it was to be offered, but at some stage it seems to have become a regular morning, and maybe also evening, offering in the Jerusalem temple (1 Kgs 18:29, 36; 2 Kgs 3:20; 16:15; Ps 141:2), or at least a part of those daily offerings.

The final sacrifice to be considered does not have an agreed name when put into English. It is the *šĕlāmîm* sacrifice, frequently these days being called the "well being" sacrifice, other names having been given to it depending on what is considered to be the etymology of the name. Thus the NRSV translation in Lev 3:1–16 has "well-being," it being understood that the Hebrew name comes from the Hebrew *šālēm*, and this is the name adopted in this work. However, the earlier RSV, understanding the name as having been derived from the Hebrew *šālôm*, translated it "peace offering"; an earlier one was "communion offering," this being dependent on the view and understanding of Robertson Smith.[28] An animal without blemish was required to be offered in this sacrifice: it could be male or female, and could be of cattle, goats or sheep. All the fat of the animal was to be offered to God, to be burnt on the altar, as an offering by fire to the Lord (Lev 3:5, 11, 16), while the blood was to be dashed against all the sides of the altar (Lev 3:3, 8, 13). Further, in this sacrifice family members could participate in the eating of parts of the offering.[29] It has to be said that the texts at our disposal in the Old Testament do not make it clear in just what circumstances this sacrifice was to be made. Lester Grabbe has suggested that the offering of this one sacrifice might have been believed to include within it a freewill offering to God on the part of the offerer, or it may have been offered so as to complete the making of a vow to God, or it may have been given by way of expression of thanks to God for his deliverance of the offerer in a time of trouble.[30]

---

28. See Smith, *Lectures on the Religion of the Semites*. See also the extract from this in Carter, *Understanding Religious Sacrifice*, 55–75.

29. On this see Méndez-Montoya, *The Theology of Food*.

30. For further details of this sacrifice and some of the problems we have in understanding it, see Grabbe, *Leviticus*, 32–34.

Sacrifices

Why did people of Ancient Israel offer sacrifices, and why do certain parts of the Old Testament go into such detail about them, in particular concerning the ways in which they are to be offered and what part or parts of the offering go to whom? As is often the case, the Hebrew Bible, alas, does not tell us nearly as much as we would wish to know about these matters, and in particular what it was believed *happened* when an offerer made a sacrifice to the Lord, and when a certain sacrifice was appropriate for the occasion but not another. Thus we have to do our best with the resources that are before us, namely, first, reading, as it were, between the lines of the accounts that we have been given in the Old Testament, and second, taking some notice of recent studies of the institutions of sacrifices in cultures where sacrifices are still offered, though naturally seeking to give due regard for differences of understanding of such things between cultures. Thus, for example, the studies of E. E. Evans-Pritchard of sacrifices in a particular African Culture, and Mary Douglas's anthropological studies have been helpful, though not without their critics.[31]

The accounts of sacrifices in the book of Leviticus speak of these offerings as being pleasing to God, sometimes expressing this through the metaphor of their presenting to the Lord a pleasing odor. Equally, it seems clear that at least some sacrifices were thought of as being costly offerings to God, and as regards monetry value they were indeed costly for the offerer. Presumably, the offering of a costly gift was deemed to be appropriate in the situation where the offerer felt a sense of real indebtedness and gratitude to the Lord. By means of this costly sacrifice the offerer made a tangible act of thanksgiving to God. Similarly, it seems that by means of the offering of the appropriate sacrifice an individual's personal vow to the Lord could be sealed or ratified. Sacrifice, alternatively, could be regarded as strengthening the fellowship between the worshipper and the Lord, and even in some cases tend to the strengthening of the relationship of family members and others.

It is also clear that a highly significant aspect of sacrifices was that some of them were believed to be of atoning worth to the offerer, or those on whose behalf the offerer brought certain of the sacrifices. In this regard it is clear that the blood of the sacrificial victim was believed to be of the greatest significance, in that it brought about purification for unwitting sins. We may take note of the fact that as a result of his African observations and researches, E. E. Evans-Pritchard was able to speak of sacrifices having piacular effect. In the Hebrew Bible, and particularly in the book of

---

31. Evans-Pritchard, *Nuer Religion*; Douglas, *Purity and Danger*; Douglas, *Leviticus as Literature*; and Carter, *Understanding Religious Sacrifice*.

Leviticus, this aspect of sacrifices tends to be expressed through the usage of the verb *k-p-r*, which it seems most appropriate to translate as "cover." That is, the effect and great gift of an atoning sacrifice is that unwitting sins are forgiven, that the relationship of the (sinful) offerer and the (holy) Lord is restored and normalized. As we have already seen—and to this we shall return—the Old Testament can speak of ways other than through sacrifice whereby a person or a community, may have their sins forgiven, such as through prayers of intercession or petition.[32]

We can perhaps understand that in the ritual of the offering of a sacrifice to God there is a certain element of what we may from a Christian perspective, and admittedly with a degree of anachronism, call "sacramental,"[33] insofar as there is something tangible and evidential, something that may be touched, handled, seen and felt that may thereby be a real aid to that worshipper, or those worshippers, so aware of sins, who may thus come to know the more surely that their sins have been forgiven. Thus the matter might appropriately be restated: we should surely consider the Hebrew Bible's sacrificial system as believed to be a great gift of the Lord to his people whereby they may be forgiven their unwitting sins, and also *know* that those sins have been forgiven.

Nevertheless, the sacrificial system that we read about in the Old Testament, one that in so many of its aspects bore marked similarities to the sacrificial systems of other nations and ethnic groups, both ancient and also more modern, was only able to make provision for the forgiveness of, the "covering" of, unwitting, that is accidental, sins, and not for those sins that had been committed knowingly, deliberately, or as the Hebrew Bible frequently refers to them, "committed with a high hand." Perhaps as far as the forgiveness of those sins that were believed to have been "committed with a high hand" other ways than through the established sacrificial system were needed. In fact, such forgiveness, so it was believed, could only be sought and found through the direct action and steadfast love of the Lord.[34]

---

32. See above, 107–111, and below, 285–87.

33. I intend the use of the word "sacramental" here in reference to its wider application than to only seven, or even just two, sacraments. Thus White says in this regard of the earlier centuries of the Christian church, "For well over a thousand years there was no consensus about just how many sacraments there were. For Augustine, the list included such things as the baptismal font, the giving of salt at baptism, the ashes of penance, the Creed, the Lord's Prayer, and Easter day. One thing mattered: that in these acted signs God was given to humans" (White, *Introduction to Christian Worship*, 172). It is in this sense that I speak of a certain "sacramental" aspect in the matter of sacrifices being offered and received.

34. On this matter see above, 114–15.

10

Feasts, Festivals, and Calendars

This chapter considers some aspects of the calendrical arrangement of various festivals and feasts we read about in the Hebrew Bible, noting, so far as is possible, when and on what occasions the prescribed feasts and festivals were to be observed. For in the Hebrew Bible there are number of references to a range of feasts and festivals, not only as spoken about in a connected way in Exod 12:1–13:22; 23:14–17; 34:18–26; Lev 23:1–44; Num 28:1—29:40; Deut 16:1–17, but also in a number of more occasional references in the historical and prophetical books. Nevertheless, although there are these various references it yet remains difficult to gain an overall picture of the annual cycle of festivals and feasts, not least because it is clear that over the centuries these matters changed. Further, it is not clear from what periods of time some of the festivals we read about in the Old Testament come. Moreover, when we do have reference to feast or festival is that intended to indicate what happened in an earlier, or else perhaps in the contemporary time of the writer or editor of that book or part of that book? Thus, in these matters, as in a good deal else in the study of the Hebrew Bible—and not least in matters to do with worship—we frequently have more questions than we have answers.

In the Beginning...

In dealing with calendrical matters something needs to be said about an aspect of the theological thought found at the beginning of the Hebrew Bible, in particular Gen 1:1—2:4a, material that it would be generally agreed comes from the so-called Priestly writers. What we are presented with here is a very formalized account of the creation of the world by God (*'ĕlōhîm*) in six stages, each stage constituting the divine work on a subsequent day of the week. Thus on the fourth day the heavenly bodies, presumably the sun and moon, were created thereby making provision for the dating, and the associated recording of dates, in the world. Further, we are told in this account that by the end of the sixth day the creation of the world was completed, and that God "blessed" (*brk*) the seventh day, he "hallowed" it, "made it holy" (*qdš*) (Gen 2:3). In Gen 2:2 we read "And on the seventh day God finished (*klh*) the work (*ml'kh*) that he had done . . ." There is nothing stated here about worship taking place on the seventh day, on the day of rest, that is "sabbath" (*šbt*), yet in the Old Testament we do have references to worship taking place on it, and to this we shall return.

In the meantime, it may be noted that what we might understand as a theological association between the completion of the divine work of creating the world and what we are told about the work of Moses in his establishing the desert tabernacle is set forth.[1] At the end of that latter account we are told "So Moses finished (*klh*) the work (*ml'kh*)" (Exod 40:33), a similarity in wording to what we read at the conclusion of the account of creation in Gen 2:2 which, in the words of Gordon Wenham, "suggests that the erection of the tabernacle is being compared to God's creation of the world."[2] What is of interest and significance for this study is the implied emphasis and importance here ascribed to the establishment of the Israelite desert place of worship, namely the tabernacle. Further, we may pursue this theme and association of significant events and the place of worship by considering the following. In 1 Kgs 6:1 we read that it was in the four hundred and eightieth year after the Israelites came out of Egypt, in the fourth year of King Solomon's reign, in the second month (Ziv), that Solomon began to build the house of the Lord. Further, when the lengths of the reigns of the Judean kings that we read about in 1 and 2 Kings are added together, and fifty years for the time in exile is added in, we have another figure of 480 years from the beginning of the building of Solomon's temple until its destruction by the Babylonian army in 586/7 BCE.[3] Again, the significance for the study of what we read in the Hebrew Bible about worship is that these "marker points" of years are made in reference to the establishment of the central places of worship, the envisaged dwelling places of the Lord whereby and wherein his people believed they may come into his holy presence. In particular they suggest a deep and profound importance on the part of at least some of those who passed on to the future generations their records and writings about the desert tabernacle and the Jerusalem temples. Then to be considered are some rather more routine and down to earth dates in the Hebrew Bible's worship calendar.

---

1. For the desert tabernacle, see above, 24-25.
2. Wenham, *Genesis 1-15*, p. 35; and Amos, *Genesis*, 14.
3. For these matters, see, e.g., Burney, *Notes on the Hebrew Text of the Books of Kings*, 58-61; and Blenkinsopp, *The Pentateuch*, 49.

The Festival of Passover

This is the first of the major festivals we read about in the Old Testament, it being the dominant subject in the whole block of material Exod 12:1—13:22. The Feast of Passover was the ritual for the celebration of the Lord's deliverance of his people from Egypt, and the Exodus account of this festival is presented in the form of instructions about the ritual being interspliced into the historical account of part of the divine deliverance of the Israelites, in particular of the final plague against Egypt. Further, it is clear that here the setting for this celebration is in families in homes.

It is widely thought that Passover was originally a nomadic pastoral festival, the blood of the slaughtered animal providing protection for the flocks in the annual migration. Yet this Passover, as portrayed in the Hebrew Bible, became for the Israelites the ceremony for the seeking of travelling mercies, both for the original celebrants as they set out on their perilous desert journey, and also for the continuing journeys in life of all their latter day successors. Above all Passover became the Israelite and Jewish celebration of the divine deliverance from suffering and slavery in Egypt.

In the Exod 12-13 account the passover lamb was to be slaughtered at twilight on the 14th day of Nisan (the first month of the ancient Israelite year), the protecting blood being put on door frames (Exod 12:7). Then the lamb was roasted and, along with unleavened bread and bitter herbs, shared in a family meal, part of which was taken up with the head of the family explaining the significance of the ritual (vv. 8-11, 25-27), thus making the festival both the pious remembrance of things historical and also the prayerful celebration of their contemporary and future deliverances. No doubt something of this can been observed in the account of the passover celebration at Gilgal when the Israelites went into the land of Canaan (Josh 5:10-12), after which, so we are informed, the Israelites began to eat the produce of the land of Canaan.

At some later stage, perhaps as a result of the changes of worship effected in the days of king Josiah and the influence of the so-called deuteronomic school, Passover became a celebration in a central sanctuary, and thus a pilgrimage festival. Such is the picture given to us in Deut 16:1-8. Various other changes were made, one of which was perhaps the linking of Passover observations with the festival of Unleavened Bread, and to this last-named feast we now turn.[4]

---

4. For further on Passover, see, e.g., Bokser, "Unleavened Bread and Passover"; Rylaarsdam, "Passover and Feast of Unleavened Bread"; and Gorman, "Passover, Feast of."

The Agricultural Festivals

In Exodus, Leviticus, and Deuteronomy we are given lists of three agricultural feasts, these being portrayed as having importance in the life of the people of Israel. These are called by the words *ḥag* and *môʿēd*, both of which can be translated either "festival," or "feast," words which have already been mentioned.[5] In Exodus we find two lists of these feasts/festivals, the first being in 23:14-17. Here we read that the Israelites are to hold a feast/festival for the Lord three times a year, the first being the feast of unleavened bread, this to take place in the month of Abib for the reason, it is said, that that was the month when Israel came out of Egypt (v. 15). There is no mention here of Passover. The second feast spoken about is the gathering of the first fruits of the harvest, while the third is the festival of ingathering at the end of the year "when you gather in from the field the fruit of your labor" (v. 16).[6]

The second list is in Exod 34:18-26, and once again the first feast spoken of is that of unleavened bread (*ḥag hamaṣṣôt*), which, again, is to be held in the month of Abib, the month when Israel came out of Egypt (v. 18). Here again, it is commanded that the Israelites shall eat unleavened bread for the seven days of the feast (Exod 23:15; 34:18). However, what is different here is that whereas the Israelites are commanded in 23:15b not to appear before the Lord empty handed, in 34:20 the requirement is set out in detail as to just what offerings are to be brought. Exodus 34:21 is taken up with the command about resting, and not working, on the sabbath day. We may observe that not without good cause, but not wholly accurately, the whole passage Exod 34:10-28 has been called the Ritual Decalogue, in distinction to the Ethical Decalogue in Exod 20:2-17.[7]

Then in Exod 34:22 are listed the two other feasts, namely, the feast of weeks (*šābūʿōt*—that is 7 weeks after Passover), and the feast of ingathering (*ḥag hāʾāsîp*). Verse 23 has the command that three times in the year all males are to attend at these pilgrimage festivals and thus appear before the Lord, the God of Israel—which looks as if pilgrimage to Jerusalem is being envisaged. Meanwhile, Exod 34:24 gives an assurance that the Israelites can feel secure about their coveted land while they are away on these pilgrimage festivals. (They cannot use that as an excuse for not going to the festival!) Exodus 34:25-26 is about festival of Passover, and the requirement that at this festival there is to be no leaven present, and that all parts of the sacrifice are to be consumed or burned before the morning. Further, it is to be the

---

5. See above, 179-80.

6. See Kraus, *Worship in Israel*, 26-45, for the Cultic Calendars in the Pentateuch. See also Jenson, *Graded Holiness*, 182-209, 227-31.

7. See, e.g., Durham, *Exodus*, 458.

best of the first fruits that are to be offered to the Lord in "the house of the Lord your God," this mention of the locality suggesting what is being envisaged is settled life in the promised land when there was a temple in Jerusalem.

There is a further list of pilgrimage festivals set out in Lev 23:1-44, a chapter more detailed about these festivals than the lists in Exod 23:14-19 and 34:18-26, and with other matters in the cultic calendar. Thus, for the present, we shall consider only what Lev 23 has to say about the three agricultural festivals, and then after looking at Deut 16:1-17, will return to the other matters spoken of in Lev 23:1-44.

Leviticus 23:4-14 speaks of two festivals that are to take place in the Spring, both being called "festivals of the Lord" (*môʿădê yhwh*), "holy convocations" (*miqrāʾê qōdeš*). On the fourteenth day of the first month there is to be a passover offering to the Lord (v. 5), and on the following day the festival of unleavened bread, when for seven days the Israelites are to eat unleavened bread (v. 6). On both first and seventh days there are to be "holy convocations" (here, *miqrāʾ qōdeš*), when no work is to be done (vv. 7-8). Thus, here are brought together the talk of unleavened bread and passover. Then follow in vv. 9-14 instructions about the festival of first fruits, accompanied by instructions about "raising the sheaf" (v. 11), the burnt offering of a lamb, the grain offering, the drink offering (vv. 12-13), after which, and only after which, the Israelites may eat of the new grain (v. 14).

Then follow in Lev 23:15-21 instructions about the Feast of Weeks, instructions in greater detail than those in Exodus: there is to be elevation offering; burnt offering as well as offerings of grain; drink and fire; and, again, no work is to be done on this day. And there is the reminder in v. 22 that some of the harvest is to be left for the poor and the alien. In Lev 23:23-32 there are details and instructions about the Day of Atonement, matters already considered.[8]

Leviticus 23:33-43 is about the festival of booths (*ḥag hasukôt*), which is to take place on the fifteenth day of the seventh month (Tishri), and to last seven days. This is an autumn festival (September-October) when the grapes and olives are picked, the name "booths" being given to indicate the living in the fields, in shelters made from branches while the harvest was gathered, no doubt to make provision for day and night security. At a more elevated level the talk of booths was intended to remind the people that in the days when the Lord brought his people out of Egypt they had perforce to live in booths, and were thus being reminded of their divine rescue from Egyptian bondage (vv. 42-43).

---

8. See above, 170-75.

The third book in the Hebrew Bible where these three agricultural festivals are spoken about is Deuteronomy. This is in ch. 16, and here they have definitely become pilgrimage festivals, it being stipulated that they are to be held "at the place that the Lord will choose as a dwelling for his name" (Deut 16:2, 6, 11; cf v. 15), which seems clearly intended to indicate that this place is the temple in Jerusalem, a matter which could not be stated in so many words while the literary form of an address by Moses to the people of Israel *before* the Israelites crossed over the Jordan into the promised land was maintained.

The same three agricultural festivals are spoken of here, the first being passover in Deut 16:1–8. In this account what seems earlier to have been an ancient ceremony in which shepherds sought to ward off danger to their flocks has become the Israelite festival that celebrated the historical event of the exodus from Egypt. The second festival is that of Weeks (*ḥag šābūʿôt*), (Deut 16:9–12) which again is to be held in the central sanctuary, and sons and daughters; male and female slaves; resident Levites; along with strangers, orphans, and widows are to be included, for the Israelites were to remember they were slaves in Egypt (v. 12). The third festival is that of booths (*ḥag hasukōt*), which is to take place when the produce of the fields and the wine press have been gathered in, and again there is the extended family group including slaves, Levites, orphans, and widows who take part, "for the Lord your God will bless you in all your produce and in all your undertakings, and you shall surely celebrate" (v. 15).

Thus Deuteronomy stresses that three times each year all males shall appear at the appointed place for the three great festivals—unleavened bread, weeks, and booths—and all shall give as they are able, according to the blessings they have received (Deut 16:16–17). We should note that what we have here is the taking over of Canaanite religious festivals, which did both retain their earlier purpose of being thanksgiving ceremonies for the land harvest, and that also came to be times of worship and thanksgiving to Yahweh for the dramatic rescue of his suffering people from Egypt.

The Day of Atonement

We have earlier given attention to the significance of this "Day," a matter set out in some detail in Lev 16:1–34.[9] We now consider its place in the Hebrew Bible's cultic calendars. As observed above, while in Lev 16:1–34 what happens on the Day of Atonement is spoken about in much detail, yet also the matter is set forth in one of the lists of annual Agricultural festivals, namely

---

9. See above, 170–75.

Lev 23:23-32, where it is said that this is to take place in the seventh month, that is in the month of Tishri (September-October). The first day of this is to be a day of complete rest, a "holy convocation" (*miqrā' qōdeš*), a day to be commemorated with trumpet blasts (v. 24). The people are to present the Lord's offering by fire, which it seems must be intended to indicate the offering of a sacrifice, or sacrifices, the latter possibility about which we read in Lev 16:1-19. Leviticus 23:24-32 goes on to stress that on the Day of Atonement the only work to be done is this very matter of the worship of the Lord, in particular the making of atonement. It is to be a day of "self-denial," each person is to humble themselves, even "afflict" (*'-n-h*) themself (v. 29). It is stressed that the most solemn, indeed vital, activity on this day is the matter of dealing with sins, seeking the divine forgiveness for them, the "covering" (*k-p-r*) of them.

What is not recorded in Lev 23:24-32, is anything about what is presented in Lev 16:1-34 as the second part of the ceremonies of this most solemn day, namely the ceremony of the two goats, and the sending away into the wilderness of one of them for the (mysterious) "Azazel," upon which Aaron had laid his hands, thus symbolically transferring the sins of the people onto the goat and which thereby was sent away into the wilderness, to a place "far away" (Lev 16:20-24).

As has been seen there are unanswered questions raised by these different accounts of what was clearly a most solemn and important day in the religious life of the people of Yahweh. The dating of these accounts, and of the ceremonies about which they speak is also a matter of much debate, with little scholarly agreement. Is the talk about the trumpet blasts in Lev 23:24 about what in later times was to be done through the sounding of the ram's horn (*šôpăr*; see for example Ps 81:3)? The major difference in these accounts is the lack of any mention of the two goats in Lev 23, one of which in the detailed account in Lev 16 is to be "for Azazel." Indeed, are the differences between the accounts of the festival in Lev 16:1-34 and 23:26-32 to be explained by changes of settings and circumstances occasioned by the movement and progression of the Israelites from wilderness wanderings to settled dwellers in cities and towns? In short, are these changes to be explained by the concern on the one hand neither to forget important discoveries and emphases in worship, in particular matters of human sinfulness and divine forgiveness, and nor on the other to neglect changes that call for adaptations and accommodation to needs and pressures of a later contemporary situation.[10]

10. In this regard, see the treatment of Gerstenberger, *Leviticus*, 347–54. However, it seems to me that Gerstenberger pushes the matter of the change from an agricultural to a city life to a degree that I do not think is realistic. I would think that in the "latter" city

The Cultic Calendar in Numbers 28 and 29

This, it is widely agreed is Priestly material coming from a late time, de Vaux saying it is "the complete list of the sacrifices offered in the second Temple after the time of Esdras."[11] It sets out in detail what sacrifices and offerings are to be presented at the various festivals through the year, and includes sacrifices that are to be offered daily (28:3–8). It goes on to list the weekly Sabbath offerings (28:9–10); monthly new moon offerings (28:11–15); feasts of Unleavened Bread (28:16-25), Weeks (28:26–31), New Year (29:1–6), Day of Atonement (29:7–11), and Tabernacles (29:12–38). In addition to these stipulated offerings, individuals could make their own personal offerings (29:39). These are all set out in a helpful tabular form by Eryl Davies.[12] Another way of expressing the provision and the requirements of the cultic feasts set out in the Hebrew Bible is as shown in the present work in the section that now follows.

The Hebrew Bible Cultic Calendar

We cannot be certain when in ancient Israel the new year was celebrated, whether in the spring or in the autumn, with possible change of spring to autumn or vice-versa.[13] The cultic calendar seems to have gone as follows, though we should take note of two factors: (a) only four of the Hebrew names of the month appear in the Hebrew Bible, namely, Abib (Nisan), Ziv (Iyyar), Ethanim (Tishri), Bul (Marhesvan), and (b) The Feast of Weeks is said to take place fifty days after Passover, but no month is stated.

Hebrew month	Equivalent	Festival
1. Nisan (Abib)	Mar/Apr	Unleavened Bread, Passover
2. Iyyar	Apr/May	Weeks?
3. Sivan	May/June	Weeks?

days, Israelite/Jewish people would still understand themselves be to a large degree dependent on the produce of the land, and that in large numbers they may still have been cultivators of land. On Day of Atonement, see Hieke and Nicklas, *The Day of Atonement*.

11. Vaux, *Ancient Israel*, 473. For the late date of this material, see also Budd, *Numbers*, 312–15; and Davies, *Numbers*, 305–7.

12. Davies, *Numbers*, 305–6.

13. David J.A. Clines has studied the matter exhaustively: see "The Evidence for an Autumnal New Year"; and "New Year."

Hebrew month	Equivalent	Festival
4. Tammuz	June/July	
5. Ab	July/Aug	
6. Elul	Aug/Sept	
7. Tishri (Ethanim)	Sept/Oct	Booths, Day of Atonement
8. Marhesvan (Bul)	Oct/Nov	
9. Kislev	Nov/Dec	
10. Tebet	Dec/Jan	
11. Shebat	Jan/Feb	
12. Adar	Feb/Mar	

The above schema is basically taken from the prescriptions set out in Exod 23:14–17 and 34:18–23, yet we should not lose sight of the reality that in Exod 29:38–42 and Num 28:2–8, as we have already seen, there were prescribed—presumably for the Jerusalem temple—that whole series of daily, sabbath, monthly offerings as well as those celebrated and solemnly remembered on the particularly special and specified occasions. We can see here a real priestly concern for a continual and continuing life and program of religious observances taking place in the temple, such that in the priestly judgment would maintain in appropriate balance the covenant relationship between the Lord and his people.[14]

Sabbath, Sabbatical Year, and Jubilee

We do not know when the beginnings of the institution of the Sabbath took place, but it is suggested that it was early, earlier that the Priestly Writings, perhaps much earlier. Nor do we know from where the concept of this day came, and Babylonia, Canaan, and elsewhere have all been suggested, but such suggestions are inevitably speculative. What is clearer is that the Hebrew word *š-b-t*, from which the word "Sabbath" is derived means "cease, stop, be at a standstill," and that in the first place is what the Hebrew Sabbath is about, a day of rest when no work apart from what is vital, or at least necessary, is to be done. Not surprisingly in the course of time regulations and advice arose that set out just what was permissible on this day and what

---

14. On the Hebrew Bible's cultic calendars, see, e.g., Vaux, *Ancient Israel*, 468–74.

was not. Exodus 12:16 does acknowledge that people still have to eat, even on the sabbath.

Yet while what we might call the earlier significance of the sabbath was concerned with a day of rest, it would seem to have become also a day when sacrifices were offered. Perhaps it was a "later" practice, this particular keeping the sabbath that is reflected in Num 28:9–10 where the offerings appropriate for this day are set out, as indeed they are also in Ezek 46:4–5. Again, the references in Neh 10:33 and 2 Chr 8:13 and 31:3 suggest that in the post-exilic period these sabbath offerings were made regularly. Various of the Hebrew prophets speak of worship taking place on the sabbath (Isa 1:13; Hos 2:11; Amos 8:5), while 2 Kgs 4:23 would seem to suggest the prophets were likely to be consulted on this day.[15]

Leviticus 25:1–7, 20–22 explains the principle of the "Sabbatical Year" (*šabātôn*), that the seventh year of a seven-year cycle is to be a "sabbath of complete rest for the land," something of an extension of the sabbath-day rest principle (Exod 20:8–11; 31:12–17). The Israelites are told that in the sixth year of a given seven-year cycle the land will yield sufficient food to last the people until the next normally-produced harvest is gathered (Lev 25:19–22). This legislation is also spoken of in Exod 23:9–12. Further, there is talk in other parts of the Hebrew Bible of the seventh year of any seven-year cycle being observed in the cancellation of loans and the freeing of slaves (Deut 15:1–3, 12–15; Jer 34:8–16). We should also note that provision which is set out in such places as Lev 19:9–10; 23:22; Deut 24:19–20 (compare Ruth 2:1–7) specifying that certain parts of the harvest are to be left for those who otherwise would not have sufficient. These matters are presented as agricultural matters, and we do not read of any associated sacrifices, offerings, or other worship.

Then there is the matter of the year of Jubilee (*yôbēl*), of which details are given in Lev 25:8–17; 27:16–24, and also in Num 36:4, which specify that after seven periods of seven years, there is to be a further fallow year, the Year of Jubilee. This was also to be a year of "release," that is both release of land to its original ownership and also release of slaves. Again, this seems to have been a matter of what we might call social welfare, and no particular aspects of worship are specified in the documents that we have. Nevertheless, we do not have any clear indication that this year of Jubilee tradition was ever actually observed.[16]

15. For a thorough survey of the Old Testament's references to sabbath as a special religious day, see Rowley, *Worship in Ancient Israel*, 90–91; Vaux, *Ancient Israel*, 475–83; Binder, *Into the Temple Courts*, 18; Hasel, "Sabbath"; and Shafer, "Sabbath." McKay, in her *Sabbath and Synagogue*, makes a vigorous case for there not having been worship on the sabbath in ancient Israel. On sabbath and worship, see also Vaux, *Ancient Israel*, 469.

16. On this matter, see, e.g., Wright, "Jubilee, Year of"; and Knauth, "Jubilee, Year of."

Any Other Festivals?

There was at one period in the modern study of the Hebrew Bible the widespread acceptance of one of the theories of the Norwegian scholar Sigmund Mowinckel (1884-1965) that there was in the ancient Israelite new year — that Mowinckel argued was in the seventh month, Tishri — a festival when the divine kingship of Yahweh was celebrated, and so also the earthly kingship of the reigning king in Jerusalem. This theory was set out in Mowinckel's large work *The Psalms in Israel's Worship*.[17] More mature deliberations on Mowinckel's theories have let to the rejection of them by a large majority of present-day scholars for the reason that there is no clear evidence in the Old Testament that such festivals did in fact take place, though something of an exception is John Day.[18] Other possibilities of annual festivals in ancient Israel being reflected in the Old Testament psalms were set forth by such scholars as Artur Weiser, a ceremony of covenant renewal, and Hans-Joachim Kraus, the kingship of Yahweh. Again on the basis that we do not read of such festal ceremonies in the book of Psalms actually taking place, it has generally been felt that such theories are inevitably speculative, and thus, in keeping with a predominant trend in contemporary study of the Old Testament, in this particular work they are not further considered.

In later Judaism there were developed a number of religious festivals not spoken about in the Hebrew Bible, such as Purim (from the book of Esther), and in the period of the Maccabees the festival of Hanukkah. In the Qumran Scrolls there is mention of further feasts, such as Firstfruits of Oil, Feast of the Firstfruits of Wine, and even Feast of Wood Offering (11QT 19-25), while Josephus mentions a Festival of Woodgathering (*War* 2.425). Perhaps what is involved in the last-named is the provision of wood for the altar in the temple (see Neh 10:34).[19]

Lectionaries?

From time to time and over the years various scholars have suggested and argued for the existence and use of lectionaries in Israelite worship, but it has to be said that there is no real evidence for such, that is until the time of the synagogue. Then again, as has already been seen, our problem is paucity of evidence about the beginnings of the institution of the synagogue, in particular whether that was in the Babylonian Exile or whether, and this

---

17. Mowinckel, *The Psalms in Israel's Worship*, 1:106-92; 2:222-50. A development of these views of Mowinckel is to be observed in Eaton, *Vision in Worship*.

18. Day, *Psalms*, 67-87.

19. For worship at Qumran, see above, 55-56. On Qumran calendars, see Stern, "Qumran Calendars."

seems the most likely option, it was in the Hellenistic period.[20] With lectionaries we are beset with similarly elusive knowledge regarding possible beginnings. While we read in parts of the Old Testament what we might wish to regard as certain leanings and leadings towards the reading of parts of what became the Hebrew Bible, such as we have in Deut 31:10–12; 2 Kgs 22:8–13; 23:1–3; and Neh 8, it is not until as late as the first century CE that we have clear evidence for the reading of the Torah and the Prophets on a regular basis. Thus we read in Acts 15:21 "For in every city, for generations past, Moses has had those who proclaim him, for he has been read aloud every sabbath in the synagogues."[21] Further, the Preface to Sirach has been cited as second century BCE evidence of the public reading of the Law by the Jews in Egypt, but that is perhaps reading more into the Preface than in reality is there.[22]

However, by the time of the Mishnah some of those texts can be read as indicating that there was a pattern of readings from the Torah in the sabbath afternoon, and Monday and Thursday services.[23] Yet the comparatively late dating of these documents can hardly be cited as evidence that in the first century CE or earlier Jewish practice involved a regular pattern of readings. By the time we get to the third century CE it would seem that the synagogue did have a regular pattern of readings from the Law and Prophets, and perhaps, as has been suggested, that was in part intended to be a substitute for temple sacrifices.[24] While some have argued that at an early date there was a fixed triennial lectionary cycle in the Jewish church—and it has been pointed out that comparatively late witnesses to such practices could possibly represent what happened in earlier times—at the same time it can be argued that on these matters definite assurance is in short supply.[25] Thus in this particular study the issue of possible Jewish temple lectionaries will not be further considered.

---

20. On the beginnings of the institution of the synagogue, see above, 51–53.

21. See also Acts 13:14–15 and Luke 4:16–17.

22. This is cited by Guilding, *The Fourth Gospel and Jewish Worship*, 6. However, we may perhaps wish to ask, was Sirach saying anything more than that he was able in Egypt to find help in his study of the Law and the Prophets?

23. For references, see Aagerson, "Early Jewish Lectionaries," 271.

24. See Reumann, "A History of Lectionaries," esp. p. 116; and Werner, *The Sacred Bridge*, 52–53.

25. Thus following on, from, and in response to Guilding, *The Fourth Gospel and Jewish Worship*, see in particular the critiques of Porter, "The Pentateuch and the Triennial Lectionary Cycle"; Morris, *The New Testament and the Jewish Lectionaries*, 14–34; and Williams, "The Fourth Gospel and Jewish Worship." See also Bunce, "The Liturgy of the Last Gospel," esp. pp. 272–73.

11

Evidences of Liturgies

As has earlier been stated in this work the word "liturgy" is used in two main senses. The first is of a complete, whole act of worship, and thus is the word used of this present Part III of the study where we have considered the significance of prayers and psalms, sacrifices, feasts, festivals and calendars in *whole acts of worship*. The second sense in which "liturgy" is used is of a particularly *worded part* of an act of worship, and the associated task here in this chapter is to inquire if among the many and varied parts of the Hebrew Bible are some of the words of worship, of individual liturgical pieces, from times long ago. In truth, many have been the suggestions of scholars as to various passages in the Old Testament that present us, so it is argued, with wordings of ancient liturgies.[1] Inevitably, only a small number of the many suggestions that have been put forward can be discussed in this chapter. Further, what may have been suggested as liturgies from long ago must inevitably be speculative, to at least some degree. Indeed, the issue of whether or not such-and-such a passage was once a liturgy or fragment thereof must of necessity be an unresolvable question — at least until and if ever we find materials confirming such. Thus the material set forth here is inevitably of a speculative nature. Nevertheless, we may begin with certain words that must be widely judged as likely to have been liturgical materials from what we might call biblical times. Thus it is to the book of Exodus that first we turn.

Exodus

In Exod 15:1–21 we have two expressions of praise celebrating the divine victory at the sea, the victory portrayed as enabling the Israelites involved in these events to escape from Egypt and embark upon their journey through the wilderness to new life in Canaan. In this passage there are two songs, the first being portrayed as that of Moses (Exod 15:1–18) with the heart of its message expressed in v. 11:

---

1. In this regard, see Porter, "Cultic Interpretation."

> Who is like you, O Lord, among the gods?
> Who is like you, majestic in holiness,
> awesome in splendor, doing wonders? (Exod 15:11)

The second is the Song of Miriam, this being portrayed as accompanied by the playing of tambourines and dancing (Exod 15:20–21):

> Sing to the Lord, for he has triumphed gloriously;
> horse and rider he has thrown into the sea. (Exod 15:21)

It is very probable that this *is* material that was used in the Israelite cult, it being widely agreed among critics and commentators that here are liturgical pieces.[2] Here is an expression of the peoples' praise at what the Hebrew Bible presents as the fundamental, archetypal expression of divine deliverance of sufferers from their distresses, in particular of what was seen as the deliverance, rescue, of the people of God. We can well believe that this had a clear and definite place in the Israelite cult, and that here we have an example, or examples, of cultic liturgies. The most obvious setting for the use of these "hymns" would seem to have been in Passover celebrations.[3]

From Exodus to Micah

We continue with a formula found in a range of places in the Hebrew Bible to which the word "liturgy" has come to be attached, a formula that we may say makes a "primary" appearance in the book of Exodus, namely, Exod 34:6–7, two verses that in NRSV are translated as follows:

> The Lord, the Lord,
> a God merciful and gracious,
> slow to anger,
> and abounding in steadfast love and faithfulness,
> keeping steadfast love for the thousandth generation,
> forgiving iniquity and transgression and sin,
> yet by no means clearing the guilty,

---

2. See, e.g., Durham, *Exodus*, 202–5; Pedersen, *Israel, III-IV*, 405–7; Muilenburg, "A Liturgy on the Triumphs of Yahweh"; Hyatt, *Exodus*, 162–63; and Blenkinsopp, *The Pentateuch*, 157–60.

3. See Hyatt, *Exodus*, 162; Freedman, "Pentateuch"; and Noth, *Exodus*, 121. See also the discussion in Childs, *Exodus*, 240–53. Durham says, "the likelihood is that the poem was used on a regular basis, throughout the cultic year, not just at Passover or at some other holy occasion. The deliverance the poem celebrates is far too basic to Israel's faith and far too pervasive in OT theology for so splendid an account of it to have had so restricted a usage" (*Exodus*, 204). Others have argued for the setting of this liturgy in the Passover celebration.

> but visiting the iniquity of the parents upon the children
> and the children's children,
> to the third and the fourth generation. (Exod 34:6-7)

It is widely agreed that this passage has a relationship with worship, it being referred to variously as a creed, or as credal,[4] as "an old cultic formula preserved in the worship of Israel,"[5] or as "a part of a confession of faith about Yahweh."[6] It is an elaborate expression of praise to the Lord, yet portrayed as if it comes directly from that Lord himself (v. 6a), and it gives expression to the steadfast love and faithfulness of the Lord that lasts for generation upon generation, and forgives iniquity and transgression. Yet also it speaks of the Lord who in the mystery of his being judges his people for their sins, even to a number of generations. Whether this was first a part of a narrative that became a liturgy, or whether rather it was a known liturgy to the compilers of what has come down to us as the book of Exodus who then incorporated it into their work, we shall likely never know. From the point of view of its setting in the narrative about on the one hand the desert sin of the manufacture of the golden calf and the judgment of Yahweh upon that, with yet on the other hand the gracious compassion of the Lord that he would continue to lead his people on towards the promised land, certainly makes for a remarkable statement, and a powerful expression of faith in God in the liturgy of worship.

A shortened form of what we have in Exod 34:6-7 is to be found in three of the biblical psalms, unsurprisingly in that with the psalms we *are* in the midst of liturgical material,[7] namely Pss 86:15; 103:8; 145:8. In each of these occurrences there is nothing about the judgmental aspect of the Lord. Psalm 86:15 is a firm statement about the Lord being merciful and gracious, slow to anger, and abounding in steadfast love and faithfulness. The same is the case with Ps 103:8, while in Ps 145:8-9 the basic formula is there again but to it has been added in v. 9 "The Lord is good to all, and his compassion is over all that he has made," which has made the formula of praise capable of further and wider application, even generalizing it. Have the judgmental words that we find in Exod 34:6-7 been purposely not stated so as to enable the more general application in worship of the formula? In this regard it should be noted that the basic theme of the divine mercy which we find in the formula in these three psalms is also to be found in a series of other

---

4. So, e.g., Gowan, *Theology in Exodus,* 241; Coggins, *Exodus,* 124.

5. Thus Hyatt, *Exodus,* 323.

6. So Durham, *Exodus,* 454; Dentan, "The Literary Affinities of Exodus XXXIV 6f.," 34-51. See also Moberly, *At the Mountain of God,* 128-31.

7. On the psalms as liturgies, see below, 197-98. See also above, 119-61.

psalms; see Pss 40:10-12, 17; 78:38; 79:5-6, 8-10; 85:2-3, 5, 7, 10; 86:2-3, 5-6, 11, 16; 99:8; 111:1, 4-5, 7.

We come across the formula once again in Num 14:18, and this comes from what is portrayed as the desert setting in the time when the Israelites were complaining about the leadership of Moses and Aaron, when the people said to one another "Let us choose a captain, and go back to Egypt" (Num 14:4). Thus we are given in the words of Moses to the Lord the full form of our formula replete with both the judgmental and the compassionate and saving parts. In this setting that is hardly surprising.

The occurrences of this text go on: in Joel 2:13 where words about the Lord's willingness to relent from punishing are added, which is unsurprising in the portrayed situation of the lament drawn forth from a psalmist through the disaster of the locusts. Again in Nahum, a book to which we shall return below, we have a shortened form of the familiar formula: "The Lord is slow to anger but great in power, and the Lord will by no means clear the guilty." (Nah 1:3) Finally, we find the text in Jonah 4:2 and Neh 9:17, both of these having the compassionate and saving emphases: in Jonah 4:2 we have "ready to relent from punishing," this from the lips of the disgruntled prophet Jonah who had clearly expected and perhaps even wished for the divine judgment upon and the destruction of the Ninevites. Rather differently, in Neh 9:17 the familiar words come from the priest and scribe Ezra who prays for divine forgiveness of the people of Israel for their (perceived) sins that brought about the crisis and the judgment of the exile. May these same people now receive the forgiving love of the Lord, and no longer his punishment.

Not dissimilar are the words in Mic 7:18-20 about the overwhelming graciousness and compassion of the Lord for his sinful people, words with which the book of Micah in its final form ends. It has been suggested that the whole of the closing passage of the book, Mic 7:8-20, a passage that comprises a concluding confession, appeal and expression of confidence in the divine mercy, could have been intended to make up a composition for liturgical use.[8] At any rate here at the close of this short but varied prophetical book are summed up the major themes of the work, and in a form that we can well read as having been intended for liturgical usage. Thus after a lament concerning the people's present distress (7:1-6), the prophet looks to the Lord (7:7); then follows what was perhaps intended to be a liturgical piece (7:8-20). Here is confession, perhaps it being intended that Zion/Jerusalem is speaking (7:8-10), followed by a reassuring oracle about rebuilding

---

8. See Mays, *Micah*, 152-56; Allen, *Joel, Obadiah, Jonah and Micah*, 390-404; Gunkel, "The Close of Micah," 115-49; Willis, "A Reapplied Prophetic Hope Oracle"; Wolff, *Micah*, 211-35; and McKane, *Micah*, 237-39.

of walls, an extended boundary, and with peoples (returning exiles?) coming from afar (7:11–13). Then comes a prayer for the future life of people and city, in particular that it will be the Lord who guides, shepherds, leads, feeds his people, delivering them from fear of enemies (7:14–17). There is a final paean of praise for the forgiving and compassionate nature of the Lord (7:18–20) a passage that looks indeed as if it could well have been used as liturgy in temple and other worship in ancient Israel.[9]

Numbers and Deuteronomy

In Num 6:22–27 we read that Moses was instructed by the Lord to have Aaron and his sons bless the Israelites using the words,

> The Lord bless you and keep you;
> The Lord make his face to shine upon you, and be gracious to you;
> The Lord lift up his countenance upon you, and give you peace.
> (Num 6:24–26)

It is widely considered by commentators on this blessing formula that the actual words, not being in the characteristic language and style of the so-called Priestly writers, come from elsewhere, quite possibly from earlier times and that this formulation may represent a style of blessing used in the Jewish temple in pre-exilic times. This may be said to have received a degree of confirmation through the archaeological discovery of two silver plaques at Ketef Hinnom in the environs of Jerusalem, both of which have words of blessing remarkably similar to the wording we find in Num 6:24–26. These plaques have been dated as coming from the seventh or sixth centuries BCE.[10] We should perhaps note the intensely personal emphasis and application of this form of blessing: the verbs in it are grammatically in the singular, thus setting forth address to individual people. Further, the language of the Lord's shining face (see also Ps 67:1) is a common Hebrew anthropomorphism intended to signify his benevolent disposition, here upon the individuals being blessed. Further, the blessing being thus invoked upon these individuals is for what we might call quite ordinary, day-to-day things in life, in particular asking for the blessing of peace, a concept that

---

9. Mays says about Mic 7:18–20, "Verses 18–20 are a hymn of praise composed to be sung by the congregation (first person plurals in vv. 19f.)" (*Micah*, 166). See also Wolff, *Micah*, 228–35.

10. For details see, e.g., Davies, *Numbers*, 66. See also Barkay, *Ketef Hinnom*, esp. p. 29.

includes as well as prosperity, also, and perhaps primarily, the personally inward experience of harmony, wholeness, and well-being.[11]

Other examples of blessings spoken about in the Hebrew Bible, some of them portrayed as being uttered at the conclusion of worship, are to be found in Lev 9:22; Deut 21:5; 2 Chr 30:27; Pss 67:1 and 121:7–8. It is indeed not beyond the bounds of possibility that the basic form of these blessings may represent the sort of wording that found a place in the cult of ancient Israelite's worship in various historical periods.

Then in Deut 26:1–15 we have two ceremonies, both linked to the harvest of the land. The first of these is in 26:1–11 and for use at the time of the first fruits, and what is of particular interest in the context of this work is that there is a liturgical recital on the part of the person bringing their offering of first fruits. This is certainly presented to us in liturgical form, though whether it was actually used in Israel's cult must be highly questionable. The composition is exceedingly deuteronomic in style and content, holding together familiar deuteronomic themes: the bringing of the people out of Egypt; the gift of the land, and the place of worship the Lord has chosen where his name shall dwell; social concern for the less well-off in society.[12]

In Deut 26:13–15 we have another short composition in the style of a liturgical piece, this time expressing the affirmation of a worshipper that the gifts of the harvest have been used aright, in particular as regards obeying the laws concerning care of the less fortunate. Thus here in Deut 26:5–10, 13–15 we can say that we have what are presented as two short liturgical pieces, but which are in truth deuteronomic theological statements presented *as if* they were parts of the official liturgy of the temple, but unlikely to have been thus used.[13]

---

11. On these and other details about the priestly blessing in Num 6:22–27, see the helpful article of Miller, "The Blessing of God."

12. The thesis of Gerhard von Rad that we have in Deut 16 two short Israelite creeds (see "The Form-Critical Problem of the Hexateuch," 3–8) is seldom accepted these days. Deuteronomy 16:5–10, though reading in the manner and style of a liturgical piece, is probably here being set forth in order to proclaim once again the deuteronomic theology.

13. Nelson says, "the interpreter must recognize that Deuteronomy was more interested in promoting theology than in establishing a coherent liturgical system. Because theology took precedence, a certain amount of liturgical imprecision was acceptable." Nelson, *Deuteronomy*, 307.

The Book of Psalms

It has been argued earlier in this work[14] that we should regard the book of psalms primarily as a collection of compositions intended to be used in worship. Thus it is surely appropriate to regard each of the psalms as a liturgy. That is, here are the *words* for a whole range of situations and aspects of worship for a people to use in their approach to God in the cult. Here are liturgies for an individual, or even a whole community experiencing distressing circumstances, or alternatively in hopeful circumstances, having apparently been delivered from the threats that earlier loomed. Here are liturgies that help a people rehearse their faith in the Lord's trustworthiness, in his greatness and his faithfulness. Here truly are many liturgies, and it is more than likely that what have been preserved for us in the book of psalms did at times in the past serve as liturgies in the Jerusalem temples. Further, it is a fact that these same psalms have continued to be used as liturgies in century after century in both the Jewish Synagogue and the Christian Church.[15]

Yet there are at the same time certain of the psalms that do have the particular form of a liturgy, some of them in that they have an antiphonal, responsive style in their composition. For example, we have already seen how Pss 15 and 24 have a responsive style, enabling them to serve as liturgies for people preparing to worship,[16] and the series of psalms that have the heading "A Song of Ascents" (Pss 120-134) would seem to be a collection of liturgies for people who possibly were on their journey to worship in the temple. The last of these, Ps 134, surely bears the marks of a liturgical composition:

> Come, bless the Lord, all you servants of the Lord,
> who stand by night in the house of the Lord!
> Lift up your hands to the holy place, and bless the Lord.
> May the Lord, maker of heaven and earth,
> bless you from Zion. (Ps 134:1-3)

There are other psalms that are in antiphonal style, such as Pss 50, 81, 95, 118, 132. Other psalms bearing a particular liturgical style are Pss 100, 146-150. Psalm 136 is a hymn, and after each clause calling for thanksgiving and praise there is the response, "for his steadfast love endures forever."

---

14. See above, 157-61.

15. For the psalms and worship, see Gillingham, *The Poems and Psalms of the Hebrew Bible*, esp. pp. 211-19, 225-30, 271-72; ibid., *Psalms Through the Centuries*; ibid., *A Journey of Two Psalms*; Holladay, *The Psalms through Three Thousand Years*; Waltke et al., *The Psalms as Christian Worship*; and ibid., *The Psalms as Christian Lament*.

16. On Pss 15 and 24, see above, 130-31 and 133.

Psalm 46, another of the hymns in the psalter, also has a response, this being used but just twice, in verses 7 and 11, "The Lord of hosts is with us; the God of Jacob is our refuge." Various of the psalm headings clearly indicate the use of psalms in worship, as also in all probability does the rather mysterious "Selah." Certain of the last verses of certain psalms look as if they have perhaps been added for liturgical purposes (see, for example, Pss 2:11b; 3:8; 4:8; 7:17 and so on). Then Pss 50, 52, and 58, it has been suggested, were prophetic liturgies, and so indeed they could have been. Psalms 15, 24, 58 have unsurprisingly been called liturgies, but in fact the whole of the biblical Psalter is surely made up of liturgical materials. This is what the Book of Psalms *is*, quite simply a collection of words for worship, of materials to be used in the liturgy of worship.

We may bring to a close this short section on the Psalms by considering Ps 100, a psalm that without doubt is to be regarded as a liturgical piece coming out of the cultic life of ancient Israel. Further, it is a psalm that has been found to be remarkably helpful and challenging to many a generation of Israelite, Jewish, and Christian worshippers. Psalm 100 is indeed a profound call to worship the Lord, this command, this call being expressed through a series of verbs in the imperative. Further, reasons for these commands to praise are given: for the Lord made us; we are his people; he is good, his steadfast love (*ḥesed*) and faithfulness (*'ĕmûnāh*) enduring for ever (vv. 3–5). Thus there is the call for joyful and gladness-filled worship to be made to him:

> Make a joyful noise to the Lord, all the earth.
> Worship the Lord with gladness;
> come into his presence with singing.
>
> Know that the Lord is God.
> It is he that made us, and we are his;
> we are his people, and the sheep of his pasture.
>
> Enter his gates with thanksgiving,
> and his courts with praise.
> Give thanks to him, bless his name.
>
> For the Lord is good;
> his steadfast love endures forever,
> and his faithfulness to all generations. (Ps 100:1–5)

Nahum

The short book of the prophet Nahum was at one time regarded by some scholars as being the work of a cultic prophet, this being the thesis of P. Haupt in 1907 and of A. Haldar in 1947.[17] As has already been noted a number of times in this work, there is no certainty that there ever was in ancient Israel such an institution as "cultic prophets"; certainly we are not told about any such group or institution in the Hebrew Bible, and thus the approach in this work has been not to pursue such a possibility. What, however, we can say with some assurance is that the language of Nahum is imbued with a real note of worship; the Lord is exalted in these chapters as a great and active God in the world, and that thus it is more than reasonable to say with Richard J. Coggins "it is right to recognize that the literary usage of Nahum may often imply an indebtedness to the language of the cult."[18] Certainly the whole approach in this short prophetic book is intensely theocentric, from the theophany hymnic material in Nah 1:2-8, continuing with the uselessness of any Assyrian resistance (1:9-11), to the threats of judgment against the enemies of Israel and the assurance of deliverance to Israel (1:12—2:2). These themes continue with words about the defeat of Nineveh (that is, enemy of Yahweh) (2:3-13), and a prophetic woe-oracle against Nineveh (3:1-19). Thus the central issue in this prophecy is that of the Lord's universal sovereignty, while the style of the language could indeed be one that owed something to the cult, maybe indeed to the Jerusalem cult. Such a conclusion may be said to be strengthened by the further observation that Nahum does show something of a tendency to borrow from earlier prophetical materials—and the borrowings would seem to be by Nahum, rather than the other way round, which would indeed make Nahum a post-exilic work and that evil forces in that prophet's day have been personalized as Assyrian. For not only do we have in Nah 1:3 a reflection of the Exod 34:6-7 statement, but also in Nah 1:15a there is a near-identical rendering of Isa 52:7a. See also Nah 1:4 and note the similarities with Isa 33:9 and 50:2; and further Nah 1:15b with Isa 52:1b. Thus it looks as if Nahum's borrowings are not only from the world and the language of the cult, but also from his prophetic predecessors, in particular those in the Isaiah tradition.

---

17. See Haupt, "The Book of Nahum"; A. Haldar, *Studies in the Book of Nahum*.

18. Coggins and Re'emi, *Nahum, Obadiah, Esther*, 10. See also Coggins, "An Alternative Prophetic Tradition"; Mason, *Micah, Nahum, Obadiah*, 73-9.

Joel

The book of the prophet Joel has sometimes been regarded as a cultic liturgy, or else that it has been written in the style of a cultic liturgy. I suggest that the former proposal is still as highly speculative as it ever was, but that the latter is a likely possibility. I shall therefore not consider this book any further in this chapter, but I shall return to it in ch. 13, "The Prophets and Worship."[19]

Lamentations

No small number of commentators on Lamentations observe that here is material that has been used liturgically, in particular in connection with national lamentations on the fall of Jerusalem and the destruction of the temple in 587 BCE. It has been pointed out that phrases from this book seem to have been familiar "to the cultic-minded Chronicler (cf. II Chron.36.16-19)."[20] We read about public laments over the fall of Jerusalem in Jer 41:4–5; Isa 61:3; Zech 7:2–7 and 8:19), and we know that in later rabbinic times Lamentations was used in public laments on the ninth day of Ab as the Jerusalem city and temple destruction was remembered. It would seem that there are good grounds for our accepting that in the book of Lamentations we do have indeed liturgical materials.[21]

Habakkuk

The prophet Habakkuk's problem is that of theodicy, in particular that the warring incursions of the Chaldeans upon the people of Judah cannot be interpreted as being the Lord's judgment upon his sinful people, for the reason that the suffering and damage the Chaldeans are causing are far greater than, and totally out of proportion with, the distresses they are being called to correct.[22] However, there is no straightforward alternative theodicy presented in this prophetical book, yet what we do have by way of any answer to the new problem of the suffering of the people of Judah is expressed in cultic terms, in the language of worship. Not only is the burden of the people's

---

19. See below, 264–65.

20. Gottwald, *Studies in the Book of Lamentations*, 112.

21. See the remarks of, e.g., Provan, *Lamentations*, 19–20; and Parry, *Lamentations*, 7.

22. In this regard, see Thompson, "Prayer, Oracle and Theophany"; and ibid., "Where is the God of Justice?," 62–76.

problem stated to the Lord in the language of biblical laments (Hab 1:2-4, 12-17), but also the resolution of that problem is presented in the psalm prayer of Hab 3:1-16, with its assurance of both the Lord's might, and also his will, to save his people. Further, the reality of this divine will to save his people is here portrayed as coming to them through the medium, indeed perhaps the very experience itself, of worship, through the cult. In this regard there is a parallel with the resolution of the theodicy problem stated and resolved in Ps 73, namely, through the psalmist's going into the temple and there finding renewed assurance about the saving will of the Lord (v. 17).[23]

Few of us these days would wish to argue that Habakkuk was a cultic prophet for reasons that have already been stated, though it is entirely understandable that scholars of an earlier generation did so. Yet at the same time there is a clear relationship of the book of Habakkuk with the Judean cult and its associated worship. At the very least we have to say that this prophet was a borrower of the language and the imagery of the Jerusalem cult. Moreover, it seems probable that he was well acquainted with that cult, and that further it is surely not unreasonable to suggest that he used some of those religious realities set forth in its worship to proclaim his message of assurance to a suffering people. Perhaps the laments of Hab 1:2-4 and 12-17, along with the psalmic like passage in 3:1-19 do reflect something of the liturgies that were known in Israel's cult.

The Book of Isaiah

I consider the wider issues of what there is about worship in the book of Isaiah in the chapter which follows;[24] here the specific concern is with what appear to have been liturgies, and the material that it has been argued were, or reflected, liturgies. While there is much in this prophecy that seems clearly to reflect the liturgy of the Jerusalem cult, what we have are likely more in the nature of borrowings from that cult, rather than quotations of actual liturgies. Thus while the account of the prophet's memorable vision of the Lord in Isa 6:1-13 would seem to be an account of what the prophet experienced or what another, or others, understood him to have experienced, we are aware at the same time that the tenor of the passage does suggest the setting of the Jerusalem temple and its worship.

---

23. On Ps 73 and the issue of theodicy and worship, see Thompson, "*Where is the God of Justice?*," 100-4.

24. See below, 245-50.

Then as far as the psalm of thanksgiving in Isa 12:1–6 is concerned, it would appear that what we have here is a composition modelled upon such psalms of thanksgiving as Ps 107, and containing a series of quotations from a number of psalms, thus presenting us with what Blenkinsopp calls "a patchwork of biblical citations and allusion, especially from the book of Psalms."[25] Thus we may say that this psalm is in the style of what may be called a liturgy, that is a psalmic liturgy. Perhaps we would say much the same about the passage concerning the pilgrimage of the nations to Zion (Isa 2:2–4). This, along with the Old Testament's other version of it which occurs in Mic 4:1–5, also uses solemn, and thrillingly promissory material, yet there is hardly the evidence to suggest that it was ever used as a liturgy, or that it is presented in the style of a liturgy.

Isaiah ch. 33 should be regarded, Hermann Gunkel argued, as a "prophetic liturgy," but it has to be said that he had the majority of scholars in disagreement and only a handful in support.[26] Two of the principal difficulties in understanding this chapter relate to the problem of dating the various parts of it, and of understanding the relationships between them. Thus I also have argued that we should understand the chapter as an extended composition, the whole being developed into the form of a liturgy. Thus we have a woe oracle (vv. 1–6); a lament (vv. 7–9); an assurance of divine saving activity (vv. 10–13); a temple entrance liturgy (vv. 14–16); a vision of the Lord (vv. 17–19); and finally a vision of the peaceful city (vv. 20–24). Whether this was ever used as a liturgy we have no way of knowing. Yet in the context of this particular study it is surely not without significance that this crucial chapter, clearly set at a nodal point in the whole span and arrangement of the Isaiah book, should be expressed in the form and style of a liturgy.[27]

Isaiah 38:9–22 is entitled "writing" (*miktāb*), but which some would amend to *miktām*, a word that only occurs in some psalm headings (Pss 16:1; 56:1; 57:1; 60:1), perhaps meaning either "inscription" or "secret prayer."[28] Further, while it does seem most likely that the material commonly known as the "Isaiah Narratives" which appears in both Kings and Isaiah, is original to the Kings version, later this material came to be incorporated, with some changes, into the growth process of the book of Isaiah. One of the changes

---

25. Blenkinsopp, *Isaiah 1–39*, p. 270. The psalmic references Blenkinsopp gives that make up his "patchwork" are, in order of occurrence, Pss 118:21; 88:22; 25:5; 118:14; 105:1; 148:13; 9:12; 30:5.

26. Gunkel, "Jesaia 33, eine prophetische Liturgie," and on this see Murray, "Prophecy and Cult," 205–14.

27. For further details on these matters, see Thompson, "Vision, Reality and Worship."

28. See *DCH* 5:276.

was the addition of the "writing", "secret prayer" now in Isa 38:9-22, where it makes a composition on the subject of illness and death, containing both lament (vv. 9-18) and also thanksgiving (vv. 19-22). While there has been some scholarly debate as to the significance of the addition to the composition as it was inserted into the Isaiah book material, in particular concerning whether or not it was intended to emphasize the divine deliverance of the people and city of Jerusalem from the siege of the Assyrian army, equally we may consider it as being fashioned in the style and manner of a liturgical prayer for a person suffering a serious illness and who cries out to the Lord for help.

For most of the time represented by the Old Testament documents there was no hope of a life after death, and thus that serious illness could mean death as the end of any meaningful life. The best that could be hoped for was the rather shadowy existence in Sheol, a place about which the Hebrew Bible is divided as to whether or not God is present (see Ps 6:5 and compare Ps 139:8). Thus, and unsurprisingly, there are psalms that speaking of the finality of death, express the prayerful hope of deliverance from illness. See Pss 30:9; 88:1-6, 10-12; 115:17; Sir 17:27-28. This situation is reflected in the passage at present being considered (Isa 38:18), but there is also here the expression of thanksgiving for the fact that the speaker, King Hezekiah, was believed to have been divinely delivered from the peril of death (Isa 38:19-20). Could not this particular expression of looming tragedy, along with the later sense of merciful deliverance, reflect some sort of relationship with a ritual, even liturgy, employed in ancient Israel in circumstances which appeared to be presaging death but in which, mercifully, death did not eventuate?

There is also Isa 59:1-4, 9-20 to be considered, material that Muilenburg argued had a relationship with liturgy. Certainly these verses read like communal laments, and it is not unlikely that they did originate in the setting of the cult. Clearly the situation concerns gross and varied sinfulness in the post-exilic Jewish community in Jerusalem, Muilenburg going as far as saying that "Few chapters in the Bible are so rich and diverse in their vocabulary of sin (cf. Ps 51). Indeed, so rich is this language that English translation fails to do justice to it."[29] It would seem that there is material here that likely did have a relationship with the re-emerging Jerusalem cult—or indeed with the cult in pre-exilic times.

Isaiah 61 and 62 have been suggested as based on possible liturgies, but there is little evidence to support such a thesis. The approach of John

---

29. Muilenburg, "Isaiah 40–66," 686. For the liturgical character of Isa 59:1–21, Muilenburg refers us to Procksch, *Theologie des Alte Testaments*, 294.

Goldingay that in these chapters there are set forth five responses to the prophetic word of Isa 60:1–22 is more likely to be correct. That is, in Isa 61:1–9 we have a call to proclaim the message; in 61:10–11 an expression of praise; in 62:1–5 the call to prayer; in 62:6–9 the commissioning of those who will remind the Lord of his promises; and in 62:10–12 the commissioning of workers.[30]

Then Isa 63:7—64:12 is to be considered, a passage that it is very generally agreed should be regarded as corporate lament.[31] Here the community, the nation, remembers with thanksgiving and praise the Lord's acts on its behalf in times past (63:7–14), and then recites something of its present plight and appeals to God for his help (63:15—64:5a). There is a confession of sin (64:5b–7), and finally a renewed appeal to God (64:8–12). All this is of a piece with other expressions of penitential piety we find present in the post-exilic, Second Temple period such as Ezra 9:6–15 and Neh 9:6–37. The book Lamentations should be included in this list, with Dan 9:4–19 further expressing the same sort of anguished confession but from a rather later time. The Isa 63:7—64:12 passage has been the subject of considerable debate as to its more precise setting in life, Williamson for example and earlier others, making a robust case for it having been a liturgical composition, maybe even having been used either on the site of the ruined temple or at some other center. Blenkinsopp agrees that such a proposal "is plausible if unprovable," adding that "the structural and metrical irregularity of the composition and its close connection with the passage that follows could with equal plausibility favor the hypothesis of a purely literary work that imitates the language and themes of the psalms of lamentation." Which is, it has to be accepted, much the same as could be said, and certainly should not be forgotten, about the contents of the whole of the present chapter. Even so, Williamson and others could be correct in postulating that the present passage reflects liturgical concerns of the post-exilic period, and that what we have here might be the type of liturgy we also read about in Zech 7:1–7 and 8:18–23, which will be considered below.[32]

Before we leave the book of Isaiah we must give consideration to the thesis of Michael Goulder that the whole of the Isaiah book may be said to constitute a liturgy, in particular that he finds the Isaiah book having eight sections each of which reflects the concerns of the Psalms of Korah, and used on the eight days of the pre-exilic celebration of the Feast

---

30. See Goldingay, *Isaiah*, 345–52.
31. On the so-called corporate laments, see above, 129, 142, 147.
32. Blenkinsopp, *Isaiah 56–66*, p. 259; and Williamson, "Isaiah 63:7—64:11."

of Tabernacles.[33] This is a thesis, large and bold, but yet hardly provable; indeed some of Goulder's statements are hardly believable. Further, the fact that the Isaiah book and a group of psalms have themes in common does not necessarily mean that one is dependent upon the other. It could be that they both reflect what is going on in the common life. We surely have to accept that as yet the case that the book of Isaiah's form and emphasis owes to parts of the liturgy of the Jerusalem temple remains unlikely. Rather more likely is the commoner view that the present form of the whole book of Isaiah is due to literary concerns and the ongoing theological thinking of a series of prophets and others through a sequence of national crises and other happenings. Yet, as we have seen, there has over the years been no shortage of suggestions that parts of the Isaiah book are owing in different ways to the life of the cult, in particular to various liturgies that had their place in that worship.

Zechariah and Song of Songs

Both these works have been suggested as presenting either in part or in entirety certain features indicating cultic usage. Thus, for example, it has been posited that much of the material in the series of visions in Zech 1:7—6:15, visions which, as Katrina Larkin expresses it, "exist betwixt and between the mundane world and the heavenly world where history is made and where Jerusalem's restoration is being ordained,"[34] and which have roots in the Jerusalem cult, perhaps drawing in particular from the liturgies of the foundation of the temple, and maybe also with a general background in Ugaritic texts.[35] In view of the fact that clearly a major concern of the prophet of Zech 1–8 is with encouraging his people to rebuild the Jerusalem temple, it is possible that part of the prophet's way of appealing to them was to remind them of what had gone before in the temple of Solomon and its liturgies. It is an attractive theory, but alas not provable and one therefore that must inevitably remain no more than a possibility

About Song of Songs there have been a number of suggestions concerning a relationship with worship and cults, both cults which in the terms of what we have in the Hebrew Bible would be regarded as official, and also those that would be deemed unacceptable importations of non-Israelite cults. A number of these proposed cultic backgrounds to the Song were set

33. Goulder, *Isaiah as Liturgy*; and ibid., *The Psalms of the Sons of Korah*.
34. Larkin, "Zechariah," 611.
35. Mason, *Preaching the Tradition*; and Halpern, "The Ritual Background of Zechariah's Temple Song."

out in detail by H. H. Rowley, and others have followed him in detailing further and later suggestions.[36] Nevertheless, it is one thing to argue that there are reflections in the text of the Song from various cults and worship practices engaged in by the people of Israel, but it is a rather different matter to argue that what we have in the Song, or in parts of it, are reflections of liturgies, or even more of actual liturgies. Of those last-named it must be said that there are no clear traces in the text of Song of Songs that has come down to us.

By Way of Summary

As stated at the beginning of this chapter what has been written here can make no claim to being the results of exhaustive study. The above is no more than a sampling of suggestions that have been made over the years as to what in the Hebrew Bible may be some relics of liturgies from the life of the Israelite cult—or what maybe have been written in *imitation* of the style and approach of certain liturgies. Further, any decisions that may be made following such suggestions must inevitably be largely subjective, for we are hardly as well informed about the liturgies of ancient Israel's cult as we may have wished, and so have little with which to compare the fruits of our searches.

As stated above, my foregoing study claims to be no more than a brief sampling of just some of the many possible pieces of liturgy that have come down to us. Time fails to speak of such possibilities as Hos 14:2b–3, of Jonah 2, of Obadiah, and of much else. Yet what has been set forth is perhaps sufficient to suggest once again the sheer pervasiveness of the influence of the cult upon the life and literature of the Hebrew Bible. The Old Testament witnesses to a tradition of worship that was not confined to shrine, tabernacle, or temple, but one whose visions and formulations informed and influenced life far beyond those holy places, and whose language, forms of speech, and vocabulary possibly became widely disseminated into the language of ordinary speech.

The one part of the Old Testament that is different in this regard is the book of Psalms, for here manifestly is a large collection of liturgies. At the other extreme we have to say that if indeed our search is for the wording of liturgies, we must inevitably be disappointed with our investigations into the book of Leviticus, for what in the main we read about there is what is

---

36. H. H. Rowley, "The Interpretation of the Song of Songs." See also more recently, e.g., Garrett and House, *Song of Songs/Lamentation*, 81–82; Exum, *Song of Songs*, 47–63, 79–80; Snaith, *Song of Songs*, 5–6; and Pope, *Song of Songs*.

to be *done* rather than what is to be *said*, and that is very largely what the priests are to do. The same goes for our study of other parts of the Hebrew Bible that scholarship has labelled "Priestly."[37]

Yet for what we do have as relics of ancient liturgies—or perhaps what we *think* we have by way of such relics—we are indeed truly grateful, for with due regard for human, and perhaps in particular scholarly, subjectivity we have perhaps been vouchsafed a series of small windows opening up onto the worship of a people of long ago. Further, these "discovered" relics perhaps show us how in varying degrees the cult of ancient Israel impinged—and in some cases not?—upon the thoughts, formulations, and writings of its thinkers and theologians.

---

37. On the so-called Priestly contributions to the Old Testament, see below, 211–17.

PART IV

Visions and Warnings

> Is not this the fast that I choose:
> to loose the bonds of injustice,
> to undo the thongs of the yoke,
> to let the oppressed go free,
> and to break every yoke?
>
> ISAIAH 58:6

There is in the Hebrew Bible no single approach to, vision of worship. Rather, there are varieties of styles, approaches, and visions of worship, some of them coming about because of background historical circumstances; some because of ills in society that needed to be faced up to and addressed in the context of worship; others perhaps because there were leaders who quite simply laid their primary emphases upon different aspects of worship, for example either of singing, or of praying, or sacrificing, or celebrating, and around such an emphasis seeking to prescribe ways of worship. A number of these approaches to worship in the Old Testament call for further consideration, in particular the Priestly approach, the Deuteronomic, those of the Chronicler and of the Wisdom writers, and something of these will be set out in ch. 12.

Chapter 13 is concerned with the books of the prophets, and considers what Hebrew prophets and their editors had to say on the subject of worship, not only about its lack of worth when accompanied by lives lived with little or no consideration for the principles of justice and righteousness, but also about wider matters concerning the worship offered to the Lord in the national shrines and elsewhere, about living and thinking, believing and acting in worshipful ways. Hopefully we will hear again that element of profound worship expressed in the books of the prophets, in such words as,

> For my thoughts are not your thoughts,
> nor are your ways my ways, says the Lord.
> For as the heavens are higher than the earth,
> so are my ways higher than your ways
> and my thoughts than your thoughts. (Isaiah 55:8–9)

12

Visions of Worship

There are certain parts of the Old Testament that have either a particular concern about the matter of worship, such as for example the so-called Priestly material in the Pentateuch/Torah, or else have something distinctive to say in their writings in regard to the worship of Yahweh, examples of these being the Deuteronomic writers; the Chronicler; and the authors of the so-called Wisdom Writings. These are our concern in the present chapter, and we begin with the Priestly writers for the fact is that a major, if not *the* major, concern and subject of their contribution to the Hebrew Bible was in the vital matter of the worship of the Lord God of Israel.

Worship in the Priestly Writings

We have already considered what these writers have to say about priests and Levites and their ministry in worship, and also about the various sacrifices that they and others offered.[1] Such matters do not need to be repeated here, but what calls to be considered is the overall content and emphases of the worship the priestly fraternity believed should be offered.

In recent decades there has taken place a renewed debate about the Pentateuch/Torah and its make-up, in particular over earlier scholarship's proposals that there were sources that were given the labels "Yahwist" and "Elohist." In the recent debate it would still be very generally agreed that while we cannot be sure just what materials belong respectively to the work of those supposed Yahwist and Elohist writers, what is clear are evidences of materials that have the "deuteronomic" stamp, and what is the literature with a "priestly" stamp. By this last-mentioned material we intend those parts of the Pentateuch/Torah that in the words of Julius Wellhausen are about "the Mosaic theocracy, with the tabernacle at its center, the high priest at its head, the priests and Levites as its organs, the legitimate cultus as its regular function."[2]

---

1. On priests and Levites, see above, 71–88; for sacrifices, see above, 162–78.

2. Wellhausen, *Prolegomena to the History of Ancient Israel*, 8–9. On this recently "renewed" debate about Pentateuch sources, see, e.g., Nicholson, *The Pentateuch in the*

In spite of debates both past and more recent about the makeup of the Pentateuch, there are nevertheless remaining questions about "Priestly" material, not only concerning its date of origin, but also whether or not it was ever an independent source. For our purposes we do not need to come to definite conclusions about these matters, save to say that there are certainly portions of material in the Torah that give the appearance of having been compiled by a priestly caste, material that was probably produced as Graham Davies expresses the matter "by priests for priests."[3] The likely period for the compilation of this material is a matter to which we will return after considering the theological thought and emphases of its contents.[4]

In the narrative parts of the Pentateuch we find that the Priestly writings tend to be speeches made by such worthies as Noah, Abraham, and Moses. The Lord is set forth in this material as having created the whole world (Gen 1), and into which in special positions he has placed humanity, which has been made "in his image"; and to these people he has given a responsibility of dominion over the earth (Gen 1:26). Particularly called to carry on the purposes of God are Noah, then later Abraham, and even later Moses. As far as the desert journey in the days of Moses is concerned the Priestly writers are much less concerned with the issue of divine guidance than the other contributors to this material, but major-in rather on matters to do with worship and the cult (see for example Exod 16:25–30)—as Wellhausen so eloquently expounded in his epoch-making book, originally published in 1878, quoted above.

Genesis 2:2–3 speaks of the divine appointment of the sabbath, which is to be a day of rest, and that may be said to constitute the first ritual commandment in the Hebrew Bible. Then as regards ritual[5] we read about the ban on the human eating of blood (Gen 9:4), and the command about circumcision (Gen 17:9–14, 22–27). In Exod 25—31 and 35—40 we have the details about and building of the desert tabernacle, these details having been revealed to Moses on Mount Sinai. The word "tabernacle" (*miškān*) means "dwelling place," and that is clearly intended to signify the "divine presence," that is in order that the Lord may dwell with his people on their desert

---

Twentieth Century; and Whybray, *The Making of the Pentateuch*.

3. Davies, "Introduction to the Pentateuch," 28.

4. As far as the contents of the so-called Priestly work are concerned, we may say that in general terms the following would be widely recognized: Gen 1:1—2:4a; most of 5; parts of the flood story; parts of 10; most of 11:10—32; 17; 23; 28:1–9; 35:9–13; most of the genealogies. Exod 6:2—7:13; 12:1–20, 40–51; 25–31; 35–40. All of Leviticus. Num 1:1—10:28; parts of 16–18; most of 25:6—36:13; 33.

5. For what is intended in this work by the word "ritual," see above, 15, and below, 215–17.

pilgrimage (see Exod 25:8; 40:34). Further, outside this tabernacle there is to be the altar, upon which sacrifices are to be offered, which were believed to be the means whereby the relationship between God and his people was to be maintained.[6]

Moreover, there is talk in these same chapters of the "Tent of Meeting," that is the place set apart where the people may meet with the Lord. Here is the Priestly emphasis on a theology of the Lord's presence with his people centered upon sanctuaries. Nor to be forgotten in this Priestly theological thought is the matter of seeking forgiveness of sins, in particular through the sacrificial system, with the associated guidance of the priests in regard to offering the correct sacrifices at the specified times, and also as to distinguishing what is holy and what is common, between the clean and the unclean (see for example Lev 10:10). For in the Priestly writings there is envisaged a large gulf between the holy Lord and the sinful people of earth, yet it is not that the Lord actually dwells, lives in a tabernacle (or indeed in a tent), but rather that he appears within it from time to time in a cloud with his "glory" (*kābôd*). Further, the Lord speaks not so much directly to the people, but rather through Moses and Aaron. This affects the layout of the desert camp where the priests and the Levites are domiciled between the sanctuary and the people, for it is through these cultic officials that the people come to the Lord. Thus "The life of the people is encompassed by the ritual law and secured by propitiation, which is the purpose of the cult."[7]

As has been noted above, there are a number of views propounded as to the date of this Priestly material in the Pentateuch, and also as to whether it reflects actual practice or whether it is an idealized program of a priestly religion. For want of certainty in these matters we may perhaps venture the opinion that this material reflects something of what took place in the first Jerusalem temple, that it was compiled in the time of the Babylonian exile, and that it was intended to be a contribution to, a program for what was to become one day the new, the second, temple in Jerusalem.

Yet this talk of possibly contributing to a second, that is renewed, temple in Jerusalem raises the issue of what these so-called Priestly writers intended to indicate through their use of the word "tabernacle," which leads to consideration of the relationship between the desert "tabernacle" we read about in the Pentateuch and the "temple" in 1 Kgs and elsewhere.

---

6. Thus the title of Hundley's work on the priestly material in the Pentateuch, *Keeping Heaven on Earth*, a study which the author explains "examines this Priestly system [in the Priestly texts of the Hebrew Bible] designed to keep heaven on earth, more specifically, to secure and safeguard the divine presence at the heart of the Israelite community" (p. 1). See also Jenson, *Graded Holiness*, 111–14, 135–38.

7. Fohrer, *Introduction to the Old Testament*, 185.

The fact is that the details of these two structures are remarkably similar; it may even be said that they are improbably similar in that while the desert tabernacle is portrayed as coming from the days of the desert journey, the temple in Jerusalem comes from the settled days of burgeoning kingship, that of Solomon, along with international co-operation in the execution of that king's large Jerusalem building project. As we have already seen it is inherently improbable that a structure as large and elaborate as Solomon's temple, dependent upon foreign help in building and supply of materials, would have been practical for use in the desert, or even that it could have been built in the setting of a desert place by a journeying people.[8]

The most satisfactory solution to this matter is to regard the account of the desert tabernacle as reflecting what was later carried out in the building of the monarchical-Jerusalem temple and that the details of the latter were retrojected back into the desert setting. Yet there is something more to be said that *miškān* (Tabernacle) was perhaps something different from what *hêkāl* (temple), or *bêth ha'ĕlōhîm/YHWH* (House of God/Yahweh, that is, temple) indicated. Was the word "tabernacle" intended to indicate the sanctuary of a people who were on a (desert) journey, while the wording for "temple" was intended to indicate the holy place for a people who had taken up occupation in and around a particular place on earth, now settled, no longer a people on pilgrimage? Certainly, the word "tabernacle" in its total of 139 appearances in the Hebrew Bible has 103 of them in Priestly material.[9] On the other hand the deuteronomistic writers have a marked tendency to use the word "house" (*bait*), that is "temple," for the place of worship. Further it would seem that while the P writers tend to use the word and concept "tabernacle" for the desert sanctuary, and regarding what takes place within it as being dominated by sacrificial worship, (with perhaps prayer taking place in the Tent of Meeting?), by contrast the Deuteronomists tend to use the designation "house" (*bait*) or "temple" (*hêkāl*), and their recording of the dedication of this "house" in 1 Kgs 8:12–61 with its great space given to prayer, and followed by a comparatively brief account of the sacrifices offered (1 Kgs 8:62–64), suggests that the predominant aspect of worship they had in mind had a real emphasis upon prayer.

Some years ago Terence Fretheim argued the case that the Pentateuch's Priestly Document was anti-temple, in particular on the basis that the Jerusalem temple represented a settledness of people and faith, and thus inevitably a desertion of the old desert ideals of a pilgrim people with their

---

8. On these issues, see above, 24–28.
9. See Kellermann "*miškān*," 59.

associated itinerant places for worship.[10] Fretheim did not make reference to the issues of the possible significance of the change of usage of the sanctuary names from tabernacle and tent to temple, but it could be that that too was part of this change of perception from earlier to later times and conditions. It could also be that eventually the word "tabernacle" did come to be employed in more general terms of a place of Yahwistic worship, which would perhaps explain the occurrence of the word in some of the Psalms (see Pss 26:8; 43:3; 46:4 (Heb. v. 5); 49:11 (Heb. v. 12); 74:7; 78:28, 60; 84:1 (Heb. v. 2); 87:2; 132:5, 7), and perhaps elsewhere.

I would not wish to go so far as Fretheim did in his argument that the priestly writers were "anti-temple," but I do think these writers wished to make a point about the apparent desertion of the old desert traditions with its emphasis upon the need for God's people to keep moving on even in the establishing of the great temple on mount Zion. For perhaps the priestly writers were writing in times of great change when, for those who had eyes to see, it could be observed that the old monarchical kingdoms of Israel and Judah had come to an end, and that in the fairly immediate situation the Lord's covenant people was indeed once again to be a pilgrim people—and would perhaps have to continue to be so. Thus, I suggest, they did do something to emphasize this by their use of the word "tabernacle" for the sanctuary about which they wrote. There was indeed a sense in which the desert sanctuary they presented in their writings in such great detail was to a certain extent a retrojection of Solomon's Jerusalem temple, but it was nevertheless a retrojection seen through the lenses of the desert sanctuary. And as a part of that retrojection they changed the name of the Jerusalem shrine from "temple" to "tabernacle."

Yet concerning these priestly writers something must be said about the language of ritual we encounter in their writings, a matter that in recent years has come to the forefront in Hebrew Bible studies.[11] Rituals are common in most cultures: they employ common and worldly language, artefacts, and symbols to express issues and events which have other-worldly dimensions. Thus significant stages in an individual's life cycle, birth, puberty, marriage or the formalizing of other relationships, death are marked with earthly rites, and in many cases those earthly rites are intended to invoke divine help, blessings, mercies, in short to bring those who are at

---

10. Fretheim, "The Priestly Document: Anti-Temple?" See, e.g., what he has to say about the priestly writers: ". . . we suggest that the writers were advocating a long-existing tradition that the Israelite sanctuary should be portable and that the conception of God which they treasured was compatible only with such an institution" (316).

11. See, e.g, the work of Gorman, in particular *The Ideology of Ritual* and "Ritual Studies and Biblical Studies."

one of life's significant stages into what is believed to be the divine realm. There is thus in such rituals something that we might describe as serving like a bridge between two worlds, the human and the divine, something that provides humans with a point of intersection between themselves and the heavenly realm.

Manifestly, there is a great deal in the Old Testament that we can understand as being connected with ritual. Thus for example many of the biblical psalms that have come down to us we can understand as having served as ritual texts in a variety of situations when something by way of religious ritual was needed to enable and give expression to an individual's or a community's thanksgiving, or plea for divine help, or continuance of blessings, or the seeking of answers to some perplexing aspects, maybe apparent setbacks, in life, for forgiveness of sins. Thus have these psalms served, and continue to serve in many settings and ages in which later individuals and groups wished to associate their own personal thanksgivings and needs with their God.[12] Another example of rituals, and this part of the Hebrew Bible has recently been studied in particular with regard to this aspect of ritual, is the book of Leviticus, along with other contributions of the so-called priestly writers.[13]

There are a number of religious issues that lie at the heart of the priestly rituals, namely clean and unclean; holy and not-holy; life and death; order and chaos. These issues and concerns make up the context for the various priestly rituals. Further, coming out of these issues and concerns are three main categories, divisions of the sacred rituals, which have respectively been called Founding Rituals, Maintenance Rituals, and Restoration Rituals.

An example of a Founding Ritual is spoken about in Lev 8–10 and concerns the establishment of worship in the Tabernacle. This had been built by Moses according to the Lord's command, so we are told in Exod 40:19–32, and that leads on in Lev 8:1–36 to the ritual of the ordination of the priests, a ceremony that includes washing, the taking of different clothes, anointing, and sacrificing. Thus are the priests consecrated for their special service of

---

12. For the biblical psalms and ritual, see above, 124–25, 129.

13. See Watts, *Ritual and Rhetoric in Leviticus*; Hundley, *Keeping Heaven on Earth*. We need to be aware of the fact that the study of ritual in the Hebrew Bible is a somewhat recent innovation, and that as present there is no agreement on what we actually mean by "ritual." See the discussion in Hundley, *Keeping Heaven on Earth*, 20–37, for a statement of the problem along with a series of suggestions regarding "What is Ritual?" We may also note that Balantine in his *The Torah's Vision of Worship* can argue that a very large block of material in the Hebrew Bible is a "ritual," namely, for example, the whole of Gen 1–2, though he tends to call this whole a "liturgy." On these terms and vocabulary, see above, 15–16 and 191.

the Lord, which in Lev 9 we read of them beginning. Thus took place the ritual of the inauguration of the worship in the desert tabernacle.[14]

Second, there are Maintenance Rituals, which, says Balantine "are designed to maintain an already established order and to prevent this order from falling into disrepair."[15] Examples of such maintenance rituals are the annual festivals spoken about in the Pentateuch: in Exod 23:12–19 Unleavened Bread, Spring Harvest, and Ingathering; in Deut 16:1–17 Passover/Unleavened Bread, Weeks, and Booths; in Lev 23 and Num 28–29 all the annual festivals, including sabbath day. We have already considered these festivals,[16] so here all we need to note is that the overall purpose of them is intended to be the maintenance of the intended and proper relationship between the people and their Lord, or in the words of Milgrom "to advance the holy into the realm of the common and to diminish the impure and thereby enlarge the realm of the pure."[17]

In the third place there are what have been called Restoration Rituals, these being intended to restore a situation, a person, a group into their intended relationship with the Lord. Thus, for example, we read in Lev 14 of the ritual for the restoration of a recovered leper to a normal life in the community. Or there are all the ceremonies of the Day of Atonement as set out in Lev 16 in which sanctuary, people, and individuals are cleansed and thus brought back into fellowship and communion with God.[18]

Thus while in Leviticus, and also in surrounding material in the Torah/Pentateuch, we have a good deal by way of accounts of rituals, it has to be said that the study of ritual matters in other parts of the Hebrew Bible frequently is limited, even hampered, by a considerable shortage of detail—for so much of the time we just do not have the amount of information we would wish in order to reconstruct various further rituals. At the same time for those rituals that are spoken about, we should be mindful that they were about the ministry of the priests which had "the objective of bringing about the sanctification of the people of God, to the end that this people would be and continue to be formed anew in the image of YHWH."[19]

---

14. On this ritual, see Gorman, *The Ideology of Ritual*, 131–35; and Balantine, *The Torah's Vision of Worship*, 152–55.

15. Balantine, *The Torah's Vision of Worship*, 155.

16. See above, 170–75, 184–87.

17. Milgrom, *Leviticus 1–16*, p. 732.

18. On the Day of Atonement, see above, 170–75, 183–87. For further details about such Restoration Rituals, see Balantine, *The Torah's Vision of Worship*, 162–67; and Gorman, *The Ideology of Ritual*, 151–79.

19. Preuss, *Old Testament Theology*, 2:65.

Deuteronomy and the Deuteronomistic History

With Deuteronomy, while its theological themes and approaches are clear, questions of authorship and date of composition continue to be debated. Regarding the first of these, various groups have been suggested, prophetic, priestly, wisdom, and all have their advocates, and equally all have their detractors. Perhaps the most satisfactory approach is that advocated by R.E. Clements who suggests that we refer simply to "a 'Reforming Party' with members drawn from more than one group of leading citizens."[20] And when might such a group have been active? Perhaps we may say in a very generalizing way that the main body of the work comes from the period of the decline of the Neo-Assyrian empire, in particular from the era of the reign of King Josiah of Judah, that it was intended to be in the nature of a unifying work, in which some of the particular traditions of both the northern and southern kingdoms were brought together, but that there are parts of the work that give the appearance of coming from later, that is exilic, times such as, for example, Deut 4:27–31; 28:36–37; 29:27; 30:1–20 and others. There is indeed a good deal more to be said about such background matters to this distinctive book of the Hebrew Bible, but perhaps enough has been said by way of necessary introduction for our particular concerns.[21]

In Deut 12:2–32 are set out some of Deuteronomy's emphases concerning worship, emphases that set forth some differences from those we encounter in other parts of the Hebrew Bible. These include a ban on the worship practices of Israel's neighbors and of those displaced in Israel's occupation of the land, and further a complete destruction of their shrines and associated altars, pillars, and sacred poles (Deut 12:2–4). Rather, the people of Israel shall seek a particular place for the worship of the Lord God of Israel, a place where the Lord will choose to put his name, and in that place *their* sacrifices and burnt offerings are to be made (12:5–14). Further, their worship of the Lord God shall be a glad offering to the Lord, a true rejoicing before him who freed them from their enemies, bringing them into the land (12:11–12).[22] Deuteronomy presents a vision of worship that is a glad and full act of thanksgiving and celebration, not least for all the gifts his people have received. Thus in the ceremony of the presenting of the firstfruits

---

20. Clements, *Deuteronomy*, 79. Compare the remarks of Nelson, who suggests that behind Deuteronomy was a movement made "up of groups with different but overlapping interests (scribes, priests, sages, aristocrats)" (*Deuteronomy*, 7).

21. On the matter of the dating of Deuteronomy, see further, Mayes, *Deuteronomy*, 81–103; and Nelson, *Deuteronomy*, 4–9.

22. See, e.g., Braulik, "The Joy of the Feast" and his "Commemoration of Passion and Feast of Joy"; and Willis, "'Eat and Rejoice Before the Lord.'"

(Deut 26:1-19) there is the instruction, "you, together with the Levites and the aliens who reside among you, shall celebrate with all the bounty that the Lord your God has given to you and to your house." (Deut 26:11)

It is nowhere stated in Deuteronomy what is the reason why there is to be only one place, a single sanctuary, for the worship of the Lord, and nor where that place is to be. In spite of various scholarly attempts to make cases for other localities, Jerusalem does seem to be the most likely place,[23] but then what was the reason for this command? Various possibilities have been advanced, and a highly probable one must be that it was a radical attempt to safeguard the purity of worship, that it was an endeavor to ensure that what took place in worship had the close attention of those who were appointed as the responsible leaders in this part of the national life, and that any irregularities in practice and observance could be promptly and suitably dealt with. It was surely also to outlaw, and hopefully bring about the demise of, non-Yahwistic worship practices which the Deuteronomists labelled and condemned as those of the Canaanites (see Deut 12:2-3).[24] This, it may be added, was a bold attempt to safeguard the purity of the Yahwistic faith, but one it would seem that did not succeed, and one that was perhaps almost bound not to succeed, not least because it called for an end to local shrines and other places of worship, rather naively expecting all manner and ages of people, including those who lived at varying distances from Jerusalem, all to go to that one place to make their acts of worship. For it would seem, from what we read in the Hebrew Bible, that those deuteronomistically-condemned practices in many a local setting continued to take place (see 1 Kgs 15:14; 22:43; 2 Kgs 12:3; 14:4; 15:4, 35; 16:4; 17:11, 32; 21:3). However, the non-sacral eating of meat was allowed to take place in more localized settings, thus posing a nice distinction as to what could, and what could not be done, in a person's or a family's local setting (Deut 12:13-19).

Deuteronomy's vision of worship is above all to sound the clear note of thanksgiving to the Lord. It is to be a rejoicing in all that the Lord has done for his people, as is made clear in Deut 12:7. Further, Deut 14:22-27 stresses that all the offerings and sacrifices are to be made in this spirit of thankfulness and praise. What is conspicuous by its absence in Deuteronomy is any analysis and instruction about which sacrifice is to be offered for particular sins and offences. To be sure, sacrifices are spoken about in Deuteronomy,

---

23. So Clements, *Deuteronomy*, 60-61; Mayes, *Deuteronomy*, 223; and Bultmann, "Deuteronomy," 144. For some other views, see McConville, *Law and Theology in Deuteronomy*, 21-38; and Rofé, *Deuteronomy*, 97-101.

24. Nelson says, "Deuteronomy promotes centralization in order to safeguard the exclusive 'Yahweh alone' worship demanded by the first commandment" (*Deuteronomy*, 146).

but how they are to be offered and for what they are to be offered this book maintains a silence. Rather, the vision of worship in Deuteronomy is something much more inward on the part of the worshipper; Deuteronomy, says Clements, "consistently and carefully spiritualizes and internalizes the understanding of worship."[25] In this book a calendar of festivals is set out (Deut 16:1–17), but these are intended to be a series of thanksgivings to the Lord for what he has done for his people.[26]

Moreover, God is not pictured here as dwelling on earth, and certainly not in a temple. Rather the place of worship, which we may perhaps assume is the temple in Jerusalem, is not envisaged as being the dwelling-place of God, but is spoken of as "the place that the Lord your God will choose as a dwelling for his name" (Deut 12:5, 11, 21; 16:6). No doubt there was no shortage of Israelite people who *did* believe that God lived in the temple, but that was not a conception that the Deuteronomists either held or wished to set forth. For them the Lord dwells in ways that cannot be seen by human beings (Deut 4:12), and therefore the Israelites are neither to make any images of him (4:9–24) nor are they to worship the host of heaven (4:19). Further, the sacred ark of the covenant is not spoken of in Deuteronomy as representing the *presence* of God on earth (as it is in, for example, 1 Sam 4:5–11), its purpose rather is to contain the commandments of the Lord, written in stone and given to Moses on Mount Horeb (10:1–5; 31:26). This is the "place" where God has "caused his name to dwell"—see Deut 12:5, 11, 21; 14:23, 24; 16:2, 6, 11; 26:2. This is a most spiritual way of speaking about the Lord; the people are being told here that in the "place" of worship they will find a (spiritual) presence of the Lord, but not a physical one.

We now consider the vision of worship set forth in the so-called Deuteronomistic History. The expression Deuteronomistic History is the invention of biblical scholars to indicate the Hebrew Bible's books of Joshua, Judges, Samuel and Kings. It was the scholar Martin Noth who in his 1943 book *Überlieferungsgeschichtliche Studien*[27] set forth the theory that the block of material Deuteronomy to Kings was an organized historical work based upon the theological principles of the book of Deuteronomy. This great work carried through the story of the people of Israel from their entry into the land of Canaan until the destruction of Jerusalem and the exile in 587 BCE. The author of the work had various sources at his disposal, some needing more adaptation than others, with the result that the hand of the Deuteronomistic Historian is to be seen particularly clearly in the

---

25. Clements, *Deuteronomy*, 61.
26. On festival calendars in the Old Testament, see above, 179–88.
27. English translation: *The Deuteronomistic History*, 1981.

books of Judges and Kings, less so in Joshua and Samuel. The theory of the Deuteronomistic History basically has stood the test of time, though various further proposals about it have been made, not least in the matter of the redactional history of the work.[28]

What is there in the Deuteronomistic History about worship? As far as the book of Joshua is concerned there is little to add to what has already been said about priests and Levites,[29] in particular the role of the priests in carrying the ark of the covenant. But it should also be added that in Josh 9:27, in connection with the establishment of a place of worship we find the characteristic Deuteronomic language about the "place," that is "the altar of the Lord . . . in the place that he should choose."[30] However, in Judges[31] there is rather more about worship, and certain of the particular emphases of Deuteronomy about worship make themselves felt here. Thus the story of Gideon's exploits (Judg 6:1—8:32) includes his making of a golden ephod and placing it in his own town, Ophrah, with the result that "all Israel prostituted themselves to it there, and it became a snare to Gideon and to his family" (Judg 8:27). In not dissimilar ways the judgment fell again in the days following the leadership of Jair the Gileadite when "The Israelites again did what was evil in the sight of the Lord, worshiping the Baals and Astartes, the gods of Aram, the gods of Sidon, the gods of Moab, the gods of the Ammonites, and the gods of the Philistines. Thus they abandoned the Lord, and did not worship him." (Judg 10:6)

With the books of Samuel,[32] there is less evidence of the editorial contribution of the Deuteronomists than there is with the preceding Judges and the following books of Kings. Nevertheless there are passages in 1 and 2 Sam on the subject of worship that appear to be Deuteronomistic, such as the polemic against a non-Jerusalemite priesthood in 1 Sam 2:27-36, which includes the Lord's words "I will raise up for myself a faithful priest" (v. 35). Another is the words of condemnation of the priesthood of the house of Eli, and the appointment instead of Samuel (1 Sam 3:11-14). Then further, the important chapter 2 Sam 7 concerning the building of the temple in Jerusalem and the succession to the throne of David has long been seen to

---

28. See Cross, *Canaanite Myth and Hebrew Epic*, 274-89; Nelson, *The Double Redaction of the Deuteronomistic History*; and Mayes, *The Story of Israel between Settlement and Exile*. For a recent treatment of the Deuteronomistic History, see Römer, *The So-Called Deuteronomistic History*. See also Jones, *1 & 2 Kings*, 1:28-47.

29. See above, 71-88.

30. See Mayes, *Story of Israel between Settlement and Exile*, 40-57; McConville, 57-58.

31. See above, 66-67; and Mayes, *Story of Israel between Settlement and Exile*, 58-80.

32. See Mayes, *Story of Israel between Settlement and Exile*, 81-105.

have Deuteronomistic additions, in particular vv. 12b–13a and 22–24. The Deuteronomist seems to have been anxious to make clear that the prohibition on the building of a temple was only of a temporary nature; while it was not to take place in the time when David was king it would indeed happen during the reign of his son and successor. Thus does David magnify the Lord—in deuteronomistic language.[33]

In the books of Kings we find the most plentiful evidences of the activity of the Deuteronomists in regard to worship in the handling of their sources, in particular the "Books of the Chronicles of the Kings of Israel," and the "Books of the Chronicles of the Kings of Judah." For example, here in Kgs the ark of the covenant is a container for the law of the Lord (1 Kgs 8:9, 21) as it is in Deuteronomy (Deut 10:1–5). Again, in Kgs there is the talk in the days when there were what the Deuteronomistic Historian regarded as "good" kings, the pulling down of the places for non-Yahwistic worship, and the cleansing of the temple of unacceptable religious artefacts. Thus did kings Hezekiah (2 Kgs 18:4–8) and Josiah (2 Kgs 23:4–24) seek to restore the worship of the Lord as decreed in, for example, Deut 12:2–4. In fact, a dominant factor in arriving at a judgment upon each Judean and Israelite king is what they have done or not done in the matter of worship. Thus, Noth made the observation, "In keeping with all his presuppositions Dtr. [that is, 'Deuteronomistic author'] has centered his history on the theme of worship of God as required by the law."[34]

The long prayer of Solomon at the inaugural moment of the temple in Jerusalem set out in 1 Kgs 8:1–53 betrays again the closeness of religious thought in Deuteronomy and the so-called Deuteronomistic History. For what might look like, or been construed as, a prayer of dedication of the newly-build temple on Zion, is in fact rather more akin to a disquisition on prayer, and it shows again that Deuteronomic emphasis on prayer rather than on sacrifice. There are sacrifices spoken about, but in none of the detail that there is when it is prayer that is being spoken about (1 Kgs 8:62–64). Nor is there that clearly expressed emphasis such as we find in Leviticus about which particular sacrifice should be offered for this or for that sin. Here is worship, as in Deuteronomy, that may be said to have prayer, rather

---

33. On the deuteronomistic treatment in 2 Sam 7, see Noth, *The Deuteronomistic History*, 55–56.

34. Noth, *Deuteronomistic History*, 92, on the same page saying about this Deuteronomistic author: "he adopts a strongly negative attitude towards particular aspects of the cult; and since, out of all the regulations on worship contained in the law, he gives special, one-sided attention to matters of cult, he forms a generally pessimistic view of the possibilities of men's worship."

than sacrifice, at its heart and center, and that further the temple in Kings is truly a place of prayer.[35]

For the Deuteronomistic Historian the temple is the "dwelling place for the Lord's name" (as in 1 Kgs 8:16; 11:36; 14:21; 2 Kgs 21:7; 23:27) in the same way that we have observed it in Deuteronomy (Deut 12:11, 21). Similarly, as in Deut 12:14, 18 it is laid down that the place God chooses will be the *sole* sanctuary, so also in the most radical religious reform that the Deuteronomistic Historians can write of—brought about by King Josiah, the Deuteronomist's very model of kingship—there is that stress on the *single* sanctuary (2 Kgs 23:8-9). Thus in these matters, as indeed in a good number of other matters concerning worship, the theological outlook of the Deuteronomistic Historian does correspond closely with that of the writer(s) of the book of Deuteronomy. Here in both Deuteronomy and in the Deuteronomistic History, but most particularly in the books of Kings, is a particular and distinctive vision of worship.

The Books of Chronicles

Little more than a cursory reading of the books of Chronicles is sufficient to make clear that the Chronicler had a real concern about the issue of worship in the life of the people of Israel.[36] It has been pointed out that frequently where the Chronicler has emphasized the issue of worship he has introduced something new from what appears to have been his *Vorlage*, namely the Deuteronomistic History.[37] Nevertheless, this somewhat different emphasis on the part of the Chronicler has not pleased all those who have studied his work, as we witness in the famous words of Julius Wellhausen (1844-1918):

---

35. Noth says, "One can be sure that Dtr. ['Deuteronomistic author'] has in mind the situation in his own time, when the temple had been destroyed and a sacrificial cult on the usual scale was therefore no longer practicable in Jerusalem, but the prayers of those who remained in the land and of those who had been deported probably were directed towards the site of the old temple, in memory of the past, although they could no longer be supported by supplicatory sacrifice" (*Deuteronomistic History*, 94).

36. By "Chronicler" I intend to indicate the author of the books of Chronicles. It seems to me unlikely that this author was also the author of the books of Ezra and Nehemiah. As far as dating the books of Chronicles (at least of 1 Chron 10—2 Chron 36), I would subscribe to the view that sees them as coming from the days of the Persian rule; certainly there is no hint within them of Hellenistic pressures or influences. Perhaps indeed Chronicles comes from the same general post-exilic period that Haggai and Zechariah 1-8 came from when there were concerns, among other things, about cult and worship.

37. See among many other works, Williamson, *1 and 2 Chronicles*, 17-23.

> See what Chronicles has made out of David! The founder of the kingdom has become the founder of the Temple and public worship, the king and the hero at the head of his companions in arms has become the singer and master of ceremonies at the head of a swarm of priests and Levites; his clearly cut figure has become a feeble holy picture, seen through a cloud of incense.[38]

We may approach our subject of the Chronicler's emphases regarding worship by considering some of the words in the above quotation from Wellhausen—though we may eschew comment on the latter's assertion that for the Chronicler David has become "a feeble holy picture," yet something should be said about the cloud of incense.

It is widely recognized that the Chronicler had a real interest in the Jerusalem temple, and further that he presents David as having a more significant role in the building of it than is presented in the work of the Deuteronomistic Historian. In the Chronicler's presentation, David and Solomon are portrayed as being jointly responsible for the establishment of the temple, and moreover in Chronicles David's reign is given generous treatment. William Riley has pointed out that in the Chronicler's treatment of the 450-year story of Israel from the reign of Saul to the edict of Cyrus no less than nineteen chapters out of a total of fifty-six, that is just about one third, are allocated to the thirty-three-year reign of David over Israel and Judah. Further, in this presentation there is the serious portrayal of David's work in preparation for the cultus which will be established and centered there.[39] Further, there is the sense that it is teamwork through the historical purpose first of David and second of Solomon that sees through the mighty establishment of the temple and its worship.[40] Moreover, we may take note of certain features about this presentation of the building enterprise. In the first place the site of the temple, according to the Chronicler, is the place where David offered the sacrifice which successfully stopped the plague that had been occasioned by David's sin (1 Chr 21:26—22:1). Then also in

---

38. Julius Wellhausen, *Prolegomena to the History of Ancient Israel*, 182. Needless to say contemporary scholarship of the Hebrew Bible assesses the books of Chronicles much more positively than did Wellhausen and many of his contemporaries. We would now emphasize the vitality of the post-exilic Jewish community and its ability to respond in original ways to the new situation in which it found itself. For a convenient and brief summary of this more recent approach to the Chronicler's work, see, e.g., Jones, *1 & 2 Chronicles*; and Ackroyd, *The Chronicler in His Age*.

39. William Riley, *King and Cultus in Chronicles*, 53–65. For texts where David's provision for the cultus is emphasized, see 1 Chr 6:31 (Heb. v. 16); 9:22; 2 Chr 1:4; 2:6; 3:1; 5:1; 6:7, 42; 7:6; 23:9, 18; 29:25, 26, 27, 30; 33:7; 35:4, 15.

40. This is emphasized by Braun, "Solomon, the Chosen Temple Builder," 581–90, esp. p. 581.

2 Chr 3:1 we are told that this temple site was on Mount Moriah, that is the place where according to Gen 22 the Lord had made his appearance to Abraham and so halted Abraham's attempt to sacrifice his son Isaac. Thus the Chronicler builds up the picture of the sacredness of the site where the temple was built.[41]

Then something about the architecture of the temple for the Chronicler. According to 1 Kgs 6:2 the height of the temple that King Solomon built was 30 cubits, but for the Chronicler that has become no less than 120 cubits (2 Chr 3:3-4)! Now although Jarick has made a bold and courageous defense for the reading of the Massoretic Text at this point, seeing this as speaking of a temple pointing to heaven, even having "a tower with its top in the heavens, and they have Solomon stand in front of that tower and pray over and over that God may hear in heaven the prayers directed toward that place (2 Chr 6:21, 23, 25, 27, 30, 33, 35, 39),"[42] a more common view is that this is an impossibly high building, or part thereof, and that we should accept that it is a corruption of the text.[43] What is less contested is the assertion in 1 Chr 28:9-18 that the plans for the temple had been passed on from David to Solomon, but that at the same time—and this is not in the Kgs account—there is portrayed the involvement of the Lord himself, even, apparently, by his direct hand (1 Chr 28:19).[44] Another point about the Chronicler's temple is the assertion that Solomon incorporated a veil, a curtain, into "the most holy place" (2 Chr 3:8-14), where the Deuteronomistic Historian has "doors" (1 Kgs 6:31-32). Clearly, the Chronicler is looking back to the details of the desert tabernacle (Exod 26:31; 36:35), and claiming association with what went on in past times—especially in this instance in the days of Moses. As also in the Chronicler's account there is the emphasis on the bringing of the sacred ark, the tent of meeting, and all the holy vessels that were in the tent, into the temple (2 Chr 5:4-5);[45] again it would appear that this was in order to bring about a real sense of continuity in this temple building with all that had gone before in the sacred history of the people of Israel.

But to return to Wellhausen and his views on the Chronicler's presentation of the reign of David, now in particular to his reference to David being the founder of public worship. This is, it goes without saying, a gross

---

41. See Williamson, "The Temple in the Books of Chronicles," 20-25.

42. Jarick, "The Temple of David in the Book of Chronicles," 366-69. See esp. p.369.

43. See, e.g., Japhet, *I & II Chronicles*, 553; and Williamson, *1 and 2 Chronicles*, 205-6.

44. On this verse, see Jarick, "The Temple of David in the Book of Chronicles," 379; and Williamson, "Temple in the Books of Chronicles," 25-26.

45. On temple vessels, see above, 44-45.

exaggeration, for clearly long before the days of David worship was taking place. And yet it is true to say that there is a real emphasis on worship in the books of Chronicles. John C. Endres has written on this subject, pointing out that in the accounts of some of the Israelite kings there is a marked emphasis on worship.[46] He points out that this can be seen in, for example, the accounts of the worship that took place at crucial moments during the reigns of four kings, namely, David (see 1 Chr 16-17), Solomon (2 Chr 6-7), Jehoshaphat (2 Chr 20), and Hezekiah (2 Chr 29-30). Further, the Chronicler has incorporated into his accounts some differences from the Deuteronomistic Historian's presentation. For example, there is a marked introduction and use of psalms: we find in 1 Chr 16:8-36 a remarkable series of quotations from no less than three different psalms, Pss 105:1-15; 96:1-13; 106:1, 47-48.[47] Then in 2 Chr 6:41-42 there is the quotation of Ps 132:8-10. Further, Ps 136:1, or part of it, appears a number of times, rather like a refrain, in a number of settings, namely 1 Chr 16:41; 2 Chr 5:13; 7:3, 6; 20:21. The Chronicler appears to have used these psalm quotations to bolster the theological issues that he was dealing with in the various parts of his whole story, and thus to give added force to those special issues he was concerned to write about. Thus for example the various psalm quotations employed in 1 Chr 16:8-36 read as if they are intended to encourage a people in their pilgrimage, in particular those who have come to the stage when the ark of the Lord is brought into Jerusalem, and who must then go on in faith, looking into the future.

The insertion of Ps 136:1, "O give thanks to the Lord, for he is good, for his steadfast love endures forever," or a part of it, a number of times into 2 Chr 5 and 7 is clearly to emphasize the notes of praise and thanksgiving at the time of the completion of the Jerusalem temple building—and in the case of 2 Chr 20:21 to raise that note in anticipation of military victory in the days of king Jehoshaphat. Thus there is a marked emphasis on the use of individual biblical psalms in Chronicles, which leads to the worship spoken about in Chronicles having a distinct psalmic emphasis. While the Chronicler has full details of those aspects of worship that are important to the "priestly" school—calling the temple "a house of sacrifice," and giving full details about sacrifices (1 Chr 6:49; 2 Chr 2:6; 7:12; 29:21-24), yet at the same time he speaks about worship that has stress on songs, praises, prayers, in fact joyous worship—which sometimes reads as if it is also loud, noisy worship! This emphasis comes out in the Chronicler's account of the time when David's

---

46. Endres, "The Spiritual Vision of Chronicles"; and ibid., "Theology of Worship in Chronicles."

47. There are some, comparatively small, changes in the texts of these psalms as taken up by the Chronicler. For full details, see Kleinig, *The Lord's Song*, 134-48.

warriors wished to make him king at Hebron (1 Chr 12:23–40; see esp. v. 40). It is also there in the note in 1 Chr 15:16 "David also commanded the chiefs of the Levites to appoint their kindred as the singers to play on musical instruments, on harps and lyres and cymbals, to raise loud sounds of joy." Joyous giving to the Lord is spoken about in 1 Chr 29:17; joyful returning to homes in 2 Chr 7:10; not to speak of the joy of the people according to 2 Chr 30:26 in the days of Hezekiah, "There was great joy in Jerusalem, for since the time of Solomon son of King David of Israel there had been nothing like this in Jerusalem." Endres has made the point that "It is unique to Chronicles that worship here is particularly associated with music and song in the temple precincts."[48] Endres ventures the further thought, "That the Chronicler had much more interest in what went on in the temple than in the facility that housed it," observing that whereas 1 Kgs 7 gives more details of an architectural nature about the temple of Solomon, the Chronicler's account has more about the worship ritual introduced by the king.[49]

We may best appreciate the Chronicler's approach to worship by considering two examples from his writing on the subject, namely 2 Chr 5:11–14, and 2 Chr 29:20–35. The first of these is no more than part of the beginning of the Chronicler's account of the acts and ceremonies involved in Solomon's dedication of the temple in Jerusalem (2 Chr 5:2—7:11). In 2 Chr 5:2–14 there is recounted Solomon's bringing of "the ark, the tent of meeting, and all the holy vessels that were in the tent" (2 Chr 5:5) into the newly-completed temple in Jerusalem. This was work carried out by priests and Levites (v. 5), while, having been assembled beforehand, were Solomon and the congregation engaged in sacrificing innumerable sheep and oxen. That is to say, the Chronicler has at this stage left intact his source as he found it, neither adding to it nor subtracting from it, procedures that in other settings he is not afraid to choose. Thus he has retained the talk of sacrifices on this solemn occasion. But then comes a change: now the Chronicler has made a significant addition to his *Vorlage*. The Deuteronomistic Historian's account reads:

---

48. Endres, "The Spiritual Vision of Chronicles," 12. Further example of this are to be found in 2 Chr 23:18; 29:25–30; 30:21.

49. Endres, "The Spiritual Vision of Chronicles," 12. See also the remarks and contribution of Kleinig, "The Divine Institution of the Lord's Song," esp. p. 75 where he speaks about the Chronicler's "repeated reference to the institution of the choral rite by David as an integral part of the regular sacrificial ritual at the temple in Jerusalem (1 Chr 6:31–32 [Heb. 6:16–17]; 16:41; 23:4–5, 30–31; 25:1; 2 Chr 8:14; 23:18; 29:25; 35:15)." Kleinig brings out more of the significance of music in the Jerusalem temple ritual in, *The Lord's Song*.

> And when the priests came out of the holy place, a cloud filled the house of the Lord, so that the priests could not stand to minister because of the cloud; for the glory of the Lord filled the house of the Lord. (1 Kgs 8:10–11)

This has been expanded, the Chronicler's account being,

> Now when the priests came out of the holy place (for all the priests who were present had sanctified themselves, without regard to their divisions), all the Levitical singers, Asaph, Heman, and Jeduthun, their sons and kindred, arrayed in fine linen, with cymbals, harps, and lyres, stood east of the altar with one hundred twenty priests who were trumpeters. It was the duty of the trumpeters and singers to make themselves heard in unison in praise and thanksgiving to the Lord, and when the song was raised, with trumpets and cymbals and other musical instruments, in praise to the Lord,
>
> "For he is good,
> for his steadfast love endures forever,"
>
> the house, the house of the Lord, was filled with a cloud, so that the priests could not stand to minister because of the cloud; for the glory of the Lord filled the house of God. (2 Chr 5:11–14)[50]

Here are some of the characteristic themes of the Chronicler *a propos* worship. Thus we have the "levitical singers," in three groups, Asaph, Heman, and Jeduthun, representing possibly a stage in the post-exilic development of guilds of singers in temple worship.[51] We also hear of levitical musicians in 1 Chr 6:31–47; 15:16—16:6; 23:5; 25:1–31; 2 Chr 20:19; 29:25–29; 35:15. These appear to be the ones who were arrayed in "fine linen," with their cymbals, harps, and lyres (see also 1 Chr 15:16; 25:1 and compare 1 Chr 13:8). Nor may we forget—nor fail, imaginatively, to hear?—the one hundred and twenty priestly-trumpeters with their trumpets. We are told that the trumpeters and singers were to be "as one [*kĕʾeḥād*]" (2 Chr 5:11–14) in making themselves known "in praise and thanksgiving to the Lord," which

---

50. The whole account in 2 Chr 5:2—7:11 of the dedication of the temple, according to Williamson, "marks one of the major climaxes in the Chronicler's presentation" (*1 and 2 Chronicles*, 213), an expression that Kleinig quotes with approval (*The Lord's Song*, 157). It has been argued by Rudolph and others that the additional material in 2 Chr 5:11–13 set out above is secondary, but his and others' arguments have been robustly countered by Williamson, *1 and 2 Chronicles*, 215–16. See also Dillard, *2 Chronicles*, 40–41.

51. See Gese, "Zur Geschichte der Kultsäienger"; and Williamson, *1 and 2 Chronicles*, 20–22.

words there employed (Ps 106:1) also being spoken about in 1 Chr 16:34, 41; 2 Chr 7:3, 6; 20:21. Moreover, we are told that this musical praise and thanksgiving having been made, the temple was filled with the cloud, at one level presumably with clouds of incense, but at a deeper level to be understood as indicating that the glory of the Lord was felt to be filling the place. We should perhaps take note of the fact that for the Deuteronomistic Historian the glory of the Lord was experienced in the temple when the ark of the covenant was brought into the holy place (1 Kgs 8:1–11), whereas for the Chronicler this occurred when fervent worship took place, when the trumpeters and singers joined those with cymbals and other musical instruments to make their glad expressions of praise and thanksgiving—and much joy (2 Chr 5:11–14).[52]

The second example of the Chronicler's approach to worship we consider is 2 Chr 29:20–35, a small part of the extensive account of the cleansing and rededication of the temple by Hezekiah, the passage here being considered is given to us only by the Chronicler. In fact his whole account of the cleansing and rededication of the temple in 2 Chr 29:1–36 is, apart from vv. 1–2, to be found only in the Chronicler's work. This then is one of the Chronicler's additions to what the Deuteronomistic Historian gives to us. It is clear that Hezekiah was a king who was held in great respect and interest by the Chronicler; in his account Hezekiah is given more space and coverage than any other king with the exception of David and Solomon. Once again we have the dual emphasis upon worship that is made up both of sacrifice and of song, but here more details are given about the different sacrifices that are offered, and that the offering of the various sacrifices is accompanied by the music and song.[53]

The Chronicler's account of the rededication ceremony may be considered in three sections. The first of these is 2 Chr 29:20–24, and concerns the various animals that were brought and the associated sacrifices that were offered, these being for sin offerings and burnt offerings, and were for all the people of Israel. It seems also that what was taking place here was a cleansing and rededication of the altar. The Chronicler gives full details of these many sacrifices, suggesting that he was seriously concerned about the place of sacrifice in worship. The closest parallels in the Old Testament

---

52. See Japhet, *I & II Chronicles*, 580–81; and Kleinig, *The Lord's Song*, 164.

53. Kleinig, *The Lord's Song*, 100–4, argues that what we have here in this order and sequence of sacrifice and song at the rededication of the temple by Hezekiah represents a "set order and sequence for the performance of sacrificial worship at the temple" (103). I believe that this is going beyond the evidence, and I would understand 2 Chr 29:20–35 as probably representing no more than what the Chronicler wished to portray as having taken place just on that particular occasion of temple rededication.

to this account of sacrifices being offered are in Num 7:87–88 and Ezek 43:18–27; 45:18–20.

Then second, 2 Chr 29:25–30 details the musical accompaniment to the offering of these sacrifices. Here again are the Levites with their cymbals, harps, and lyres, and the priests with their trumpets (vv. 25–26). Then, the burnt offering having begun, so commenced "the song to the Lord" (v. 27) along with the whole assembly worshipping, the singers singing, and the trumpeters sounding—"until the burnt offering was finished" (v. 28). Then "the king and all who were present with him bowed down and worshiped" (v. 29) Finally the Levites sang praises to the Lord with gladness, and they bowed down and worshipped (v. 30).

Third, in 2 Chr 29:31–35 the whole tone becomes much more "congregational," and we read of the people being given opportunity to make their own sacrifices, "the first and only event in which the Chronicler ascribes to the people active participation in the contribution of sacrifices,"[54] Sara Japhet saying that "The thrust of the Chronicler's presentations is the transformation of the royal/courtly events into public and popular ones, not merely by the presence of crowds, but by the people's active participation in the events themselves."[55] We should perhaps also take note of the fact that the people who had brought burnt offerings were those "of a willing heart" (v. 31). Thus, in willingness of heart, in sacrifice and song, was the service of the house of the Lord restored (v. 36). Once again we observe the Chronicler's emphasis on the contributions of both sacrifice and music to the worship of the Lord, King Hezekiah and his people all rejoicing (v. 36).

Before we leave Chronicles we should take note that in this work there is a significant series of what might be called "sermons," that being the term employed when many years ago Gerhard von Rad wrote his essay "The Levitical Sermon in I and II Chronicles."[56] It is generally thought that through these sermons something of the Chronicler's essential message comes through, this being in the general terms of exhortations to trust in God, such as to believe in him, fear him (e.g. 2 Chr 15:2–7; 19:6–7; 20:20), not to put human trust in other places (e.g. 2 Chr 16:7–9), not to be afraid of this or that crisis (2 Chr 20:15–17; 32:7–8a). Another of these "sermons," not in fact cited by von Rad, is the sermon preached by the prophet Oded to the victors of the so-called Syro-Ephraimite war, exhorting them to be compassionate to the vanquished, to make peace, and to seek for reconciliation.[57]

---

54. Japhet, *I & II Chronicles*, 929.
55. Ibid.
56. Rad, "The Levitical Sermon in I and II Chronicles."
57. For details of this, see Thompson, *Situation and Theology*, 94–103.

In the context of this study of worship there are two matters to note. The first is to pursue the theme pointed out to us those years ago by von Rad, along with his further remark about the Chronicler's use of the term "as it is written,"[58] and the impression we are thus given that we have something here about the evolution of the exhortation, even of what we might call the "sermon," as indeed in his study von Rad did. It is true that these particular "sermons" were not preached in a particular worship setting, but nevertheless there is here something in the nature of an exposition for a present and contemporary situation of themes that had long been embraced, some of them even having come to be included within written documents.[59] The second concerns that issue made clear by Williamson that far from emphasizing detailed liturgical points, the emphasis in these "sermons"—either from a Levite, a prophet, or a king—is very much on practical matters of how the ancient faith is to be lived out in a new age, going on to say that thus the Chronicler "successfully demonstrates that his religion was not grounded in a cold formality."[60]

Wisdom Literature

By the Old Testament Wisdom literature we intend the books Proverbs, Job, Ecclesiastes, Sirach (Ecclesiasticus), Wisdom of Solomon, and Wisdom psalms (here regarded as Pss 37, 49, 73, 112, 127, 128, 133, 139).[61] It is not easy to give a definition for the particular type of biblical literature that we call the Wisdom writings, and not a few writers on the subject take a deal of space in trying to come up with what adequately embraces the thought of this particular genre of literature. In this approach there is the emphasis on intellectual search for meaning in those phenomena of life that are observed and experienced, and not only by the people of Israel, for the Old Testament wisdom tradition would seem to have been dependent to at least some degree upon similar searches for understanding on the parts of nations round about. Yet in the particular manifestation of wisdom thought we find in the Old Testament there is a definite place for what might be called the theological aspect. That is, we should not think of the so-called wisdom writers as emphasizing a solely-intellectual approach to the problems of, and questions

---

58. See 2 Chr 23:18; 25:4; 30:5, 18; 31:3. For this, see Rad, "The Levitical Sermon in I and II Chronicles," 279–80.

59. See above, 84–86, for more on this theme of preaching and interpreting of a document in the post-exilic period.

60. Williamson, *1 and 2 Chronicles*, 31.

61. On the so-called Wisdom Psalms, see above, 137–38.

about, the meaning of life in the world. Rather, in these writings the attempt is made to bring intellectual reasoning to matters that under the Lord occur in life, to give what explanation is possible to what happens to individuals, groups, and even nations, and further to attempt to give guidance to people about how life should be lived.

There are many questions left unanswered by life's experiences, and there are definite limits laid upon those who would give merely-intellectual responses. Such are to be observed in the various wisdom books and traditions that we have in the Old Testament. Further, as Katharine Dell has pointed out it is not possible in the Jewish context to exclude the theological perspective,[62] and as part of that a place is accorded to the worship of the Lord in the thought of the Old Testament's wisdom writers, to be sure to different degrees, and something of this is set out in what follows.

Some consideration has already been given in this work to the Hebrew verb y-r-', which is usually translated "fear." In a minority of this verb's usages in the Hebrew Bible it indicates what is caused by a threatening situation, by circumstances that give rise to the feeling of being scared, afraid.[63] Yet in a majority of usages the meaning is rather fearing God in the sense of being in awe of him in his greatness and otherness. Further this is a verb which, along with its other parts of speech, occurs with some frequency in the Hebrew Bible's wisdom literature, the word in fact having a preponderance of occurrences in Psalms, Deuteronomy, and the Wisdom Literature. Fuhs goes as far as saying that the "fear" of God, or Yahweh, is a key concept in Wisdom Literature.[64]

First, there is the relatively brief writing attributed to Qoheleth, Ecclesiastes, where we read of his various problems in trying to make sense of life in the world, and what are the responses that he makes as far as his religious beliefs are concerned. For there at the end of the work in Qoh 12:13 we read, "The end of the matter; all has been heard. Fear (y-r-') God, and keep his commandments; for that is the whole duty of everyone." Qoheleth has also commended to his readers the fear of God in 3:14; 5:7; 7:18 and 8:12. Roland Murphy says that in his references to the fear of the Lord Qoheleth "is referring to the unchangeability, and ultimately the mystery (3:11), of divine activity, before which 'fear' is the appropriate response."[65] Qoheleth

---

62. Dell, "Get Wisdom, Get Insight," 1–13.

63. For a full treatment of the verb y-r-', "fear," see, e.g., the article by Fuhs, "*yārē'*." Also see above, 3–4, 3nn7, 8.

64. Fuhs, "*yārē'*," 311.

65. Murphy, *Ecclesiastes*, lxv. Perdue, it should be noted, however, takes "fear" (*yārē'*) as meaning in Qoheleth "actual fear, fear of an unknowable power who has the ability to destroy or to reward, to dispense joy or to withhold it" (*Wisdom and Cult*,

speaks of the cult in 5:1–7, enjoining his readers to be respectful of it, guarding one's steps on the approach to the house of God, humbly drawing near to listen (v. 1), remembering that God is in heaven and that the humans are on the earth, therefore let the words of the earthbound ones be few (v. 2). When one makes a vow to the Lord, one should fulfil it without delay; if not do not make the vow (v. 4-5). Further, be aware of speaking sinful words (v. 6), and above all *fear* God (v. 7). Thus is Qoheleth positive about the cult and its ministries, not criticizing it, but emphasizing that true worship of the Lord must be accompanied by the attempt to lead a worthy life. Do not be like those spoken of by Qoheleth in 8:10, whose lives, contrary to how they appeared in their goings in and out of the holy place, were in fact unworthy. Such people do not have a true fear (awe) of God (8:11-13).

The book of Proverbs, it would be generally agreed is made up of a number of different collections of proverbs.[66] In the first collection, that in Prov 1:1—9:18, we find the words, no later than 1:7, "The fear (*yārē'*) of the Lord is the beginning of knowledge," and Toy in his commentary said this "may be regarded as the motto of the whole book."[67] There are further references to "the fear (*yārē'*) of the Lord" in Prov 2:5; 8:13; 9:10; 10:27; 14:26, 27; 15:16, 33; 16:6; 19:23; 22:4; 23:17; 24:21; 31:30. Further, as regards the book of Proverbs we should note a modest series of references to prayer (Prov 15:8, 29; 28:9), and also to sacrifice (Prov 15:8; 17:1; 21:3, 27). With the references to prayer in 15:8 and 29, and 28:9 there is emphasis upon the need for an attempt at living a worthy life on the part of the one praying, while in 16:3 it is the assurance that the committing of one's ways to the Lord will be an aid to establishing one's plans. Again, with the references to sacrifice the emphasis is on the necessity of the offerer seeking to lead a worthy life. Thus, it is as if the sages of Proverbs assume the existence and blessings of being able to pray to the Lord and to offer him sacrifices, but that yet these must be offered out of lives where there is some striving after worthiness, and faithfulness to the Lord. Very much the same goes for the making of vows to the Lord, spoken about in Prov 7:14; 20:25; 31:2. Again there is the emphasis on the worthiness of the one making the vow. Proverbs 16:6 seems to be acknowledging the established institutions of the cult for the benefit of of those who are in "awe" (*yārē'*) of the Lord.

Before we leave the book of Proverbs we should give some attention to the series of references to the "strange woman", who is differently described in the various references, in Prov 2:16-19; 5:1-14, 20; 6:24-35; 7:5. Whybray

---

178–88, esp. p. 180.)

66. On such matters in the book of Proverbs, see, e.g., Martin, *Proverbs*.

67. Toy, *Proverbs*, 10.

says, "All these passages refer to her seductive speech, and all refer to the fatal or at least disastrous consequences of association with her."[68] Way back in 1935 G. Boström proposed a cultic interpretation in which he understood that Israelite young men were being lured into involvement in the Babylonian/Canaanite fertility rite of the goddess Ishtar/Astarte. In general Boström's thesis has not been followed, the references rather having been interpreted as to a "foreign, unknown, unfamiliar," woman, maybe a prostitute. However, a number of recent scholars have retained some aspects and features of the cultic interpretation including William McKane and Leo Perdue.[69] This is one of those many issues in the study of the Old Testament about which we have to say the jury is still out; perhaps we have to say that in all probability there is no formal polemic against the Canaanite fertility cult in the book of Proverbs, but that yet there is the possibility of such a presence.

The book of Job is taken up with a sustained discussion about issues of personal suffering,[70] and in the prologue to the work in Job 1:1-22 the man Job in the face of the various misfortunes that crowd in upon him comes over as a pious person who as the head of his family leads them in the due cultic rites. Thus in 1:4-5 we read of him offering burnt offerings, and the feasts that are spoken about may well have been cultic feasts.[71] Then Job 3:1—27:23 is taken up with three cycles of speeches by Job and his three friends Eliphaz, Bildad, and Zophar, Job for his part questioning how it can be that he is suffering so greatly when he has led a devout and upright life. The point of view of his friends is that Job *must* have sinned and so brought all this grievous suffering upon himself. Much of what Job has to say in this debate is expressed in the style and language of the Old Testament lament tradition, while part of the friends' response is to seek the Lord, and his forgiveness, through the normal means of the cult (Job 5:8; 8:5-6; 11:13; 22:27), this point of view also being presented in the speeches of Elihu (32:1—37:24) especially in 33:26-28. Yet Job consistently refuses to accept that these words of the friends are meaningful to him, and that there is something much more mysterious happening to him than can be explained by his lack of cultic observances, and such is clearly the consistent point of view of the author of the book.

Some light, however, begins to emerge with the poem about God's unfathomable wisdom in Job 28:1-28, which lays stress upon the fact that

---

68. Whybray, *Proverbs*, 54.

69. See McKane, *Proverbs*, 287-88; Perdue, *Wisdom and Cult*, 146-55.

70. I treat the book of Job at some length in my work *"Where is the God of Justice?,"* 105-56.

71. See, e.g., Clines, *Job 1-20*, p. 5.

God's being and his ways are mysterious to humans, even to the most exploratory of the human race, and the only answer that can be given to the questions "But where shall wisdom be found? And where is the place of understanding?" (Job 28:12, cf. v. 20) lies in the mystery of God, "And he [God] said to humankind, 'Truly, the fear [$yārē'$] of the Lord, that is wisdom; and to depart from evil is understanding.'" (28:28). Which is to say that there is no intellectual solution to the question of human suffering, but that some understanding of it will come through the "fear" ($yārē'$) of the Lord, that is in reverencing him, worshipping him. Which does indeed lead on to what is presented in the book of Job as the nearest that any human being will get to an answer to those inscrutable problems of human suffering, an "answer" that comes out in the two great speeches of the Lord in Job 38:1—40:2 and 40:6—41:34. These speeches are about the greatness and sheer otherness of the Lord, matters that the man Job has hardly considered, and that are totally beyond his comprehension, and thus Job expresses himself in terms both of deepest personal contrition and worship of the great Lord of all (40:3-5; 42:1-6). All this is perhaps to say that there are definite limits to what humankind can know about the Lord, and in particular in seeking to fathom the mysteries of life in the world. Perhaps the true way to live life is to accept that the Lord is great and awesome, a mysterious being, with works of creation, ongoing purposes, and ways, all far beyond what the members of the human race can imagine, much less understand. Thus the main part of the book of Job ends on this deep and profound note of the surpassing greatness and wonder of the Lord, and Job quietly saying, "I had heard of you by the hearing of the ear, but now my eye sees you; therefore I despise myself, and repent in dust and ashes." (42:5-6) Meanwhile, in what looks like the addition of an Epilogue to the book (42:7-17), the Lord says that Elihu, along with Eliphaz, Bildad, and Zophar, should offer up sacrifices for their having spoken as they did, and that for them Job too will offer prayer (42:7-9). Thus, in various ways there is a considerable emphasis upon the worship of the Lord in the book of Job.[72]

So to Pss 37, 49, and 73, three psalms that are widely accepted as being called "Wisdom Psalms." Some scholars include more of the biblical psalms in this category, but the above three make the irreducible minimum over which few scholars would disagree. Each of these psalms deals with an aspect of theodicy, yet none presents a solution to the theological problem. Rather, each in its own way acknowledges the inscrutability of the Lord and his purposes, and in each a psalmist expresses a sense of awe and creaturely

---

72. On worship in Job, see the rather different approach in Perdue, *Wisdom and Cult*, 166-78.

dependence, even trust in the Lord, all of which closely border upon the aspect of the worship of God. Thus the psalmist of Ps 37 expresses his dependence upon God in the last verse, so bringing his psalm to a close with words about those who put their trust in the Lord, "The Lord helps them and rescues them; he rescues them from the wicked, and saves them, because they take refuge in him." (Ps 37:40) Within Ps 49 we have one of the few references in the Old Testament that indicate a movement towards a belief in life after death: "But God will ransom my soul from the power of Sheol, for he will receive me." (Ps 49:15) Finally, with Ps 73 we have a remarkably confident expression of faith and trust in the Lord, even in the face of the most inexplicable of life's mysteries, and such is surely an expression of the spirit of worship, for these aspects of hope and confidence in the Lord came to the psalmist in the place of worship (Ps 73:17), namely,

> Whom have I in heaven but you?
> And there is nothing on earth that I desire other than you.
> My flesh and my heart may fail,
> but God is the strength of my heart and my portion forever.
> (Ps 73:25–26)[73]

Within the Deutero-Canonical Books (Apocrypha) there are two works commonly regarded as wisdom writings, and both call for brief consideration. First there is The Wisdom of Solomon, a work that perhaps comes from the setting of Egypt in the first century BCE, written perhaps by an Alexandrian Jewish sage.[74] As regards matters of worship and the cult the writer of this work attacks the manifestations in his people's worship of various pagan religions, the religion of nature (Wis 13:1–9), idol worship (13:10—15:17), animal worship (15:18–19). In more positive mode the writer speaks of prayer as in Wis 7:7, and later in 16:28–29, where prayer both in the morning and at night is commended. Also the more formal worship events of the cult are spoken of here, keeping of Passover (18:6–9), and thinking of the wilderness tradition reference is made to the ministry of intercession of one who must be Aaron (18:20–25). This man is portrayed as good and blameless, by whose prayers and actions catastrophe was averted. Here in Wisdom of Solomon, alongside the condemnation of various foreign religious cults, is a positive assessment and commendation of the traditional worship and cult of the Israelites.[75]

---

73. For more about these three psalms, 37, 49, 73, see Thompson, "Where is the God of Justice?", 58–61, 81–84, 100–4.

74. The matters of date and place of writing are much debated. For full details, see Grabbe, *Wisdom of Solomon*.

75. See further in Perdue, *Wisdom and Cult*, 211–25.

Finally, there is The Wisdom of Jesus Son of Sirach, otherwise known as The Wisdom of Jesus Ben Sira, otherwise known as Ecclesiasticus, a work that we are told was originally composed in Hebrew but now known to us only through the Greek translation of his grandson who informs the reader in his Prologue to the book that he came to Egypt in the eighth year of the reign of Euergetes, that is 132 BCE. There is a good deal about worship and the cult in this book, such that Perdue observes, "Sirach regards cultic religion as an essential and important part of both Israel's religious heritage and the wise man's own religious devotion."[76] There are, in the first place many prayers in Ben Sira, including some lengthy ones such as hymns of praise that we find in 39:12-35 and 42:15—43:33 which extol the Lord for his work of creation, and thus let the worshippers "Ascribe majesty to his name and give thanks to him with praise" (Sir 39:15a; see also 43:30). There are also prayers of petition in 22:27—23:6 (a prayer for self-discipline), and 36:1-22 (a prayer for the deliverance of Israel). Finally, and as something in the nature of an appendix to the book there is in 51:1-12 what is portrayed as a prayer of Ben Sira, one that takes in both praise and petition.

Yet Sira is concerned about the spirit in which prayer and praise is offered, and what lies behind the prayer and praise in the life of the worshipper. Thus Sira says, "Praise is unseemly on the lips of a sinner, for it has not been sent from the Lord. For in wisdom must praise be uttered, and the Lord will make it prosper" (15:9-10). For this writer the issue of social justice is important, and he says that sacrifice and worship must be accompanied by social justice—see 34:21-27. In fact, Sira opines that the keeping of the moral law is the highest form of sacrifice and worship (35:1-5, 9a, 14-15).

Further, Ben Sira's commendations include both the established priesthood and the temple and its liturgies. While Sira condemns the pursuit of false and useless cultic ways such as divination, omens and dreams (34:5), he calls upon his readers to revere and honor the priests (7:29-31), and to join him in giving thanks for the life and ministry of the High Priest Simon son of Onias II, in particular speaking of his duties on the annual Day of Atonement (50:1-21). Further, he has many good things to say about Aaron of old, not forgetting his robes, his duties and his rights (45:6-22), and also for king David's singing the praises of God with all his heart (47:8), who thus "gave beauty to the festivals, and arranged their times throughout the year, while they praised God's holy name, and the sanctuary resounded from early morning." (47:10) So Sira also gave thanks for the provision that

---

76. Perdue, *Worship and Cult*, 188-211; the above quotation is from p. 211. On the subject of Ben Sira and worship, see also Skehan and Di Lella, *The Wisdom of Ben Sira*, 87-88; Snaith, "Ben Sira's Supposed Love of Liturgy"; and Davidson, *Wisdom and Worship*, 98-117.

Solomon had made for the temple worship (47:13), and for what at later times faithful kings such as Hezekiah and Josiah would work (49:1–4). Also Sira twice refers to Jerusalem as the "city of the sanctuary" (36:18; 49:6), the first of which comes in the prayer for Israel's deliverance and about which Perdue rightly observes, "In this prayer, Sirach calls for divine intervention on Israel's behalf on the basis of the temple in Jerusalem, the place of the divine abode. This underlines Sirach's devotion to the temple and the Jerusalem cult and his desire that the temple cultus should continue to be a revered institution in the Jewish nation."[77]

What then can we say by way of summary about worship in the wisdom writings in the Hebrew Bible and the Deutero-canonical books? In the first place in some of these writings there is considerable usage of the Hebrew verb y-r-', "fear," a word which, as has been said, encapsulates something of the spirit of one who worships, something experienced by a humble worshipper before the mighty and holy God, and which induces in the worshipper the sense of awe and reverence, even worship. The verb y-r-' occurs with some frequency in the Wisdom Literature, and it has been suggested is something of a key concept in this literature. It is present, for example in the book of Qoheleth, a writer who speaks positively of the cult in 5:1–7, exhorting those he addresses to have this "fear" of the Lord, and at the same time attempt to lead worthy lives.

The same word, $yārē'$, "fear" is also to be found in the book of Proverbs and, as we have seen, it has been suggested that the phrase "the fear of the Lord is the beginning of wisdom" could almost stand as the "motto" of the whole of the book of Proverbs. As well as making reference to this "fearing God/the Lord," there are other matters in the book of Proverbs about aspects of worship such as prayer, sacrificing, at the same time seeking to engage in worthy living, and steadfastly avoiding contact with the false cults of the Canaanites.

It has been observed above that within the book of Job there is significant talk of various established cultic rites and practices, and that any purely intellectual solution to the vexed problem of theodicy is absent. Yet something happens by the end of the chapter on "wisdom" (Job 28) with the introduction of the expression "Truly, the fear ($yārē'$) of the Lord, that is wisdom; and to depart from evil is understanding" (Job 28:28). Then soon follow the speeches of the Lord, suggesting as they inevitably do that the only true way to live in the world is to accept that the Lord is holy and awesome, planning things and doing things far, far beyond human comprehension, so that Job is left in awesome and reverent submission before the Lord, indeed in what is surely a true spirit of worship. Much the same could be

---

77. Perdue, *Wisdom and Cult*, 210.

said about those three so-called Wisdom Psalms, namely 37, 49 and 73, that we considered, for each of these ends not in intellectual understanding, but rather in worshipful awe before the mystery of God.

The author of Wisdom of Solomon while on the one hand condemning use of foreign—and inevitably thereby false—cults, on the other hand commends praying to the Lord, engaging in the ministry of intercession, and keeping the celebration of Passover. Finally, there is the Wisdom of Ben Sira, the author of which is one who according to Leo Perdue, "regards cultic religion as an essential and important part of both Israel's religious heritage and the wise man's own religious devotion."[78] For Ben Sira does indeed include in his work a goodly number of prayers, making the point that prayer should be accompanied by the living out of social justice; he ascribes majesty and praise to the Lord; he condemns false cults; he commends the respecting of priests; he exhorts the faithful keeping of the Day of Atonement. Further, he twice refers to Jerusalem as the "city of the sanctuary"; he has a devotion to the temple and the Jerusalem cult; and he looks back with thanksgiving and praise to those worthies of the past, such as Aaron, David, Solomon, Hezekiah, and Josiah who through their devotion to this tradition of worship developed it and passed it on to future generations.

---

78. Perdue, *Wisdom and Cult*, 211.

13

The Prophets and Worship

This chapter is concerned with the Hebrew Bible's books of the latter prophets, Isaiah, Jeremiah, Ezekiel, and the Twelve (so-called Minor Prophets), and what there is in them about worship. How much in these books of the prophets record the actual words of the prophets named there, and how much the wording owes to their editors inevitably remains a matter of debate. Another prophetical matter of debate—and this debate in the main took place some years ago—concerns those whom scholarship labelled cultic prophets. We read of communal groups of prophets in parts of the Hebrew Bible (see for example 1 Sam 10:5; 1 Kgs 22:10-12); was it to make clear the fact that Amos of Tekoah was not a member of such a group that he made his statement to Amaziah the priest of Bethel, "I am no prophet, nor a prophet's son"? (Amos 7:14) Further, in the past a number of scholars have argued that there were groups of what were called these cultic prophets, in particular Sigmund Mowinckel and Aubrey R. Johnson.[1] Johnson's study was thorough and detailed, though not all his arguments and examples were convincing. In his recent thorough study of the evidence Robert R. Wilson has concluded that in the days of the judges some prophets in Ephraim were connected with some of the sanctuaries, but apart from Samuel prophets do not seem to have been priests, and their role in the cult is unclear. Perhaps also we have to acknowledge our ignorance of the employment of such groups of prophets in the cultic life of ancient Israel and Judah.[2] At any rate in a matter that is inevitably speculative I shall not be paying further attention to possible groups of cultic prophets in ancient Israel.

What is clearer is the ministry of a number of individual prophets playing crucial roles both in the religious and also the political establishments

---

1. See Mowinckel, *The Psalms in Israel's Worship*, 2:53-73; and Johnson, *The Cultic Prophet in Ancient Israel*.

2. See Wilson, *Prophecy and Society in Ancient Israel*, 300-1. See also the rather cautious remarks about theories regarding cultic prophets of Rowley in *Worship in Ancient Israel*, 152-60. See further, Murray, "Prophecy and the Cult," 201. I shall not be referring in this chapter to Eaton, *Vision in Worship*, a work that assumes the existence of various cultic rites and festivals in ancient Israel whose existence is hypothetical. See above, 199, 201.

of their day. Thus, for example, Samuel is portrayed as being involved in a priestly role, offering sacrifice at Mizpah (1 Sam 7:9-10), building an altar at Ramah (1 Sam 7:17), planning to do so also in Gilgal (1 Sam 10:8); yet at the same time he is portrayed as engaged in issues that would later become associated with the prophetical office. Thus he condemned the worship of foreign gods and sought to have them put away (1 Sam 7:3); he prayed for his people, interceding for them, both that they might be rescued from their enemies, the Philistines (1 Sam 7:5, 8), and also that they might have a king to rule over them and fight their battles (1 Sam 8:6, 21; 12:19). It should also be borne in mind that in some quarters in ancient times Moses was regarded as *the* prophet par excellence (see Deut 34:10, but compare 18:15-18), and we read that he made intercession for his people in the wake of their grave sin of making the golden calf in the desert, bowing down to it, praying that it would lead them on in their desert march (Exod 32:11-14, 30-34; Deut 9:25-29; see also Ps 106:23).[3]

Something of this sort of prophetical ministry in later times is set forth in the prophetical books of the Old Testament. Yet also we can observe this in what we might call embryo form, in the activities and ministry of Elijah—but not perhaps in the same way in the accounts that we have of his successor Elisha. For a very central theme in Elijah's life was the condemnation of the worship of other gods and his attempt to bring about the cessation of these practices in Israel. Thus there were his challenges to King Ahab of Israel, and Ahab's queen, Jezebel the daughter of King Ethbaal of Sidon, in a particular way over the matter of the establishment of the cult of Baal in Samaria (1 Kgs 16:29-34). This crusade of Elijah is portrayed in the Hebrew Bible as coming to something of a climax with the contest on Mount Carmel between the multitude of prophets of Baal and the Lord's lone prophet Elijah, with the Lord and his prophet being completely victorious (1 Kgs 18:20-40). This is an aspect of the prophetic ministry that we shall come across when we turn to the later, so-called canonical prophets.

A further aspect of the prophetical work of Elijah—and again one that we shall find recurring in the proclamation and condemnations of some of the canonical prophets—was that of the censure of exploitation on the part of the powerful and wealthy over those who were poor and weak. This issue is vividly portrayed through the account of the seizing of the vineyard of a certain Naboth by King Ahab, this taking place through the connivance, authority, and power of Queen Jezebel (1 Kgs 21:1-24). This notorious incident comes to its climax with Ahab having taken possession of the vineyard, and taking his evening walk in it, being interrupted by Elijah: "Ahab said to

---

3. On the intercessions of Moses, see Thompson, *I Have Heard Your Prayer*, 103-10.

Elijah, 'Have you found me, O my enemy?' He answered, 'I have found you. Because you have sold yourself to do what is evil in the sight of the Lord, I will bring disaster on you . . .'" (1 Kgs 21:20–21a) This theme we shall find being developed in the proclamation of the prophet Amos.

Also in the records we have of the ministries of Elijah and Elisha is the matter of the prophet interceding for certain people. This, we may observe in passing, is given expression in that note about Abraham praying for Abimelech—"for he is a prophet, and he will pray for you" (Gen 20:7)—and this, again, is a ministry we observe being exercised by some of the canonical prophets.

Amos

In the book of Amos we read of four main matters regarding the Amos and the cult: non-Yahwistic worship; the so-called doxologies; the relationship of worship and social justice; the making of prayers of intercession.

It is clear that in spite of various condemnations the worship of non-Yahwistic deities and idols continued to take place.[4] This is made clear in Amos, as for example in 5:26 with its references to Sakkuth and Kaiwan, which seem to have been astral deities of the cult of Saturn.[5] It is widely felt that the worship of what for strict Yahwistic worshippers would have been idols might have come into Israel during one or more of the stages of the Assyrian expansion into territories to their west in the eighth century BCE. This verse therefore, along possibly with other parts and verses of what we now have in the book of Amos, may be reflecting the situation in Israel in times later than that of the historical prophet Amos.

Further, we should take note of Amos 2:8 and 8:14. In 8:14 there is mention of what appears to be another deity, Ashimah of Samaria, whose cult, it seems, was brought in with the Assyrian incursions or occupations in the eighth century and about which we also read in 2 Kgs 17:30. If so, this again would be reflecting what was happening in a later time than that of the prophet Amos, but alongside this consideration we should also place what we read in Amos 2:8 about Israelites lying down on garments taken in pledge alongside a plurality of altars. Now the reference could be to Yahwistic altars, but the use of the plural form here does perhaps suggest that

---

4. See above, 61–66.

5. See, e.g., Gray, "Sakkuth and Kaiwan"; Meier, "Sakkuth and Kaiwan"; and Dijkstra, "Sakkuth."

such practices occurred either also, or perhaps instead, in the environs or sanctuaries of non-Yahwistic altars.[6]

Then in Amos there are what have been called the Doxologies, these being found in Amos 4:13; 5:8-9; 9:5-6, and have been the subject of much scholarly investigation.[7] Many of the details of what has come out of this scholarship—such as whether or not there was originally one doxological composition which later came to be set out in three short ones, and what was the date of this/them; whether they were earlier than the historical Amos or later—need not concern us, for the fact is that the three doxologies by some process or other of transmission were incorporated in the completed book of Amos, thereby giving to that work through this expression of praise a real emphasis on the greatness and otherness of the Lord. Crenshaw argues that the setting of these doxologies is in passages about the judgment of Yahweh, and we may go along with that. That is, the three passages in which the doxologies are set are warnings of divine judgment that is to come upon the people for their sinful and careless lives. Further, these doxologies magnify the authority and strength of the Lord, asserting that he, the Lord, is the one who has the real power in the world, in this case to effect his judgment upon his people. Crenshaw says, "the doxologies were an expression of faith in Yahweh by a people smarting from wounds inflicted upon them by their God, but confident that he was able to deliver them if he so desired."[8] That is, in what either the prophet or else his later tradents had to say about human sinfulness and divine judgment, there were also these powerful statements setting forth the greatness of the Lord Yahweh in creation and history. Further, in answer to the (hypothetical) question about where lies the real power and authority in the world there is given the answer clearly, distinctly, worshipfully, "The Lord, the God of hosts, is his name!" (Amos 4:13; compare 5:8; 9:6).

Then there is in the book of Amos a distinct emphasis on social justice—see, for example 2:6-8 with its talk of selling righteous people for silver, and the needy for a pair of sandals (2:6); the same theme is expressed in 3:15; 4:1 and elsewhere. Yet what causes the ire of the prophet is that the society that indulges in such sinful practices is guilty of what in the book of Amos is portrayed as a further crime, for this immorality is being committed in the context of the worship of the Lord God of Israel. This receives its first expression in Amos 4:4-5, a short but powerful oracle which, in

6. On the deity Ashimah, see Gray, "Ashimah"; and Fulcro, "Ashima."

7. Among much that has been written in this regard, mention should be made of the two works, Watts, *Vision and Prophecy in Amos*, 51-67; and Crenshaw, *Hymnic Affirmation of Divine Justice*.

8. Crenshaw, *Hymnic Affirmations of Divine Justice*, 143.

tones of deep irony, speaks of the people coming to Bethel to worship at the shrine there and at the same time to transgress, and coming also "to Gilgal—and multiply transgression." (4:4a) What is going on here is that "The prophet is attacking the empty show of a scrupulously correct ritual which has no real religion behind it,"[9] and the issue climaxes in 5:18–24 with its affirmation that the "day of the Lord" will be a day not of liberation and positive happenings for the people of Israel but rather one of doom and darkness (5:18–20). Regarding more normal times there is the divine word that worship of God coming out of lives of unrighteousness is nothing less than an abomination and affront to the Lord. This is hateful worship to the Lord to whom it is offered, and details given are piercing in their intensity (5:21–22). Thus, "Take away from me the noise of your songs; I will not listen to the melody of your harps" (v. 23). And what is it that instead is required? "But let justice roll down like waters, and righteousness like an ever-flowing stream." (5:24) This is a theme that we shall find in others of the Hebrew prophets: Hosea (6:6; 8:13), Isaiah (1:10–17), Micah (6:8), later Jeremiah (6:19–21; 14:11–12), even later Malachi (1:10; 2:13), yet perhaps there is a sense in which these others are dependent in some ways upon the eighth century prophet Amos.

Yet what is it that here is being condemned? Is it worship *per se*? Or is it rather that what is unacceptable to this prophet is worship of the Lord being offered by those whose lives are steeped in sinful pursuits, in particular in practices that involve the oppression and captivity of the poorest and least strong members of society? Though the former possibility has some advocates, the majority view is that it is the latter, and such does indeed seem to be the most likely.[10] It is hardly conceivable that prophet and editors would advocate the banning of the worship of God, but entirely reasonable that they should use strong words to express the totally unacceptable worship coming from such sinful lives. We are reminded of Ps 15 with its opening questions, "O Lord, who may abide in your tent? Who may dwell on your holy hill?" (Ps 15:1), which draws forth a number of ways of expressing the matter (Ps 15:2, 4-5).[11]

In the fourth place the prophet Amos is portrayed as praying for his people. In a vision of locusts eating up the land the prophet is portrayed as praying for his people (Amos 7:1–3), interceding for them that they may be spared this destruction. Thus the prophet prays, "O Lord God, forgive, I

---

9. Snaith, *Amos, Hosea and Micah*, 25. See also, Porteous, "Ritual and Righteousness"; and ibid., "Actualization and the Prophetic Criticism of the Cult."

10. See, e.g., Rowley, "Ritual and the Hebrew Prophets"; and Kapelrud, *Central Ideas in Amos*, 75–77.

11. On Ps 15, see above, 130–31.

beg you! How can Jacob stand? He is so small!" (Amos 7:2). And when the threat of fire was impending Amos in similar words makes his intercession for his people, "O Lord God, cease, I beg you! How can Jacob stand? He is so small!" (7:5). It has been pointed out that in the third vision recorded in the book of Amos there is no intercession (7:7-9), but that is a vision of a plumb-line being set by the Lord in the midst of his people, which is presumably intended to test their righteousness or otherwise. That is, this is in the nature of a divine warning, one in which there is as yet nothing specific for the prophet to intercede about.[12]

Isaiah

By this title I intend that prophetical tradition represented in the book of Isaiah, all the material in those sixty-six chapters which comes, many of us understand, from at least three prophets, maybe even more, and a number of editors, yet with the whole work displaying a sense of commonality, even a degree of unity, in theological outlook and in various linguistic ways.[13] Thus in what follows I am considering what there is about prophets and worship in the whole of the book of Isaiah.

In the first place there is here, as there in Amos,[14] the condemnation of worship that comes from settings of immorality on the part of those offering worship. This finds expression in the opening chapter of the Isaiah book, a chapter that is widely regarded as being in the nature of an introduction to what follows, setting forth at the beginning of the work some of the themes which will recur. Thus in Isa 1:10-17 we have the Lord portrayed as addressing "rulers of Sodom . . . people of Gomorrah" and saying,

> What to me is the multitude of your sacrifices?
> says the Lord;
> I have had enough of burnt offerings of rams
> and the fat of fed beasts;
> I do not delight in the blood of bulls,
> or of lambs, or of goats. (Isa 1:11)

Thus the diatribe continues until "even though you make many prayers, I will not listen; your hands are full of blood" and finally, "learn to do good;

12. On this and about the intercessions of Amos, see Thompson, *I Have Heard Your Prayer*, 111-12.

13. For a recent study of these issues, see, e.g., Clements, *Jerusalem and the Nations*.

14. In this regard, see the remarks of Blenkinsopp in *Sage, Priest, Prophet*, where he says, "it can be shown that Isaiah is applying the message of Amos . . . to the situation of the Judean state a few decades later" (143).

seek justice, rescue the oppressed, defend the orphan, plead for the widow" (Isa 1:15b, 17). Both Amos and Isaiah highlight the offence to the Lord when worship of him comes from people who are caught up in sinful ways in their lives. (Amos 4:4; Isa 29:13). Yet again, here in Isaiah, as in Amos, it would seem that the words of condemnation are not intended to be of worship root and branch, but rather a judgment upon those manifestations of worship that for the prophet are not deemed to be *acceptable* to the Lord because of the sinful, domineering, oppressive lives of worshippers. Wildberger says what is being manifested here is "a superficial cultic piety" and that "cultic correctness, and even zealous cultic activity, are of no value if one is apparently making no effort to fulfill ethical responsibilities."[15] The same concern is spoken about in the third part of the Isaiah book, chs 56–66. In Isa 58:1–14 the prophet exposes the fact that in at least some quarters the religious fast days are used to oppress workers, and the perpetrators of such things are warned that such "fasting" as this will not make the worshippers' voices heard on high (Isa 58:4). What constitutes an acceptable fast day to the Lord is set out in 58:6–14, and is one in which religious devotions are combined with the living of godly and caring lives.

It should be emphasized that throughout the book of Isaiah there is a strong theocentric and worshipful strain. This is to be observed early in the book in the account in Isa 6:1–13 of the intense holiness and otherness of the Lord of Hosts, or as he is frequently called in the book "The Holy One of Israel" (Isa 1:4; 5:19, 24; 10:20; 12:6; 17:7; 29:19; 30:11, 12, 15; 31:1; 37:23; 41:14, 16, 20; 43:3, 14; 45:11; 47:4; 48:17; 49:7; 54:5; 55:5; 60:9, 14). The encounter of Isaiah with this holy God has some of the hallmarks of those encounters with the divine that from time to time are presented to us in the Hebrew Bible, such as Jacob at Bethel (Gen 28:10–17), Moses at Horeb (Exod 3:1–6), Elijah at Horeb (1 Kgs 19:11–18). In these encounters there is on the part of the human beings concerned that profound sense of holy awe, even "fear," for there is the awareness that the deity who is so "other" than humanity has appeared and even is speaking to a human person. In the case of the account in Isa 6 this experience is if anything heightened through the descriptive details given of the Lord, his exalted throne, so high and lofty, (even!) the hem of his robe being portrayed as sufficient to *fill* the temple, and through the account of the seraphs who with their faces veiled called in praise "Holy, holy, holy is the Lord of hosts; the whole earth is full of his glory" (Isa 6:1–3). So also here is the expression of Isaiah's deeply-felt sinfulness, leading to his response, "Woe is me! I am lost, for I am a man of unclean lips, and I live among a people of unclean lips; yet my eyes have

---

15. Wildberger, *Isaiah 28-39*, p. 618.

seen the King, the Lord of hosts!" (Isa 6:5)—as there is also with Moses, "And Moses hid his face, for he was afraid to look at God" (Exod 3:6), and perhaps also with Elijah, "he wrapped his face in his mantle and went out and stood at the entrance of the cave" (1 Kgs 19:13).

Further, Isaiah having been so dramatically confronted by the Lord was commissioned to a particular task in the divine service—as also were Moses and Elijah (see Exod 3:7-22; 1 Kgs 19:15-21). As far as Isaiah was concerned this was commissioning to a particular ministry in the national Judean crisis occasioned by the attack of Syria and Israel upon Judah and Jerusalem, the so called Syro-Ephraimite war. The details of the prophet's ministry in this crisis, which need not trouble us here,[16] are set out in the various oracles in Isa 7 and 8, and the whole block of material Isa 6:1—9:7 has been understood by many to be something of a statement ("Denkschrift") of the prophet or his editors about the prophet's ministry in the crisis.

It is the shape and arrangement of the "Denkschrift" that is of interest to us in the present work on the subject of worship. For while the central part of of this account has the actual details of the crisis and the prophet's words therein (Isa 7:1—8:22), both of which are presented as closely bound up with immediate political realities, yet this is framed by two passages that lift the reader into higher and wider realms of consideration: in Isa 6:1-13 by the prophet's commissioning account and in 9:2-7 by the divine promise of the future king who would show wisdom and statecraft, qualities lamentably absent in king Ahaz in the Syro-Ephraimite crisis. I do not wish to suggest that these, what I have called framing passages, are worship materials *per se*, but I do see them both as being suffused with the spirit of reverence and worship. In Isa 6:1-13 it is the intense awareness of the holiness and otherness of the Lord which brings about in the prophet his awareness of his own and his people's sinfulness; while in 9:2-7 it is the almost hymn-like quality of the promise of a future wise and caring national leader. Altogether, we may say that the so-called "Denkschrift" is made up of a remarkable combination of the writing of an account of the living through an earthly political crisis along with a framing of worship-like oracles, the latter setting the former into a religious, reverential, worshipful setting.[17]

---

16. For details, see the standard commentaries, and further, Thompson, *Situation and Theology*, 22–62.

17. Corley, "Elements of Coronation Ritual in Isaiah 11.1–10," argues that Isa 11:1–10 is a reflection of a royal coronation ritual. He makes a good case, but it is inevitably a speculative proposal. Nevertheless the passage, Isa 11:1–10, may be said to continue the tendency and the style of the preceding Isa 6:1—9:7 block of material, namely being in the nature of a presentation about a political issue set in the frame of

Further, there are expressions of praise and thanksgiving that appear at various junctures in the Isaiah book, such as the thanksgiving to the Lord in Isa 12, and reminiscent of a number of the biblical psalms. Great thanksgiving is offered to the Lord either that some historical crisis has been successfully overcome—either the Syro-Ephraimite crisis, or alternatively a more general expression in an "eschatalogical song of thanksgiving."[18] There are also appearances of "hymnic" material in Isa 25:1—26:21 in the section of the book that is expressed in apocalyptic language (Isa 24–27). Certainly Isa 25:9–12 reads like an eschatalogical song of thanksgiving, while 25:1–5 and 26:1–6 appear to be songs of thanksgiving, the former for the destruction of an enemy city, the latter for the deliverance of a city that would appear to be Jerusalem. Moreover, Isa 35, standing as it does between the earlier part of the Isaiah book (chs 1–32) and what will follow, so brimming with hope and promise for the future (chs 40–55), is certainly expressed in hymnic style and is nothing but theocentric. In fact, much of the content of Isa 40–55 is expressed in language that resonates with the themes of worship. Again, it may be described as theocentric, and the matter has hardly ever been better expressed than it was by James Muilenburg in his contribution to the *Interpreter's Bible*. Muilenburg said about the prophet of Isa 40–55: "The intensity of the prophet's thought and feeling is expressed in many ways. He lifts his voice in exalting triumph as he sees the approach of Israel's conquering Lord. He breaks into ecstatic hymns again and again as the event takes place before his enraptured eyes (cf. 42:10–13; 44:23; 45:8; 49:13). The theme of redemption almost invariably stirs him to songs of praise."[19]

What is there in the book of Isaiah about the Jerusalem temple? Though it does not say so explicitly, the setting of the prophet's inaugural vision in Isa 6 would seem to be that of the temple. Further this temple would seem to be the place to which religious offerings were brought (1:12), the place to which the king would go and pray in a time of crisis (37:14–20). Then that visionary promise in 2:2–4, very probably coming from a time considerably later, envisages the temple as the destination of religious pilgrimage, the place where search is made for the word of the Lord. Perhaps Isa 4:2–6 should be regarded as an oracle on the same theme. Isaiah 18:7 envisages people of Nubia bringing their gifts to Zion, "the place of the name of the Lord of hosts." Perhaps above all Isa 19:19 has the most remarkably expansive portrayal of Yahweh worship taking place: "On that day there will be an altar to the Lord in the center of the land of Egypt." This is followed

---

deeply religious matters.

18. See, e.g., Clements, *Isaiah 1–39*, pp. 127–29.
19. Muilenburg, *Isaiah 40–66*, p. 386.

by "and the Egyptians will know the Lord on that day, and will worship with sacrifice and burnt offering, and they will make vows to the Lord and perform them" (19:21). Another similarly hopeful passage, this too with inevitable scholarly-disputed date, is Isa 30:27-33. It reads as if a pilgrimage to Jerusalem is envisaged, rather along the lines of what we glimpse in Pss 120-134. Thus, "You shall have a song as in the night when a holy festival is kept; and gladness of heart, as when one sets out to the sound of the flute to go to the mountain of the Lord, to the Rock of Israel." (Isa 30:29)

However, there is remarkably little about a temple in Isa 40-55, Solomon's temple having been destroyed by the Babylonians in 587 BCE, some of its artefacts being taken away to Babylon (2 Kgs 25:8-17). With the possibilities of exiles being able to return to Jerusalem there is indeed the promise that not only will Jerusalem be rebuilt but also that new temple foundations will be laid (Isa 44:28). This we are told was part of the work ordered by the new Persian ruler, Cyrus (Ezra 1:1-4; 3:7), indicating, as Blenkinsopp expresses it that there was "imperial sponsorship of the restored Jerusalem cult."[20] But then there is nothing more said in Isa 40-55 about the temple, thus giving the impression that to the prophet of these chapters this possible rebuilding of the temple was of neither paramount nor immediate importance.

By contrast, in Isa 56-66 we encounter more frequent references to the temple.[21] It is spoken of by the Lord as "my glorious house" (60:7), and that it will be beautified through the use of choice materials in its construction (60:13). Presumably these must be promises for the future, for in Isa 61:4 it sounds as if the temple is still in ruins. See also 63:18 and 64:11. Yet when the temple is rebuilt it will indeed "be called a house of prayer for all peoples" to which all, including the foreigners, will be welcomed, and whose gifts and sacrifices will be accepted (56:6-7). For "Thus says the Lord God, who gathers the outcasts of Israel, I will gather others to them besides those already gathered" (56:8). But we should take note of the fact that the emphasis is on the temple being a place of prayer: it would appear that in comparison with sacrifice prayer is here portrayed as gaining in importance. Are we to assume that this is something that has come out of the religious experience of exile? Is there something here in embryo that at some later time will result in the institution of the synagogue? This is also to be seen perhaps in the various prayerful, communal confessions of sin such as we read in Isa 59:9-15a, and with which we may compare the prayers of

---

20. Blenkinsopp, *Isaiah 56-66*, pp. 85-88.

21. On worship in Isa 56-66, see Blenkinsopp, *Isaiah 56-66*, pp. 85-88; and Tiemeyer, *Priestly Rites and Prophetic Rage*.

confession coming from the same era in Ezra 9:6-15; Neh 9:6-37, and from perhaps rather later Dan 9:4-19. Further, within this (envisaged?) sanctuary there are foreigners serving as officials (Isa 66:21).

Nevertheless alongside all such matters there is also in parts of the Isaiah book an ongoing polemic against idols and the worship of them, these matters being to the fore in chs 1-39 and 56-66. Thus in the opening chapter of the whole book we have the condemnation of corrupt worship practices in 1:29-31, this being renewed in 2:8 and 18, and 10:10-11. There is also in Isa 17:7-8 and 10-11 a condemnation of religious practices perpetuated by Israelite people. Meanwhile in 28:7-8 it is priests who are being condemned for their conduct. In the third part of the book we have an extended passage in 56:9—57:13 about corrupt leaders and corrupt worship, the latter detailed in 57:3-13.

As far as prophetic intercession is concerned there is only one place in the whole of the book of Isaiah where this appears to be mentioned, this being in the third part of the book, in Isa 63:7—64:12. Although Isaiah is asked to pray for King Hezekiah in Isa 37:4, this is recorded in material that began life as deuteronomistic (see 2 Kgs 19:4), and at that point represents deuteronomistic thought rather than Isaianic. We should perhaps say that in general the understanding of prophecy we find in the book of Isaiah has a firm emphasis on prophets being those who are called to speak from the Lord to his people, this so predominating that as far as we are able to perceive the accompanying ministry of speaking *for* people *to* their God does not have great emphasis here. It is perhaps not without significance that in the Assyrian crisis for Hezekiah it is the king himself, and not Isaiah the prophet, who is portrayed as taking the letter he has received from the Assyrians into the temple, where he "spread it before the Lord" and prayed to the Lord (Isa 37:14-20), while it is the prophet Isaiah who brings the resulting message from the Lord to the beleaguered king (Isa 37:21-35).

Hosea

There is emphasis in the book of Hosea over the prophet's indictment of his people's sin in the travesty of worship they offer to the Lord God of Israel. This is highlighted in the early chapters of the book through the talk in Hos 1-3 of Hosea's marriage to Gomer, and her subsequent unfaithfulness to him. Whichever way this is intended to be understood, either as acted parable or else as insight through earlier experience, the theme of unfaithfulness is applied to the people of Israel in their covenant relationship with their Lord. Indeed, the issue of Israelite unfaithfulness to Yahweh is a dominant theme in the book right from the opening verses. Thus in Hos 1:2 we read, "the land commits great whoredom (*z-n-h*) by forsaking the Lord." In this way so many of the people have gone astray (Hos 4:10, 11, 12, 13; 5:3, 4; 6:10), and Hosea is critical of the failure of both prophets (Hos 4:5; 9:7, 8) and (in particular it would seem) priests (Hos 4:4, 6, 9, 5:1) to change this situation for the better.[22] We read about sexual orgies in Hos 4:14, and thus the talk of marital unfaithfulness that the prophet portrays himself as experiencing was clearly intended to be understood both in a physical and also metaphorical sense. Thus says Macintosh, "Promiscuity, caught in the cult and in its associated idolatry, was for Hosea the term which best epitomised all the nation's depraved and immoral behaviour."[23]

What, however, we miss in the received prophecy of Hosea is any vision the prophet and/or his editors might have had for the worship they believed *should* have taken place in the land of Israel. There is no vision here of either renewed worship or any reformation of temple ordering. This comes to us as something of a surprise, for there are in this prophecy deep and profound expressions of Yahweh's ongoing purposes for his people, of his ongoing commitment to them, and of his burning desire to receive them back to himself in faithfulness (Hos 1:10-11; 2:14-23; 3:1; 6:1-3, 11b; 11:1-9; 14:4-8), but alas nothing here about a desired renewal of worship.

There is nevertheless an issue this prophecy speaks of which is characteristic of some of the prophetical ministries. It is not that Hosea actually prays for his people in their sinful plight, but he is portrayed as giving his people the words *they* may use as they seek to return to the Lord.[24] Thus we are told that Hosea instructed his people to take with them these words as they returned to the Lord,

> Take away all guilt;
> accept that which is good,

---

22. See Ackerman, *Under Every Green Tree*, 3, who in her study of some of the prophets who prophesied in later times than Hosea speaks of those who worshipped other gods instead of or in addition to Yaweh, or in ways that were considered illegitimate by those who were responsible for passing on the records that have come down to us. See further, Andersen and Freedman, who say concerning Hos 4–14 "The major aberrations are cultic, in the most basic sense of the term, and political. False worship of the true God or true worship of false gods—one leads to the other—has its counterpart in false politics . . ." (*Hosea*, 48).

23. Macintosh, *Hosea*, xvi.

24. However, Macintosh refers to Hos 14:1-8 as "Hosea's Prayer *De Profundis*," understanding these verses as a prayer of the prophet said over Israel in the Lord's name (*Hosea*, 558-81). I take them in the way understood by Davies, as comprising "a prophetic exhortation which incorporates a model prayer of penitence (vv. 1-3)" (*Hosea*, 298).

> and we will offer
> the fruit of our lips.
> Assyria shall not save us;
> we will not ride upon horses;
> we will say no more, "Our God",
> to the work of our hands.
> In you the orphan finds mercy. (Hos 14:2b–3)

To which is the Lord's reply:

> I will heal their disloyalty;
> I will love them freely,
> for my anger has turned from them. (Hos 14:4)

Micah

The various parts of the book of Micah are widely thought—though there is considerable scholarly disagreement on specific details—to come from different times. While parts of the book bear marks of probably having come from the eighth century, at the same time other parts read as though they more likely come from the post-exilic period. While I shall speak about possible dating for some of this material, I shall yet be considering the completed book as it has come down to us, in its canonical form.

As regards the matter of the contents of this short prophetic book, on the subject of worship there are a number of themes we have already come across in other books of the Old Testament. Thus here in Mic 1:7, is talk about images (*pesel*) and idols (*'āṣāb*), artefacts that are to do with false and unacceptable worship on the part of the people of Israel and Judah. Here in Mic 1:2–16, in materials that would seem to come from various times but which have been melded into a literary unity, are portrayed sins sufficient to explain divine judgment being executed by a foreign nation. Thus what has become a familiar condemnation of Israelite worship practice is sounded again here. Further in 1:5 we have the condemnation of "high places" (*bāmôt*), perhaps "cult shrines," these being found even in Jerusalem. In fact, here both Samaria and Jerusalem are apostrophized for their sins of engaging in worship that prophets, and certainly those who espoused deuteronomistic thought, regarded—and it seems loudly proclaimed—as unacceptable and sinful. Perhaps there is a further condemnation of false and unacceptable worship in the talk of "whore's fee," (*'etnan*, NRSV "wages," but compare REB's "earnings for prostitution," for the word is sometimes used in a specific sense of "harlot's pay").[25] Another aspect of unacceptable worship, spoken about in Mic 3:11, is priests teaching "for a price," that is, presumably, being paid for it. Such practices and other aspects of unacceptable worship, especially of consulting sorcerers and soothsayers, of the use of images and pillars, sacred poles and other human devised artefacts, are singled out in Mic 5:12-14 as being under threat of divine extermination.

Micah 6:6-8 is about the spirit of acceptable worship, and poses the question of what is an acceptable offering or sacrifice with which one may come before the Lord. Does it lie in bringing burnt offerings of calves, or rams, or oil? Does it consist in the offering of a child, that is in the offering of a worshipper's own child? In v. 8 it is affirmed that these people have been divinely told that what is required by God from his people is not in fact correct offerings, sacrifices and liturgies, but rather good living, in particular doing justice (*mišpāṭ*), loving mercy (*ḥesed*), and walking humbly, attentively (*ṣĕnēaʿ leket*) with their God. It is not easy to believe that what is intended to be said here is that the worship of God is not important, but rather that worship and life do go together. The answer to the questions posed in fact moves the discussion from the nature of what is to be offered to the Lord, to "a focus on the quality of life that is lived. Good is what YHWH requires and what is good is the one thing needful to know. The answer does not revert to divine first-person style or use any other device to authorize itself. The declaration belongs to tradition and one needs only to be reminded."[26]

This passage reminds us of the condemnation in the book of Amos at the divine displeasure with festival assemblies and the giving of sacrifices and offerings unless or until it is accompanied by justice and righteousness (Amos 5:21-24). With this we may associate Isa 1:12-17, in particular its condemnation of practices in which lives stained with the blood of violence are declared unacceptable on the part of those who come before the Lord to make their prayers and bring their offerings and sacrifices. These people are told that the Lord "cannot endure solemn assemblies with iniquity" (Isa 1:13).[27]

Jeremiah

We may divide our discussion of what there is in the book of Jeremiah concerning worship into three parts, the first and third parts dealing with what

---

25. See *DCH* 1:462.

26. Mays, *Micah*, 141.

27. On Amos 5:21-24, see above, 243-44, and for Isa 1:12-17, 245-46. See also above, 194-95, on Mic 7:18-20 as a possible liturgy.

the prophet Jeremiah is portrayed as saying and doing, the second part what we are told the people of Judah were doing.[28]

First then, we need to consider what is said about Jeremiah in the book that bears his name. We are told that he came from Anathoth, was of a priestly family (Jer 1:1), but at the same time was critical of the Judean priests of the day. Jeremiah said that they, along with kings, officials, and prophets, will be shamed (2:26, see also v. 9), for even the priests, along with others, were dealing falsely (6:13; 8:10), and were ungodly (23:11). Not surprisingly Jeremiah is portrayed as suffering at the hands of the priest Pashur, the chief officer in the house of the Lord, who we are told struck Jeremiah and had him put in the stocks for a night (20:1-2).

We find remarkably little in the traditions in the book of Jeremiah about any future temple of the Lord. While there is much in the book about the Babylonian destruction of the land, of Jerusalem, and of the temple (see 52:13), Jeremiah—having already warned his people that the temple may one day become like that temple at Shiloh (26:6), that is, we assume, a ruin, destroyed—does not seem to say anything specific about a future temple, though there is a possible presumption that there will be one in the future (see 33:11, 18, 21-22). Rather, the emphasis about renewal in this book concerns renewed inward religion (see Jer 31:31-34), and perhaps the renewed worship envisaged here is of a similarly inward nature. What, however, is of a more tangible nature in this regard is the talk in the book of temple vessels, that they shall be carefully and reverently conveyed to Babylon, the place of exile (27:21-22; 52:18-23), and brought back (28:3-6). This a concern we find also in other parts of the Hebrew Bible.[29]

We can now turn to what, according to the book of Jeremiah, was taking place in Judah, in particular to what sins the people were said to have been committing. For there is a major polemic in this book concerning the people of Judah going after other gods, and engaging in rites that were deemed to be Yahwistically unacceptable. Thus time and again in this book

---

28. There continue to be considerable differences in scholarly approaches to the book of Jeremiah, in particular as to how much of what is portrayed as being the words of Jeremiah is to be attributed to the prophet, and how much represents the work of his editors; and also the matter of the historical contribution of the prophet. There are also varying evaluations of the historical accuracy of what we read in this biblical book, and further there are complex issues over differences between the Hebrew and Greek texts of Jeremiah. All these matters are to be observed in the different approaches in the commentaries of Holladay, *Jeremiah*, vols. 1 and 2; Carroll, *Jeremiah*; McKane, *Jeremiah*, vols. 1 and 2; and Allen, *Jeremiah*. In this present work my approach is to take the received Hebrew Text as the biblical basis for my comments, and to regard what is attributed to Jeremiah as coming from the prophet of that name.

29. On the theme of temple vessels, see above, 44-45.

we read of the people going in religiously false directions (see 2:28; 5:19; 7:1—8:3), going after the Baals, the gods of the Canaanites (9:14; 32:29, 35), and engaging in pagan worship (11:1–17; 13:10, 27; 16:11, 18; 17:2; 18:15). They are even indicted for having built high places and to have engaged in child sacrifice (19:4–5, 13; 32:35), and further making offerings to the queen of heaven (44:17–23, 25).[30] For Jeremiah the Lord had clearly said "do not go after other gods to serve and worship them, and do not provoke me to anger with the work of your hands." (25:6)

What then, with this sort of ministry that Jeremiah was called to exercise, is there in this book about this prophet's responses as regards the matter of worship? In the first place, there is a remarkable series of personal outpourings in prayer on the part of the prophet himself to the Lord. These (Jer 11:18–23; 12:1–6; 15:15–21; 17:14–18; 18:19–23; 20:7–18) are generally known as "Confessions," but they would perhaps more accurately and helpfully be described as personal laments, such individual laments that we find in the biblical Psalter.[31] Certainly in these passages the prophet cries out in a real sense of agony to the Lord for the difficult and demanding way in which as a prophet he has been forced to travel.[32]

It has already been observed that part of the ministry of some of the Israelite prophets appears to have been concerned with praying for their people. In the case of Jeremiah he is recorded as having received instructions that he was *not* to pray for his people (7:16; 11:14; 14:11; 15:1). It is generally taken that this apparently strange command is to be understood in the sense that his people are in such depths of sinfulness that the prophet would be, as it were, wasting his time in praying for them. In that sense Jeremiah is not to pray for his people.[33] Nevertheless we read in the book that the prophet does in fact pray for his people: he confesses their corporate sins (14:7–9), and he intercedes for them, this being portrayed as having taken place a number of times (14:13; 14:19—15:9; 37:3; 42:2, 4, 20). Further, this prophet is portrayed as making his own prayers to God, not only in the so-

---

30. For details of these and other such rites, see above, 62–65, and also Ackerman, *Under Every Green Tree*, esp. pp. 5–35.

31. See above, 124–25.

32. On these Confessions of Jeremiah, see my earlier treatments in Thompson, *I Have Heard Your Prayer*, 130–40; and "Where is the God of Justice?," 35–37, 115–16, 126, 177.

33. Allen understands this command somewhat differently saying, "Intercession on behalf of the people was a regular part of a prophet's ministry since a prophet was not only Yahweh's representative in addressing the people but the people's representative in addressing Yahweh . . . In this case the people's religious offenses are judged to be so flagrant that the normal prophetic service had to be suspended, letting Yahweh's anger take its destructive course, as v. 20 will affirm . . ." (*Jeremiah*, 98).

called "Confessions" but also in affirmation of his faith in God (16:19–20), and in praise of him (10:1–16); moreover, Jeremiah exhorts the Israelites to pray for the people in the land in which they, Judeans, find themselves to be exiles, far away from home (29:7, 12).

Ezekiel

Like Jeremiah, Ezekiel was of a priestly family, and was himself, a priest. Thus in the Hebrew Bible he is presented as being both priest and prophet, one whose ministry was among the exiles in Babylon (Ezek 1:1–3). There are scenes in the book of Ezekiel that can be read as if the prophet was at times present in Jerusalem, but the general view of scholarship is that after his deportation in the fifth year of the reign of King Jehoiachin (1:2), that is the year 597 BCE, the prophet was located solely in Babylon, and that those passages in the book which might be read as coming from one resident in Jerusalem represent what he saw in vision of his "home" city while he was in Babylon.[34]

Ezekiel in his call to the prophetic ministry was commanded that he was to give words only of judgment (see 8:1; 33:30–33), and indeed it is at a comparatively late stage in the book that we read of him actually interceding for his people (36:37–38). As far as the subject of worship is concerned it has to be said that the opening call narrative in ch. 1 gives the impression of being intensely worshipful, for it gives a vision of the deity himself, ending with the words, "Like the bow in a cloud on a rainy day, such was the appearance of the splendor all around. This was the appearance of the likeness of the glory of the Lord" (1:28) But then soon begins the prophetic complaint about the worship being practiced and offered by at least some of the people, worship which for the prophet is totally unacceptable, being indeed a mockery of what worship is intended to be, in particular not being focussed on the Lord God of Israel. Thus there is talk in 5:11 of the people defiling the Jerusalem sanctuary; the artefacts of false and unacceptable worship will be thrown down (6:4–7); the idols and other foci of false worship will be destroyed (6:13). In 8:7–18 we have a particularly full description of at least some aspects of abominations in worship,[35] followed by the warning that divine judgment will begin at the sanctuary (9:6)—but portrayed in this book as going on from there into many places. For time and again we read of the involvement in idol worship (14:3–8; 20:16, 24, 39; 22:3, 4; 23:30); of those who are apostrophized as "playing the whore," by which we assume

---

34. See, e.g., Joyce, *Ezekiel*, 5–6.
35. On Ezek 8:7–18, see in particular, Ackerman, *Under Every Green Tree*, 37–99.

that cultic and sexual apostasy is intended (16:15-22); and the sanctuary being profaned (23:38-39; 25:3). Further, drink and other offerings are presented on high hills, and under leafy trees (6:13; 20:28-31); and there is talk of child sacrifice (20:31; 23:39).[36]

The book of Ezekiel ends in a way very different from that of Jeremiah. For in Ezek 40-48 we are given no less than nine consecutive chapters on the subject of the Jerusalem temple and the worship therein, which, it would be generally agreed, come from the sixth century BCE, some scholars arguing that these chapters are a unity and come from the prophet Ezekiel, others that we do not have a holistic composition, but rather a series of strata of writings coming from different hands.[37] I shall proceed on the assumption that here we are dealing with a holistic block of material that one way or another has come from Ezekiel, and further I am content to regard the chapters with their at times apparently rather strange language, as being both in the nature of a dream and also what might have been envisaged as one day becoming a reality. That is, we have here something in the nature of an interweaving of the visionary and the realistic. I realize that these are large assumptions to make about these nine chapters that have been much studied and discussed over many years, but they seem not unreasonable to serve as a basis for this particular study.[38] The text of Ezek 40-48 deals with three main subjects and issues: first, in 40:1—43:12 a vision of the new temple; second, in 43:13—46:24 regulations for and details about the worship in the new temple; third, 47:1—48:35 about the river, the allocation of land, and the ongoing presence of the Lord. We shall deal with these in turn.

Ezekiel 40:1—43:12 affords considerable detail about Ezekiel's vision of the new temple. After words of introduction to the whole experience (40:1-4), in which we are told that in vision the prophet was set down on a very high mountain, this presumably being intended to indicate a link with Moses of old who received instructions "on the mountain" about the tabernacle he was to build on the earth (Exod 25:1—31:18). Then we read in Ezek 40:5-16 about an outer wall to the temple and the east gate. We are not told that the geographical setting for this, and what is to come, is the city of Jerusalem, yet it is difficult to believe that anywhere but Jerusalem is being spoken about. Again, Zion is not spoken about—but then Zion is not spoken

---

36. On all these aspects of unacceptable and false worship, see above, 61-66.

37. See, e.g., Joyce, *Ezekiel*, 219, for details and references to various views on these matters.

38. For consideration of some of these issues, see Block, *Ezekiel 25-48*, pp. 494-506; Zimmerli, *Ezekiel 2*, pp. 325-28; Greenberg, "The Design and Themes of Ezekiel's Program of Restoration"; Niditch, "Ezekiel 40-48 in Visionary Context"; and Darr, "The Wall around Paradise: Ezekielian Ideas about the Future."

about anywhere in Ezekiel. Further, what we have in the prophet's vision is not to be built actually in the city, but rather on a high mountain with the city towards the south (40:2). Presumably the mountain being envisaged is at one level Zion, the mountain where Solomon's temple was built, and at a deeper level Mount Sinai. Thus here is a further link with Moses of old and all that he was commanded "on the mountain" to build on earth, suggesting that this new temple had a firm relationship with, and be in a succession to, what had been divinely given of old, namely, the desert tabernacle. And what about the "wall all around the outside of the temple area" (40:5), to "make a separation between the holy and the common" (42:20)? That is, the wall was not so much to keep intruders or enemies out, but rather to designate, to mark out the area, the space, that was holy—that is, to separate the sacred from the profane. For although this Ezekielian temple does not have the three parts as did Solomon's, with their distinctively different gradations of holiness, yet it does have both this outer wall to separate profane and sacred and also a "holy of holies" within the actual temple.

On the east side of this wall there was a gateway with steps up into the inner area, with recesses (40:6–16), and there were similar gates on the northern and southern sides (40:20-27), all of which led into the outer court, the place of worship for the people (vv. 17–19). However, the western wall had a building next to it (41:12), and thus had no gate. Within the outer walled area was another wall, also with its gates, making the court of the priests (40:28–37). Provision was incorporated for the preparation, by way of washing and slaughtering, of the sacrificial offerings (vv. 38–43), as well as rooms for the Zadokite priests and the Levites (vv. 44–47). This is followed by details of the dimensions of the various parts of the temple (40:48—41:4), the vestibule (40:48–49), the sanctuary (NRSV "nave" 41:1–2), and the inner sanctuary called the "most holy place"—what is otherwise known as the "holy of holies" (41:3–4). The dimensions of the nave were 40 cubits in length and 20 cubits in width. This unit of measurement we are told in 40:5 was "long cubits", that is "a cubit and a handbreadth in length," that is about 20.6 inches, or 520mm. Thus the nave/sanctuary was about 70 feet by 35 feet, 21 meters by 10.5 meters.

The account then goes on to speak about the decoration, and details about the interior, of this temple (41:5–26), there being side chambers, and an upstairs area along with the necessary staircase, mostly in fact rather on the lines of what we are told there had been in Solomon's temple (1 Kgs 6:5–10), and also it should be said of what we are told was in the desert Tabernacle of Exod 25–31. However, a somewhat striking exception was that Ezekiel's temple was, in comparison with Solomon's, distinctly empty; in Ezekiel's there was not even the ark of the covenant. It may be that in the

Ezekiel account there is a striving to express a sense of the presence of God that was less anthropomorphic than one demanding the presence of a cultic object such as the historic ark of the covenant. Rather, here in Ezek 43:5 we perhaps have the presence of God expressed in "the glory of the Lord filled the temple." Paul Joyce observes, "Such is Ezekiel's focus on YHWH himself that much else is simply eclipsed."[39] However, there was, so we are told in 41:21–22, an altar in front of the "holy place," one that is not to be confused with the stone altar of sacrifice which stood outside the temple itself (43:13–27).

Details of the priests' rooms are set out in 42:1–14, though in places the text is in some disarray, so we cannot be sure just what it is saying. It suffices to say that here are rooms for the priests, to be their vestries or sacristies, where they could robe and disrobe, whereby worshippers were protected from having contact with the holy—and also the holy not being defiled by contact with what was profane. There is further a note on the dimensions of the whole temple area, namely a square of 500 cubits on each side (42:15–20). Moreover, we are told once again that there was the wall all round the complex "to make a separation between the holy and the common" (42:20).[40] Finally, about these temple arrangements, and as the climax of them—and the climax also of the vision the prophet had been vouchsafed—we are given in 43:1–12 details of the return of the glory of the Lord into the holy space of the temple. We are no doubt intended to be taken in thought back to Ezek 11 when the Lord departed from the city and from his people, now reading that those people were promised the presence of their Lord with them, and 43:1–12 portraying the magnificent scene of the Lord's return. Thus in 43:4–5: "As the glory of the Lord entered the temple by the gate facing east, the spirit lifted me up, and brought me into the inner court; and the glory of the Lord filled the temple." No doubt we are intended to be reminded of Exod 40:34 and 1 Kgs 8:11, telling respectively of the glory of the Lord filling the desert tabernacle and the house of the Lord. Further we have in the Ezekielian account the divine words to the prophet, "He said to me: Mortal, this is the place of my throne and the place for the soles of my feet, where I will reside among the people of Israel forever" (43:7)

Then Ezek 43:13—46:24 gives regulations for and details about worship in the new temple. These begin in 43:13–27 with the altar of burnt offering, of similar dimensions to those given by the Chronicler (2 Chr 4:1). This altar was raised up, having steps up to it on its eastern side, and this

---

39. Joyce, *Ezekiel*, 225. See also Joyce, "Temple and Worship in Ezekiel 40–48," esp. pp. 150–52.

40. On this subject and theme, see Jensen, *Graded Holiness*, 89–114.

would be the focus of the sacrificial cult of the temple. While there is the holy of holies, for Ezekiel the *pěnîmāh* (literally "inside"), and envisaged as the symbolic place of the presence of God, here at the stone altar is at the same time the center of worship, in particular of the sacrificial worship.[41] Also given here are details of special arrangements and sacrifices to be offered for the dedication of this altar, with the reassurance to the worshippers, "When these days are over, then from the eighth day onward the priests shall offer upon the altar your burnt offerings and your offerings of well-being; and I will accept you, says the Lord God." (Ezek 43:27)

Ezekiel 44:1-4 takes us back to the gate on the eastern side of the temple, now shut because that had been the way that the glory of the Lord had entered (43:4)—it had become "hallowed because the deity has passed through it to return to the place of his special abode," says Joyce.[42] Then follow instructions about who may and who may not come into the sanctuary, and although the words may sound harsh and somewhat exclusive, the concern is to preserve a sense of holiness and to ensure that what is "holy" does not become "common," nor what is "unclean" become accepted as "clean" (44:4-14). It is clear from study of Ezra, Nehemiah, Isa 56-66, and Chronicles that in the post-exilic community there was a lively debate, perhaps inevitably, about who was and who was not to be included in that community.[43] At any rate, Ezekiel seems here to taking very much the priestly point of view in such matters.

The account continues with regulations for the priests,[44] and what are being spoken about here are the Zadokite priests, it being emphasized that they have a status superior to that of the Levites (44:15-31), for the reason—so it is said here—that when Israel went astray so too did the Levites, going after idols (44:10). However, the Levites *are* permitted to offer their service in the temple (44:11, 14), "But the levitical priests, the descendants of Zadok, who kept the charge of my sanctuary when the people of Israel went astray from me, shall come near to me to minister to me; they shall attend me to offer me the fat and the blood, says the Lord God." (44:15-16) We are hardly surprised that the account then sets out in detail regulations concerning levitical priests' vestments and other conditions attaching to their temple duties, including that these priests do not have possession of

---

41. On these two centers of worship in Ezekiel's temple, see Stevenson, *The Vision of Transformation*. About this stone altar, see Block, *Ezekiel 25-48*, pp. 595-604.

42. Joyce, *Ezekiel*, 231.

43. See the remarks in Thompson, *Isaiah 40-66*, xxxi.

44. In this regard, see McConville, "Priests and Levites in Ezekiel"; and Joyce, *Ezekiel*, 232 (this last esp. for a summary of the debate concerning the priority of the Priestly work and Ezekiel). Also see above, 77-81.

lands, nor inheritances, but are to live on the various offerings stipulated as due to them (44:15–31). Yet, as has been pointed out to us,[45] there is no mention here of a High Priest, but we are unable to be certain why this is so.

Ezekiel 45:1–8 speaks about the distribution of land and the associated boundaries, matters that appears again in 47:13—48:35. In particular, there is a "holy district" (45:1), and within this are sections for the Levites in the north and the Zadokite priests in the south. There is also land allocated to the "prince" (*nāśî'*), the one who in effect is the successor to the king of old (45:7–8).[46] Ezekiel never speaks of a human king, going no further than speaking of the "prince," and no doubt this is a reflection both of pre-exilic Israel's varied experiences with the rule of kings and also of the realities of the new political situation. Overall, the Old Testament could be said to give the impression that kings were something of a mixed blessing. At any rate, here in Ezekiel's plan for the future it is the "prince" and no more, yet due provision of land is made for him. The following verses outline the prince's responsibilities (45:9–17), in particular that he is not to oppress the people—and included is the warning, "Thus says the Lord God: Enough, O princes of Israel! Put away violence and oppression, and do what is just and right. Cease your evictions of my people, says the Lord God." (45:9) Rather, justice is to be done, and while the prince has his privileges he is also to make due provision of offerings so that thus atonement may be made for the whole house of Israel (45:10–17). Chapter 45 closes with regulations for the keeping of various national religious festivals, vv. 18–24 seem to be talking about Passover, v. 25 possibly about Booths, but there is nothing here about Weeks, or even about the Day of Atonement.

Ezekiel 46 reverts to the matter of the "prince" (*nāśî'*). Here are outlined his duties and role as well as privileges in worship. Whereas on the six working days of the week that gate of the inner court remains closed—for it was through that gate that the glory of the Lord had entered the temple (43:3–5)—yet on the sabbath day, and on the day of the new moon, it was to be opened, and it would be through this that the prince would come into the place, and watch the sacrifices being made (46:1–2). This would be privilege indeed! And yet, while he was responsible for bringing offerings for himself and for his people, he himself did not actually offer sacrifices, for he was not a priest. Rather, the picture presented to us in Ezek 46:1–2 is of the prince who comes through the inner east door, remaining standing there and watching the cultic activity of the priests, then like any other worshipper

---

45. In particular by Rooke, *Zadok's Heirs*, 116–19. See also Levenson, *Theology of the Program of Restoration*, 141–44; Fishbane, *Biblical Interpretation in Ancient Israel*, 295; and Kasher, "Anthropomorphism, Holiness and Cult."

46. See Levenson, *Theology of the Program of Restoration*, 55–107.

prostrating himself (v. 2 *hištaḥăwāh*), and leaving. Further, the chapter contains yet more about the prince's responsibility to care for his people: "The prince shall not take any of the inheritance of the people, thrusting them out of their holding; he shall give his sons their inheritance out of his own holding, so that none of my people shall be dispossessed of their holding." (46:18) Chapter 46 closes in vv. 19-24 with a description of the places allocated for the preparation of food for the priests and the people, these matters having already been spoken about in 42:1-14—once again the concern seems to be about what was holy not being contaminated by what was profane. About this material in Ezek 43-46 concerning the worship in the new temple Leslie C. Allen says, "Overall these chapters present sketches of the working temple, often taking over earlier cultic traditions and sometimes evidently creating new details of cultic expression. The unit gives the practical outworking of a theology of an overwhelmingly transcendent God immanent among his covenant people."[47]

Third, we consider Ezek 47:1—48:35 and what this has to say about the river, the allocation of land, and the ongoing presence of the Lord. Ezekiel 47:1-12 constitutes the prophet/priest's final word about his vision of the temple; it is his vision of a river flowing from below the threshold of the temple, which as it flows eastwards becomes progressively deeper and deeper (47:1-6). Then as it flowed onward there were trees growing in the land on either side of it, and the prophet's angel guide—the one who first appeared at 40:3—was still interpreting for Ezekiel, explaining to him that wherever the river[48] flows "every living creature that swarms will live, and there will be many fish, once these waters reach there. It will become fresh; and everything will live where the river goes" (47:9) When thus watered the leaves of the trees will not wither, but will bear fresh fruit every month, "because the water for them flows from the sanctuary. Their fruit will be for food, and their leaves for healing" (47:12). This makes a powerful picture and imagery of the life-giving, and transforming (as of the desert into fruitful land) presence of the Lord which finds its earthly starting point, its fount of life in the temple, and presumably in the worship that is maintained there: "The temple is the place where Yahweh's presence is to be found, and

---

47. Allen, *Ezekiel 20-48*, p. 270.

48. In Ezek 47:9 the MT has the word "river" in the Hebrew dual form, "two rivers." Has the text here been influenced by the two rivers in Zech 14:8? Or perhaps by the two rivers spoken about in Gen 2:10 and 13? The LXX has just the one river, and so too the Vulgate, and further we may note that NRSV translates "river" in the singular. See Zimmerli, who says that this dual form of the word is "incomprehensible and not attested by any version" (*Ezekiel 25-48*, p. 507).

as a result of this divine indwelling in its midst, Israel is to experience the richness of the divine blessing in its land."[49]

Ezekiel 47:13–23 is in very different style, being about the allocation of the land, and the subject continues in ch. 48. The concern seems to be that there shall be proper divisions of land between the twelve tribes, with two portions being allocated to Joseph, these being for Manasseh and Ephraim, which conveniently maintains the tribal portions to twelve as the Levites are allocated space in the sacred area. For Ezekiel the eastern boundary of these lands is the River Jordan, whereas the arrangements spoken about in Num 34:1–12 go to the other, the eastern side of the river. Further, the aliens (Hebrew *gērîm*) who live among the people of Israel are not to be forgotten (47:22–23): if the words of Ezek 44:9–14 had a somewhat harsh sound about them, this gives another side to the matter, and we are reminded of that approach proclaimed in Isa 56:1–8. We are also reminded of the words of Deut 10:19, "You shall also love the stranger [*gēr*], for you were strangers [*gērîm*] in the land of Egypt."[50]

Chapter 48 continues the theme of the allocation of lands to the tribal groups of the people of Israel, this being spoken about in vv. 1–7 and 23–29. Between these two blocks of material, the provision for the priests and the Levites (vv. 8–22) is spoken about once again, now in more detail (see 45:1–8). The allocation of land for the priests—and these are the Zadokite priests—is set out in vv. 10–12, an area that also includes the temple in the middle of it (v. 10). There was also the area for the Levites (v. 13), and none of these lands were to be sold or exchanged; they were all a part of the "holy area", part of the sacred "reserve, portion" (*tĕrûmāh*) that was dedicated to particular usage (v. 8). There was also an area set apart for the "prince" (*nāśî'*, vv. 21–22), lying between the territories of Judah and Benjamin.

The chapter—and in fact this block of material about temple and worship, and indeed the whole of the book of Ezekiel, making this part something of a climax to the whole work—comes to a close with a note about the gates of the city and also the name of the city (48:30–35). The whole section, it may be noted, is very much concerned with naming. That is, as far as the gates are concerned there are three on each of the four sides of the city, and each of them is named after an Israelite tribe—here the tribe of Levi is counted as one of them, and thus Joseph has also just one, and not separate ones for Manasseh and Ephraim (compare 48:4–5). And finally we are told "the name of the city from that time on shall be, The Lord is There" (48:35) Paul Joyce says, "A magnificently theocentric note for this

---

49. Clements, *God and Temple*, 107.
50. See the remarks of Blenkinsopp, *Ezekiel*, 234.

most God-centered of biblical books to end on! 'The Lord is There.'"[51] This city when it is spoken of in this biblical book is neither Jerusalem nor Zion, and no doubt the reasons for that absence lie in the theological thinking of the prophet and/or his editors, but its (new?) name used here at the climax of the work may be regarded as saying all that there is to be said about the holy city, "The Lord is There."

Ezekiel 40–48, as we have seen, is expressed in language that is both visionary and yet at the same time remarkably down-to-earth in its detail and specificity, and further all-embracing in its concern and provision. Thus it goes into detail about priests and Levites and their allotted lands; about tribal people and their allocation of lands; about worship in the temple and about provision and sustentation for the people; about due offerings and sacrifices in the temple; and about life and wholeness for the nations. At the heart and center of all this is the temple with its worship, where is the glory of the Lord that is to be glimpsed, and from which there flows the life-giving stream that nourishes and fructifies the lands through which it flows, that causes deserts to become fruitful, plants and trees to grow, and in particular those leaves that are for the healing of the nations. Above all what is being spoken about here is a theocracy whose name will be "The Lord is There." Perhaps Jon Levenson has expressed what is of abiding worth in this vision with which the Book of Ezekiel both ends and also comes to its climax:

> Two and a half millennia after the composition of the program of restoration of Ezek. 40-48, it still stands as a judgment upon all human history and as a beacon to all who, even in the bleakest days, continue to hope for what it promises and to labor for what it mandates, humbly, in the expectation of standing on that "very high mountain" (40:2) and catching a glimpse of the city whose name is "The Lord is there" (48:35).[52]

Joel

Though Joel is a short book its study is difficult for a series of reasons: it has been variously dated, from the second to the ninth centuries BCE, and there is no agreement over whether it is a unity or a collection of varied oracles.[53] A number of scholars have proposed that we should regard the book as a cultic liturgy, or else that it is written in the style of a cultic liturgy.

---

51. Joyce, *Ezekiel*, 241.

52. Levenson, *Theology of the program of Restoration*, 163.

53. On all these matters see the full yet concise discussion in Barton, *Joel and Obadiah*, 3–36.

It is perhaps most reasonable that we should opt for the *style* of a cultic liturgy, and thus does Barton seem to regard the book, saying, "It seems to me . . . that Joel *draws on* liturgical forms rather than *being* itself a liturgy."[54] In particular there are two somewhat parallel passages, each of which sets out the particular disaster, followed by the call to lament, followed by the lament itself, in the following way:

1:2–4	Details of disaster
1:5–14	Call to lament
1:15–20	The lament
. . .	
2:1–11	Details of disaster
2:12–17a	Call to lament
2:17bc	The lament

This does not take account of the rest of the book of Joel, but perhaps it is best to consider Joel 1:2—2:17 as a piece of writing in the style of, after the matter of, a lament. Further, in view of the frequently-noted feature of widespread quoting from a range of the prophets and other parts of the Old Testament we perhaps do well to see the book of Joel as coming from post-exilic times. This consideration is strengthened by the observation of Rex Mason, pointing out to us a certain closeness of relationship of themes between Joel and Zech 9–14, suggesting that there seems to be in both of these two works something of those various challenges that faced the post-exilic community as it re-established life in and around Jerusalem.[55]

Obadiah

There is a reasonable degree of scholarly agreement that the background setting of the short prophecy of Obadiah is the Babylonian destruction of Jerusalem in 587 BCE. This view is especially espoused by Wolff, followed by a good number of others, though some dissent.[56] Wolff understands that what we have in Obadiah is a lament for the fall of Jerusalem that might have been used on those occasions of lamentation spoken about in Zech

---

54. Barton, *Joel and Obadiah*, 21 (his italics). See also Ogden, "Joel 4."
55. See Mason, *Zephaniah, Habakkuk, Joel*, 120.
56. See Wolff, *Obadiah and Jonah*, 42–44; and Barton, *Joel and Obadiah*, 120–23. For the view that Obad 12–14 is not so much a description of what has taken place but rather a warning of what might come to take place at some future time, see Bartlett, "The Brotherhood of Edom"; and ibid., "Edom and the Fall of Jerusalem."

7:3, 5; 8:19, and in 2 Kgs 25:1, 3-4, 8-9; Jer 41:1-3.[57] He also considers that the laments in the book of Lamentations might also have been used on such occasions.[58]

Jonah

With the book of Jonah there are references to aspects of worship that call for notice, first in the portrayal of Jonah as a recalcitrant prophet in ch. 1, then in the great storm at sea, the sailors are spoken of as praying to the Lord for their safe deliverance while Jonah, the supposed prophet of the Lord was asleep in the lower part of the boat. Thus the captain called upon Jonah to pray, "Get up, call on your god." Yet in the same scene we are told that not only did the sailors throw Jonah into the sea, but they also offered a sacrifice to the Lord and made vows (Jonah 1:16). Thus are these sailors portrayed as more faithful to their god than was Jonah to his. The same goes for the situation in Nineveh when Jonah proclaimed his message "Forty days more, and Nineveh shall be overthrown!" (Jonah 3:4). Yet when the people of Nineveh, taking the lead of their king, repented of their sins so that God forgave them and did not bring the calamity upon them (3:6-10), Jonah was displeased, even angry, and went, sulking and brooding, to sit in the shade to see what world happen to the city (4:1-5).

The message of the short book of Jonah would seem to be that the people of Israel have failed in their task of proclaiming to other nations the ways and will of the Lord God of Israel, whom they believed to be the Lord of the whole earth. Thus Jonah is portrayed as a useless prophet, a parody of what one who is called to go to a foreign nation to proclaim a message about the Lord God of Israel should actually be.[59] Further, the story conveys its message through the ironic, perhaps even comic, use of some of the elements of worship, in particular prayer,[60] but also through a composition in the form of a psalm in which it is proclaimed that "Deliverance belongs to the Lord!" (2:9b), an assurance that presumably is intended to apply both to recalcitrant Hebrew prophets and also to repentant foreign nations.

---

57. See below, 269-70.

58. For judicious comments on this possibility that the laments in Lamentations may have been used in post 587 BCE public rituals of lamentation, see Parry, *Lamentations*, 7. See also Provan, *Lamentations*, 19-20; and Salters, *Jonah and Lamentations*, 70-71.

59. See Thompson, "The Mission of Jonah."

60. See Good, *Irony in the Old Testament*, ch. 2; Holbert, "'Deliverance Belongs to Yahweh!'"; and Whedbee, *The Bible and the Comic Vision*, 191-220.

We cannot say either that the book of Jonah is about worship, or that it is expressed in liturgical form, but we can surely say that it uses some of the elements of the liturgy of worship to proclaim its message. It is surely striking that the author of this work proclaims such an original message through such original use of language.

Nahum

Although from a literary point of view this is a short book, yet it has generated much scholarly debate, due first to the harsh tone of much that is expressed in the prophecy in anticipation of the forthcoming fall of Nineveh, and its portrayal of Yahweh as "A jealous and avenging God . . . the Lord takes vengeance on his adversaries and rages against his enemies" (Nah 1:2). Secondly, it is because over a good number of years it has been suggested that what we have in the book is liturgical material,[61] it having been further suggested that Nahum might have been a "cult prophet." As the existence of such prophets cannot be more than speculative, that suggestion is best left on one side.[62] Yet there is in Nahum reference to Jerusalem festivals (*ḥag*, 1:15; Heb 2:1); further, there is the incomplete acrostic in 1:2-8 plus 1:9—2:2 all of which is in psalm-like form, speaking of a coming divine judgment on Nineveh. The further suggestions that Nah 2:3-10 being about the fall of the city and, along with 3:8-17 and 18-19, expressing further words of judgment, are both expressed in cultic language seems not unreasonable.[63]

To these considerations there should be added the further one concerning the words of 1:3, "The Lord is slow to anger but great in power, and the Lord will by no means clear the guilty," which have already been considered as in all probability owing something to the realm of worship.[64] Thus, all things considered we may say that the book of Nahum does appear reflective of the language of the Israelite cult.

---

61. See, e.g., Mason, *Micah, Nahum, Obadiah*, 76-79; Coggins, "An Alternative Prophetic Tradition"; and Coggins and Re'emi, *Nahum, Obadiah, Esther*, 9-10. See also above, 199.

62. On cult prophets, see above, 199-201, 240. Then there is the further suggestion that what appears to be cultic language in Nahum derives from some *particular* cultic occasion or Jerusalem festival. I would prefer to say that what we have in Nahum is the use of the language of the Jerusalem cult to express what the prophet and his editors wished to say.

63. This suggestion owes to Humbert, "Le problème du livre de Nahoum." See also the remarks of Christensen, *Nahum*, 20-25.

64. On the various occurrences of this formulation, see above, 192-95.

Habakkuk

The problem addressed in the short book of Habakkuk is theodicy, in particular why do the Lord's people suffer grievously from the warlike activities of the Chaldeans (Hab 1:5-11). That common solution to the theodicy problem, namely that the suffering is because of sin in no way satisfies this prophet, for the evil and suffering the Chaldeans cause among the (admittedly) sinful Israelites (Hab 1:2-4) is so greatly out of all proportion to the original sins that supposedly brought it about (Hab 2:12-17).[65] In fact this book does not come up with a theodicy that explains the Israelite people's sufferings, but what it does have, apart from two prophetic oracles (1:5-11; 2:1-5) and a series of woe oracles (2:6-19), are two laments (1:2-4, 12-17) and a psalm (*těpillāh*, 3:1-19). Anything approaching a possible resolution to the theodicy problem is expressed in terms of the content of this psalm of Hab 3. Not surprisingly it has in the past been suggested that the prophet Habakkuk was a cultic prophet, but as has been earlier observed that can only be speculative. What I suggest is something clearer, namely that the theodicy problem for this prophet is expressed through the language of worship, that is in the psalm of Hab 3. In fact when the prayers of lament (1:2-4 and 12-17) are taken into account along with the psalm, entitled a prayer (3:1-19), it is to be observed that over half the verses of this prophecy are of the language, and from the realm, of worship. Thus I suggest with Habakkuk's prophecy the theological problem and its solution is to a large degree expressed in the language of the cult, that is of worship. It may be more than this, and as it apparently happened for the psalmist of Ps 73 the resolution to the theodicy problem was found through the actual experience of engaging in worship in the temple (Ps 73:17).[66]

Zephaniah

According to the genealogy in Zeph 1:1 not only did Zephaniah receive the word of the Lord in the days of King Josiah of Judah, but also that he was descended through a number of generations from King Hezekiah. This mention of two kings, both of whom we are told were responsible for sweeping religious reforms in Judah and Jerusalem, suggests that at least to some degree the ministry of Zephaniah was concerned with purity, or lack of it, in

---

65. On theodicy in Habakkuk, see Thompson, "*Where is the God of Justice?*," 63-76.

66. For a more detailed statement of, and justification for, this interpretation of the book of Habakkuk, see Thompson, "Prayer, Oracle and Theophany," 33-53.

the cult of his own day.⁶⁷ Further, we do not have to read far into this short prophecy before we come across the prophet's proclamation of the Lord's judgment on the worship of Baal, and other aspects of cultic apostasy (Zeph 1:4-5). Further, there is talk in 1:7 of the Lord having "prepared a sacrifice, he has consecrated his guests," this perhaps intended to indicate the worshippers are being, or have been, sanctified, that is, those who have been summoned to "seek the Lord" (2:3; in fact the whole passage 2:1-3 is a call to penitence). Yet this short prophecy ends by speaking of the divine judgment upon and the resulting purification of Jerusalem (3:1-13), and with a psalm-like composition (3:14-20). It has not-infrequently been observed that this psalm has parallels with the so-called "Enthronement Psalms" which proclaim and celebrate the rule of Yahweh as king of the world (see Pss 47, 93, 96, 97, 98, 99).⁶⁸

Haggai and Zechariah 1-8

Both the prophets Haggai and Zechariah are, according to the notices in the books that bear their names, to be dated in the post-exilic period, in particular in the second year of the Persian king Darius, that is in the year 520 BCE.⁶⁹ About this period Wolff says, "It is the end of the exilic period. The dark shadows of the catastrophe of 587 are still hanging heavy over Jerusalem. The temple, which had burned to the ground, is still a heap of rubble, the haunt of jackals (Hag 1:4, 9; Lam 5:18)."⁷⁰

The ministries of both these prophets was concerned with the rebuilding of the temple; thus we are told that part of the proclamation of Haggai to his people was, "Is it time for you yourselves to live in your paneled houses, while this house lies in ruins?" (Hag 1:4), with the call in 1:7-14 to build the temple. However, in 2:9 there is the word, "The latter splendor of this house shall be greater than the former," which rather gives the impression that that there was a certain strand of thought abroad in Jerusalem that the rebuilt temple would *not* match up to the glories of Solomon's temple. Yet also here is the promise that the treasures of the nations would be brought to this new temple, and thus it would be filled with the splendor of the Lord

---

67. On this, see Wilson, *Prophecy and Society in Ancient Israel*, 279-80.

68. See, e.g., Mason, *Zephaniah, Habakkuk, Joel*, 25; and Smith, *Micah-Malachi*, 143-44. On the Enthronement Psalms, see above, 153.

69. It is generally agreed that Zech 9-14 comes from a later time and will be treated below, along with Malachi.

70. Wolff, *Haggai*, 15. On the subject of worship in Haggai, Zechariah 1-8, and Malachi, see Tiemeyer, *Priestly Rites and Prophetic Rage*.

(2:7). Beckwith observes about Hag 2:6–9, "This is a new form of the old prophetic promise that in the latter days all nations shall flow to the mountain of the Lord's house, to be taught his ways, and to cease from warfare against one another (Isa 2:1–4; Mic 4:1–5), and that his house will become a house of prayer for all peoples (Isa. 56:7); but the promise is now applied to the Second Temple."[71] Just what other theological thought was held by Haggai, or his editors, regarding this temple—was it intended to represent the Lord's presence in his people's midst, or was it perhaps intended to be the place where sacrifices, or maybe prayers, were offered?—we are not told. Yet there is this: it is suggested in Haggai that the fortunes of the people would change for the better, and that it would bring about their peace, their *shalom* (Hag 2:9b, cf 2:19b). Perhaps it was believed that when this work was done then the way would have been prepared for the forthcoming work of the Lord (Hag 2:20–23).

In Zech 1–8 we are in a rather different thought world from that of Haggai. The latter seems intended to be read for its facts, but with the former there is the emphasis on the visionary; in particular Zech 1:7—6:8, having been called "Eight Night Visions and Oracles."[72] Probably much of this imagery has cultic roots.[73] For within this vision cycle there is an emphasis on the importance of rebuilding the temple, and perhaps the pilgrimage theme met with in Haggai (2:7) is again here in Zech 2:11. Zechariah 8:9 seems to be looking back to the time when the foundations of the new temple were laid, while Zech 4:8–9 speaks of the importance of continuing the building work on the foundations already laid. Further, in Zech 6:12–15 there are some details given of what is envisaged as being characteristic of its future life: there would be a high priest, Joshua, and further what looks like a person designated the Branch, the latter being perhaps a king, or one who would be as near a king as would be possible in those changed situations.[74] Again, there is talk of those who will come from afar, both in Zech 6:15, and particularly in 8:18–23.

Zechariah 9–14 and Malachi

There is a considerable difference between chs 1–8 and 9–14 of the book of Zechariah, both in the style and in the content of the materials. In chs 9–14

---

71. Beckwith, "The Temple Restored," 74.

72. So Smith, *Micah-Malachi*, 185.

73. Larkin, "Zechariah," 611–12.

74. On "Branch," see also Zech 3:8; Jer 23:5; 33:14-16; Corney, "Branch"; and Bracke, "Branch."

there are no visions, and nor is there anything about rebuilding the temple. What, however, is present is talk of pilgrimage to Jerusalem in 14:16–21. This is envisaged as being a pilgrimage of the survivors of the nations who come to celebrate the festival of booths, tabernacles.[75] There will be a sentence of judgment upon those who do not come, but those who do come will be the sanctified, and so too will the vessels they use. Further these pilgrims are portrayed as those who once came up *against* Jerusalem, but who "now must appear for ritual purposes, namely, to venerate the deity who was responsible for their defeat and to celebrate a Yahwistic festival. Travel to do battle has been transformed into an annual pilgrimage."[76] There in Jerusalem at this festival they shall indeed "worship the King, the Lord of hosts" (Zech 14:17), and this will take place in the house of the Lord, where there is the altar, and where sacrifices will be offered (14:20–21).

We have to say that we know remarkably little about Malachi, which in all probability is not this prophet's name but rather his divine designation "My Messenger," or even "My Angel." Yet given the brevity of this book, it has to be said that there is a significant amount of material here about worship, giving rise to suggestions that Malachi may have been a cult prophet. As in such previous cases we can leave that possibility on one side,[77] but what is clearer is that in all probability we are dealing in this prophetic book with a post-exilic situation. There is talk in the first chapter about blemished sacrifices, and that priests have been involved in this unsatisfactory matter (Mal 1:6–14). Then, almost as if following on from what has been spoken about there are in Mal 2 instructions to priests about appropriate conduct and correct execution of their duties. This is called by Rogerson, "a powerful condemnation of the priests,"[78] and is followed in ch. 3 by the announcement of the coming of the messenger of the Lord, the one who will come to purify the descendants of Levi "until they present offerings to the Lord in righteousness" (Mal 3:3).

By Way of Summary

The foregoing somewhat lengthy discussion of the Hebrew prophets and worship calls for an attempt at summarizing the present part of this study.

---

75. On this festival, see above, 183–89. We may also note that Zech 9–11 and 12–14 have the title *maśśā'*, "oracle" (lit. "burden"), as also does Malachi 1–3, and the three passages are considered together in this work.

76. Petersen, *Zechariah 9–14 and Malachi*, 155.

77. See above, 199–201, 240, 267, 268.

78. Rogerson, "Malachi," 616.

First, it is manifestly clear that while the protest about unacceptable worship on the part of some of the prophets is an aspect of what the prophets had to say on our subject, yet it is by no means the whole story. Further, there are some themes held in common between various of these prophets, as we have observed in the course of this study; yet equally there are differences between the accounts we have of these various prophetic emphases, and we observe what comes over as some prophets demonstrating a real originality of thought. There are further differences manifest in the scale and extent of certain of these presentations, in particular the sheer size of the writings in the three great scrolls, Isaiah, Jeremiah, and Ezekiel. Moreover, within these three works that of Isaiah may be said to be on a scale all of its own, covering as it does times pre-exilic, apparently assuming an exile, and going on to speak of worship in the Jerusalem setting in the post-exilic period. Within this extensive book there is the prophetic condemnation of the non-Yahwistic deities, alongside an emphasis on the goodness, sheer greatness, and incomparableness of the Lord God of Israel, whose glory the prophet Isaiah, glimpsed in the Jerusalem temple, and whose presence and purposes this prophet and other prophets are portrayed as interpreting in both the post-exilic and the pre-exilic eras. Thus about the divine provision of a triumphant way prepared for the Israelite people freely to leave their Babylonian exile, there are abundant expressions of world-wide praise and wonder. In a later time, as life is begun to be re-established in Jerusalem, there is given the vision of worship for a wider than Israelite group alone: this has become the promise of an invitation to, and offer of engagement in worship, for both Israelites and aliens in the new age.

As far as the Jeremiah book is concerned, as well as finding here an impassioned invective about the sin of participation in non-Yahwistic worship and cults, and also the works of priests who were corrupt, there is further the employment of anguished personal prayer on the part, we presume, of the prophet Jeremiah himself, who in the difficulties experienced in being the Lord's prophet had to endure much suffering, not least at the hands of members of his family and friends in Anathoth. While we know from other parts of the Hebrew Bible about this distinctive style of lamenting, crying out to the Lord, the style is not common in the prophets. Thus this makes for a distinctive approach to prayer on the part of one of the Hebrew prophets. There is also here the prophet praying for his people, interceding for them—though commanded *not* to do so.

In the book of Ezekiel while there are those oft-observed polemics about corrupt priests, about worship of non-Yahwistic deities, and about the worship of Israel's incomparable Lord, what is distinctive is that whole block of material in chs 40–48 setting forth the prophet's vision of a new temple of the Lord, where not only does his worship take place, but also from where so many benefits and blessings follow and flow. This is nothing less than a remarkable vision of the place of worship, and of the exaltation of the Lord God, in this extended vision of the future Jerusalem and its special place of divine presence and worship in the renewed national life.

What then of some commonality of themes within these books of the prophets in the issues of worship? What in this regard perhaps calls for first mention is the recorded words, even invective, of certain of the prophets about various abuses of worship and the associated unsatisfactory offering of such parodies of worship. Perhaps the most serious of these was the offering of worship on the hills and under the green trees to the gods of the Canaanites, the most serious expression of condemnation being in the book Hosea, yet the issue had earlier been there in the ministry of Elijah. It makes an appearance too in the Amos book, and so also in Micah, in Jeremiah to a certain extent, and in a small way in Ezekiel. So too there is very little of it in the book of Isaiah. In this regard it is perhaps significant that in the third part of the Isaiah book there is the invitation to worshippers from all peoples to come together bringing their burnt offerings and sacrifices which will be accepted on the altar in the temple, for that holy place will be called "a house of prayer for all peoples" (Isa 56:7). Is there something here of the issue that if Israelite people cannot be prevented from worshipping in the ways of the Canaanites, let all the peoples come together in worship of the Lord God of Israel?

The second aspect of perceived unworthiness in the worship offered to the Lord by his people was the worship coming out of lives that were being lived unworthily, particularly where advantage and exploitation of weaker members of the community prevailed. This drew forth some of the most memorable yet seriously judgmental words of the prophets such as are found in Amos 5:23-24 and Mic 6:8:

> Take away from me the noise of your songs;
> I will not listen to the melody of your harps.
> But let justice roll down like waters,
> and righteousness like an ever-flowing stream. (Amos 5:23-24.
> Compare Mic 6:7-8)

Yet the issue had been earlier proclaimed by the prophet Elijah, and it is there too in the first part of the book of Isaiah, recurring in the last part, Isa 56-66.

The third aspect of unworthiness in worship highlighted in the Hebrew Bible is in its leadership by unworthy priests. The issue is raised in the book of Micah ("its priests teach for a price," Mic 3:11) and also in Malachi where we read of the charge against them of offering on the altar polluted food, and imperfect animals (Mal 1:6b–8a), and it is also there in Isaiah and Amos.

In this brief attempt at summarizing the messages of the prophets concerning worship, it perhaps needs to be emphasized that there is a real sense of theocentricity allied to worship in these books. This is manifested most obviously in the so-called doxologies in the Amos book (Amos 4:13; 5:8; 9:5–6), but it is there in the Isaiah book not only as a major feature of awe and worship in the style of the proclamation of the new exodus in Isa 40–55 yet further in Isa 1–39, perhaps above all in the way the political message of the prophet in the Syro-Ephraimite war (Isa 7:1—8:22) is sandwiched between passages that speak of the glory and the marvellous purposes of the Lord (Isa 6:1–13; 9:2–7). Further, in the books of Jonah and Habakkuk something of the central message of each of the works is given expression through the use of a psalmic composition expressing the centrality of the Lord and his purposes in the challenging matters being discussed. In Zechariah we have the vision of travel to fight a battle being transformed into a pilgrimage to Jerusalem "to worship the King, the Lord of hosts" (Zech 14:17), while Nahum's message is redolent with what appears to be the language and imagery of the Jerusalem cult. Finally, in the matter of theocentricity the book of Ezekiel is in a league all of its own, with its nine chapters at the conclusion of the work where, expressed in the language of vision, is a new temple which is to be at the center of life for the new city and people, and making its own particular contribution to the affirmation of divine presence therein, in the new name of the city "The Lord is There" (Ezek 48:35).

Did the prophets intercede for their people? In particular was intercession an expected part of the prophetic ministry? In answer to the first question we can answer in the affirmative: we are told of the intercessions of Moses, of Elijah and also of Elisha. It is certainly there in the Amos book, but the theme is not strong in the book of Isaiah except perhaps in the third part. Hosea can give his people a prayer to take with them when they return to the Lord, but Jeremiah is told *not* to pray for his people. Perhaps that prohibition upon Jeremiah is the strongest evidence we have that the prophets *were* expected to pray for their people, and yet a doubt must remain in our minds because with a good number of them there is no mention of the matter.

What, we may also ask was the attitude of the prophets to the temple and its worship? We have mixed evidence in our biblical sources: although what is portrayed as Isaiah's inaugural call experience appears to take place in the temple, yet there is little further about that place until we come to the third part of the book (Isa 56–66). It is also there in Haggai, but above all the theme is presented in a superabundant manner in the prophecy of Ezekiel, the man who was both priest and prophet, who manifestly sees the place and worship of a temple in Jerusalem as the very heart of the city, the holy place where above all the presence of the Lord is made manifest, thus giving to the city its new name "The Lord is There." It should also be said that there seem to be at least some echoes of the worship of the temple, reflections perhaps of parts of its rituals in the books of some of the prophets, borrowings from its language, such as for example the laments in the books of Jeremiah, in Joel and Obadiah, in some of the language of Zech 9–14, and in the use of psalmic language in Jonah and Habakkuk.

PART V

Worship in the Hebrew Bible

> One thing I asked of the Lord,
> that will I seek after:
>
> to live in the house of the Lord
> all the days of my life,
> to behold the beauty of the Lord,
> and to inquire in his temple.
>
> PSALM 27:4

Worship is the search for, and the response of, the human creature for the Eternal, in the particular case of the Hebrew Bible of, in the main, for those people who looked to Abraham as their ancestor it was to the Deity who had appeared to them in sundry places, and also in and through various deliverances, and who became known to them as Yahweh, their Lord God. As we have seen in the preceding chapters this worship was manifested in a series of varieties, with at times changes in styles and emphases in that worship effected by various religious, and sometimes even, national leaders. We are hardly able to speak in little more than vague statements about "developments" in that worship, for we are not sufficiently clear about the course of historical events, and certainly not to assign dates for the adoption of this and that worship. Thus we perhaps have to be content to emphasize matters of *variety* in Israel's worship rather than *developments*.

Thus in what follows we shall proceed by considering four main aspects of this worship, first the places where this worship took place; second the various types, styles, kinds of worship that we read about in the Hebrew Bible; third the various leaders of worship spoken about in these documents; fourth some final comments about what we might call the spirituality of this worship, and the sense of religious reality of these offerings of praise and prayer, confession and sacrifice.

14

Concluding Reflections

Walter Brueggemann in his *Theology of the Old Testament* says, "The place and activity of public worship, the cult, overseen by authorized priests, plays an enormously important role in the faith and life of the Old Testament community."[1] He goes on to observe that this cult claims a large portion of Old Testament texts, a fact that was set out in some detail in the Introduction to this present work,[2] and then fleshed out in subsequent chapters. We now seek to gain some conspectus of these studies, to offer something by way of summary concerning the worship spoken about in the Hebrew Bible. First then, in the words of Brueggemann, "The place . . . of public worship."

The Places of Worship

Various are the places spoken of in the Old Testament where worship may be offered.[3] In the stories in Gen 12–50 the Patriarchs are portrayed as worshipping in sundry places, not infrequently in geographical settings where the Lord had appeared to them, where a mercy or a deliverance had been experienced, in a place where it was deemed there had been an appearance of the divine to someone or other. Such places, so we are told, are sometimes thereafter regarded as sacred, and worthy to be places of future worship—thus, for example, Bethel where the Lord appeared to Jacob, who marked the place with a standing stone, and which may have been the place where subsequently a temple came to be built (Gen 28:10–22; 1 Kgs 12:25–33). Further, perhaps such places came to be regarded as venues for what would later be called pilgrimages, at which devotees would seek a sense of the presence of the Lord in a place where in the past that presence had been found powerfully and significantly.

---

1. Brueggemann, *Theology of the Old Testament*, 650.
2. See above, 6–11.
3. See above, 17–56, for the various places of Israelite worship.

Yet these Scriptures also speak of more permanent and dedicated places where the Lord could be sought and worship offered. Perhaps such a place, as yet, however, portable, was the Tent of Meeting according to the tradition, set up in the wilderness after the deliverance from Egypt (Exod 33:7–11; Num 11:16–30; 12:1–16). Yet by the time the Israelites became settled in their promised land we read of shrines and temples, in the fullness of time this coming to its apotheosis in the building and establishment of the temple in king David's city of Jerusalem. Yet we also read of worship taking place in individual homes, and in recent years it has been suggested that more worship than we are actually told about in the Old Testament took place in the settings of homes. Nor should there be forgotten those places of worship under green trees, on high hills, on high places to which Israelites resorted, and for which actions they would be condemned by some of their religious leaders. Thus the approach of the Deuteronomic writings was that there was only one official and acceptable place of worship, and that must have been the temple in Jerusalem. Even so, and certainly not receiving any approval from the Deuteronomists there had been temples built in the northern kingdom of Israel, but these it seems fell to the Assyrian in 722 BCE.

Nevertheless, even that most holy and sacred shrine on Zion's hill was not to last for ever, it being destroyed by the conquering Babylonian army in 587 BCE, yet on the return of some of the Israelites to Jerusalem by permit of the Persians there was the call to rebuild the temple, which indeed did eventually take place. Meanwhile, other temples had been built in foreign places and their worship life seems to have flourished for a period in lands where Jewish people were exiled. Further, following on from the edict of the Persian ruler Cyrus a new temple (Zerubbabel's) was built in Jerusalem, and this seems to have become, as Solomon's temple of old had been, *the* place of worship for Jewish people, that holy shrine than which no greater could at that time be imagined.

We can surely appreciate something of the special nature of the Jerusalem temple as a place for worship, set as it was in such a prominent place in ancient Israel's "world," its very premises arranged with ascending degrees of holiness, from entrance (*'ûlām*), leading to nave (*hêkal*) and so towards the most holy part (*dĕbîr*), what became known as the "holy of holies." All this must surely have been something of a non-verbal sign on a major scale "speaking" of the God of the Israelites and of his relationship with his people Israel, while the presence there of the ark of the covenant, and a possible burning light, and other appurtenances and artefacts, decorations and additions, would have added to the sense of presentation on earth of aspects of divinity, and to the urge to seek the Lord, to worship him. Manifestly there is something profoundly significant and important for religious people who in their search for continued communion with, and worship of their invisible and at many-a-time apparently hidden God, do so need such earthly shrines and temples to help them in what are for the devotees vitally important matters concerning what may be called the spirit-world. This may be because in the face of the mysteries of belief in a heavenly and eternal deity, earthly words quite simply give out, and matters of faith defy even the profoundest and boldest attempts at explanation. Thus in place of words of explanation a new language, mode of thinking and explaining is needed for the extreme situation. Hence come religious buildings, and their various parts, appurtenances, artefacts, and above all the devotions and rituals that take place within them. For the call for the holy building, and what is present there, and what goes on within it, is needed to express, to "say" what mere words cannot say.[4] Something of this would seem to be reflected in the words of at least two of the Psalms of Ascent:

> I was glad when they said to me,
> "Let us go to the house of the Lord!"
> Our feet are standing
> within your gates, O Jerusalem. (Ps 122:1–2)

> Lift up your hands to the holy place,
> and bless the Lord.
> May the Lord, maker of heaven and earth,
> bless you from Zion. (Ps 134:2–3)

This is perhaps also demonstrated insofar as within the religious communities who were successors to the people spoken about in the Hebrew Bible, there arose in future time the deeply perceived need for their own holy places, in Judaism the institution of the synagogue, and in Christianity a marked urge to build churches and cathedrals, and the energy and conviction to continue to do so.

It was clearly of very great importance for at least some of the leaders in the post-exilic era that a new temple on Zion's hill should as a priority be established. This emphasis we have seen strongly present in the prophecies of Haggai, Zechariah 1–8, and Malachi, and also in the seriously expansive description and justification in the book of Ezekiel, chs 40–48. In this vision of Ezekiel there is the conviction that this holy building speaks of the presence of the Lord, in such a profound and pronounced way that through it the very city will come to receive a new name, "And the name of the city from that time on shall be, The Lord is There" (Ezek 48:35) Further, for those

---

4. I am indebted to Williams, *The Edge of Words*, esp. pp. 168–70, for his discussion of non-verbal signs.

who live around this holy city and temple there is the gift of ever-flowing life, for from this temple and its worship there springs forth fructifying life and wellbeing, expressed in the imagery of the stream that flows from the temple area bringing life and fruitfulness, food and healing, to the many surrounding lands. Thus:

> On the banks, on both sides of the river, there will grow all kinds of trees for food. Their leaves will not wither nor their fruit fail, but they will bear fresh fruit every month, because the water for them flows from the sanctuary. Their fruit will be for food, and their leaves for healing. (Ezek 47:12)

Different Types of Worship

Yet while there may be this agreement as to the importance and significance of the particular place for worship, there is at the same time in the Hebrew Bible the witness to the fact that differing styles of worship took place in the actual physical temple building, and elsewhere. However, there is the matter of our not always being told what it might have been intended *should* take place in various settings and even holy places. For example, what it was envisaged should be taking place in the worship in Ezekiel's temple we are not told. Nevertheless, the offering of sacrifices must seem highly likely to have been an envisaged activity in that place. As far as the historical Jerusalem temples are concerned we perceive three main strands of the worship that took place, all of which have been considered in the preceding pages of this work.

The first of these is what we may call the priestly approach, so called because of our perception that those who speak of these matters in parts of the book of Exodus, in Leviticus, and in parts of Numbers give all the appearances of setting forth in their writings the concerns of priests and Levites. The emphasis in this worship is on sacrifices, and while these writers do not generally give us words that were said at the sacrificial services, they emphasize what is to be done when a sacrifice is offered, and further tell us what particular sacrifice is to be offered for this or that occasion, and what by way of offering is to be presented for each of the various sacrifices.

For these priestly writers the temple was the place of the divine glory (Exod 40:34–38), and their serious concern, and that of the whole priestly class, was that it was through the sacrificial system that an individual, a group, a community, a nation was granted the means to be given assurance of the forgiveness of their sins. In the eyes of these writers the sacrificial system was the divine gift to God's people that they, the people, might be granted the forgiveness of those sins that had been committed inadvertently. The priests led their people in a series of rituals, that is they used common and worldly language, artefacts, and symbols to express issues and events which had other-worldly dimensions and significance. It was believed that it was by means of such rituals that a "bridging" was taking place between the two worlds, the human and the divine. Here in these sacred rites there was a point of intersection betwixt, between the ever-sinful people of earth and the holy God of heaven. What lay at the heart of this whole business of these priestly rituals was human uncleanness, sinfulness, chaos, and death on the one hand, and on the other hand heavenly purity, holiness, order, and life. For these situations there were particular rituals, in particular what have been called Founding Rituals (like the inauguration of worship in a sanctuary); Maintenance Rituals (for example, a series of festivals observed through the year to maintain the divine-human relationship); Restoration Rituals (to restore a person into their intended relationship with the Lord, such as took place, for instance on the Day of Atonement).[5]

In the priestly estimation there was a serious gulf between the heavenly and the earthly realms, this in particular because the Lord of heaven was perfection and holiness, while the people of earth were indeed earth-bound and sinful, ever failing to live up to the expectations of their covenant relationship with the Lord. The ministries of the priests and the Levites lay in the betwixt of these two worlds and modes of existence. It was as if they occupied a dangerous frontier between God and his people, and their calling was to bridge these worlds of the holy and the profane. Thus they existed to minister what were believed to be the various divinely-provided rituals and sacrifices whereby heaven and earth, the Lord and his people, could be kept in harmony. Yet thus, those priests and Levites were indeed those who were thereby required to live very much in a state of perpetual liminality.

What we may call the second main strand, kind, style of the worship that is portrayed as taking place in the Jerusalem temple was Deuteronomic, that which we read about in the book of Deuteronomy and in the so-called Deuteronomistic History.[6] A key feature of Deuteronomy's teaching about worship concerns the keeping of that worship wholly and purely Yahwistic, in particular free of taint from the influence and contamination of the worship practices of the neighboring Canaanites. Even more, the Israelites must

---

5. On Sacrifices, see above, 162–78; on Priests and Levites, see above, 71–78; on Priestly rituals, see above, 215–17.

6. On worship in Deuteronomy and the Deuteronomistic History, see above, 218–23.

do their best to eliminate the Canaanitish worship practices from the land. Thus:

> You must demolish completely all the places where the nations whom you are about to dispossess served their gods, on the mountain heights, on the hills, and under every leafy tree. Break down their altars, smash their pillars, burn their sacred poles with fire, and hew down the idols of their gods, and thus blot out their name from their places. You shall not worship the Lord your God in such ways. (Deut 12:2–4)

Rather, the people of Israel are to worship the Lord their God in the one central place that the Lord has chosen where his name will dwell (Deut 12:5–7). The place is certainly intended to be Jerusalem, though that could not be stated while still maintaining that the book Deuteronomy is setting-forth the words of Moses to the Israelites on the eve of their crossing the Jordan to take-up occupation in the land of promise. Further, we should notice that Deuteronomy does not speak of the Lord actually *dwelling* in the temple, only that he has *caused his name* to be there—whereas it could have been that other theologians of ancient Israel did think more in terms of a divine presence, a divine dwelling, in particular in the most holy part, the "holy of holies" (*děbîr*), of the temple. Thus does Deuteronomy speak of a *spiritual* presence of the Lord with his people. A corollary of this is that in Deuteronomy the ark of the covenant rather than being some representation of Yahweh's presence is a container for the tablets of stone on which were inscribed the words of the law given by the Lord to Moses on the mountain (Deut 10:1–5; 31:26). A yet further corollary is that what Deuteronomy espoused was what we might call a religion of the heart, an internalized faith that would issue in worship that came from the very depths of the inner being of the worshippers. Thus:

> You shall love the Lord your God with all your heart, and with all your soul, and with all your might. Keep these words that I am commanding you today in your heart. (Deut 6:5–6)

Deuteronomy is deeply concerned with the matter of purity of worship, and therefore stresses that the only place where sacrifices are to be offered is at the central shrine, though no instructions are given here about what individual sacrifices are to be made for the forgiveness of particular sins. At the same time the people in their towns and villages are allowed the non-sacral eating of meat (Deut 12:13–19). Yet when sacral offerings are made—at the central place of worship—these are to be glad offerings of thanksgiving for all that God has done for his people, "rejoicing in all the undertakings in which the Lord your God has blessed you" (Deut 12:7). Thus all offerings are to be made in a spirit of thankfulness and praise (Deut 14:22–27).

The deuteronomic emphasis on the theme of the maintenance of the pure Yahwistic worship is to be observed clearly in the so-called Deuteronomistic History, the books of Joshua, Judges, Samuel, and Kings, in particular in the last of these. Here, as in Deuteronomy, the ark of the covenant is a container for the law of the Lord (1 Kgs 8:9, 21), but the deuteronomic themes are clearly to be traced in, on the one hand the condemnation of the majority of the kings who permitted the worship of the Canaanite gods still to be taking place during their reigns, and on the other hand the high praise accorded to the two kings Hezekiah (2 Kgs 18:4–8) and Josiah (2 Kgs 23:4–24) who each took steps to purify the cult, in particular seeking to rid it of Canaanitish cultic additions. Further, in the Books of Kings there is a real emphasis on the importance and significance of the offering of prayer as well as that of making sacrifices. This is to be observed in the prayer of dedication of the Jerusalem temple by king Solomon (1 Kgs 8:1–53), where there is the extended talk of offering prayer in that place, or even towards that place, for individuals and groups in all manner of troublesome situations. Again, here is the emphasis that it is not that God dwells in the temple, but rather that this place is the "dwelling place for the Lord's name" (see 1 Kgs 8:16; 11:36; 14:21; 2 Kgs 21:7; 23:27), and further that this is to be Israel's *single* sanctuary (see 2 Kgs 23:8–9).

What can we say about this single-minded approach to the purity of the Israelite worship found in the deuteronomic literature? On the one hand we may commend the thoroughness with which these leaders sought to safeguard what they conceived as being true Yahwistic worship, but on the other hand it may be felt that there is a certain strain of intolerance towards the people and worshippers of another religious faith. Undoubtedly there are things to be said about these two viewpoints, both for and against, but we may perhaps reflect upon the fact that it was perhaps to at least some extent thanks to the Deuteronomists that ancient Israel was able to pass on to its successors in the monotheistic faiths some of the basic foundational beliefs and practices.

The third main strand or kind of worship we read about in the Hebrew Bible is what we may call the Psalmic, a style of worship which we can be sure had a place in the worship of the Jerusalem temple.[7] Here is worship expressed in words and prayers, worship that does not include sacrifice.

---

7. On the Psalms and worship, see above, 119–61.

Yet all the familiar aspects of the Hebrew Bible's prayers are found here in the book of Psalms. There is the praise of God, as set forth in the so-called psalms of confidence and in those psalms which have been called hymns. In fact the whole of the psalter ends on something of an extravaganza of praise in Ps 150, "Let everything that breathes praise the Lord! Praise the Lord!" (Ps 150:6) Yet at the same time the Psalter gives more than adequate space to a remarkable series of psalms in which both individuals and also whole groups, even whole communities, cry out to the Lord, sometimes in the strongest and most-outspoken language available, thus bringing their problems and grievances to God, matters which it appears the Lord is not addressing. Nevertheless in so many of what have been called Psalms of Lament there is by the end of the psalm a real, deeply-profound expression of confidence in the immediacy of the Lord's delivering presence with the sufferers from their present distresses.

Equally, the psalms give due space for a person, or group, to make their confession of sin to the Lord; to recite their history in cadences of praise; to express their theological questionings occasioned by the sufferings of apparently innocent people and at the same time the apparent prosperity of those who appear to be leading unworthy, even sinful lives; to give a series of Songs of Ascents, psalmic material probably for those who ascend Zion's hill in order to engage in the worship of the Lord at the temple.

Perhaps above all the ongoing, abiding significance, and perceived value of the biblical psalms lies in the sheer range of expressions and formulations of Yahwistic faith and life that are present in this Hebrew Bible compilation, providing a wealth of material for individual and communal use. Here are expressions of thanksgiving for all that is past (for example Ps 92), yet also prayers for the future (for example Pss 40:17; 106:47); here is the call to depart from evil and at the same time to do good (for example Ps 34:14; compare Ps 37:27); here is the call to seek the Lord and all that he has to offer those who follow (for example Pss 105:4; 119:2, 10, 45, 94); here is the quiet and prayerful individual approach to the Lord (for example Ps 16), and at the same time in the so-called Wisdom Psalms (at the least Pss 37, 49, 73) the serious yet devout questioning of the ways of the Lord, particularly in regard to the sufferings and difficulties apparently devout followers of the Lord experience in their lives; nevertheless here also in the concluding verses of Ps 73 is one the Old Testament's most profound responses to this ever-present theodicy problem, the issue of how it can be that righteous and godly people have to endure sufferings:

> Whom have I in heaven but you?
> And there is nothing on earth that I desire other than you.

My flesh and my heart may fail,
but God is the strength of my heart and my portion forever.
(Ps 73:25–26)

The biblical Psalter, so it has been argued above, is essentially a *worship book*; here are the Songs of Ascents, and various other collections which appear to have been "compiled" for worship purposes. While there are, as we have seen, in the so-called Priestly writings full details about which sacrifices and offerings are to be presented and made on this and that occasion, and when particular rituals are appropriate for the situation, the book of psalms presents us rather with a whole series of suitable *words* for the worship. It is surely not without significance that there seems to have been in the religious community at Qumran a deep concern for the preservation of the texts of the psalms, and maybe also for the usage of the psalms in their own community's worship.[8] Further, as has been many times observed it is the Book of Psalms that has been the part of the Hebrew Bible that Christians have ever found the most straightforward to incorporate into their liturgies and worship. Meanwhile the Jewish religious communities have continued to make wide use of the psalms in their worship, and thus have praises been expressed in times past and present about the enormous contribution of the biblical psalms to the ongoing worship of the Lord's people. Perhaps what in particular has enabled this passing on of worship materials from a people of ancient times and so to be used in the various communities of the Abrahamic faiths is that it is none other than *worship* material, indeed *material for worship*. Thus says William P. Brown:

> Whereas other books of the Bible contain God's words and the narratives of God's work, both in history and in creation, the Psalter conveys something of Israel's vociferous response to God—the community's cries and acclamations, its proclamations and discursive reflections. The psalms present, in short, a sanctuary of shouting and singing.[9]

It is appropriate here to speak about the approach to worship of the author of the books of Chronicles, the so-called Chronicler. While we should

---

8. On the Psalms and the Qumran community, see above, 55–56, 161.

9. Brown, *Psalms*, 160. For the interest in the psalms that seems to be evidenced in the Qumran community, see above, 55–56, 161. For the usage of the psalms in Christian worship, see, for example, what is said in Pentiuc, *The Old Testament in Eastern Orthodox Tradition*, esp. pp. 260–62; Woolfenden, "Eastern Christian Liturgical Traditions"; Spinks, "Eastern Christian Liturgical Traditions"; and Lamb, *The Psalms in Christian Worship*. For the usage of the Psalms in Jewish worship, see Maher, "The Psalms in Jewish Worship"; Jacobovits, *The Authorised Daily Prayer Book of the United Hebrew Congregations*; and Simpson, *Jewish Prayer and Worship*, esp. pp. 60–62.

perhaps not make too much of this factor, it would nevertheless appear that the Chronicler did have a particular interest in psalms, and a certain concern to speak of them, and quote from them in what he wrote about worship, for this author's quotations from the psalms is plentiful. This we have already noted, along with the Chronicler's apparent predilection for music and song in the temple precincts.[10] As we have observed there is in 1 Chr 16:8–36 a whole series of quotations from Pss 105:1-15; 96:1-13; 106:1, 47–48; in 2 Chr 6:41-42 there is the quotation of Ps 132:8–10; also the quotation of Ps 136:1 is made in 1 Chr 16:41; 2 Chr 5:13; 7:3, 6; 20:21. Nevertheless, while the Chronicler does call the temple "a house of sacrifice" in 1 Chr 6:49; 2 Chr 2:6; 7:12, the various references to worship expressed in songs, praises, prayers suggest to us joyous worship, worship that was at times loud and noisy. We may quote again what the Chronicler has to say in 1 Chr 15:16, "David also commanded the chiefs of the Levites to appoint their kindred as the singers to play on musical instruments, on harps and lyres and cymbals, to raise loud sounds of joy." With the Chronicler, further, we do seem to have worship which when it was sacrificial was also accompanied by joyful songs and praises, as for example we are told took place at the time when, according to the Chronicler's account, Hezekiah rededicated the temple (2 Chr 29:25–30).

There is a sense in which the ongoing worship of the Jewish people retained a serious usage of the psalms, even to increasing that usage. Thus to a certain degree there came about something of a new orientation of worship away from sacrificial emphasis and towards the psalmic. This may partly have been owing to the demise of the temple in 70 CE,[11] but we may question whether that was the sole reason for this new orientation. May it not also have been led by a growing appreciation of the depths of understanding there is in the psalms, on the one hand of the human psyche and its deep needs, and on the other of the reality of the Lord God in his eternity, greatness, and mystery, in his faithfulness and loving kindness, in his judgment upon sin yet also his willingness to forgive? Thus too would the infant Christian Church in its worship embrace the use of the Psalter.

---

10. See above, 223–31.

11. The author of the Letter to the Hebrews in 13:15 would seem to be making use of the "old" language of sacrifice in his formulation for the "new" dispensation, "sacrifice of praise." The Qumran *Rule of the Community* (1QS ix.4-5) speaks of "the proper offering of the lips is like a soothing (odour) of righteousness, and perfection of way like an acceptable freewill offering . . ." See Bruce, *Hebrews*, 405–6; and Knibb, *Qumran Community*, 138

There are yet further styles, types of worship spoken about in the Hebrew Bible, these being forms of worship not confined to temple settings. Thus what I call a fourth style of worship is that expression of awe, wonder, praise occasioned by some revelation to, generally, an individual normally on a manifestly unexpected occasion. An example of such a theophanic experience spoken about in the Hebrew Bible is the divine appearance to Jacob on his flight from home, with its, "Then Jacob woke from his sleep and said, 'Surely the Lord is in this place—and I did not know it!' And he was afraid [*yr'*], and said, 'How awesome is this place! This is none other than the house of God, and this is the gate of heaven.'" (Gen 28:16–17) This is surely the language of worship, and what is being spoken about is the experience of the divine to which any human response almost must be one of awe and praise. Another obvious example of such an experience is that of Isaiah in what looks likely to have been the Jerusalem temple, where again the human words of response to the divine appearance resound with the language of praise:

> In the year that King Uzziah died, I saw the Lord sitting on a throne, high and lofty; and the hem of his robe filled the temple. Seraphs were in attendance above him; each had six wings: with two they covered their faces, and with two they covered their feet, and with two they flew. And one called to another and said: "Holy, holy, holy is the Lord of hosts; the whole earth is full of his glory." (Isa 6:1–3)

Further examples of such experiences are those of the surprise encounter with the deity by Moses (Exod 3:1–6), where once again there is talk of the sense of fear, awe on the part of the human party involved; or the experience of the fleeing Elijah and the Lord coming to him on Mount Horeb (1 Kgs 19:11–13). These are encounters of human beings with the holy God, and the accounts of them stress the elements of surprise and awe, and are nothing if not suffused with the element of worship.

We should consider further expressions of worship, and these may be spoken of more briefly. What I would call a fifth type, or style of worship only appears in our texts as the beginning stage of a style of worship that will come to have an ongoing and burgeoning significance not alone in the Jewish worshipping community but also in the worship of the other Abrahamic faith communities. This is the worship that is centered on the Lord as he and his ways and deeds are spoken about in what emerged as the community's sacred documents. These matters we read about in the book of Nehemiah, in particular of the activity of hearing words being spoken which were from a document which was gaining some authority and standing in the community as setting forth aspects of the ways and the will of the Lord God. Such documents as those we read about in the book of Nehemiah seem to have been writings and records that had their genesis in the Babylonian exile, and are portrayed as having some standing in and authority for the slowly-being-re-established Jewish community back in the homeland. At any rate in Neh 8:1–18 we hear of Ezra reading from what is described as "the book of the law of Moses," and of what he was reading being interpreted by Levites who "helped the people to understand the law" (Neh 8:7). In subsequent times in both Jewish and Christian communities this style of worship in which portions of the scriptures are read and which is followed by exposition and the proclamation of what is perceived to be the message, or the messages, of the passage, or passages, for the worshippers in their daily lives would become regular and widespread.[12]

Nor should we forget as a sixth style the worship that took place in individual homes. At one time it appears this was the setting, place for the keeping of Passover (Exod 12:1—13:22), while various rites of passage, and maybe other family prayers and devotions took place here.[13]

There is also, in the seventh place, that worship receiving sustained criticism in the Hebrew Bible, but that judging by the number of references to it in these documents did take place, and continued to take place, with uncommon frequency, namely the worship at high places and under green trees. This was worship that was essentially Canaanite, and which in the pages of the Hebrew Bible is subject to the strongest of criticisms, indeed outright condemnation, not least by those of the deuteronomic and deuteronomistic persuasions. The fact that we read of such condemnations time and time again in both the Former and the Latter Prophets suggests that these were practices that went on and on over a considerable span of time, in spite of various attempts to eliminate them.[14]

Yet it should be remembered that the above, what I have called these seven styles, kinds of worship, are all aspects of one great matter, the issue that is present, as we have seen, in so much of the Hebrew Bible, namely the worship of the holy and eternal Lord, in fact the response in a sense of wonder, love, and praise on the part of his frail and sinful followers to ever-fresh awarenesses of the divine glory and greatness, and of the Lord's presence and provision for his people. The fact that we can enumerate these various types, styles of worshipful approach to the Lord, itself speaks eloquently of what was deemed to be at least on the part of some of the Israelite leaders

---

12. On this emerging aspect of worship, see above, 84–87.
13. On worship in individual homes, see above, 49–51.
14. On worship at high places and under green trees, see above, 53–55.

the importance and vitality of the ongoing approach to and worship of the Lord God of Israel.

Further, what is surely worthy of note is the variety, the multiplicity within this series of differing styles of worship. Not only is there the formality of the priestly ritual in worship, there is also the presentation of the moment of spontaneous worship when a person has had some particular experience of the divine; not only is there the deuteronomic emphasis on the vitality of inward and personal worship, there is also the joyful celebratory style of the Chronicler; not only is there the preserved expression of prayer and praise in the succession of different psalms, there is also the quiet, even private, worship in individual homes; not only is there the emphasis on the yearning for purity of worship, there is also the warning of possible trespass into realms that would better be regarded as dangerous for the purity of the faith and that therefore should be regarded as forbidden. Yet equally, with the presentation in the book of Nehemiah of a new way in which the purposes of the Lord, both ancient and contemporary, with his people was heard, expounded, rejoiced over, and prayed about, it may be said that in the Hebrew Bible there is not only the emphasis on old, established, tried and tested ways of worship, but there is also an openness to other, and newer, styles of worship.

The Leaders of Worship

We may perhaps say that there were in ancient Israel two main professional groups responsible for the leadership of worship, priests and Levites, alongside some others we have considered in the preceding chapters, such as kings, and prophets, not forgetting those heads of households.

As has already been explained the task of trying to set forth a history of the Old Testament priesthood is not attempted in this work for the reasons that we do not have in the Hebrew Bible the literary resources to do so. Rather, the more limited aim of describing how various parts of the Hebrew Bible speak of priests and Levites has been attempted. The priests were above all called to facilitate the working of the Israelite cult, in particular of the sacrificial cult. They were called to be the authorized persons in these important matters, those who knew when and what sacrifices were to be offered. The matter is well summed up by the writer of the New Testament Letter to the Hebrews who, admittedly speaking of the high priest, observed "Every high priest chosen from among mortals is put in charge of things pertaining to God on their behalf, to offer gifts and sacrifices for sins." (Heb

5:1)[15] The ministry of the priests was at the altar, and was about offering gifts and sacrifices, in particular being concerned in the crucial matter of the sacrificial blood, the blood being believed, as Lev 1–7 explains in some detail, to be the means of securing the forgiveness of a wide range of unwitting, involuntary sins, and thus the continuation of ongoing life in the presence of the Lord. This is to say that if the ancient sacrificial system was of importance for national life and individual lives, then so too was the vitally associated ministry of the authorized priesthood, that is of those who had the necessary skills and understandings to carry out these holy matters. The priests, as we have noted, were also involved in teaching the people, explaining to them the things of the Lord and what should be their responses to his holiness and his gracious care of them; it was also their responsibility to give judgments on various matters, rulings on sundry questions of a moral nature.

It was most likely in post-exilic times that there came about the office of the High Priest, though the institution of such, and details of their responsibilities, have been written back into the accounts of the Sinai revelations. Further, perhaps it was in the days after the conquest of Jerusalem that the mysterious personage and priesthood of Melchizedek made his historical appearance, one who comes before us both as priest and king. Our own conclusions are that we should regard Melchizedek first and foremost as a king, one who in that kingly capacity acted as a priest.

Then there are the Levites, who are portrayed in different parts of the Old Testament as occupying various roles and fulfilling a variety of responsibilities. While in Leviticus they are mentioned but twice (Lev 25:32, 33), and with no details given as to their cultic or other responsibilities, yet their existence is written about: perhaps indeed they assisted the priests in their duties, and cared for various matters in the tabernacle. In Numbers they are more spoken about, being cultic functionaries, assistants to the priests, responsible for the fabric of the worship place, and in particular responsible for the safe and successful transportation, and re-erection, of the desert sanctuary. Then, in the book of Deuteronomy with its somewhat dual talk of Levites and also of levitical priests we are not sure what we are intended to understand. Clearer however, are indications about their responsibilities, about their work at the altar, of their teaching tasks, caring for, and proclaiming the law, giving help in judging difficult legal matters and cases, consulting the divine lots, Urim and Thummim, in attempting to discern the will of God.

---

15. On Priests and Levites, and also on the High Priest, see above, 71–88.

It is also clear from the Old Testament that the king was involved in matters we would associate with leadership of worship.[16] Clearly in the thought of the Hebrew Bible the king was an important and significant person in national life, this extending to responsibilities in worship and the leadership thereof. The king's special place in that nexus of relationships of the Lord God and his people Israel, seems to have meant that the king could at times perform functions we would think of as being those of the priests. It would seem that we should not regard the king *as* a priest, but rather that the king—*as king*—did fulfil various priestly responsibilities, not least on great state occasions. Further, the Old Testament's so-called deuteronomistic literature points to the great responsibility of the reigning king for the maintaining the purity of the Israelite cult, and for the elimination of foreign religious influences.

Something needs to be said by way of summary about the Hebrew prophets and worship.[17] Not only is there in the books of the prophets significant reference to the Lord in terms of profound praise, there is also loud criticism of certain aspects of the worship that comes out of unworthy, unrighteous lives. Thus we get in some of the prophets, in particular in the books of Isaiah, Amos, and Micah, scathing words of condemnation of the worship offered by such outright sinners. This worship, and other such travesties of worship, these prophets and others of the prophets proclaimed were grossly offensive to God, and unacceptable to him who is all holiness and compassion. As the matter is expressed in the book of Micah,

> He has told you, O mortal, what is good;
> and what does the Lord require of you
> but to do justice, and to love kindness,
> and to walk humbly with your God? (Mic 6:8)

Yet at the same time we may observe on the part of at least some of the prophets a real appreciation of the nation's need of the Jerusalem temple and all that would thereby be provided and represented. Thus post-exilic prophets such as Haggai, Zechariah 1–8, and Malachi urged upon the community the importance of rebuilding the temple, thus re-establishing all that it had earlier stood for and signified.

Finally very little can be said about heads of households as leaders of the worship that seems to have taken place in individual homes; our documents give us few details of such things. While some of heads of households may have been able to appoint a Levite or a priest to fulfil such duties

---

16. On the king and worship, see above, 89–102.
17. On the prophets and worship, see above, 240–75.

(Judges 17), no doubt most householders were much more thrown back on their own resources.[18]

Joseph Blenkinsopp has pointed out that "The Israelite priesthood and its literary productions have not had a good press in Christian Old Testament scholarship since the Enlightenment."[19] Perhaps we may be permitted to widen that statement somewhat, and observe that all too often those who are appointed to lead the worship of the holy God inevitably render themselves open to criticism, not only because they may not be carrying out their tasks correctly, sufficiently assiduously, or because it is believed that their lives are unworthy of their high calling, or even because they are not perceived to be carrying out those duties in the ways others would wish. Such is perhaps a not unlikely fate for those who are appointed to such high and sacred tasks, many of such tasks inevitably being carried out in somewhat public settings. Yet the work of the leadership of worship, whether on the parts of priests or Levites, or whether on the parts of kings or heads of households, was of a highly important and indeed holy nature, and deflections and falls from the necessary high standards would necessitate the intervention of a prophet or perhaps a king. And all of these were thus engaged in holy ministries, ministries that were believed to be vital for the well-being of the nation and all its peoples and communities. For these leaders were the ones appointed to stand on holy ground, and before the holy God to minister on behalf of their sinful people. They were indeed standing, living, serving between heaven and earth.

Once Again, the Worship

We may usefully remind ourselves of those words of the late Evelyn Underhill (1875-1941) in her book entitled *Worship*.

> Worship in all its grades and kinds, is the response of the creature to the Eternal: nor need we limit this definition to the human sphere. There is a sense in which we may think of the whole of the Universe, seen and unseen, conscious and unconscious, as an act of worship, glorifying its Origin, Sustainer, and End.[20]

This sense of the reality of worship is, as we have seen in the preceding study an abiding theme throughout the Old Testament. As has been

---

18. On worship in the home, see above, 49–51.

19. Blenkinsopp, *Sage, Priest, Prophet*, 66.

20. Underhill, *Worship*, 3. We may take note of the fact that various contemporary scholars of the Hebrew Bible speak in similar tones of the sense of worship in the account of the creation in Gen 1:1—2:4. See, e.g., Blenkinsopp, *The Pentateuch*, 60–63; Barker, *Temple Theology*, 13–32.

observed there is a real and sustained prevalence of the talk about, and about the activity of worship in these documents. There is as Ronald Clements has pointed out to us a cultic dimension to what we are told in the Hebrew Bible about the faith of Israel, and further, that as a part of this "what is of paramount importance in the Old Testament is the presence of God, rather than any doctrine of his existence."[21] In this worship there is on the part of the people of God a real reaching out to him, a seeking of his presence with them for their journeys of life, a profound sense on their part of an unworthiness to seek his aid and to be recipients of his forgiving love and guidance for the future times. This is a human reaching out into what we might these days speak about as the spiritual realm, a search for those parts of life that are neither confined to, nor constricted by, the things of merely earthly life. Thus prayer assumes a large part of the total span of worship in the Hebrew Bible, and also seeking divine forgiveness for sins committed. Hence the need for those specialists in the life of the cult—those priests and Levites—those whose lives were dedicated to the calling of serving in the interface between earth and heaven, betwixt and between, liminal people, those who could communicate between these worlds of existence.

There are times when this worship is being spoken about where human language runs out, and when perhaps there are surprise encounters between the Lord and individual people. What we may perhaps find somewhat strange is the near absence in the Old Testament of a call for silence in worship. Habakkuk is nearly on his own in calling for this: "But the Lord is in his holy temple; let all the earth keep silence before him!" (Hab 2:20). and not dissimilar is Zechariah, "Be silent, all people, before the Lord; for he has roused himself from his holy dwelling" (Zech 2:13). It is rather that in general terms the worship the Hebrew Bible sets forth is hardly short of words, and as we have noted can at times be portrayed as noisy—yet indeed vibrant.[22]

It would be unrealistic to expect that worship offered by people of earth to the praise of the holy Lord would always be worthy of his perfection and compassion, and the Hebrew Bible does not shy away from recording some of the Hebrew prophets' excoriations about such matters. Among the callings of at least some of the prophets was this conviction that the people were under judgment for their various failures in the living out of human relationships and their worship of the holy Lord. Yet at the same time perhaps one of the deep meanings of the worship we read about in the Old Testament is that it was in the felicitous expression of Brueggemann a matter of

---

21. Clements, *Old Testament Theology*, 40.

22. On silence in worship, see, e.g., MacCulloch, *Silence: A Christian History*. For some other occurrences of the notion of silence in the Old Testament, see Job 4:16; Isa 41:1; Qoh 3:7; Ps 4:4 (Heb v. 5).

"Redescribing Reality,"[23] that is in worship there is set forth something of the greatness, the otherness, the sheer perfection and loving forgiveness of the Lord, and a call to worshippers therefore to confess their sins, to rejoice in their continued divine guidance and calling, and to give thanks for reassurance they have received for their lives through that worship.

In the book of Psalms we are afforded many a glimpse into the joy and assurance afforded by worship and the place of worship, such as for instance that which we find in Ps 26:

> O Lord, I love the house in which you dwell,
> and the place where your glory abides. (Ps 26:8)

And what we read about in the Wisdom of Jesus ben Sirach, coming almost certainly from a later time than Ps 26, bears witness to the ongoing reality of this worship. Ben Sirach is speaking here in all probability of the liturgy of the Day of Atonement.

> Then the sons of Aaron shouted;
> they blew their trumpets of hammered metal;
> they sounded a mighty fanfare
> as a reminder before the Most High.
> Then all the people together quickly
> fell to the ground on their faces
> to worship their Lord,
> the Almighty, God Most High.
> Then the singers praised him with their voices
> in sweet and full-toned melody.
> And the people of the Lord Most High offered
> their prayers before the Merciful One,
> until the order of worship of the Lord was ended,
> and they completed his ritual. (Sir 50:16–19)

Thus, as we began, so we may end, with a final reminder of that spirit of worship which as we have observed is at the very heart of the Hebrew Bible:

> For great is the Lord, and greatly to be praised;
> [. . .]
> Ascribe to the Lord, O families of the peoples,
> ascribe to the Lord glory and strength.
> Ascribe to the Lord the glory due his name;
> bring an offering, and come into his courts.
> Worship the Lord in holy splendor;
> tremble before him, all the earth. (Ps 96:4a, 7–9)

---

23. This is the title of a book referring strictly to the Old Testament in general, rather than to worship in particular. See Brueggemann, *Redescribing Reality*.

Bibliography

Aagerson, James W. "Early Jewish Lectionaries." In *ABD*, 4:270–71.
Abba, Raymond. "Priests and Levites." In *IDB*, 3:876–89.
———. "Priests and Levites in Deuteronomy." *VT* 27 (1977) 257–67.
Ackerman, Susan. "Household Religion, Family Religion, and Women's Religion in Ancient Israel." In *Household and Family Religion in Antiquity*, edited by John Bodel and Saul M. Olyan, 127–58. Oxford: Blackwell, 2008.
———. *Under Every Green Tree: Popular Religion in Sixth-Century Judah*. Harvard Semitic Monographs 46. Atlanta: Scholars, 1992.
———. "Who is Sacrificing at Shiloh? The Priesthoods of Ancient Israel's Regional Sanctuaries." In *Levites and Priests in Biblical History and Tradition*, edited by Mark Leuchter and Jeremy M. Hutton, 25–43. Ancient Israel and Its Literature 9. Atlanta: Society of Biblical Literature, 2011.
Ackroyd, Peter R. *The Chronicler in His Age*. JSOTSup 101. Sheffield, UK: Sheffield Academic, 1991.
———. "The Temple Vessels: A Continuity Theme." In *Studies in the Religious Tradition of the Old Testament*, 46–60. London: SCM, 1987.
Aharoni, Yohanan. *The Archaeology of the Land of Israel*. Translated by Anson F. Rainey. London: SCM, 1982.
Albertz, Rainer. *A History of Israelite Religion in the Old Testament Period*. Translated by John Bowden. 2 vols. London: SCM, 1994.
———. "Personal Piety." In *Religious Diversity in Ancient Israel and Judah*, edited by Francesca Stavrakapoulou and John Barton, 134–46. London: T. & T. Clark, 2010.
Albright, William F. *Yahweh and the Gods of Canaan: A Historical Analysis of Two Contrasting Faiths*. London: Athlone, 1968.
Alexander, Philip S. "Aqedah." In *A Dictionary of Biblical Interpretation*, edited by R. J. Coggins and J. L. Houlden, 44–46. London: SCM, 1990.
Allen, Leslie C. *Ezekiel 20–48*. Word Biblical Commentary 29. Dallas, TX: Word Books, 1990.
———. *Jeremiah: A Commentary*. Old Testament Library. Louisville, KY: Westminster John Knox, 2008.
———. *Joel, Obadiah, Jonah and Micah*. The New International Commentary on the Old Testament. London: Hodder and Stoughton, 1976.
———. *Psalms 101–150*. Word Biblical Commentary 21. Waco, TX: Word Books, 1983.
Alter, Robert. *The Book of Psalms: A Translation with Commentary*. New York: Norton, 2007.
Amos, Clare. *Genesis*. Epworth Commentaries. Peterborough, UK: Epworth, 2004.
Andersen, Francis I., and David Noel Freedman. *Hosea*. Anchor Bible. New Haven: Yale University Press, 1980.
———. *Micah*. Anchor Bible. New York: Doubleday, 2000.

Anderson, Arnold A. *The Book of Psalms*. 2 vols. New Century Bible Commentary. London: Oliphants, 1972.
Anderson, George W. "Enemies and Evildoers in the Book of Psalms." *BJRL* 48 (1965) 18–29.
———. "'Sicut cervus': Evidence in the Psalter of Private Devotion in Ancient Israel." *VT* 30 (1980) 388–97.
Ap-Thomas, Dafydd R. "Notes on Some Terms Relating to Prayer." *VT* 6 (1956) 225–41.
———. "Some Aspects of the Root HNN in the Old Testament." *JSS* 2 (1957) 128–48.
———. "Some Notes on the Old Testament Attitude to Prayer." *SJT* 9 (1956) 422–29.
Ashby, Godfrey. *Sacrifice: Its Nature and Purpose*. London: SCM, 1988.
Astour, Michael C. "Melchizedek (Person)." In *ABD*, 4:684–86.
Auffret, Pierre. *The Literary Structure of Psalm 2*. JSOTSup 3. Sheffield, UK: JSOT Press, 1977.
Barkay, Gabriel. *Ketef Hinom: A Treasure Facing Jerusalem's Walls*. Jerusalem: The Israel Museum, 1986.
Balentine, Samuel E. *Prayer in the Hebrew Bible: The Drama of Divine-Human Dialogue*. Overtures to Biblical Theology. Minneapolis: Fortress, 1993.
———. *The Torah's Vision of Worship*. Overtures to Biblical Theology. Minneapolis: Fortress Press, 1999.
Barker, Margaret. *The Gate of Heaven: The History and Symbolism of the Temple in Jerusalem*. London: SPCK, 1991.
———. *The Great High Priest: The Temple Roots of Christian Worship*. London: T. & T. Clark, 2003.
———. *On Earth as it is in Heaven: Temple Symbolism in the New Testament*. Edinburgh: T. & T. Clark, 1995.
———. *Temple Themes in Christian Worship*. London: T. & T. Clark, 2008.
———. *Temple Theology: An Introduction*. London: SPCK, 2004.
Barrett, C. Kingsley. *Acts 15–28*. International Critical Commentary. London: T. & T. Clark International, 1998.
Barrick, W. Boyd. "High Place." In *ABD*, 3:196–200.
Bartlett, John R. "The Brotherhood of Edom." *JSOT* 4 (1977) 2–27.
———. "Edom and the Fall of Jerusalem." *PEQ* 114 (1982) 13–24.
———. "Zadok and His Successors at Jerusalem." *JTS*, n.s., 19 (1968) 1–18.
Barton, John. *Joel and Obadiah*. Old Testament Library. Louisville: Westminster John Knox, 2001.
Beale, Gregory K. *The Temple and the Church's Mission: A Biblical Theology of the Dwelling Place of God*. Downers Grove, IL: InterVarsity, 2004.
Beckwith, Roger T. "The Jewish Background to Christian Worship." In *The Study of Liturgy*, edited by Cheslyn Jones et al., 39–51. London: SPCK, 1978.
———. "The Temple Restored." In *Heaven on Earth: The Temple in Biblical Theology*, edited by T. Desmond Alexander and Simon Gathercole, 71–79. Carlisle, UK: Paternoster, 2004.
Bernhardt, Karl-Heinz. "Ugaritic Texts." In *Near Eastern Religious Texts Relating to the Old Testament*, edited by Walter Beyerlin and translated by John Bowden, 185–226. Old Testament Library. London: SCM, 1978.
Binder, Donald D. *Into the Temple Courts: The Place of the Synagogues in the Second Temple Period*. SBL Dissertation Series 169. Atlanta: SBL, 1999.

Bird, Phyllis. "The Place of Women in the Israelite Cultus." In *Ancient Israelite Religion: Essays in Honor of Frank Moore Cross*, edited by Patrick D. Miller, Paul D. Hanson, and S. Dean McBride, 397–419. Philadelphia: Fortress, 1987.
Blenkinsopp, Joseph. *Ezekiel*. Interpretation Commentary. Louisville: John Knox, 1990.
———. *Ezra-Nehemiah*. Old Testament Library. London: SCM, 1988.
———. *Isaiah 1–39*. Anchor Bible. New York: Doubleday, 2000.
———. *Isaiah 40–55*. Anchor Bible. New York: Doubleday, 2000.
———. *Isaiah 56–66*. Anchor Bible. New York: Doubleday, 2003.
———. *The Pentateuch: An Introduction to the First Five Books of the Bible*. London: SCM, 1992.
———. *Sage, Priest, Prophet: Religious and Intellectual Leadership in Ancient Israel*. Louisville: Westminster John Knox, 1995.
———. *Wisdom and Law in the Old Testament: The Ordering of Life in Israel and Early Judaism*. Oxford Bible Series. Oxford: Oxford University Press, 1983.
Block, Daniel I. *Ezekiel 25–48*. New International Commentary on the Old Testament. Grand Rapids: Eerdmans, 1998.
Boccaccini, Gabriele. "High Priest." In *EDB*, 589–90.
Boda, Mark J., Daniel K. Falk, and Rodney A. Werline, eds. *Seeking the Favour of God*. Vol. 1, *The Origins of Penitential Prayer in Second Temple Judaism*. Atlanta: SBL, 2006.
Bodel, John and Saul M. Olyan, eds. *Household and Family Religion in Antiquity*. Malden, MA: Blackwell, 2008.
Bokser, Baruch M. "Unleavened Bread and Passover, Feasts of." In *ABD*, 6:755–65.
Boyce, Richard Nelson. *The Cry to God in the Old Testament*. SBL Dissertation Series 103. Atlanta: Scholars, 1988.
Bracke, John M. "Branch." In *ABD*, 1:776.
Brady, Christian M. M. "Sun." In *EDB*, 1257.
Braulik, Georg. "The Joy of the Feast: The Conception of the Cult in Deuteronomy." In *The Theology of Deuteronomy: Collected Essays of Georg Braulik, O.S.B.*, 27–65. N. Richland Hills, TX: BIBAL, 1994.
———. "The Rejection of the Goddess Asherah in Israel." In *The Theology of Deuteronomy: Collected Essays of Georg Braulik, O.S.B.*, 165–82. N. Richland Hills, TX: BIBAL, 1994.
Braun, Joachim. *Music in Ancient Israel/Palestine*. Grand Rapids: Eerdmans, 2000.
———. "Music, Musical Instruments." In *EDB*, 927.
Braun, Roddy L. "Solomon, the Chosen Temple Builder: The Significance of 1 Chronicles 22, 28, and 29 for the Theology of Chronicles." *JBL* 95 (1976) 581–90.
Broyles, Craig C. *The Conflict of Faith and Experience in the Psalms: A Form-Critical Study*. JSOTSup 52. Sheffield, UK: Sheffield Academic, 1989.
Brown, William P. *Psalms*. Interpreting Biblical Texts. Nashville: Abingdon, 2010.
Bruce, F. F. *The Epistle to the Hebrews*. New International Commentary on the New Testament. London: Marshall, Morgan & Scott, 1964.
Brueggemann, Walter. "Bounded by Obedience and Praise: The Psalms as Canon." *JSOT* 50 (1991) 63–92.
———. "Psalms and the Life of Faith: A Suggested Typology of Function." *JSOT* 17 (1980) 3–32.
———. *Redescribing Reality: What We Do When We Read the Bible*. London: SCM, 2009.

———. *Theology of the Old Testament: Testimony, Dispute, Advocacy*. Minneapolis: Fortress, 1997.

———. *Worship in Ancient Israel: An Essential Guide*. Nashville: Abingdon, 2005.

Budd, Philip J. *Leviticus*. New Century Bible Commentary. London: Marshall Pickering, 1996.

———. *Numbers*. Word Biblical Commentary 5. Waco, TX: Word Books, 1984.

Bultmann, Christoph. "Deuteronomy." In *The Oxford Bible Commentary*, edited by John Barton and John Muddiman, 135–58. Oxford: Oxford University Press, 2001.

Bunce, James W. "The Liturgy of the Last Gospel." *ExpT* 126 (2014–15) 270–80.

Burnett, Joel. "Tammuz." In *EDB*, 1274.

Burney, C. F. *Notes on the Hebrew Text of the Books of Kings*. Oxford: Clarendon, 1903.

Callaway, Phillip R. *The Dead Sea Scrolls for a New Millennium*. Eugene, OR: Cascade, 2011.

Carroll, Robert P. *Jeremiah*. Old Testament Library. London: SCM, 1986.

Carter, J., ed. *Understanding Religious Sacrifice: A Reader*. London: Continuum, 2003.

Childs, Brevard S. *Exodus*. Old Testament Library. London: SCM, 1974.

———. *Old Testament Theology in Canonical Context*. London: SCM, 1985.

Christensen, Duane L. *Nahum*. Anchor Yale Bible. New Haven: Yale University Press, 2009.

Clements, Ronald E. *Deuteronomy*. Old Testament Guides. Sheffield, UK: JSOT Press, 1989.

———. *God and Temple*. Oxford: Basil Blackwell, 1965.

———. *Isaiah 1–39*. New Century Bible Commentary. London: Marshall, Morgan & Scott, 1980.

———. *Jerusalem and the Nations: Studies in the Book of Isaiah*. Sheffield, UK: Sheffield Phoenix, 2011.

———. "The Meaning of Ritual Acts in Israelite Religion." In *Eucharistic Theology Then and Now*, 1–14. SPCK Theological Collections. London: SPCK, 1968.

———. *Old Testament Theology: A Fresh Approach*. London: Marshall, Morgan & Scott, 1978.

———. "Worship and Ethics: A Re-examination of Psalm 15." In *Worship and the Hebrew Bible: Essays in Honor of John T. Willis*, edited by M. Patrick Graham, Richard R. Marrs, and Steven L. McKenzie, 78–94. JSOTSup 284. Sheffield, UK: Sheffield Academic, 1999.

Clifford, Richard J. "In Zion and David a New Beginning: An Interpretation of Psalm 78." In *Traditions in Transformation: Turning Points in Biblical Faith*, edited by Baruch Halpern and Jon D. Levenson, 121–41. Winona Lake, IN: Eisenbrauns, 1981.

Clines, David J. A. "The Evidence for an Autumnal New Year in Pre-exilic Israel Reconsidered." *JBL* 93 (1974) 22–40.

———. *Ezra, Nehemiah, Esther*. New Century Bible Commentary. London: Marshall, Morgan & Scott, 1984.

———. *Job 1–20*. Word Biblical Commentary 17. Dallas, TX: Word Books, 1989.

———. "Nehemiah 10 as an Example of Early Jewish Biblical Exegesis." *JSOT* 21 (1981) 111–17.

———. "New Year." In *IDBSup* 625–29.

Coats, George W. "Abraham's Sacrifice of Faith: A Form-Critical Study of Genesis 22." *Int* 27 (1973) 389–400.

Cody, Aelred. *A History of Old Testament Priesthood*. Rome: Pontifical Biblical Institute, 1969.

Coggins, Richard J. "An Alternative Prophetic Tradition." In *Israel's Prophetic Tradition: Essays in Honour of Peter Ackroyd*, edited by Richard J. Coggins, Anthony Phillips, and Michael Knibb, 77–94. Cambridge: Cambridge University Press, 1982.

———. *Exodus*. Epworth Commentaries. Peterborough, UK: Epworth, 2000.

Coggins, Richard J., and S. Paul Re'emi. *Nahum, Obadiah, Esther*. International Theological Commentary. Edinburgh: Handsel, 1985.

Corley, Jeremy. "Elements of Coronation Ritual in Isaiah 11.1–10." *PIBA* 35 (2012) 1–29.

Corney, Richard W. "Branch." In *IDB*, 1:460–61.

Craigie, Peter C. *Psalms 1–50*. Word Biblical Commentary 19. Waco, TX: Word Books, 1983.

Crawford, Cory D. "Between Shadow and Substance: The Historical Relationship of Tabernacle and Temple in Light of Architecture and Iconography." In *Levites and Priests in Biblical History and Tradition*, edited by Mark Leuchter and Jeremy M. Hutton, 117–133. Ancient Israel and Its Literature 9. Atlanta: SBL, 2011.

Crenshaw, James L. *Hymnic Affirmation of Divine Justice: The Doxologies of Amos and Related Texts in the Old Testament*. SBL Dissertation Series. Missoula, MT: Scholars, 1975.

Cross, Frank Moore. *Canaanite Myth and Hebrew Epic: Essays in the History of the Religion of Israel*. Cambridge, MA: Harvard University Press, 1973.

Curtis, Adrian H. W. "Canaanite Gods and Religion." In *Dictionary of the Old Testament Historical Books*, edited by Bill T. Arnold and Hugh G. M. Williamson, 132–42. Downers Grove, IL: InterVarsity Press, 2005.

———. *Psalms*. Epworth Commentaries. Peterborough, UK: Epworth, 2004.

———. *Ugarit: Ras Shamra*. Cambridge: Lutterworth, 1985.

Danby, Herbert. *The Mishnah*. Oxford: Oxford University Press, 1933.

Darr, Katheryn Pfisterer. "The Wall around Paradise: Ezekielian Ideas about the Future." *VT* 37 (1987) 271–79.

Davidson, Robert. *Wisdom and Worship*. London: SCM, 1990.

Davies, Eryl W. *Numbers*. New Century Bible Commentary. London: Marshall Pickering, 1995.

Davies, G. Henton. "Ephod." In *IDB*, 2:118–119.

———. "High Places." In *IDB*, 2:602–604.

———. "Tabernacle." In *IDB*, 4:498–506.

Davies, Graham I. *Hosea*. New Century Bible Commentary. London: Marshall Pickering, 1992.

———. "A Note on the Etymology of *hištaḥ^{a}wāh*." *VT* 29 (1979) 493–95.

———. "The Theology of Exodus." In *In Search of True Wisdom; Essays in Old Testament Interpretation in Honour of Ronald E. Clements*, edited by Edward Ball, 137–52. JSOTSup 300. Sheffield, UK: Sheffield Academic, 1999.

Davies, John G. "Cult, Cultus." In *A New Dictionary of Liturgy and Worship*, edited by John G. Davies, 202–203. London: SCM, 1986.

Day, John. "The Destruction of the Shiloh Sanctuary and Jeremiah VII 12, 14." In *Studies in the Historical Books of the Old Testament*, edited by John A. Emerton, 87–94. VTSup 30. Leiden: Brill, 1979.

———. "How many Pre-exilic Psalms are there?" In *In Search of Pre-Exilic Israel*, edited by John Day, 225–50. JSOTSup 406. London: T. & T. Clark, 2004.

———. *Molech: A God of Human Sacrifice in the Old Testament*. Cambridge: Cambridge University Press, 1989.

———. *Psalms*. Old Testament Guides. Sheffield, UK: JSOT Press, 1990.

———. "Whatever Happened to the Ark of the Covenant?" In *Temple and Worship in Biblical Israel*, edited by John Day, 250–70. London: T. & T. Clark, 2007.

———. *Yahweh and the Gods and Goddesses of Canaan*. JSOTSup 265. Sheffield, UK: Sheffield Academic, 2002.

DeClaissé-Walford, Nancy L. *Reading from the Beginning: The Shaping of the Hebrew Psalter*. Macon, GA: Mercer University Press, 1997.

Dell, Katharine J. *'Get Wisdom, Get Insight': An Introduction to Israel's Wisdom Literature*. London: Darton, Longman & Todd, 2000.

———. "'A Time to Dance;' Music, The Bible and the Book of Ecclesiastes." *ExpT* 126 (2014–2015) 114–121.

Dentan, Robert C. "The Literary Affinities of Exodus XXXIV 6f." *VT* 13 (1963) 34–51.

DeVries, LaMoine F. "Jachin and Boaz." In *EDB*, 665.

Dijkstra, Meindert. "Sakkuth." In *EDB*, 1152.

Dillard, Raymond B. *2 Chronicles*. Word Biblical Commentary 15. Waco, TX: Word Books, 1987.

Douglas, Mary. *Leviticus as Literature*. Oxford: Oxford University Press, 1999.

———. *Purity and Danger: An Analysis of Concepts of Pollution and Taboo*. Harmondsworth: Penguin, 1970.

Dozeman, Thomas B. "Urim and Thummim." In *EDB*, 1349.

Driver, Samuel R. *Deuteronomy*. International Critical Commentary. Edinburgh: T. & T. Clark, 1896.

Durham, John R. *Exodus*. Word Biblical Commentary 3. Waco, TX: Word Books, 1987.

Eaton, John H. *Kingship and the Psalms*. The Biblical Seminar. Sheffield, UK: JSOT Press, 1986.

———. "The Psalms and Israelite Worship." In *Tradition and Interpretation*, edited by George W. Anderson, 238–73. Oxford: Clarendon, 1979.

———. *Vision in Worship: The Relation of Prophecy and Liturgy in the Old Testament*. London: SPCK, 1981.

Eddinger, Terry W. "Ephod." In *EDB*, 415.

———. "Teraphim." In *EDB*, 1286.

Edelman, Diana. "Cultic Sites and Complexes beyond the Jerusalm Temple." In *Religious Diversity in Ancient Israel and Judah*, edited by Francesca Stavrakopoulou and John Barton, 82–103. London: T. & T. Clark, 2010.

———. "Hezekiah's Alleged Cultic Centralization." *JSOT* 34.4 (2008) 395–434.

Eisenman, Robert and Michael Wise. *The Dead Sea Scrolls Uncovered*. Shaftesbury, UK: Element, 1992.

Emerton, John A. "The Etymology of *Hištaḥᵃwāh*." In *Instruction and Interpretation: Studies in Hebrew Language, Palestinian Archeology and Biblical Exegesis*, edited by Hendrik A. Brongers et al., 41–55. OTS 20. Leiden: Brill, 1977.

———. "Priests and Levites in Deuteronomy: An Examination of Dr G. E. Wright's Theory." *VT* 12 (1962) 129–38.

———. "The Riddle of Genesis xiv." *VT* 21 (1971) 403–39.

Endres, John C. "The Spiritual Vision of Chronicles: Wholehearted, Joy-filled Worship of God." *CBQ* 69 (2007) 1–21.

———. "Theology of Worship in Chronicles." In *The Chronicler as Theologian: Essays in Honor of Ralph W. Klein*, edited by M. Patrick Graham, Steven L. McKenzie, and Gary N. Knoppers, 165–88. JSOTSup 371. London: T. & T. Clark, 2003.

Evans-Pritchard, E. E. *Nuer Religion*. Oxford: Clarendon Press, 1956.

Exum, J. Cheryl. *Song of Songs*. Old Testament Library. Louisville: Westminster John Knox, 2005.

Finkelstein, I., and Neil Silberman, "Temple and Dynasty: Hezekiah, the Remaking of Jerusalem and the Rise of the Pan-Israelite Ideology." *JSOT* 30 (2006) 259–85.

Fishbane, Michael. *Biblical Interpretation in Ancient Israel*. Oxford: Oxford University Press, 1985.

Fohrer, Georg. *Introduction to the Old Testament*. Translated by David Green. London: SPCK, 1974.

Frazer, James G. *The Golden Bough: A Study of Magic and Religion*. Abridged Edition. London: Macmillan, 1922.

Freedman, David N. "Pentateuch." In *IDB*, 3:720.

Freedman, David N., Jack. R. Lundbom, and Heinz-Josef Fabry. "ḥānan." In *TDOT*, 5:22–36.

Fretheim, Terence E. "The Priestly Document: Anti-Temple?" *VT* 18 (1968) 313–29.

Friedman, Richard Elliott. "Tabernacle." In *ABD*, 6:292–300.

Fuhs, H. F. "*yārēʾ*." In *TDOT*, 6:290–315.

Fulcro, William J. "Ashima." In *ABD*, 1:487.

Garrett, Duane, and Paul R. House. *Song of Songs/Lamentations*. Word Biblical Commentary 23B. Nashville: Thomas Nelson, 2004.

Gaster, Theodor H. "Sun." In *IDB*, 4:463–65.

George, Mark K. *Israel's Tabernacle as Social Space*. Ancient Israel and Its Literature 2. Atlanta: SBL, 2009.

Gerstenberger, Erhard S. *Leviticus*. Translated by Douglas W. Stott. Old Testament Library. Louisville: Westminster John Knox, 1996.

———. "ʿatar." In *TDOT*, 11:458–60.

Gerstenberger, Erhard S., and Heinz-Josef Fabry. "pll." In *TDOT*, 11:567–78.

Gese, Hartmut. "Zur Geschichte der Kultsänger am zweiten Tempel." In *Vom Sinai zum Zion: Alttestamentliche Beiträge zur biblischen Theologie*, 147–58. Munich: Chr. Kaiser Verlag, 1974.

Gillingham, Susan. *A Journey of Two Psalms: The Reception of Psalms 1 and 2 in Jewish and Christian Tradition*. Oxford: Oxford University Press, 2013.

———. *The Poems and Psalms of the Hebrew Bible*. The Oxford Bible Series. Oxford: Oxford University Press, 1994.

———. *Psalms Through the Centuries*. Vol. 1. Blackwell Bible Commentaries. Oxford: Blackwell, 2008.

———. "Studies of the Psalms: Retrospect and Prospect." *ExpT* 119 (2007–2008) 209–16.

Goldingay, John. "The Dynamic Cycle of Praise and Prayer in the Psalms." In *The Poetical Books: A Sheffield Reader*, edited by David J. A. Clines, 67–72. Sheffield, UK: Sheffield Academic, 1997.

———. *Isaiah*. New International Biblical Commentary. Carlisle, UK: Paternoster, 2001.

Gordon, Cyrus H. "Terephim." In *IDB*, 4:574.
Gordon, Robert P. *1 & 2 Samuel: A Commentary*. Exeter, UK: Paternoster, 1986.
Gorman, Frank H., Jr. *Divine Presence and Community: A Commentary on the Book of Leviticus. International Theological Commentary*. Grand Rapids: Eerdmans, 1997.
———. *Ideology of Ritual: Space, Time and Status in the Priestly Theology*. JSOTSup 91. Sheffield, UK: Sheffield Academic, 1990.
———. "Passover, Feast of." In *EDB*, 1013–14.
———. "Ritual Studies and Biblical Studies: Assessment of the Past; Prospects for the Future." *Semeia* 67 (1995) 12–36.
Gottwald, Norman K. *Studies in the Book of Lamentations*. London: SCM, 1954.
Good, E. M. *Irony in the Old Testament*. Sheffield, UK: Almond, 1981.
Goulder, Michael D. *Isaiah as Liturgy*. Society for Old Testament Study Monographs. Aldershot, UK: Ashgate, 2004.
———. *The Psalms of the Sons of Korah*. JSOTSup 20. Sheffield, UK: JSOT Press, 1982.
Gowan, Donald E. *Theology in Exodus: Biblical Theology in the Form of a Commentary*. Louisville: Westminster John Knox, 1994.
Grabbe, Lester L. *Judaism from Cyrus to Hadrian*. London: SCM, 1994.
———. *Leviticus*. Old Testament Guides. Sheffield, UK: Sheffield Academic, 1993.
———. *Priests, Prophets, Diviners, Sages: A Socio-Historical Study of Religious Specialists in Ancient Israel*. Valley Forge, PA: Trinity, 1995.
———. *Wisdom of Solomon*. T. & T. Clark Study Guides. London: T. & T. Clark, 2003
Grant, Jamie A. "The Psalms and the King." In *Interpreting the Psalms: Issues and Approaches*, edited by David Firth and Philip S. Johnston, 101–18. Downers Grove, IL: InterVarsity Press, 2005.
Gray, John. "Ashimah." In *IDB*, 1:252.
———. "Sakkuth and Kaiwan." In *IDB*, 4:165.
Greenberg, Moshe. *Biblical Prose Prayer: As a Window to the Popular Religion of Ancient Israel*. Berkeley: University of California Press, 1983.
———. "The Design and Themes of Ezekiel's Program of Restoration." *Int* 38 (1984) 181–208.
Grisbrooke, W. Jardine. "Incense." In *A New Dictionary of Liturgy and Worship*, edited by John G. Davies, 265–66. London: SCM, 1986.
Guilding, Aileen. *The Fourth Gospel and Jewish Worship: A Study of the Relation of St. John's Gospel to the Ancient Jewish Lectionary System*. Oxford: Clarendon, 1960.
Gunkel Hermann. "Jesaia, eine prophetische Liturgie." *ZAW* 42 (1924) 77–208.
———. "The Close of Micah." In *What Remains of the Old Testament and Other Essays*, 115–49. New York: Macmillan, 1928.
Haak, Robert D. "Altar." In *ABD*, 1:162–67.
Haldar, Alfred. *Studies in the Book of Nahum*. Uppsala: Almqvist & Wiksell, 1947.
Halpern, Baruch. "The Ritual Background of Zechariah's Temple Song." *CBQ* 40 (1978) 167–90.
Handy, Lowell K. "Tammuz." In *ABD*, 6:318.
Haran, Menahem. *Temples and Temple-Service in Ancient Israel*. Winona Lake, IN: Eisenbrauns, 1985.
Hartley, John E. *Leviticus*. Word Biblical Commentary 4. Dallas, TX: Nelson, 1992.
Hasel, Gerhard F. "Sabbath." In *ABD*, 5:849–56.
Haupt, Paul. "The Book of Nahum." *JBL* 26 (1907) 1–53.
Hausmann, J. "*rānan*." In *TDOT*, 13:515–22.

Hayward, C. T. Robert. "The Jewish Temple at Leontopolis: A Reconsideration." *JJS* 33 (1982) 429–43.

———. *The Jewish Temple: A Non-Biblical Sourcebook*. London: Routledge, 1996.

Heider, George C. *The Cult of Molek: A Reassessment*. JSOTSup 43. Sheffield, UK: Sheffield Academic, 1985.

———. "Molek." In *ABD*, 4:895–98.

Heiler, Friedrich. *Prayer: A Study in the History and Psychology of Religion*. Translated by Samuel McComb. Oxford: Oxford University Press, 1932.

Herbert, Arthur S. *Worship in Ancient Israel*. Ecumenical Studies in Worship. London: Lutterworth, 1959.

Hieke, Thomas, and Tobias Nicklas, eds. *The Day of Atonement: Its Interpretation in Early Jewish and Christian Traditions*. Themes in Biblical Narrative 15. Leiden: Brill, 2012.

Holbert, John C. "'Deliverance Belongs to Yahweh!': Satire in the Book of Jonah." *JSOT* 21 (1981) 59–81.

Holladay, William L. *Jeremiah*. 2 vols. Hermeneia Commentary. Philadelphia: Fortress, 1986–89.

———. "On Every High Hill and under Every Green Tree." *VT* 11 (1961)170–76.

———. *The Psalms through Three Thousand Years: Prayerbook of a Cloud of Witnesses*. Minneapolis: Fortress, 1996.

Hossfeld, Frank-Lothar, and Eric Zenger. *Psalms 2*. Translated by Linda M. Malony. Hermeneia Commentary. Minneapolis: Fortress, 2005.

———. *Psalms 3*. Translated by Linda M. Malony. Hermeneia Commentary. Minneapolis: Fortress, 2011.

Houston, Walter. "Exodus." In *The Oxford Bible Commentary*, edited by John Barton and John Muddiman, 67–91. Oxford: Oxford University Press, 2001.

Humbert, Paul. "Le problème du livre de Nahoum." *RHPR* 12 (1932) 1–15.

Hundley, Michael B. *Keeping Heaven on Earth: Safeguarding the Divine Presence in the Priestly Tabernacle*. FAT 2, Reihe 50. Tübingen: Mohr Siebeck, 2011.

Hutchinson, James Hely. "The Psalms and Praise." In *Interpreting the Psalms: Issues and Approaches*, edited by David Firth and Philip S. Johnston, 85–100. Downers Grove, IL: InterVarsity Press, 2005.

Hyatt, J. Philip. *Exodus*. New Century Bible Commentary. London: Marshall, Morgan & Scott, 1980.

Inge, John. *A Christian Theology of Place*. Ashgate, UK: Aldershot, 2003.

Jakobovits, Immanuel, ed. *The Authorised Daily Prayer Book of the United Hebrew Congregations of the Commonwealth*. 3rd rev. ed. London: Singer's Prayer Book Publication Committee, 1990.

Japhet, Sara. *I & II Chronicles*. Old Testament Library. London: SCM, 1993.

Jarick, John. "The Temple of David in the Book of Chronicles." In *Temple and Worship in Biblical Israel*, edited by John Day, 365–81. London: T. & T. Clark, 2007.

Jenson, Philip P. *Graded Holiness: A Key to the Priestly Conception of the World*. JSOTSup 106. Sheffield, UK: Sheffield Academic, 1992.

Johnson, Aubrey R. *The Cultic Prophet in Ancient Israel*. Cardiff, UK: University of Wales Press, 1962.

———. "Psalm 23 and the Household of Faith." In *Proclamation and Presence: Old Testament Essays in Honour of Gwynne Henton Davies*, edited by John I. Durham and Gwynne H. Davies, 255–71. Richmond, VA: John Knox, 1970.

———. *Sacral Kingship in Ancient Israel*. Cardiff, UK: University of Wales Press, 1967.

Johnston, Philip S. "The Psalms and Distress." In *Interpreting the Psalms: Issues and Approaches*, edited by David Firth and Philip S. Johnston, 63–84. Downers Grove, IL: InterVarsity, 2005.

Jones, Clifford M. *Old Testament Illustrations*. Cambridge Bible Commentary. Cambridge: Cambridge University Press, 1971.

Jones, Gwilym H. *1 & 2 Chronicles*. Old Testament Guides. Sheffield, UK: Sheffield Academic, 1993.

———. *1 and 2 Kings*. 2 vols. New Century Bible Commentary. London: Marshall, Morgan and Scott, 1984.

Josephus, Flavius. *Jewish Antiquities: Books 12–14*. Translated by Ralph Marcus. Cambridge, MA: Harvard University Press, 1986.

———. *The Jewish War*. Translated by G. A. Williamson and revised by E. M. Smallwood. Harmondsworth: Penguin, 1981.

Joyce, Paul M. *Ezekiel: A Commentary*. LHBOTS 482. London: T. & T. Clark, 2007.

———. "Temple and Worship in Ezekiel 40–48." In *Temple and Worship in Biblical Israel*, edited by John Day, 145–63. London: T. & T. Clark, 2007.

Kapelrud, Arvid S. *Central Ideas in Amos*. Oslo: Oslo University Press, 1961.

Kasher, R. "Anthropomorphism, Holiness and Cult: A New Look at Ezek 40–48." *ZAW* 110 (1998) 192–208.

Kellermann, D. "*miškān*." In *TDOT*, 9:58–64.

Kierkegaard, Søren. *Fear and Trembling*. Translated by Alastair Hannay. London: Penguin, 2003.

Kirkpatrick, A. F. *The Book of Psalms (1–41)*. The Cambridge Bible. Cambridge: Cambridge University Press, 1917.

Kleinig, John W. "The Divine Institution of the Lord's Song in Chronicles." *JSOT* 55 (1992) 75–83.

———. *The Lord's Song: The Basis, Function and Significance of Choral Music in Chronicles*. JSOTSup 156. Sheffield, UK: Sheffield Academic, 1993.

Knauth, Robin J. DeWitt. "Jubilee, Year of." In *EDB*, 743.

Knibb, Michael A. *The Qumran Community*. Cambridge Commentaries on Writings of the Jewish and Christian World 200 BC to AD 200. Cambridge: Cambridge University Press, 1987.

Koester, Craig R. *The Dwelling of God: The Tabernacle in the Old Testament, Intertestamental Jewish Literature, and the New Testament*. Catholic Biblical Quarterly Monograph Series 22. Washington, DC: Catholic Biblical Association of America, 1989.

Kraus, Hans-Joachim. *Psalms 1–59*. Translated by Hilton C. Oswald. Continental Commentary. Minneapolis: Augsburg, 1988.

———. *Psalms 60–150*. Translated by Hilton C. Oswald. Continental Commentary. Minneapolis: Augsburg, 1989.

———. *Worship in Israel: A Cultic History of the Old Testament*. Translated by G. Buswell. Oxford: Blackwell, 1966.

Kunim, Seth. "Judaism." In *Sacred Place*, edited by Jean Holm with John Bowker, 115–48. Themes in Religious Studies. London: Continuum, 1994.

Lamb, John A. *The Psalms in Christian Worship*. London: Faith Press, 1962.

Larkin, Katrina J. A. "Zechariah." In *The Oxford Bible Commentary*, edited by John Barton and John Muddiman, 610–15. Oxford: Oxford University Press, 2001.

Levenson, Jon D. *The Death and Resurrection of the Beloved Son: The Transformation of Child Sacrifice in Judaism and Christianity*. New Haven: Yale University Press, 1993.

———. "From Temple to Synagogue: 1 Kings 8." In *Traditions in Transformation: Turning Points in Biblical Faith*, edited by Baruch Halpern and Jon D. Levenson, 143–66. Winona Lake, IN: Eisenbrauns, 1981.

———. *Theology of the Program of Restoration of Ezekiel 40–48*. Harvard Semitic Monographs. Missoula, MT: Scholars, 1976.

Lim, Timothy H., et al., eds. *The Dead Sea Scrolls in their Historical Context*. Edinburgh: T. & T. Clark, 2000.

Lioy, Dan. *Axis of Glory: A Biblical and Theological Analysis of the Temple Motif in Scripture*. Studies in Biblical Literature 138. New York: Peter Lang, 2010.

Lowery, Richard H. *The Reforming Kings: Cult and Society in First Temple Judah*. JSOTSup 120. Sheffield, UK: Sheffield Academic, 1991.

MacCulloch, Diarmaid. *Silence: A Christian History*. London: Penguin, 2014.

Macintosh, A. A. *Hosea*. International Critical Commentary. Edinburgh: T. & T. Clark, 1997.

Maher, Michael. "The Psalms in Jewish Worship." *PIBA* 17 (1994) 9–36.

Maiberger, P. "*pāga'*." In *TDOT*, 11:470–76.

Martin, James D. *Proverbs*. Old Testament Guides. Sheffield, UK: Sheffield Academic, 1995.

Mason, Rex. *Micah, Nahum, Obadiah*. Old Testament Guides. Sheffield, UK: Sheffield Academic, 1991.

———. *Preaching the Tradition: Homily and Hermeneutics after the Exile*. Cambridge: Cambridge University Press, 1990.

———. *Zephaniah, Habakkuk, Joel*. Old Testament Guides. Sheffield, UK: JSOT Press, 1994.

Mauchline, John. *1 and 2 Samuel*. New Century Bible. London: Oliphants, 1971.

Mayes, Andrew D. H. *Deuteronomy*. New Century Bible. London: Marshall, Morgan & Scott, 1979.

———. *The Story of Israel between Settlement and Exile: A Redactional Study of the Deuteronomistic History*. London: SCM, 1983.

Mays, James L. *Micah*. Old Testament Library. London: SCM, 1976.

———. *Psalms*. Interpretation Commentary. Louisville: John Knox, 1994.

McCann, J. Clinton, Jr., ed. *The Shape and Shaping of the Psalter*. JSOTSup 159. Sheffield, UK: JSOT Press, 1993.

McConville, J. Gordon. *Joshua: Crossing Divides*. Phoenix Guides to the Old Testament 6. Sheffield, UK: Phoenix, 2013.

———. *Law and Theology in Deuteronomy*. JSOTSup 33. Sheffield, UK: JSOT Press, 1984.

———. "Priests and Levites in Ezekiel: A Crux in the Interpretation of Israel's History." *TynB* 34 (1983) 3–31.

McKane, William. *Jeremiah*. 2 vols. International Critical Commentary. Edinburgh: T. & T. Clark, 1986–96.

———. *Micah: Introduction and Commentary*. Edinburgh: T. & T. Clark, 1998.

———. *Proverbs*. Old Testament Library. London: SCM, 1970.

———. *Studies in the Patriarchal Narratives*. Edinburgh: Handsel, 1979.

McKay, Heather A. *Sabbath and Synagogue: The Question of Sabbath Worship in Ancient Judaism*. Religions in the Graeco-Roman World 112. Leiden: Brill, 1994.

McKay, John. *Religion in Judah under the Assyrians 732–609 BC*. London: SCM, 1973.

McMillion, Phillip. "Worship in Judges 17–18." In *Worship and the Hebrew Bible: Essays in Honor of John T. Willis*, edited by M. Patrick Graham, Richard R. Marrs, and Steven L. McKenzie, 225–43. JSOTSup 284. Sheffield, UK: Sheffield Academic, 1999.

Meier, Samuel A. "Sakkuth and Kaiwan." In *ABD*, 5:904.

Méndez-Montoya, Angel F. *The Theology of Food: Eating and the Eucharist*. Oxford: Wiley-Blackwell, 2012.

Meyers, Carol. "Ephod." In *ABD*, 2:550.

———. "Household Religion." In Francesca Stavrakopoulou and J. Barton. *Religious Diversity in Ancient Israel and Judah*, 118–34. London: T. & T. Clark, 2010.

———. "Jachin and Boaz." In *ABD*, 3:597–98.

———. "Jachin and Boaz in Religious and Biblical Perspective." CBQ 45 (1983) 167–78.

———. "Temple, Jerusalem." In *ABD*, 6:350–69.

Milgrom, Jacob. *Leviticus 1–16*. Anchor Bible. New Haven: Yale University Press, 1991.

———. *Leviticus 17–22*. Anchor Bible. New Haven: Yale University Press, 2000.

Miller, Patrick D. "The Blessing of God: An Interpretation of Numbers 6:22–27." Int 29 (1975) 240–51.

———. *They Cried to the Lord: The Form and Theology of Biblical Prayer*. Minneapolis: Fortress, 1994.

———. "Prayer and Divine Action." In *Israelite Religion and Biblical Theology: Collected Essays*, 445–69. JSOTSup 267. Sheffield, UK: Sheffield Academic, 2000.

———, "Prayer as Persuasion: The Rhetoric and Intention of Prayer." In *Israelite Religion and Biblical Theology: Collected Essays*, 337–44. JSOTSup 267. Sheffield, UK: Sheffield Academic, 2000.

———. "Prayer and Sacrifice in Ugarit and Israel." In *Israelite Religion and Biblical Theology: Collected Essays*, 84–100. JSOTSup 267. Sheffield, UK: Sheffield Academic, 2000.

———. *The Religion of Ancient Israel*. Louisville: Westminster John Knox, 2000.

Mitchell, Christopher Wright. *The Meaning of BRK "To Bless" in the Old Testament*. SBL Dissertation Series 95. Atlanta: Scholars, 1987.

Mitchell, David C. "Resinging the Temple Psalmody." *JSOT* 36.3 (2012) 355–78.

Moberly, R. Walter L. *At the Mountain of God: Story and Theology in Exodus 32–34*. JSOTSup 22. Sheffield, UK: JSOT Press, 1983.

———. *Genesis 12–50*. Old Testament Guides. Sheffield, UK: JSOT Press, 1992.

Morris, Leon. *The New Testament and the Jewish Lectionaries*. London: Tyndale Press, 1964.

Moore, Megan Bishop and Randall W. Younker. "Terebinth." In *EDB*, 1286.

Mowinckel, Sigmund. *The Psalms in Israel's Worship*. Translated by D. R. Ap-Thomas. 2 vols. in 1. Oxford: Blackwell, 1982.

———. *Religion and Cult: The Old Testament and the Phenomenology of Religion*. Edited by K. C. Hanson and translated by John F. X. Sheehan. Eugene, OR: Cascade Books, 2012.

Muddiman, John. "Fast, Fasting." In *ABD*, 2:773–76.

Muilenburg, James. "Isaiah 40–66." In *Interpreter's Bible*, vol. 5, edited by G. A. Buttrick, 381–773. New York: Abingdon, 1956.

———. "A Liturgy on the Triumphs of Yahweh." In *Studia Biblica et Semitica*, 233–51. Wageningen: H. Veenman & Zonen, 1966.

Murphy, Roland. *Ecclesiastes*. Word Biblical Commentary 23A. Dallas, TX: Word Books, 1992.

Murray, Robert. "Prophecy and Cult." In *Israel's Prophetic Tradition: Essays in Honour of Peter Ackroyd*, edited by Richard J. Coggins, A. Phillips, and M. Knibb, 200–216. Cambridge: Cambridge University Press, 1982.

Nakhai, Beth Alpert. "Altar." In *EDB*, 45–48.

——— "High Place." In *EDB*, 588–89.

Nelson, Richard D. *Deuteronomy*. Old Testament Library. Louisville: Westminster John Knox, 2002.

———. *The Double Redaction of the Deuteronomistic History*. JSOTSup 18. Sheffield, UK: JSOT Press, 1981.

———. *Kings*. Interpretation Commentary. Louisville: John Knox, 1987.

———. *Raising Up a Faithful Priest: Community and Priesthood in Biblical Theology*. Louisville: Westminster John Knox, 1993.

Nicholson, Ernest W. *The Pentateuch in the Twentieth Century: The Legacy of Julius Wellhausen*. Oxford: Oxford University Press, 1988.

Niditch, Susan. "Ezekiel 40–48 in Visionary Context." *CBQ* (1986) 208–24.

———. "Judges." In *The Oxford Bible Commentary*, edited by John Barton and John Muddiman, 176–91. Oxford: Oxford University Press, 2001.

———. *Judges*. Old Testament Library. Louisville: Westminster John Knox, 2008.

Nielsen, Kjeld. "Incense." In *ABD*, 3:404–9.

———. *Incense in Ancient Israel*. VTSup 38. Leiden: Brill, 1986.

Noort, Ed. "Genesis 22: Human Sacrifice and Theology in the Hebrew Bible." In *The Sacrifice of Isaac: The Aqedah (Genesis 22) and its Interpretations*, edited by Ed Noort and Eibert J. C. Tigchelaar, 1–20. Leiden: Brill, 2002.

Noth, Martin. *The Deuteronomistic History*. Translated by D. R. Ap-Thomas et al. JSOTSup 15. Sheffield, UK: JSOT Press, 1981.

———. *Exodus*. Translated by John S. Bowden. Old Testament Library. London: SCM, 1962.

———. *Leviticus*. Translated by J. E. Anderson. Old Testament Library. London: SCM, 1977.

Ogden, Graham S. "Joel 4 and Prophetic Responses to National Laments." *JSOT* 26 (1983) 97–106.

Olyan, Saul M. *Biblical Mourning: Ritual and Social Dimensions*. Oxford: Oxford University Press, 2004.

Otto, Rudolph. *The Idea of the Holy: An Enquiry into the Non-Rational Factor in the Idea of the Divine and its Relation to the Rational*. Translated by John W. Harvey. London: Oxford University Press, 1936.

Otzen, Benedikt. "'ābad." In *TDOT*, 1:19–23.

Pajunem, Mika S. "Perspectives on the Existence of a Particular Authoritative Book of Psalms in the Late Second Temple Period." *JSOT* 39.2 (2014) 129–63.

Palmer, James, "Exodus and the Biblical Theology of the Tabernacle." In *Heaven on Earth: The Temple in Biblical Theology*, edited by T. Desmond Alexander and S. Gathercole, 11–22. Carlisle, UK: Paternoster, 2004.

Parrinder, Geoffrey. *West African Religion*. London: Epworth, 1969.
Parry, Robin A. *Lamentations*. The Two Horizons Old Testament Commentary. Grand Rapids: Eerdmans, 2010.
Pedersen, Johannes. *Israel: Its Life and Culture III–IV*. London: Oxford University Press, 1959.
Pentiuc, Eugen J. *The Old Testament in Eastern Orthodox Tradition*. Oxford: Oxford University Press, 2014.
Perdue, Leo G. *Wisdom and Cult: A Critical Analysis of the Views of Cult in the Wisdom Literatures of Israel and the Ancient Near East*. SBL Dissertation Series 30. Missoula, MT: Scholars, 1977.
Petersen, David L. *Zechariah 9–14 and Malachi*. Old Testament Library. London: SCM, 1995.
Peterson, David. *Engaging with God: A Biblical Theology of Worship*. Downers Grove, IL: InterVarsity, 1992.
Pfeiffer, R. H., "The Fear of God," *IEJ*, 5(1955), 41–48.
Pitkänen, Pekka. "From Tent of Meeting: Presence, Rejection and Renewal of Divine Favour." In *Heaven on Earth: The Temple in Biblical Theology*, edited by T. Desmond Alexander and Simon Gathercole, 23–34. Carlisle, UK: Paternoster, 2004.
Pope, Marvin H. *Song of Songs*. Anchor Bible 7C, New York: Doubleday, 1977.
Porten, Bezalel. "Elephantine Papyri." In *ABD*, 2:445–55.
Porteous, Norman W. "Actualization and the Prophetic Criticism of the Cult." In *Living the Mystery: Collected Essays*, 127–41. Oxford: Blackwell, 1967.
———. "Ritual and Righteousness: The Relation of Ethics to Religion in the Prophetic Literature." In *Living the Mystery: Collected Essays*, 61–75. Oxford: Blackwell, 1967.
Porter, J. Roy. "Cultic Interpretation." In *A Dictionary of Biblical Interpretation*, edited by Richard J. Coggins and J. L. Houlden, 153–55. London: SCM, 1990.
———. "The Pentateuch and the Triennial Lectionary Cycle: An Examination of a Recent Theory." In *Promise and Fulfilment: Essays Presented to Professor S. H. Hooke in Celebration of his Ninetieth Birthday*, edited by F. F. Bruce, 163–74. Edinburgh: T. & T. Clark, 1963.
Preuss, Horst Dietrich. *Old Testament Theology*. Translated by Leo G. Perdue. 2 vols. Edinburgh: T. & T. Clark, 1995–96
Pritchard, James B., ed. *Ancient Near-Eastern Texts relating to the Old Testament*. Princeton: Princeton University Press, 1969.
Procksch, Otto. *Theologie des Alte Testaments*. Gütersloh: C. Bertelsmann, 1950.
Provan, Iain. *Lamentations*. New Century Bible Commentary. London: Marshall Pickering, 1991.
Quellette, J. "Temple of Solomon." In *IDBSup*, 872–4.
Rad, Gerhard von. "The Form-Critical Problem of the Hexateuch." In *The Problem of the Hexateuch and Other Essays*, translated by E. W. Trueman Dicken, 1–78. Edinburgh: Oliver & Boyd, 1966.
———. *Genesis*. Translated by John H. Marks. London: SCM, 1963.
———. "The Levitical Sermon in I and II Chronicles." In *The Problem of the Hexateuch and Other Essays*, translated by E. W. Trueman Dicken, 267–80. Edinburgh: Oliver & Boyd, 1966.
———. "The Royal Ritual in Judah." In *The Problem of the Hexateuch and Other Essays*, translated by E. W. Trueman Dicken, 222–31. Edinburgh: Oliver & Boyd, 1966.

———. "The Tent and the Ark." In *The Problem of the Hexateuch and Other Essays*, translated by E. W. Trueman Dicken, 103–24. Edinburgh: Oliver & Boyd, 1966.
Rambo, Lewis R. "Cult." In *A New Dictionary of Christian Theology*, edited by Alan Richardson and John Bowden, 137. London: SCM, 1983.
Ramsey, George W. "Zadok." In *ABD*, 6:1034–36.
Rehm, Merlin D. "Levites and Priests." In *ABD*, 4:297–310.
Reif, Stefan C. *Judaism and Hebrew Prayer: New perspectives on Jewish liturgical history*. Cambridge: Cambridge University Press, 1993.
Reumann, John. "A History of Lectionaries: From the Synagogue at Nazareth to Post-Vatican II." *Int* 31 (1977) 116–30.
Richardson, Peter. *Herod: King of the Jews and Friend of the Romans*. Edinburgh: T. & T. Clark, 1999.
Riley, William. *King and Cultus in Chronicles: Worship and the Reinterpretation of History*. JSOTSup 160. Sheffield, UK: JSOT Press, 1993.
Ringgren, Helmer. "*hll*." In *TDOT*, 3:404–410.
Rodd, C. S. "Psalms," in *The Oxford Bible Commentary*, edited by John Barton and John Muddiman, 355–405. Oxford: Oxford University Press, 2001.
Rofé, A. *Deuteronomy: Issues and Interpretation*. Edinburgh: T. & T. Clark, 2002.
Rogerson, John W. *The Art of Biblical Prayer*. London: SPCK, 2011.
———. "Malachi." In *The Oxford Bible Commentary*, edited by John Barton and John Muddiman, 615–17. Oxford: Oxford University Press, 2001.
———. "Music." In *The Blackwell Companion to the Bible and Culture*, edited by John F. A. Sawyer, 286–98. Oxford: Blackwell, 2006.
———. "Myth." In *A Dictionary of Biblical Interpretation*, edited by Richard J. Coggins and J. L. Houlden, 479–82. London: SCM, 1990.
Römer, Thomas. *The So-Called Deuteronomistic History: A Sociological, Historical and Literary Introduction*. London: T. & T. Clark, 2007.
Rooke, Deborah W. "Kingship as Priesthood: The Relationship between the High Priesthood and the Monarchy." In *King and Messiah in Israel and the Ancient Near East*, edited by John Day, 187–208. LHBOTS 270. London: Bloomsbury T. & T. Clark, 2013.
———. *Zadok's Heirs: The Role and Development of the High Priesthood in Ancient Israel*. Oxford Theological Monographs. Oxford: Oxford University Press, 2000.
Rowley, Harold H. *The Faith of Israel*. London: SCM, 1956.
———. "The Interpretation of the Song of Songs." In *The Servant of the Lord and other Essays on the Old Testament*, 187–234. London: Lutterworth, 1952.
———. "The Meaning of Sacrifice in the Old Testament." In *From Moses to Qumran: Studies in the Old Testament*, 67–110. London: Lutterworth, 1963.
———. "Papyri from Elephantine." In *Documents from Old Testament Times*, edited by D. Winton Thomas, 256–69. New York: Harper & Row, 1961.
———. "Ritual and the Hebrew Prophets." In *From Moses to Qumran: Studies in the Old Testament*, 111–38. London: Lutterworth, 1964.
———. *Worship in Ancient Israel: Its Forms and Meaning*. London: SPCK, 1967.
Rylaarsdam, J. C. "Passover and Feast of Unleavened Bread." In *IDB*, 3:663–68.
Salters, Robert B. *Jonah and Lamentations*. Old Testament Guides. Sheffield, UK: JSOT Press, 1994.
Sanders, E. P. *Judaism: Practice and Belief*. London: SCM, 1994.

Sansom, Michael C. "Laying On of Hands in the Old Testament." *ExpT* 94 (1982-83) 323-26.
Sawyer, John F. A. "Types of Prayer in the Old Testament: Some Semantic Observations on Hitpallel, Hithanen, etc." *Semitics* 7 (1980) 131-43.
Scharbert, Joseph. "*brk*." In *TDOT*, 2:279-308.
Schley, Donald G., and Michael S. Spence. "Zadok." In *EDB*, 1406-7.
Schofield, John N. "Megiddo." In *Archaeology and Old Testament Study*, edited by D. Winton Thomas, 309-28. Oxford: Clarendon, 1967.
Schramm, Brooks. *The Opponents of Third Isaiah: Reconstructing the Cultic History of the Restoration*. JSOTSup 193. Sheffield, UK: Sheffield Academic, 1995.
Schunk, K.-D. "*bāmāh*." In *TDOT*, 2:139-45.
Shafer, B. E. "Sabbath." In *IDBSup* 760-62.
Simpson, William W. *Jewish Prayer and Worship: An Introduction for Christians*. London: SCM, 1965.
Singer, Itamar. *Hittite Prayers*. Writings from the Ancient World 11. Atlanta: Society of Biblical Literature, 2002.
Skehen, Patrick W. and Alexander A. Di Lella. *The Wisdom of Ben Sira*. Anchor Bible. New York: Doubleday, 1987.
Sklar, Jay. *Sin, Impurity, Sacrifice, Atonement: The Priestly Conceptions*. Hebrew Bible Monographs 2. Sheffield, UK: Sheffield Phoenix, 2005.
Smith, Mark S. "The Near Eastern Background of Solar Language for Yahweh." *JBL* 109 (1990) 29-39.
Smith, Ralph L. *Micah-Malachi*. Word Biblical Commentary. Waco, TX: Word Books, 1984.
Smith, W. Robertson. *Lectures on the Religion of the Semites: The Foundational Institutions*. Edited by S. Cook. London: A. & C. Black, 1927.
Smith-Christopher, Daniel L. "Fasting." In *EDB*, 456.
Snaith, John G. "Ben Sira's Supposed Love of Liturgy." *VT* 25 (1975) 167-74.
———. *Song of Songs*. New Century Bible Commentary. London: Marshall Pickering, 1993.
Snaith, Norman H. *Amos, Hosea and Micah*. London: Epworth, 1956.
———. *Leviticus and Numbers*. New Century Bible. London: Nelson, 1967.
———. "The Sin Offering and the Guilt Offering." *VT* 15 (1965) 73-80.
Soggin, J. Alberto. *Judges*. Translated by John Bowden. Old Testament Library. London: SCM, 1981.
Spencer, John R. "Levites and Priests." In *ABD*, 4:297-310.
Spinks, Bryan D. "Eastern Christian Liturgical Traditions: Oriental Orthodox." In *The Blackwell Companion to Eastern Christianity*, edited by Ken Parry, 339-67. Oxford: Wiley-Blackwell, 2014.
Stavrakopoulou, Francesca. "'Popular' Religion and 'Official' Religion: Practice, Perception, Portrayal." In *Religious Diversity in Ancient Israel and Judah*, edited by Francesca Stavrakopoulou and John Barton, 37-58. London: T. & T. Clark, 2010.
Stern, Sacha. "Qumran Calendars: Theory and Practice." In *The Dead Sea Scrolls in Their Historical Context*, edited by Timothy H. Lim et al., 179-86. Edinburgh: T. & T. Clark, 2000.
Stevenson, Kalinda R. *The Vision of Transformation: The Territorial Rhetoric of Ezekiel 40-48*. SBL Dissertation Series 154. Atlanta: Scholars, 1996.
Stinespring, William F. "Temple, Jerusalem." In *IDB*, 4:534-60.

Sweeney, Marvin A. *I & II Kings*. Old Testament Library. Louisville: Westminster John Knox, 2007.
Talstrar, Eep. *Solomon's Prayer*. Kampen: Kok Pharos, 1993.
Tate, Marvin E. *Psalms 51–100*. Word Biblical Commentary 20. Dallas, TX: Word Books, 1990.
Taylor, J. Glen. *Yahweh and the Sun: Biblical and Archaeological Evidence for Sun Worship in Ancient Israel*. JSOTSup 111. Sheffield, UK: Sheffield Academic, 1993.
Taylor, John B. "The Temple in Ezekiel." In *Heaven on Earth: The Temple in Biblical Theology*, edited by T. Desmond Alexander and Simon Gathercole, 59–70. Carlisle, UK: Paternoster, 2004.
Thelle, Rannfrid Irene. *Approaches to the "Chosen Place": Accessing a Biblical Concept*. LHBOTS 564. London: T. & T. Clark, 2012.
Thomas, D. Winton. *Documents from Old Testament Times*. New York: Harper and Row, 1961.
Thompson, Michael E. W. *I Have Heard Your Prayer: The Old Testament and Prayer*. Peterborough, UK: Epworth, 1996.
———. *Isaiah 40–66*. Epworth Commentaries. Peterborough, UK: Epworth, 2001.
———. "The Mission of Jonah." *ExpT* 105 (1993–94) 233–36.
———. "New Life Amid the Alien Corn: The Book of Ruth." *EQ* 65:3 (1993) 197–210.
———. "Prayer, Oracle and Theophany: The Book of Habakkuk." *TynB* 44.1 (1993) 33–53.
———. *Situation and Theology: Old Testament Interpretations of the Syro-Ephraimite War*. Sheffield, UK: Almond, 1982.
———. "Vision, Reality and Worship: Isaiah 33." *ExpT* 113 (2001–2) 327–33.
———. "What Happens When we Pray?: A Contribution from the Old Testament." *ExpT* 114 (2002–2003) 367–72.
———. "Where is the God of Justice?": The Old Testament and Suffering*. Eugene, OR: Pickwick Publications, 2011.
Tiemeyer, Lena-Sofia. *Priestly Rites and Prophetic Rage: Post-Exilic Prophetic Critique of the Priesthood*. FAT 2, Reihe 19. Tübingen: Mohr Siebeck, 2006.
Tomes, Roger. "'Our Holy and Beautiful House': When and Why was 1 Kings 6–8 Written?" *JSOT* 70 (1996) 33–50.
Toorn, Karel van der. *Family Religion in Babylonia, Syria and Israel: Continuity and Change in the Forms of Religious Life*. Leiden: Brill, 1996.
———. *From Her Cradle to Her Grave: The Role of Religion in the Life of the Israelite and the Babylonian Woman*. Biblical Seminar 23. Sheffield, UK: JSOT Press, 1994.
———. "Sun." In *ABD*, 6:237–39.
Toy, Crawford H. *Proverbs*. International Critical Commentary. Edinburgh: T. & T. Clark, 1899.
Trever, John C. "Terebinth." In *IDB*, 4:574.
Underhill, Evelyn. *Worship*. London: Nisbet, 1937.
Vaughan, Patrick H. *The Meaning of 'BAMA' in the Old Testament: A Study of Etymological, Textual and Archaeological Evidence*. Society for Old Testament Study Monograph Series 3. Cambridge: Cambridge University Press, 1974.
Vaux, Roland de. *Ancient Israel: Its Life and Institutions*. Translated by John McHugh. London: Darton, Longman and Todd, 1965.
———. *Studies in Old Testament Sacrifice*. Cardiff, UK: University of Wales Press, 1964.
Vermes, Geza. *The Dead Sea Scrolls in English*. Sheffield, UK: JSOT Press, 1987.

Vos, Clarence J. *Woman in Old Testament Worship*. Delpht: Judels & Brinkman, 1968.
Waltke, Bruce K., James M. Houston, and Erika Moore. *The Psalms as Christian Lament: A Historical Commentary*. Grand Rapids: Eerdmans, 2014.
———. *The Psalms as Christian Worship: A Historical Commentary*. Grand Rapids: Eerdmans, 2010.
Watts, James W. *Ritual and Rhetoric in Leviticus: From Sacrifice to Scripture*. Cambridge: Cambridge University Press, 2007.
Wedbee, J. William. *The Bible and the Comic Vision*. Cambridge: Cambridge University Press, 1988.
Weinfeld, Moshe. "kābôd." In *TDOT*, 7:22–38.
Weiser, Artur. *Psalms*. Translated by Herbert Hartwell. Old Testament Library. London: SCM, 1962.
Wellhausen, Julius. *Prolegomena to the History of Ancient Israel*. Gloucester, MA: Peter Smith, 1973.
Wenham, Gordon J. *Genesis 1–15*. Word Biblical Commentary 1. Waco, TX: Word Books, 1987.
———. *Genesis 16–50*. Word Biblical Commentary 2. Nashville: Thomas Nelson, 1994.
———. *Leviticus*. New International Commentary on the Old Testament. Grand Rapids: Eerdmans, 1979.
———. "The Religion of the Patriarchs." In *Essays on the Patriarchal Narratives*, edited by Alan R. Millard and Donald J. Wiseman, 157–88. Leicester, UK: InterVarsity, 1980.
Werner, Eric. *The Sacred Bridge: The Interdependence of Liturgy and Music in Synagogue and Church during the First Millennium*. New York: Columbia University Press, 1959.
Westermann, Claus. *Genesis 12–36*. Continental Commentary. Translated by John J. Scullion. London: SPCK, 1986.
———. *The Living Psalms*. Translated by J. R. Porter. Edinburgh: T. & T. Clark, 1989.
White, James F. *Introduction to Christian Worship*. Nashville: Abingdon, 1990.
Whybray, R. Norman. *The Making of the Pentateuch: A Methodological Study*. JSOTSup 53. Sheffield, UK: JSOT Press, 1987.
———. *Proverbs*. New Century Bible Commentary. London: Marshall Pickering, 1994.
———. "The Wisdom Psalms." In *Wisdom in Ancient Israel: Essays in honour of J. A. Emerton*, edited by John Day, Robert P. Gordon, and Hugh G. M. Williamson, 152–60. Cambridge: Cambridge University Press, 1995.
———. *Reading the Psalms as a Book*. JSOTSup 222. Sheffield, UK: Sheffield Academic, 1996.
Wildberger, Hans. *Isaiah 28–39*. Translated by Thomas H. Trapp. Continental Commentary. Minneapolis: Fortress, 2002.
Williams, John Tudno. "The Fourth Gospel and Jewish Worship: Guilding's Theory Revisited." In *The Reception of the Hebrew Bible in the Septuagint and the New Testament: Essays in Memory of Aileen Guilding*, edited by David J. A. Clines and J. Cheryl Exum, 126–45. Hebrew Bible Monographs 55. Sheffield, UK: Sheffield Phoenix, 2013.
Williams, Rowan. *The Edge of Words: God and the Habits of Language*. London: Bloomsbury, 2014.
Williamson, Hugh G. M. *Israel in the Books of Chronicles*. Cambridge: Cambridge University Press, 1977.

———. "The Origins of the Twenty-Four Priestly Courses: A Study of 1 Chronicles xxiii–xxvii." In *Studies in the Historical Books of the Old Testament*, edited by J. A. Emerton, 251–68. VTSup 30. Leiden: Brill, 1979.

———. *1 and 2 Chronicles*. New Century Bible Commentary. London: Marshall, Morgan & Scott, 1982.

———. *Ezra, Nehemiah*. Word Biblical Commentary 16. Waco, TX: Word Books, 1985.

———. "Isaiah 63:7—64:11. Exilic Lament or Post-Exilic Protest?" *ZAW* 102 (1990) 48–58.

———. "The Temple in the Books of Chronicles." In *Templum Amicitiae: Essays on the Second Temple presented to Ernst Bammel*, edited by William Horbury, 15–31. JSNTSup 48. Sheffield, UK: Sheffield Academic, 1991.

Willis, John T. "A Reapplied Prophetic Hope Oracle." In *Studies on Prophecy*, 64–76. VTSup 26. Leiden: Brill, 1974.

Willis, Timothy M. "'Eat and Rejoice Before the Lord': The Optimism of Worship in the Deuteronomic Code." In *Worship and the Hebrew Bible: Essays in Honor of John T. Willis*, edited by M. Patrick Graham, Richard R. Marrs, and Steven L. McKenzie, 276–84. JSOTSup 284. Sheffield, UK: Sheffield Academic, 1999.

Wilson, Gerald H. *The Editing of the Hebrew Psalter*. SBL Dissertation Series 76. Chico, CA: Scholars, 1985.

———. "Shaping the Psalter: A Consideration of Editorial Linkage in the Book of Psalms." In *The Shape and Shaping of the Psalter*, edited by J. Clinton McCann, 72–82. JSOTSup 159. Sheffield, UK: JSOT Press, 1993.

Wilson, Ian. "Merely a Container? The Ark in Deuteronomy." In *Temple and Worship in Biblical Israel*, edited by John Day, 212–49. London: T. & T. Clark, 2007.

Wilson, Robert R. *Prophecy and Society in Ancient Israel*. Philadelphia: Fortress, 1984.

Wolff, Hans Walter. *Haggai*. Translated by Margaret Kohl. Continental Commentary. Minneapolis: Augsburg, 1988.

———. *Micah*. Translated by Gary Stansell. Continental Commentary. Minneapolis: Augsburg, 1990.

———. *Obadiah and Jonah*. Translated by Margaret Kohl. Continental Commentary. Minneapolis: Augsburg, 1986.

Woolfenden, Graham. "Eastern Christian Liturgical Traditions: Eastern Orthodox." In *The Blackwell Companion to Eastern Christianity*, edited by Ken Parry, 319–38. Oxford: Wiley-Blackwell, 2010.

Wright, Christopher J. "Jubilee, Year of." In *ABD*, 3:1025–30.

Wright, David P. *The Disposal of Impurity: Elimination Rites in the Bible and in Hittite and Mesopotamian Literature*. SBL Dissertation Series 101. Atlanta: Scholars, 1987.

———. "Unclean and Clean (Old Testament)." In *ABD*, 6:729–42.

Wyatt, Nicolas. "Royal Ritual in Ancient Judah." In *Religious Diversity in Ancient Israel and Judah*, edited by Francesca Stavrakopoulou and John Barton, 61–81. London: T. & T. Clark, 2010.

Zimmerli, Walter. *Ezekiel 2: Chapters 25–48*. Hermeneia Commentary. Translated by James D. Martin. Philadelphia: Fortress, 1983.

Index of Subjects

Aaron, 73
Agricultural festivals. *See* Festivals and feasts
Altars, 8, 22–23, 27–28, 31, 38, 38n27, 99
Anat, 63
Ark of the covenant, 8, 28–30, 32–33, 37, 60, 174, 174n25, 222, 225, 227, 258–59, 280, 284
Asherah, 63, 100
Ashimah of Samaria, 242, 243n6
Astarte, 63
Atonement, 165, 166, 170–75
Azazel, 171–72, 175, 185

Baal, 8, 62, 63, 99
Baal Epic, 63
Bethel, 21–22, 31, 78, 99, 279
Blessing, 195–96
Blood, 173–74
"Branch," 270, 270n74

Child sacrifice. *See* Molech
Christians and worship in the Old Testament, 11, 121, 161–62, 287–88, 294
Circumcision, 50, 67
Creed, creedal, 193
Cult centralization, 101, 218–23, 280, 283–85
Cult, definition of, 14–15
Cultic calendars, 179–89
Cultic prophets. *See* Prophets
Cultic prostitution, 9–10, 250–52

Dan, 31, 76, 78
Day of Atonement, 1–2, 72, 72n4, 83, 166, 170–75, 183–87, 217, 237, 239, 261, 283, 296
Desert sanctuaries, 26–29
Desert tabernacle, 24–25
Deuteronomy and Deuteronomistic History, 218–23
Divination, 87–88

Elephantine, temple at, 47–48
Ephod, 31–32, 50n2, 82, 86
Ezra, 84–86

Fasting, 174, 174n23
Festivals and feasts, 179–89
    Agricultural festivals, 182–87, 217, 261
    Booths, 183–84, 186–87, 217, 261, 271
    Hanukkah, 189
    Passover, 50–51, 181–82, 186, 192, 192n3, 217, 239, 261
    Pilgrimage festivals, 183–84
    Purim, 189

Golden calves, 30–31

High hills and green trees, worship at, 54–55, 62
High Places, worship at, 32–33, 53–54, 62, 99, 100, 101–2
High Priest, 80, 80n16, 270, 292
Home as place of worship, 49–51, 293
Horeb, 23–24

INDEX OF SUBJECTS

Household religion, 66–68
Hymns, 121–45, 149–50, 153, 153n77, 156–57, 159
Incense, 32, 39, 83–84
Incense altar, 27, 39, 99
Irregularities in worship, 61–66

Jachin and Boaz, 36, 36nn21, 22
Jerusalem temple. *See* Temple, Jerusalem
Jubilee year, 188, 188n16

Kedushoth, 1
Kings and worship, 87–88, 89–102, 261–62, 293
    Coronation Psalms, 91–97
    Kings as priests, 97–98
    Kings as religious leaders, 98–102
    Royal Psalms, 91–97

Leaders of worship, 291–94
    Heads of households, 49–51
    Kings, 89
    Levites, 71–88
    Priests, 71–88
Lectionaries, 189–90
Leontopolis, temple at, 47
Levites, 9, 12, 71–88, 263–64, 292
Levitical singers and musicians, 228–29
Liturgy and liturgies,
    Definitions of, 15–16
    Liturgies in Hebrew Bible, 130–31, 154, 191–207, 267

Megiddo, place of worship at, 50, 53
Melchizedek, 21, 21n6, 78, 87–88, 97–98
Mercy seat, 27, 171, 171n18, 172
Molech, 49, 61, 64, 64n17, 99–100, 167–68, 257
Moses, 3, 8, 23–25, 83
Musical instruments and worship, 120, 120n4, 121
Myth, 19, 19n1

Numinous, 3–4, 24

Patriarchal worship, 19–23
People at worship, 59–70

Personal piety and devotion, 68–70
Place of worship, 17–56, 279–82
Prayer, 11, 105–18, 222–23, 265–66
    Formal Prayers, 113–15
    Prayers of confession, 111, 269
    Prayers of lament, 112–13, 255, 265–66, 268
    Prayers of intercession, 8, 108–11, 178, 255
    Prayers of petition, 107–8, 178
    Prayers of thanksgiving, 111
    Prayer in worship, 285
    Vocabulary of Prayer, 106–7
Priests and Levites, 71–87
Priests and priestly concerns, 12–13, 71–88, 164, 263–64, 272–73, 282–83, 291–92
Priestly vestments, 82, 82n20
Priestly writings, 4, 26, 212n4
    Worship in, 211–17
Prophets, Hebrew, and worship, 9–10, 240–75
    Cultic prophets, 199, 201, 240, 240n2, 267, 268
    Prophetic intercession, 108–11, 242, 244–45, 250–52, 255–56, 274
    Prophets and temple, 256–64, 269–70, 274–75
Psalms, book of, 119–61
    Five books of, 122
    First book of, 124–39
    Second book of, 140–45
    Third book of, 145–51
    Fourth book of, 151–54
    Fifth book of, 154–57
    Psalm "clusters" and collections, 122–23
    Psalm types, 121
    Psalms and sacrifice, 160
    Psalms and worship, 157–61, 197–98, 285–87
    Psalms of Confidence, 128–29, 143, 153, 155, 159
    Psalms of Corporate (Communal) Lament, 113, 129, 142, 147–48, 152, 155, 159

Psalms of Individual Lament, 112n23, 124, 129, 135, 140, 149, 153, 159
Psalms of penitence, 141–42
Psalms of prophetic liturgy, 143–44, 149, 153
Psalms of thanksgiving, 135, 135n42, 145, 153, 155, 159
Psalms: Liturgies: 130–31, 154, 159
Psalms, Enthronement, 153, 269
Psalms, Historical, 153
Psalms, Royal psalms, 91–97, 123–24, 142, 151, 153–55
Psalms, Wisdom, 137, 137n44, 146–47, 155, 160
Psalmic hymns, 127, 149, 153, 153n77, 156, 159

Queen of Heaven, 61
Qumran, worship at, 55–56, 161, 189, 287

Ritual in worship, 15, 177–78, 212, 212n5, 215–17, 283

Sabbath, 80, 187–88, 188n15, 217, 261
Sabbatical year, 188
Sacrifices, 11, 31–32, 81–82, 162–78, 219–20, 226, 282–83
   Burnt offerings, 164–68
   Day of Atonement. *See* above.
   Expiatory sacrifices, 168–70
   Grain offering, 175–76
   Intended purpose, 163, 177–78
   Well-Being offering, 175–76
Sakkuth and Kaiwan, 242, 242n5
Sanctuary at Kuntillet 'Ajrud, 47
Saturn, 242
Sea, molten/bronze, 37
Selah, 120–21, 198
Shrines in Canaan, 30–33
Sinai/Horeb, Mount, 3, 23–24
Singing in worship, 121, 226–30
Sun worship, 63–64
Synagogues, 51–53, 189–90, 281, 287
   At Gamla, 51
   At Herodium, 51
   At Masada, 51

Tabernacle, 8, 24–25, 26–27, 28, 212, 213, 214, 215, 258
   see also, Desert tabernacle
Tammuz, 61, 61n3
Temples, 33–48
Temple, Jerusalem, 9, 24–29, 33–47, 63, 212, 213, 215, 220, 223–25, 227, 288
   Building and layout of, 34–39
   Destruction of, 44–45
   Ezekiel's temple, 256–64, 272–73
   In Isaiah book, 245–50
   Place of pilgrimage, 42–43, 59–60
   Purpose of, 39–42, 280–81, 281n4, 282, 285
   Temple vessels, 44–45, 225, 227–28, 254
   Worship in, 60, 153, 156–57, 161
   Zerubbabel's temple, 45–47, 280
Temples at Dan and Bethel, 43–44, 62
   at Leontopolis and Elephantine, 47–48
Temple at Shechem, 30
   at Shiloh, 30, 30n8, 32, 60, 76
Tent and Tent of Meeting, 8, 25, 27, 28, 116, 213–25, 225, 227, 280
Teraphim, 31, 32, 32n13, 49–50
Terebinth, 32, 32n14
Tiglath-pileser, 38

Ugarit, and worship at, 63–64, 90, 105
Unleavened bread, festival of, 181–84
Urim and Thummim, 86, 86n30, 87

Wisdom Literature, worship in, 231–39
Women in Israelite cultus, 68
Worship, 2–6, 294–96
   Of Canaanites, 53–55, 62–65, 234, 252–53, 254–55, 256–57, 269, 272, 285, 290
   Centrality and prevalence of in Hebrew Bible, 6–11
   Definition of, 2–3
   Historical development of, 12
   In Amos, 10, 242–45
   In Chronicles, 223–31, 287–88
   In Daniel, 11, 67

Worship *(continued)*
   In Deuteronomic literature, 29,
      195–96, 218–23
   In Ecclesiastes (Qoheleth), 232–33
   In Exodus, 7–8, 23–25, 192–93
   In Ezekiel, 4, 9, 256–64
   In Ezra, 11, 85–86
   In Genesis, 7, 19–23
   In Habakkuk, 10, 200–201, 268
   In Haggai, 10, 269–70
   In Hosea, 250–52
   In Isaiah, 9, 201–5, 245–50
   In Jeremiah, 9, 253–56
   In Job, 10, 234–35
   In Joel, 10, 200, 264–65
   In Jonah, 266–67
   In Joshua, 8
   In Judges, 8–9
   In Kings. *See above*, in
      Deuteronomic literature
   In Lamentations, 200
   Language of, 4–6
   In Leviticus, 71–74, 162–78
   In Malachi, 10, 270–71
   In Micah, 10, 252–53
   In Nahum, 10, 199, 267
   In Nehemiah, 11, 85–86
   In Numbers, 73–74, 195
   In Obadiah, 206, 265–66
   In priestly writings, 162–78, 211–17
   In Psalms, 10, 70, 119–61, 197–98,
      206–7, 235–36, 285–88
   In Proverbs, 233–34
   In Ruth, 11, 110, 110n18
   In Samuel. *See above*, in
      Deuteronomic literature
   In Sirach (Ecclesiasticus), 237–38
   In Song of Songs, 205–6
   In Wisdom Literature, 231–39
   In Wisdom of Solomon, 236
   In Zechariah 1–8, 10, 205, 270
   In Zechariah 9–14, 270–71
   In Zephaniah, 10, 268–69
   Language (vocabulary) of, 3–6
   Silence in, 295, 295n22
   Unrighteous living, and, 65–66,
      241–42, 243–46, 252–55,
      255n30, 272
Worship Types/styles in Hebrew Bible,
   Centred on sacred documents, 52,
      84–87, 289–90
   Chronicler's, 223–31, 287–8
   Deuteronomic, 218–23, 283–85
   Expression of awe and praise, 289,
      290–91
   At high places and under green
      trees, 53–55, 62, 99, 101–2
   In homes, 49–51, 290
   Multiplicity of worship styles,
      282–91
   Priestly approach, 71–88, 162–78,
      282–83
   Psalmic, 119–61, 285–88

Zadok, 73, 77–79, 81, 260, 263

Index of Authors

Aagerson, James W., 190n23
Abba, Raymond, 75n8
Ackerman, Susan, 55n17, 61nn2, 3, 62nn5, 6, 10, 66, 66nn22, 23, 67nn25, 28, 251n22, 255n30, 256n35
Ackroyd, Peter R., 44–46, 45n41, 46n44, 224n38
Aharoni, Yahanan, 22n12
Albertz, Rainer, 49, 49n1, 50, 50nn2, 5, 6, 60n1, 66, 66n22, 69n32
Albright, William F., 62n7
Alexander, Philip S., 168n9
Allen, Leslie C., 61, 61n2, 95n12, 194n8, 254n28, 255n33, 262, 262n47
Alter, Robert, 130n27
Amos, Clare, 180n2
Andersen, Francis I., 62n9, 64n17
Anderson, Arnold A., 131, 131nn29, 32, 136n43, 139n50, 142n52, 150, 150n72
Anderson, George W., 69n32, 125n16
Ap-Thomas, Dafydd R., 106n5, 107n10
Astour, Michael C., 87n32
Augustine, Saint, 178n33
Auffret, Pierre, 124n14

Balentine, Samuel E., 216n13, 217, 217nn14, 15, 18
Barkay, Gabriel, 195n10
Barker, Margaret, 27n2, 28nn4, 5, 120n4, 294n20
Barrett, C. Kingsley, 175n26
Barrick, W. Boyd, 33n16, 53n12
Bartlett, John R., 78n12, 80n16, 265n56
Barton, John, 264n53, 265, 265n54
Beckwith, Roger T., 270n71
Bernhardt, Karl-Heinz, 64n14

Binder, Donald D., 51n8, 52n9, 188n15
Bird, Phyllis, 68, 68nn29, 30
Blenkinsopp, Joseph, 42n36, 53n10, 61n4, 71n1, 81, 82n19, 84n25, 85n26, 180n3, 192n2, 202, 202n25, 204n32, 245n14, 249nn20, 21, 263n50, 294, 294nn19, 20
Block, Daniel I., 257n38, 260n41
Boccaccini, Gabriele, 80n16
Boda, Mark J., 111n22
Bodel, John, 66, 66n21
Bokser, Baruch, 181n4
Boström, G., 234
Boyce, Richard Nelson, 116n30
Bracke, John M., 270n74
Brady, Christian M. M., 64n15
Braulik, Georg, 55n17, 218n22
Braun, Joachim, 120n4
Braun, Roddy L., 224n40
Broyles, Craig C., 125n16
Brown, William P., 11, 70, 70n33, 122nn9, 127n19, 129n24, 135n42, 137n44, 158n82, 160n85, 287, 287n9
Bruce, F. F., 288n11
Brueggemann, Walter, 146n66, 159n84, 279, 279n1, 296n23
Budd, Philip J., 166n6, 169n10, 186n11
Bultmann, Christoph, 219n23
Bunce, James W., 190n25
Burnett, Joel, 61n3
Burney C. F., 36n23, 180n3

Callaway, Phillip R., 56n19
Carroll, Robert P., 254n28
Carter, J., 163n1, 176n28, 177n31
Childs, Brevard S., 42n36, 192n3

INDEX OF AUTHORS

Christensen, Duane L., 267n63
Clements, Ronald E., 6, 6n15, 27n2, 131n28, 218, 218n20, 219n23, 220, 220n25, 245n13, 248n18, 263n49, 295n21
Clifford, Richard J., 151n73
Clines, David J. A., 46n45, 84n24, 186n13, 234n71
Coats, George W., 168n9
Cody, Aelred, 71, 71n1
Coggins, Richard J., 28, 28n5, 193n4, 199, 199n18, 267n61
Corley, Jeremy, 247n17
Corney, Richard W., 270n74
Craigie, Peter C., 125, 126n17, 135n41, 136n43, 144n60
Crenshaw, James L., 243, 243nn7, 8
Cross, Frank Moore, 78n12, 221n28
Curtis, Adrian H. W., 63n13, 134, 134n39, 135n41, 138n48, 139n50

Danby, Herbert, 175n26
Darr, Katheryn Pfisterer, 257n38
Davidson, Robert, 237n76
Davies, Eryl W., 54, 54n13, 186, 186nn11, 12, 195n10
Davies, G. Henton, 27n2, 32n12, 33n16
Davies, Graham I., 3n5, 8n18, 212n3, 251n24
Davies, J. G., 14, 14n31
Day, John, 28n6, 30n8, 43n37, 55n17, 62n7, 63n13, 64nn15, 17, 91n5, 111n21, 123n12, 127n19, 129nn23, 24, 130n26, 135n42, 137n44, 168n9, 174n25, 189, 189n18
DeClaissé-Walford, Nancy L., 122n9
Dell, Katharine J., 120n4, 232, 232n62
Dentan, Robert C., 193n6
DeVries, LaMoine F., 36n22
Dijkstra, Meindert, 242n5
Dillard, Raymond B., 228n50
Douglas, Mary, 42, 163n1, 177, 177n31
Dozeman, Thomas B., 86n30
Driver, Samuel R., 55n16
Durham, John R., 27n2, 182n7, 192nn2, 3, 193n6

Eaton, John H., 91n6, 121n7, 122n8, 189n17, 240n2
Eddinger, Terry W., 32nn12, 13
Edelman, Diana, 53n12, 100n19
Eisenman, Robert, 56n19
Emerton, John A., 3n5, 75n9, 87n32
Endres, John C., 226, 226n46, 227, 227nn48, 49
Evans-Pritchard, E. E., 177, 177n31
Exum, J. Cheryl, 206n36

Finkelstein, I., 100n19
Fishbane, Michael, 261n45
Frazer, J. G., 172n19
Freedman, David N., 192n3
Fretheim, Terence E., 214–5, 215n10
Friedman, Richard Elliott, 27n2
Fuhs, F. H., 3nn7, 8, 232nn63, 64
Fulcro, William J., 243n6

Garrett, Duane, 206n36
Gerstenberger, Erhard S., 169n10, 172n19, 173n21, 185n10
Gese, H., 228n51
Gillingham, Susan, 56n19, 91n5, 121nn5, 6, 7, 122n11, 123n12, 124n14, 125n16, 127n19, 129nn23, 24, 130n26, 133n37, 135n42, 137n44, 143n58, 154n78, 197n15
Goldingay, John, 119n3, 159n83, 203–4, 204n30
Gordon, Cyrus H., 32n13
Gordon, Robert P., 77n11
Gorman, Frank H., 15n33, 181n4, 215n11, 217nn14, 18
Gottwald, Norman K., 200n20
Good, E. M., 266n60
Goulder, Michael D., 204–5, 205n33
Gowan, Donald E., 193n4
Grabbe, Lester L., 42n36, 45n42, 47nn47, 49, 72, 72n3, 75, 75n9, 80n17, 164n2, 169, 169n12, 170n13, 176, 176n30, 236n74
Grant, Jamie A., 91n5
Gray, John, 242n5, 243n6
Greenberg, Moshe, 105, 105n3, 257n38
Grisbrooke, W. Jardine, 84, 84n23

INDEX OF AUTHORS

Guilding, Aileen, 190nn22, 25
Gunkel, H., 91, 121, 122, 194n8, 202, 202n26

Haak, Robert D., 38n27
Haldar, A., 199, 199n17
Halpern, B., 205n35
Handy, Lowell K., 61n3
Haran, Menahem, 25n18, 32n12, 33n16, 38n27, 39n30, 44n39, 82n20, 100n19
Hartley, John E., 42n36, 73n5, 165n5, 166n6, 169, 169n11, 171n18, 173n22
Hasel, Gerhard F., 188n15
Haupt, Paul, 199, 199n17
Hayward, C. T. Robert, 47nn47, 48
Heider, G. C., 64n17, 168n9
Heiler, Friedrich, 105, 105n1
Herbert, Arthur S., 3, 3n6, 5, 5n11, 14
Hieke, Thomas, 172n19, 175n26, 185n10
Holbert, J. C., 266n60
Holladay, William L., 55n16, 56n19, 121nn5, 6, 133n37, 197n15, 254n28
Hossfeld, Frank-Lothar, 94n8, 95n9, 142nn52, 53, 54, 144nn61, 62, 63; 145n64, 150, 150n70, 152n75
Houston, Walter, 8, 8n17, 27n2
Humbert, Paul, 267n63
Hundley, Michael B., 216n13
Hutchinson, James Hely, 127n19
Hyatt, J. Philip, 192nn2, 3, 193n5

Jakobovits, Immanuel, R., 287n9
Japhet, Sara, 37n24, 225n43, 229n52, 230nn54, 55
Jarick, John, 225, 225nn42, 44
Jenson, Philip P., 42n36, 83n20, 84n23, 164n2, 182n6, 259n40
Johnson, Aubrey R., 94n8, 133n36, 240, 240n1
Johnston, Philip S., 125n16, 129n24
Jones, Clifford M., 35n17
Jones, Gwilym H., 37n25, 38n28, 90n3, 221n28, 224n38

Josephus, Flavius, 46n46, 47n48, 189
Joyce, Paul M., 174n24, 256n34, 257n37, 259n39, 260, 260nn42, 44, 263, 264n51

Kapelrud, Arvid S., 244n10
Kasher, R., 261n45
Kellermann, D., 214n9
Kierkegaard, Søren, 168n9
Kirkpatrick, A. F., 133n35
Kleinig, John W., 226n47, 227n49, 228n50, 229nn52, 53
Knauth, Robin J. DeWitt, 188n16
Knibb, Michael A., 55, 55n18, 288n11
Kraus, Hans-Joachim, 12n27, 94n7, 95nn10, 11, 122n8, 126, 126n18, 128n22, 136n43, 138n49, 139n50, 142n55, 182n6, 189,

Lamb, John A., 121n6, 287n9
Larkin, Katrina J. A., 205n34, 270n73
Levenson, Jon D., 64n17, 114n27, 168n9, 261nn45, 46, 264, 264n52
Lim, Timothy H., 56n19
Lowery, Richard H., 100n19, 101n20
Luther, Martin, 156

MacCulloch, Diarmaid, 295n22
Macintosh, A. A., 62, 62n11, 251, 251nn23, 24
Maher, Michael, 121n6, 287n9
Martin, James D., 233n66
Mason, Rex, 205n35, 265, 265n55, 267n61, 269n68
Mauchline, John, 77n11
Mayes, Andrew D. H., 218n21, 219n23, 221nn28, 30, 31, 32
Mays, James L., 43n37, 128n21, 134n40, 138n47, 195n9, 253n26
McCann, J. Clinton, Jr, 122n9
McConville, J. Gordon, 219n23, 221n30, 260n44
McKane, William, 20n4, 194n8, 234, 234n69, 254n28
McKay, Heather A., 188n15
McMillion, Philip, 76n10
Meier, Samuel A., 242n5

Méndez-Montoya, Angel F., 176n29
Meyers, Carol, 32n12, 35nn17, 20, 36n22, 50n3, 51, 66, 66n22, 67nn25, 28
Milgrom, Jacob, 166n6, 171n16, 173n22, 217, 217n17
Miller, Patrick D., 66n22, 68, 68n29, 89n1, 105, 105nn2, 4, 115n29, 117, 117n32, 118n35, 196n11
Mitchell, David C., 5n14, 120n4
Moberly, R. Walter L., 19n2, 21n7, 193n6
Morris, Leon, 190n25
Moore, Megan Bishop, 32n14
Mowinckel, Sigmund, 4n9, 14n31, 121, 150n71, 189, 189n17, 240, 240n1
Muddiman, John, 174n23
Muilenburg, James, 192n2, 203, 203n29, 248n19
Murphy, Roland, 232, 232n65
Murray, Robert, 202n26, 240n2

Nakhai, Beth Alpert, 33n16, 38n27, 53n12
Nelson, Richard D., 35, 35n19, 196n13, 218nn20, 21, 219n24, 221n28
Nicholson, Ernest W., 211n2
Niditch, Susan, 33n15, 50n3, 76n10, 257n38
Nielsen, Kjeld, 83, 83n21, 84n22
Noort, Ed, 168n9
Noth, Martin, 169n10, 192n3, 220, 220n27, 222nn33, 34, 223n35

Olyan, Saul M., 66, 66n21, 67n28
Otto, Rudolph, 1, 1n1, 3, 4, 4n9, 24, 24n16
Otzen, Benedikt, 5n11

Pajunem, Mika S., 121n6
Parrinder, Geoffrey, 172n19
Parry, Robin A., 200n21, 266n58
Pentiuc, Eugen J., 287n9
Perdue, Leo G., 232n65, 234, 234n69, 235n72, 236n75, 237n76, 238n77, 239n78
Petersen, David L., 271n76

Pfeiffer, R. H., 3
Pope, Marvin H., 206n36
Porten, Bezalel, 47n50
Porteous, Norman W., 244n9
Porter J. Roy, 190n25, 191n1
Preuss, Horst Dietrich, 40n32, 217n19
Procksch, Otto, 203n29
Provan, Iain, 200n21, 266n58

Quellette, J., 35n17

Rad, Gerhard von, 25n18, 89, 90n2, 168n9, 196n12, 230, 230n56, 231, 231n58
Rambo, Lewis R., 15n32
Ramsey, George W., 78n12
Rehm, Merlin D., 78n12
Reumann, John, 190n24
Richardson, Peter, 47n47
Riley, William, 224, 224n39
Ringgren, Helmer, 5n13
Rofé, A., 219n23
Rogerson, John W., 19n1, 120n4, 271n78
Römer, Thomas, 221n28
Rooke, Deborah W., 80n16, 88, 88n33, 97n15, 261n45
Rowley, H. H., 12n27, 25n18, 47n50, 66n18, 131n30, 139n50, 168n9, 188n15, 206n36, 240n2, 244n10
Rylaarsdam, J. C., 181n4

Salters, Robert B., 266n58
Sanders, E. P., 47nn47, 49
Sansom, M. C., 166nn6, 7
Sawyer, John F. A., 106n5
Scharbert, Joseph, 5n14
Schley, Donald G., 78n12
Schofield, John N., 50n4
Schramm, Brooks, 12n27
Schunk, K.-D., 53n12
Shafer, B. E., 188n15
Simpson, William W., 287n9
Skehen, Patrick W., 175n26, 237n76
Sklar, Jay, 42n36
Smith, Mark S., 64n16
Smith, Ralph L., 269n68, 270n72
Smith, W. Robertson, 176, 176n28

INDEX OF AUTHORS

Smith-Christopher, Daniel L., 174n23
Snaith, John G., 206n36, 237n76
Snaith, Norman H., 169n12, 171n16, 244n9
Soggin, J. Alberto, 50n3
Spencer, John R., 75, 75n8
Spinks, Bryan, 287n9
Stern, Sacha, 189n19
Sweeney, Marvin A., 37n26

Talstrar, Eep, 113n25
Tate, Marvin E., 144n63, 149n69, 150, 150n72, 152n75
Taylor, J. Glen, 64nn15, 16
Thelle, Rannfrid Irene, 40n31, 62n11
Thomas, D. Winton, 63n12
Thompson, Michael E. W., 11n24, 110nn18, 19, 113nn24, 25, 114n26, 115nn28, 29, 117nn31, 33, 123n13, 125n16, 131nn28, 31, 137n45, 138n46, 143n57, 147n67, 200n22, 201n23, 202n27, 230n57, 234n70, 236n73, 241n3, 245n12, 247n16, 255n32, 260n43, 266n59, 268nn65, 66
Tiemeyer, Lena-Sophia, 249n21, 269n70
Tomes, Roger, 35n18, 114n27
Toorn, Karel van der, 64n15, 66n22, 68n29
Toy, C. H., 233, 233n67
Trever, John C., 32n14
Tyndale, William, 172

Underhill, Evelyn, 2, 2nn3, 4, 294, 294n20

Vaughan, Patrick H., 33n16, 53n12
Vaux, Roland de, 22n11, 53n11, 78n12, 80n16, 86n28, 89n1, 90n2, 168n9, 169n12, 174n23, 186n11, 187n14, 188n15

Vermes, Geza, 56n19
Vos, Clarence J., 68n29

Waltke, Bruce K., 197n15
Watts, James W., 163n1, 164n4, 216n13, 243n7
Weinfeld, Moshe, 4n10
Weiser, Artur, 189
Wellhausen, Julius, 211n2, 212, 223–24, 224n38, 225–26
Wenham, Gordon J., 20, 20n5, 21n7, 22nn9, 10, 73n5, 87n32, 168n9, 180n2
Werner, Eric, 190n24
Westermann, Claus, 22n9, 87n32, 91n5, 125n16, 129n24, 133n37, 158, 158n82, 168n9
White, James F., 178n33
Whybray, R. Norman, 122n9, 137n44, 144n60, 158n82, 212n2, 234n68
Wildberger, Hans, 246n15
Williams, John Tudno, 190n25
Williams, Rowan, 165n5, 281n4
Williamson, Hugh G. M., 37n24, 46n45, 53n10, 80n17, 84nn24, 25, 204, 204n32, 223n37, 225nn41, 43, 44, 228nn50, 51, 231, 231n60
Willis, John T., 194n8
Willis, Timothy M., 218n22
Wilson Gerald H., 122, 122n9, 157, 157n81
Wilson, Ian, 29n7
Wilson, Robert R., 240, 240n2, 269n67
Wolff, Hans Walter, 194n8, 195n9, 265, 265n56, 269n70
Woolfenden, Graham, 287n9
Wright, Christopher J., 188n16
Wright David P., 172n19
Wyatt, Nicolas, 90, 90n4, 97n15

Zimmerli, Walter, 257n38, 262n48

Index of Biblical References

Old Testament/Hebrew Bible

Genesis

1:1—2:4a	179, 294n20
1:1—2:3	28
1—11	19
1	212
2:2–3	180, 212
4:3–5	175
4:13–14	7
4:26	20
6—9	42
6:5	42
7—9	7
8:20	7, 167
8:20–21	22, 38
8:21	42
9:4	212
12:6–7	30
12:7–8	38
12:8	23
12—50	19, 20–23, 49, 88, 279
12—36	7
12:6	32
12:8	20, 22
13:3—4, 18	67
13:4	20, 22, 23, 38
13:18	31, 32
14:1–24	31
14:13	32
14:18–20	88, 97
14:18	31, 78
14:19–20	87
17:9–14	212
17:22–27	67, 212
18:1	32
18:23–33	22, 110
20:7	242
20:27	22
21:33	20, 22
22:1–19	23, 38, 49, 64, 167–68, 225
23:8	106
24:1–67	108, 108n14, 111
25:21	67
26:23–25	31
26:25	20, 23, 38, 67
28:10–22	21, 22, 23, 31, 78, 246, 279, 289
31:19–54	22, 31, 32, 49
32:29–31	22
33:19–20	38, 67
35:1, 7	38, 67
37—50	7, 115
43:11	175
43:14	115
45:5, 8	7, 21
48:15–20	115
50:10	67
50:20	7, 21

Exodus

1:1—18:27	23
3:1–15	23–24
3:1–6	3, 4, 14, 246, 289
3:1	23
3:6	3, 247
3:7–22	247
3:14–15	20
5:1–31	8
6:3	20

Exodus (continued)

8:8	106
12:1—13:22	179, 181, 290
12	51
12:16	188
13:2, 12–13, 15	64
15:1–21	7, 8, 191
15:1	120
15:11	192
15:20–21	8, 68, 120, 192
16:25–30	212
17:6	23
17:15–16	38
19:1—24:18	23
20:2–7	182
20:8–11	188
20:24	51
23:9–12	188
23:12–19	179, 182, 183, 187
25:1—40:38	23, 24, 25, 26, 170
25:1—39:43	86
25:1—31:18	28, 71, 212, 257, 258
25:1—30:38	164
25:1—27:20	27
25:1–40	27
25:3–7	27
25:17–22	29
25:8	27, 213
25:10–16	28
25:31–40	27
26:1–6	27
26:7–14	27
26:31	225
28:6–12	82
28:15–35	32, 86
28:36–42	82
29:38–42	82
30:1–38	83
30:1–10	83
30:7–8	83
30:18–19	37
31:12–17	188
32:1–35	31, 62
32:11–14, 31–34	108, 114, 106, 108n16
32:11	106, 108n16
32:11–14	110, 114n26, 117, 241
32:18–19	120
32:20–21	120
32:30–34	241
32:31–32	110
33:6	23
33:7–11	25, 27, 116, 280
34:6–7	118, 192–93, 199
34:10–28	182
34:18–26	179, 182, 183, 187
35:1—40:38	27, 28, 212
35:10–19	27
35:27	32
36:35	225
38:8	68
39:1–26	32
39:2–7	82
39:27–31	82
39:28	82
39:43	28
40:9–13	21
40:19–32	216
40:33	180
40:34–38	282
40:34	213

Leviticus

1—16	163
1—7	82, 164, 292
1—3	170
1	164, 165, 167
1:3–9	165
1:5–9	167
1:14–17	72
1:4	165
1:5	72, 82
1:9, 13, 17	165
1:12	72
2	175
2:1-3	176
3	175, 176
3:2, 8, 13	72, 82
3:3, 5, 11, 16	176
3:17	173
4—7	170

4:1—5:13	167, 168, 170
4:2, 13, 22, 27	168
4:6–34	72
4:24–33	82
5:1–13	169
5:14–18	168
5:14–16	169
6—7	73
6:12–13	72
7:1–6	168, 169
7:11–21	72
7:11	173
7:14, 30	72
7:26	173
7:31, 32	73n5
7:38	164
8—10	170, 216
8:1–36	216
8:8	86n30
8:10–12	21
9	217
9:22	196
10:1	83
10:10	213
11—15	41, 170
11—13	72
11:24–40	67
12:2–8	67
12:3	67
12:6–7	68
14	217
14:34–53	67
15:1–33	67
15:28	72
16	72, 165, 170–75, 173n21, 184–85, 217
16:2	83
16:12–13	72, 83
16:12	72
16:21	166
16:29	174
16:32	72
16:34	1–2
17:11, 14	82
17:11	174
17:12	173
18:21	64, 168
19:9–10	188
20:2–5	64, 168
21:5	67n27
21:10	74
23	179, 183, 217
23:22	188
23:23–32	185
23:27–32	174
23:33–43	183
24:8	72
25:1–7, 20–22	188
25:1	164
25:8–17	188
25:9	174
25:19–22	188
25:32–33	73, 292
26:46	164
27:8, 12, 18	72
27:16–24	188
27:34	164

Numbers

1:48–54	74
1:53	74
3:1–13	74
3:38	74
4:1–49	74
6:2	68
6:22–27	195–96
7:1	21
7:87–88	230
8:14–19	74
9:25–29	241
11:16–30	25, 280
12:1–16	25, 280
14:4	194
14:18	118n34, 194
16:1–11	74
18:1–32	74
19:1–22	67
27:12–23	86
27:18–21	74
28—29	179, 186–87, 217
28:2–8	187
28:11–15	67
29:7–11	174

Numbers (continued)

30:3-15	68, 174
31:6	74
31:25-31	74
33:52	53
34:1-12	263
35:25-32	74
36:4	188

Deuteronomy

4:9-24	220
4:9	64
4:12	220
4:19	64, 220
4:27-31	218
6:4-9	69
6:5-6	284
6:6-9	50
7:1-5, 25-26	101
8:10	5
9:8-21	31
9:9-10	174
9:25-29	114n26, 241
10:1-5	29, 220, 222, 284
10:8-9	75
10:8	29n7
10:9	74
10:19	263
11:30	32
12:2-32	218
12:2-4, 29-31	101
12:2-4	101, 218, 284
12:2-3	219
12:5, 11, 21	220
12:5-14	101, 218
12:5, 11, 14, 21	40
12:5-14	101
12:5-7	284
12:7	219, 285
12:11-21	223
12:11-12	218
12:11	29
12:12	74
12:12, 18-19	74
12:13-19	219, 284
12:14, 18	223
12:29-31	101
13:1-8	101
14:1	67n27
14:22-27	101, 219, 285
14:23-24	29, 220
14:24-26	101
14:27-29	74
15:1-3, 12-15	188
16:1-22	68, 184
16:1-17	179, 183, 217, 220
16:1-8	181
16:1-7	101
16:2, 6, 11	29, 220
16:6	220
16:11-14	74
16:16	43
16:21—17:1	101
17:2-7	101
17:3	64
17:9, 18	74
17:8-13	75
17:12	75
17:14-20	101
18:1-2	74
18:6-8	75
18:6-7	74
18:15-18	241
18:9-14	101
19:17	75
21:5	75, 196
24:8	74
24:19-20	188
26:1-19	219
26:1-15	196
26:2	29, 220
26:3-4	75
26:11-12	74
26:11	219
26:14	68
27:9	74
28:36-37	218
29:10-11	68
29:27	218
30:1-20	218
31:9-13, 24-26	75, 84
31:10-12	190
31:26	220, 284

33:1–29	83	20:26	8
33:8–11	75, 84, 86	20:27	22
34:10	241	21:19, 21	68

Joshua

Ruth

5:10–12	181	1:6–18	110
6:26	64	1:8–9	110
7:5–9	129	1:9	107
8:30–35	75	1:16	106
9:27	221	2:1–17	110
10:1	78	2:1–7	188
13:14	75	2:12	107, 110
21:1–45	75	2:20	68
21:1–2	76	3:6–15	110
		3:10	107, 110
		4:1–12	110
		4:10	110
		4:11–12	107, 110
		4:14	68

Judges

1 Samuel

2:5	8	1:1–28	60
2:13	8	1:1–20	67
3:7	8	1:1–13	76
3:15	8	1:3	68
4:4	68	1:10–16	68
5:1	68	1:11, 24–28	68
5:2	5	2:1–11	60
6:1—8:32	221	2:18	32
6:6	8	2:27–36	32, 176, 221
6:18	176	2:28	32
6:24	8, 38	3:1–21	30
6:25	63	3:1–3	30
6:28–32	8	3:11–14	221
7:15	8	4:3–7	30
8:27	32, 86, 221	4:5–11	220
9:4, 27, 46	30	6:14	167
10:6	221	6:15	76
11:31	67	7:3	241
11:34–40	64	7:5–17	31
13:2–24	67	7:5–9	110
13:16	8	7:5	241
13:19–23	51, 67	7:6	129
13:19	176	7:8	241
17—18	9, 31, 66, 76, 78, 86	7:9–10	241
17:4–5	33, 67		
17:5	32		
17:7–13	50, 76		
18:14, 17, 20	32		
20:23, 26	129		

1 Samuel (continued)

7:9	167
7:13–17	77
7:17	241
8:1–22	77
8:6, 21	241
9:3–20	77
9:12	53
10:1	77
10:5	240
10:8	241
11:14–15	31
12:17–23	110–11
12:19	241
13	77
13:9–10	97
14:3	32
15	77
15:23	32
18:6–7	120
19:13, 16	32
22:18	32
22:20	77
23:6, 9	32
28:8–19	68
29:5	120
30:7	32

2 Samuel

1:11–12	67
3:31	67
5:7–11	33
6:1–19	30
6:5	60
6:13, 17–18	97
6:14	32
6:17	33, 167
7	221
7:1–7	33
7:2–3	97
7:12–13, 22–24	222
8:17–18	77, 97
15:24–37	78
15:24	76
20:25	97
23:1	120
24:10	111
24:25	38, 97

1 Kings

1:38–39	89
2:26–27	97
2:35	78
3:4–5	97
4:2	78, 97
4:21	175
5:1—8:61	34
5:1—8:66	97
5:1–12	34
5:11	34
6:1—8:61	35n18
6:1–38	34
6:1	180
6:2	40, 225
6:3	35
6:4–6	35
6:5–10	258
6:16	36
6:18	36
6:19	37
6:20–22	38
6:31–32	37, 225
6:38	39
7:1–51	227
7:1	39
7:2–8	39
7:2	40
7:9–12	39
7:15–22	36
7:23–26	37
7:27–50	37
7:38–39	37
7:40–47	37
7:47	38
7:48–50	36
8:1–61	70
8:1–53	222, 285
8:1–11	229
8:1–9	30
8:1–2	60
8:5	41

8:5, 62–64	97
8:9	23, 42
8:9, 21	222, 285
8:10–11	228
8:11	259
8:12–61	214
8:13	40
8:14–53	113
8:16	223, 285
8:22–53	41, 114–15
8:22	38
8:27	40
8:54	38
8:62–64	38, 41, 113, 214, 222
8:64	167
9:25	97
11:7	53, 64, 168
11:36	223, 285
12:1–24	78
12:1–11	43
12:25–33	279
12:25–31	54
12:25–29	78
12:26–33	97
12:28–30	62
12:28–29	30
12:28	43
12:29–33	44
12:31	78
12:33—13:2	99
12:33	78, 97
13:1–6	78
13:1–2	97
14:2–5	68
14:21	223, 285
14:23–24	101
14:23	54n15, 161
15:12–16	101
15:14	54n15, 161, 219
16:26	98
16:29–34	99, 241
17:17–24	67
18:20–40	241
18:29, 36	176
19:8	23, 24
19:9b–18	3
19:11–18	246
19:11–13	247, 289
19:15–21	247
21:1–24	241
21:20–21a	242
21:27	174
22:10–12	240
22:41–50	101
22:43	54n15, 161, 219

2 Kings

3:2	176
3:20	176
3:27	167
4:22–23	68
4:23	188
4:32–37	67
6:15–20	117
10:29	44
11:11	90
11:12	89–90
12:3	54n15, 219
12:10	74
14:4	54n15, 219
15:3–4	99
15:4, 35	54n15, 219
16:3	64, 168
16:3b–4	99
16:4	54n15, 219
16:10–18	99–100
16:10–15	38
16:12–15	97
16:15	176
16:17	37
16:29–34	99
17:9, 11, 29, 32	54n15
17:11, 32	219
17:17	167, 168
17:30	242
18:1—20:21	100
18:4–8	222, 285
20:1–7	109
20:1–3	67
20:7	67
21:1–18	100
21:3	219
21:3–5	100

2 Kings (continued)

21:3, 5	64
21:6	168
21:7	223, 285
22:1—23:30	100
22:4, 8	74
22:8–13	190
23:1–3	190
23:3	60
23:4–24	222, 285
23:5	54
23:8–9	223, 285
23:8	31
23:9	82
23:10	64, 168
23:15–20	44
23:24	32
23:27	223, 285
24:13	44
25:1, 3–4, 8–9	266
25:8–17	249
25:13–17	44
25:13	37
25:14–15	44

1 Chronicles

6:3–8	77
6:31–47	228
6:31	227n49
6:49	226, 288
12:23–40	227
13:8	228
15:6—16:6	228
15:16	227, 228, 288
16—17	226
16:8–36	226, 288
16:34, 41	229
16:41	226, 227n49, 288
18:8	37
21—22	80
21:26—22:1	224
22—29	97
23—26	80
23:4–5, 30–31	227n49
23:5	228
24:1–31	80–81
25:1–31	81, 228
25:1	227n49, 228
25:6	81
26:1–32	81
28:9–19	225
28:18	39
29:17	227
22:20	5

2 Chronicles

2:1—8:16	34
2:4	39
2:6	226, 288
3:1	225
3:3–5	225
3:8–14	225
3:15	36n21
4:1	259
5:1–14	226
5:2—7:11	227
5:4–5	225
5:5	227
5:10	23
5:11–14	227, 228, 229
5:13	226, 228, 288
6:1—7:22	226
6:1–42	70
6:3–42	113
6:12–42	114
6:21–39	225
6:41–42	226, 288
7:1–22	226
7:3, 6	226, 229, 288
7:4–5	113
7:4	60
7:10	227
7:12	226, 288
8:13	188
8:14	227n49
11:15	101
13:11	39
14:3–5	100
15:2–7	230
15:8–17	101
16:7–9	230

17:6	101	6:5	44
19:6–7	230	6:15	45
20:1–37	226	7:1—10:43	84n24
20:3–12	129	7:1–28	85
20:19	228	7:11–21	79
20:15–17	230	7:12	79
20:20	230	7:19	44
20:21	226, 229, 288	8:21–23	174
23:18	227n49	8:26–28	44
26:1–23	99	8:33–34	44
26:16, 19	39	9:1—10:44	79
29:1—30:27	226	9:1–15	114
29:1–36	229	9:6–15	204, 250
29:7	39	10:1–44	85
29:20–35	227, 229	10:1	68
29:21–24	226	10:10, 16	79
29:25–29	228		
29:25–30	230, 288	## Nehemiah	
29:25	227n49		
29:31–36	230	1:1—13:31	223n36, 260
30:26	227	3:1	74
30:27	196	4:7, 9	110
31:2–4	57	5:19	108
31:3	188	6:14	108
32:7–8a	230	7:39–60	79
33:1–20	100	7:65	86n30
33:2–9	100	7:72–73	79
33:10–17	100	7:73b—8:18	70
33:17	53, 101–2	8:1—10:39	84n24
34:1—35:27	100	8:1–18	84, 85, 190, 290
35:15	227n49, 228	8:1–13	79
36:7, 18	44	8:1–8	53
		8:2	68
## Ezra		9:1–38	60, 114
		9:1	174
1:1—10:44	223n36, 260	9:5	5
1:7–11	44	9:6–37	204, 250
1:1–4	249	9:17	118n34, 194
2:36–63	79	9:18	31
2:63	86n30	10:29–30	68
3:1—6:19	79	10:31	46
3:7	249	10:32–39	46
3:10–11	120	10:33	188
4:1–24	45	10:34	46, 189
5:13–16	45	10:39	44
5:14–15	44	12:1–47	85
6:1–22	45	12:26, 36	79

Nehemiah (continued)

12:43	68
12:44–47	46
13:5, 9	44
13:14–31	108

Job

1:1—41:17	231, 234–35
1:1–22	234
1:4–5	234
1:5	167
3:1—27:23	234
4:16	295n22
5:8	234
8:5–6	234
11:13	234
21:15	106
22:27	234
28:1–28	234–35
28:12	11, 235
28:20	11, 235
28:28	11, 235, 238
32:1—37:24	234
33:26–28	234
38:1—40:2	11, 117, 235
40:3–5	235
40:6—41:34	11, 235
42:1–6	235
42:5–6	11, 235
42:7–17	235
42:8	167

Psalms

1	123–24
2–41	124–39
2	91, 124
2:11b	198
3–41	122
3–7	112n23, 124
3	124–26
3:8	198
4	126
4:4	295n22
4:8	198
5	126
6	126
6:4	117n32
6:5	203
7	126–27
7:17	103, 198
8	120, 127–28
9, 10	112n23, 122, 124, 128
9:14	5
11	128–29
12	113, 129
13	112n23, 124, 129–30
14	130
15	130–1, 133, 197, 198, 244
16	131, 286
16:1	202
17	106, 112n23, 124, 131–2
18	91, 132
19	132
19:4b–6	64
19:7–14	123
20	91, 93, 132
21	91, 93, 132
22	69, 112n23, 120, 124, 132–33
22:1	116
22:3	5
22:25	5
23	69, 133
24	133, 197, 198
24:3–6	130
24:6, 10	120
25	69, 112n23, 124, 133–34
25:7	117n32
26	112n23, 124, 134, 296
26:7	6
26:8	215, 296
27	112n23, 124, 134
27:4	277
28	112n23, 124, 134–35
29	135

INDEX OF BIBLICAL REFERENCES

29:5	34	49	123n13, 131, 137, 143, 231, 235–36, 239, 286
30	111, 135		
30:9	203		
31	112n23, 124, 135–36	49:11	215
		50	143–44, 197, 198
31:16	117n32	50:13	139, 173
32	111, 135, 136	51—72	123
33	122, 136	51	69, 111, 112n23, 124, 141–42
34	111, 135, 136–37		
34:3	6	51:1	117n32
34:14	286	51:6	139
35	112n23, 124, 135, 137	52	112n23, 124, 143, 198
35:13	174	52:3, 5	120
36	135, 137	53	130n25
37	123n13, 137, 231, 235–6, 239, 286	54	112n23, 124
		55	112n23, 124
37:27	286	56	112n23, 120, 124
37:35	34	56:1	202
38	112n23, 124, 135, 137–38	57	112n23, 120, 124
		57:1	202
39	112n23, 124, 135, 138	57:5	6
		58	113, 120, 143, 198
40	112n23, 124, 135, 138–39	59	112n23, 120, 124
		60	113, 120, 124
40:10–12, 17	194	60:1	202
40:11–17	139	61	112n23, 124
40:17	286	62	143
41	111, 135, 139	64	112n23, 124
42–89	122	65	145
42–83	123	66	145
42—72	140–45	66:8–12	111
42	112n23, 124, 141	67	111, 145
42:4	43	67:1	195–96
43	112n23, 124, 141	68	145
43:3	215	68:25–6	68
43:1	69	68:34–35	145
44	113, 142	69	112n23, 120, 124
44:2, 24	69	69:13, 16	117n32
44:26	117n32	70	112n23, 124
45	91, 94, 120, 142	71	112n23, 124
46	120, 143, 198	72	91, 94, 142
46:4	215	73—89	145–51
46:7, 11	120	73–83	123
47	123, 143, 269	73	69, 123n13, 131, 137, 146–47, 201, 231, 235–36, 239, 286
48	143		
48:9	6		

Psalms (continued)

73:17	268
73:25–26	160, 286–87
74	113, 147
74:7	215
75	120, 149
76	149–50
77	112n23, 124, 147–48
78	150
78:28, 60	215
78:38	194
78:60–61	30, 30n8
79	113
79:5–6, 8–10	194
80	113, 120
80:10	34
81	120, 149, 197
81:3	185
82	148
83	113, 148
84–85, 87–88	123
84	43, 59, 69, 120, 149, 150
84:1–12	59
84:1	215
85	113, 148–49
85:2–3, 5, 7, 10	194
86	106, 112n23, 124, 149
86:2–3, 5–6, 11, 16	194
86:5, 15	117n32
86:15	118n34, 193
87	149, 150
87:2	215
88	112n23, 124, 149
88:1–6, 10–12	203
89	91, 94–95, 123, 151
90—106	151–54
90	106, 113, 152
91	153
92	123, 153, 286
93	123, 153, 269
94	112n23, 124, 152
94:1–11	113
95–99	123
95	153, 197
95:6–7a	103
96	1, 269
96:1–13	226, 288
96:4	5
96:4a, 7–9	296
96:7–9	154
97	269
98	269
99	269
99:8	194
100	197, 198
100:2	4–5
101	91, 95, 153
102	106, 112n23, 123, 124, 153
103:1	5
103:8	118n34, 193
103:22	5
104	153
104:1	5
105	153
105:1–15	226, 288
105:4	286
106	152
106:1, 47–48	226, 288
106:1	5, 229
106:19–23	31
106:19	23
106:23	116, 241
106:47	286
107	155–56, 202
107:1–32	111
107:1	5
109	112n23, 124
109:21, 26	117n32
110	91, 95–96
110:4	87, 88, 98
111–17, 146–50	123
111:1, 4–5, 7	194
115:17	203
116	111, 156
118	156, 197
118:1–4	5
118:29	5
119	123, 154
119:2, 10, 45, 94	286

INDEX OF BIBLICAL REFERENCES

120–34	43, 59–60, 123, 197, 249
120	112n23, 124
121:7–8	196
122	43
122:1–2	281
122:1	17, 60
124	111
126	113
126:1–6	60
129	111
130	69, 112n23, 124
130:1–8	60
130:3	2
131:1–3	60
132	91, 96, 197
132:5, 7	215
132:8–10	226, 288
134	154
134:1–3	197
134:2–3	281
136	197
136:1–26	5
136:1	226, 288
137	113
138	111, 156
139	69, 112n23, 124
139:8	203
140	112n23, 124
141	112n23, 124
141:2	176
142	106, 112n23, 124
143	112n23, 124
143:12	117n32
144:1–11	91, 96
145:8–9	193
145:8	118n34
146–150	123, 197
149:1–3	120
150	120, 123–24, 156–57, 286
150:6	286

Proverbs

1:1—9:18	233–34
1:7	233
2:5	233
2:16–19	233
5:1–14, 20	233
6:24–35	233
7:5, 14	233
8:13	233
9:10	233
10:27	233
14:26, 27	233
15:8, 29	233
15:16, 33	233
16:3, 6	233
17:1	233
19:23	233
20:25	233
21:3, 27	233
22:4	233
23:17	233
24:21	233
28:9	233
31:2	233
31:30	233

Ecclesiastes (Qoheleth)

3:7	295n22
3:11, 14	232
5:1–7	232–3, 238
7:18	232
8:10–13	233
8:12	232
12:13	232

Song of Songs

1:17	34
3:6	39
4:6, 14	39

Isaiah

1—39	250, 274
1—32	248
1:4	246
1:10–17	9, 245–46
1:11	173, 245
1:12–17	253

Isaiah (continued)

Reference	Page
1:12	248
1:13	39, 188
1:15	65
1:15b, 17	246
1:16–17	65
1:29–31	250
2:2–4	202, 248, 270
2:3	84
2:8, 18	250
2:13	34
4:2–6	248
5:19, 24	246
6:1—9:7	247, 247n17
6:1–13	201, 246, 247, 274
6:1–8	4, 14
6:1–3	289
6:3	1, 4
6:5	2, 247
7:1—8:22	247, 274
9:2–7	247, 274
9:10	34
10:10–11	250
10:20	246
11:1–10	247n17
12:1–6	9, 202
12:6	246
17:7–8, 10–11	250
17:7	246
18:7	248
19:16–25	9
19:19	248
19:21	249
24—27	248
25:1—26:21	248
29:13	246
25:1–5	248
25:9–12	248
26:1–6	248
28:7–8	250
29:19	246
30:11, 12, 15	246
30:22	32
30:27–33	249
31:1	246
33	202
33:9	199
33:14–16	130
35	248
37:4	250
37:14–35	250
37:23	246
38:1–6	109
38:2–3	107
38:9–22	202, 203
38:21	67
40—55	248, 249, 274
41:1	295n22
41:14, 16, 20	246
42:10–13	9, 248
43:1	69
43:3, 14	246
44:2, 24	69
44:23	248, 249
45:8	248
45:11	246
47:4	246
48:17	246
49:7	246
49:13	9, 248
50:2	199
52:1b	199
52:7a	199
54:5	246
55:5	246
55:8–9	210
55:10–13	9
56—66	46, 52, 79, 249, 250, 260, 273, 275
56:1–8	263
56:6–8	9
56:6–7	249, 270
56:7	41, 46, 273
56:8	249
56:9—57:13	250
57:3–13	61–62, 250
58:1–14	174, 246
58:4	246
58:6	209
59:1–4, 9–20	203
59:9–15a	249
60:1–22	204
60:6	39
60:7	249
60:9, 14	246

60:13	249
61—62	203–4
61:1–9	204
61:3	200
61:4	249
61:10–11	204
62:1–12	204
63:7—64:12	204, 250
63:7—64:11	113, 129
63:18	249
64:11	249
65:1–7	62
66:3	168
66:21, 23	80, 250

Jeremiah

1:1	79, 254
2:8	84
2:9	254
2:26	254
2:28	255
5:19	255
5:31	79
6:13–14	79
6:13	254
6:19–21	244
6:26	67
7:16	106, 255
7:1–8:3	255
7:12–15	30, 30n8
7:16–20	61, 68
7:16	106, 108, 255
7:31	54n15
8:2	64
8:10–11	79
8:10	254
9:14	255
9:17–20	67
10:1–16	256
11:1–17	255
11:14	108, 255
11:18–23	112, 255
11:21, 23	79
12:1–6	112, 255
13:10, 27	255
14	113, 129
14:2–9, 19–22	113, 129
14:7–9	255
14:11–12	244
14:11, 13	108, 255
14:18	79
14:19—15:9	255
15:1	109, 255
15:15–21	112, 255
16:11, 18	255
16:19–20	256
17:2	255
17:3	54n15
17:14–18	112, 255
18:15	255
18:19–23	112, 255
19:4–5, 13	255
19:5	54n15
20:1–3	79
20:1–2	254
20:7–18	112, 255
22:7, 14	34
23:5	270n74
23:11	254
25:6	255
26:6	254
27:18	106
27:21–22	254
28:3–6	254
29:7, 12	256
31:31–34	254
32:29	255
32:35	54n15, 64, 168, 255
33:11, 18, 21–22	254
33:14–16	270n74
33:18–22	79
34:8–16	188
37:3	255
41:1–3	266
41:4–5	200
42:2, 4, 20	255
43—44	47
44:15–29	61, 68, 255
44:17–23, 25	255
48:35	53, 54n15
52:13	254
52:17–19	44
52:17	37
52:18–23	254

Lamentations

5:1–22	113, 129

Ezekiel

1:1—3:27	3
1:28	256
1:1–3	256
1:2	256
5:11	256
6:3, 6	54n15
6:4–7	256
6:3	256, 257
6:13	256, 257
8:1	256
8:7–18	256
8:14	61
8:16	64
9:6	256
11	259
14:3–8	256
16:15–22	257
16:16	54n15
20:16, 24, 39	256
20:28–31	257
20:31	257
22:3, 4	256
22:23–31	81
23:30	256
23:38–39	257
23:39	257
25:3	257
33:30–33	256
36:2	54n15
36:37–38	256
40—48	81, 257–64, 272–73, 281
40:1—43:12	257–59
40:45–46	81
42:13	81
43:13—46:24	257, 259–62
43:18–27	230
43:19	81
44:18	82
45:18–20	174n24, 230
46:4–5	188
46:19–20	81
47:1—48:35	257, 262–64
48:35	274, 281

Daniel

1:2	44
6:10	60, 67
9:3	174
9:4–19	204, 250
12:2–3	131

Hosea

1—3	250–51
1:2	251
1:10–11	251
2:11	188
2:14–23	251
3:1	251
4:4, 6, 9	251
4:4–6, 9	78
4:5	251
4:6	84
4:10–19	63
4:10–13	251
4:13	32
4:14	251
5:1–2	78, 251
5:3, 4	251
6:1–3, 11b	251
6:6	244
6:9	78
6:10	251
8:4–6	31
8:5, 6	62
8:13	244
9:7, 8	251
9:15	62
10:1–8	62
10:5	31, 78
10:15	78
11:1–9	251
12:11	62
13:2	62, 168

14:1–3	10
14:2b–4	251–52
14:2b–3	206
14:4–8	251

Joel

1—3	264–65
1—2	113, 129
1:2—2:17	265
2:12–17	10
2:12–13	174
2:13	118n34

Amos

2:6–8	243
2:8	242
3:15	243
4:1	243
4:4–5	243
4:4	246
4:4a	244
4:13	243, 274
5:8–9	243
5:8	243, 274
5:18–24	10, 244
5:21–24	65, 253
5:23–24	273
7:1–3, 4–6	108
7:1–3	244
7:2–9	245
7:9	54n15
7:12	44
7:13	31
7:14	240
8:5	188
8:14	242
9:5–6	243, 274

Obadiah

1:1–21	265–66

Jonah

1:1—4:11	266–67
1:16	266
2:1–10	206
2:2–9	106
2:9b	266
3:4	266
3:6–10	266
4:1–5	266
4:2	118n34, 194

Micah

1:2–16	252
3:11	79, 253, 273
4:1–5	270
4:1–4	10
4:2	84
5:12–14	253
6:6–8	66, 253
6:6–7	64
6:7–8	273
6:7	167
6:8	244, 273, 293
7:1–7	194–95
7:1–6	194
7:7	194
7:8–20	194–95
7:18–20	10, 194

Nahum

1:1—3:19	267
1:3	118n34, 194
1:3b–8	10

Habakkuk

1:2–4, 12–17	201
2:20	295
3:1–19	10, 120, 201

Zephaniah

1:1—3:20	268–69

Haggai

1:1—2:23	223n36, 269–70, 281, 293
1:1–14	80
1:1	74
2:2–4	80

Zechariah

1:1—8:23	205, 223n36, 270, 281, 293
1:7—6:15	46, 205
2:3	295
3:1–9	80
3:1	74
3:8	270n74
6:11	80
7:1–7	204
7:2–7	200
7:3, 5	129, 265–66
8:18–23	204
8:19	129, 174, 200, 265–66
9:1—14:21	265, 270–71, 275
11:1	34
14:17	274

Malachi

1:1—4:6	270–71, 281, 293
1:6—2:10	10
1:6—2:9	80
1:6b–8a	274
1:10	244
2:13	244
4:4	23

Apocrypha

Baruch

1:8–9	44

1 Esdras

4:43–46, 57	44
4:57	45

2 Esdras

10:21–22	44

Judith

4:9–15	129

1 Maccabees

1:23	44
4:49	44
14:15	44

2 Maccabees

1:1—2:32	44

Sirach (Ecclesiasticus)

1:1—51:12	231
7:29–31	237
15:9–10	237
22:27—23:6	237
30:18	68
34:5	237
34:21–27	237
35:1–5, 9a, 14–15	237
36:1–22	237
36:18	238
39:12–35	237
39:15a	237
42:15—43:33	237
43:30	237
45:6–22	237
47:8	237
47:10	237
47:13	238

INDEX OF BIBLICAL REFERENCES

49:1–4	238	7:7	236
49:6	238	13:1–9	236
50:1–21	237	13:10—15:17	236
50:5–7	174	15:18–19	236
50:16–19	296	16:28–29	236
51:1–12	237	18:6–9	236
		18:20–25	236

Tobit

4:17	68

Dead Sea Scrolls

11Qmelch	88
1QS ix.4–5	288n11

Wisdom of Solomon

1:1—19:22	231, 236

New Testament

Mark

6:1–5	52

13:14–15	190n21
15:21	190
27:9	174

Luke

4:16–30	52
4:16–17	190n21

Hebrews

5:1–4	87
5:1	81, 291–92
5:6	87
5:10	88
6:10—7:19	88
9:13–14	162
13:15	288n11

Acts

13:13–16	52

www.ingramcontent.com/pod-product-compliance
Lightning Source LLC
Chambersburg PA
CBHW061424300426
44114CB00014B/1530